Pahlavi Iran's Relations with Africa

This book presents the first comprehensive study of Iran's complex relationship with Africa during the late Pahlavi era. While many studies of Iran's foreign relations during the Cold War present Iranian policy as fully aligned with the United States, Robert Steele reveals Iran as an independent actor capable of forging its own path, and shows that Africa was central to Iran's economic policy and security strategy during the reign of Shah Mohammad Reza Pahlavi. Africa was where the shah sought allies to balance the radicalism of Nasser, often through Iranian aid, customers for Iranian oil and potential sources of uranium. Bolstered by the British withdrawal from the Persian Gulf in 1971 and the oil price hike of 1973, Steele also shows how the shah saw an opportunity for his Iran to play a leading role in the Indian Ocean, revealing the central place of Africa in Iran's global strategy.

ROBERT STEELE is a postdoctoral fellow at the Institute of Iranian Studies, Austrian Academy of Sciences. He is the author of *The Shah's Imperial Celebrations of 1971: Nationalism, Culture and Politics in Late Pahlavi Iran* (2020), and co-editor of *Iran and Global Decolonisation: Politics and Resistance After Empire* (2023).

Pahlavi Iran's Relations with Africa

Cultural and Political Connections in the Cold War

ROBERT STEELE
Austrian Academy of Sciences

CAMBRIDGE
UNIVERSITY PRESS

CAMBRIDGE
UNIVERSITY PRESS

Shaftesbury Road, Cambridge CB2 8EA, United Kingdom

One Liberty Plaza, 20th Floor, New York, NY 10006, USA

477 Williamstown Road, Port Melbourne, VIC 3207, Australia

314–321, 3rd Floor, Plot 3, Splendor Forum, Jasola District Centre, New Delhi – 110025, India

103 Penang Road, #05–06/07, Visioncrest Commercial, Singapore 238467

Cambridge University Press is part of Cambridge University Press & Assessment, a department of the University of Cambridge.

We share the University's mission to contribute to society through the pursuit of education, learning and research at the highest international levels of excellence.

www.cambridge.org
Information on this title: www.cambridge.org/9781009473149

DOI: 10.1017/9781009473132

When citing this work, please include a reference to the DOI 10.1017/9781009473132

First published 2024

A catalogue record for this publication is available from the British Library

A Cataloging-in-Publication data record for this book is available from the Library of Congress

ISBN 978-1-009-47314-9 Hardback

Contents

Figures

Acknowledgements

While researching at the National Archives in London in summer 2019, I came across a report of the visit of Empress Farah Pahlavi of Iran to London in 1976. The report mentioned that the empress had recently travelled to Senegal where she had laid the foundation stone of a joint Iranian–Senegalese city which would be named after her, Keur Farah Pahlavi. I searched the secondary literature on Iran's foreign relations in the Pahlavi period and found very few references to this extraordinary initiative. In fact, there were very few studies on Iran's relations with Africa at all. To discover more, I travelled to McGill University library, which holds the archives of the architect Moshe Safdie, who was hired by the Iranian and Senegalese governments to design the Keur Farah Pahlavi city. There I found a wealth of material, including reports, minutes of meetings, letters and newspaper articles, which formed the basis of an article that was published in the journal *Iranian Studies*. In the years that followed, I discovered more and more fascinating facets of Iran's entanglement with Africa during the late Pahlavi period and became convinced that the subject merited a book.

I am grateful to the Department of Near East Languages and Cultures at the University of California, Los Angeles, where I spent two years as a postdoctoral fellow from 2019 to 2021, for giving me the encouragement to start this project, and supporting my research, including funding my trip to Montreal and the acquisition of documents from the Dutch national archives. I was fortunate to be able to continue the project as a visiting fellow at the department of International History at the London School of Economics and Political Science.

My knowledge of Pahlavi Iran and its global interactions during the Cold War has been enriched by conversations with many colleagues, among them Arash Azizi, Roham Alvandi, Thomas Bédrède and Lior Sternfeld. I am grateful to Houchang Chehabi, who has always been gracious in giving advice and sharing sources, and he very kindly read through my chapters on Southern Africa. Throughout this project, I have spent many hours discussing Iran and Africa with Firoozeh Kashani-Sabet, whose scholarship and insights have had huge impact on my work. I thank her for her encouragement, and for her generosity in sharing documents with me. I am grateful also to Safa Mahmoudian, for checking my Persian transliteration and to Marziyeh Bazyar for assistance with research. At Cambridge University Press, I wish to acknowledge the excellent work of Biju Singh, Natasha Burton and Maria Marsh. Finally, I would like to thank the Institute of Iranian Studies at the Austrian Academy of Sciences for facilitating the completion of this project in Vienna, and for supporting my research.

The research for this book has taken me to many places, from London, the Hague, Nantes and Paris, to Los Angeles, Stanford, Dakar and Montreal. My wife, Maria, has been my constant companion throughout this time, accompanying me all over the world, helping to read sources in Dutch and French, and reading (and critiquing) my work. She was more excited than I was to discover the tapestry portrait of Léopold Sédar Senghor that was given as a gift for attending the 1971 celebration at Persepolis, hanging outside his office at his home (now a museum) in Dakar. This book would not have been possible without her steadfast support.

Note on Transliteration

The transliteration follows the system employed by the journal *Iranian Studies*, which adopts the long a (ā), ayn (ʿ) and hamza (ʾ). Names which are commonly understood in English, for example Mohammad Reza Pahlavi, have not been converted into this style, so as not to confuse non-specialists. Translations are my own, unless otherwise stated.

Introduction

On 8 May 1974, an unexpected visitor arrived at Tehran's Mehrābād Airport. Despite the impromptu nature of the visit, efforts were made to make the guest feel welcome in Tehran. He was granted full military honours, and was met at the airport by the prime minister, Amir ʿAbbās Hoveydā, as well as several other important figures, including the Saudi ambassador to Iran.[1] This guest was the president of Uganda, the authoritarian military dictator Idi Amin. In February that year, during the Islamic Summit Conference in Lahore, Amin had spoken of his wish to establish a Ugandan embassy in Tehran.[2] He also spoke on that occasion about the need for rapprochement between Iran and Iraq, and even suggested that he be provided with a plane so that he could travel to Tehran to convince the shah to come with him in person to the Lahore conference to try and solve this problem together.[3] This offer was clearly not taken particularly seriously, because Amin's visit to Iran in May, which came at the end of a tour of the Middle East, caught everyone off guard. The visit was said in the press to have been 'completely unexpected and sudden', and there was a sense of bewilderment at Amin's arrival among Iranian officials.[4]

Eager to make the most of this unanticipated visit in terms of public relations – since such visits from foreign leaders substantiated the shah's credentials as a global statesman – the daily newspaper *Ettelāʿāt* printed an image of Prime Minister Hoveydā greeting Amin at the airport on its front page. Amin was the guest of the prime minister for lunch and in the evening a banquet was held in his honour by the shah. In spite of Iran's observations of the formalities of

[1] *Ettelāʿāt*, 18 Ordibehesht 1353/ 8 May 1974, 4.
[2] P. A. E. Renardel de Lavalette to minister of foreign affairs, 13 March 1974, Nationaal Archief (The National Archives of the Netherlands), The Hague (henceforth NA) 2.05.191/433.
[3] *Ettelāʿāt*, 19 Ordibehesht 1353/ 9 May 1974, 4. [4] Ibid.

receiving heads of state, Iranian officials were annoyed at Amin's attempts to meddle in Iran's affairs. The US ambassador in Tehran, Richard Helms, wrote that 'Iranian officials were not happy at [the] prospects of Amin's visit and his conduct here confirmed their expectations'.[5] One of these officials was the shah's court minister, Asadollāh ʿAlam, whose diary entry for that day reads:

> In the evening Idi Amin, the president of Uganda, who without any prior warning, decided to come from Jeddah to Iran, in order to reconcile Iran and Iraq, was the guest of the shah. It is most ridiculous; he was a boxer and a corporal in the British army, now he is a general! He says strange and ludicrous things...[6]

ʿAlam confirmed to Helms that 'Amin was on a self-appointed mission of mediation to resolve [the] difficulties affecting relations between Iran, Iraq and Syria'.[7] Amin's crude and unpolished manner also irritated the sensibilities of some of the Pahlavi political elite, particularly the cultivated and erudite prime minister. According to Helms, 'During [the] shah's banquet Amin's behaviour was so bumptious, boisterous and burpy that Hoveyda was heard to mutter to an aide, "get him out of [the] country by 10:00 tomorrow morning"'.[8]

In spite of how distasteful Amin seemed to the Pahlavi elite, his charm offensive was not entirely unsuccessful, for just five months later, on 12 October 1974, Iran announced that it had established diplomatic relations with Uganda.[9] Idi Amin's visit is exceptional for its spontaneity, but throughout the 1970s, the arrival of leaders or emissaries from Africa in Tehran was a very common occurrence. They

[5] Richard Helms telegram, 13 May 1974, WikiLeaks Cable 1974TEHRAN03762_b.

[6] Diary entry 18 Ordibehesht 1353, *Yāddāsht-hā-ye ʿAlam*, vol. 4, ed. ʿAli-Naqi ʿĀlikhāni (Tehran: Ketābsarā, 2014), 84.

[7] Helms telegram, 13 May 1974.

[8] Ibid. Hoveydā reported to the US ambassador Richard Helms that Amin told him that he wished to re-establish relations with the United States, which had just one year earlier recalled its ambassador in anger after Amin sent a message to Nixon wishing him a 'speedy recovery from the Watergate affair'. Hoveydā reacted with 'some surprise' at this and asked Amin why, in light of his 'insulting message', he felt the United States would want to re-establish relations with him. Hoveydā told the ambassador that 'Amin professed injured innocence and said that he intended no slight or insult but was simply expressing his "true" feelings.' Helms telegram, 19 May 1974, WikiLeaks Cable 1974TEHRAN03965_b.

[9] Helms telegram, 14 October 1974, WikiLeaks Cable 1974TEHRAN08633_b.

came to Iran to request economic or military aid, political support, trade deals and other agreements, and in a relatively short period of time Iran built up extensive political and trade connections across the continent. For example, Ethiopia under Emperor Haile Selassie developed a close relationship with Iran in the 1960s and was for a period Iran's key strategic ally in East Africa. Haile Selassie travelled to Iran in 1964 and 1971, and the shah himself travelled to Ethiopia in 1968, on what would be his only visit to sub-Saharan Africa during his reign. Iran developed a close relationship with Senegal in the 1970s, the culmination of which was the visit of Empress Farah in 1976 to lay the foundation stone of a Senegalese–Iranian city that would bear her name, Keur Farah Pahlavi. As one of only two monarchs with the title 'emperor' – the other was Emperor Hirohito of Japan – the shah was invited as a special guest to attend the coronation of the self-proclaimed emperor of Central Africa, Jean Bedel Bokassa, in December 1977.[10] The shah also cultivated close ties with the president of Zaire, Mobutu Sese Seko, to whom he gave military aid, as well as favourable prices for oil.

Despite efforts to build close ties with non-Arab Africa in the 1960s, the shah maintained a strong presence in North Africa, too. Egyptian president Gamal ʿAbd al-Nasser had severed ties with Iran in 1960 and became for the next decade the shah's main adversary. The shah thus developed strong ties with Tunisia and Morocco, conservative, pro-Western states that he felt could help to exploit frictions in the brand of Arab unity promoted by Egypt's firebrand president. With the decline of Nasser after the Six-Day War of June 1967, Iran re-established relations with Egypt. With Nasser's successor, Anwar Sadat, the shah developed a close personal and political relationship, and Egypt became Iran's closest ally in Africa during the 1970s. This remarkable turnaround was particularly striking considering the deep animosity between Iran and Egypt under Nasser. Iran's rapprochement with

[10] The shah and Emperor Hirohito were apparently at the top of Bokassa's invitation list, and he had been in contact with the shah as early as April 1977. Apparently, Bokassa also sought the help of Iran, Japan and Morocco in putting together an imperial constitution. *Ettelāʿāt*, 17 Farvardin 1356/ 6 April 1977; and Brian Titley, *Dark Age: The Political Odyssey of Emperor Bokassa* (Liverpool: Liverpool University Press, 1998), 84 and 92. The other emperor, Haile Selassie, had lost his throne in 1974.

Egypt removed a local threat and allowed the shah to pursue more boldly his ambitions beyond Iran's immediate geographical sphere.

As Haile Selassie's authority waned in the early part of the 1970s, and after his fall in 1974, Iran sought to develop ties with other countries in East Africa. Most important among these countries were Sudan under President Ja'far Nimeiry and Somalia under President Siad Barre. Such was the strategic shift in the Horn of Africa that Iran actually provided military support to Siad Barre's Somalia for use against its former ally Ethiopia. Barre even travelled to Iran in December 1977, just days before President Carter's visit that month, to implore the shah to use his influence with the US president to try to convince him to give military support to Somalia. President Carter's visit is often remembered for his infamous New Year message, in which, just weeks before the intensification of the protests that would result in the overthrow of the Pahlavi regime, he declared Iran to be 'an island of stability'. However, at the time, the issue at the top of the agenda during meetings between the shah and President Carter was the situation in the Horn of Africa. The issue was also discussed extensively and prominently in the Iranian press.

In spite of the extensive ties Iran developed with the countries of Africa during the 1970s, and despite the fascinating ways in which the interplay between decolonisation, the Cold War and Iran's sudden oil wealth influenced its foreign policy, there have been few studies on Iran's African relations in this period. One of the reasons for this is that the expansion of these relations occurred during a relatively short period between 1970 and 1978. Indeed, for most of the first five decades of Pahlavi rule, Iran had very few interactions with Africa beyond the Arab north. There were two main reasons for this: first, Iran's concerns were primarily local; and second, the vast majority of Africa was still under some form of colonial rule. The decolonisation of Africa, which began in earnest towards the end of the 1950s, changed the situation completely. By the 1960s, Africa was no longer divided between various European colonial powers; it was now made up of some fifty independent nations, each looking for allies to help them shake off the remnants of colonialism, and avoid being dragged into the Cold War. Mohammad Reza Pahlavi, meanwhile, had faced a tumultuous first twelve years on the throne, but in the years following the removal of Mohammad Mosaddeq as prime minister in 1953, his position became more secure, his economy achieved stable growth, and he was able to think more clearly about the role Iran could play on the global stage.

To put the vast expansion of Iran's ties across the African continent during the 1970s into perspective, in 1969, Iran had political relations with only five countries in the whole of Africa – just one of those, Ethiopia, outside the Arab north. By the mid-1970s, Iran had established links with over thirty countries, and by the revolution, Iran had a presence in most African countries.[11] Among the countries Iran established diplomatic relations with in this period were: Lesotho, Swaziland and South Africa in 1970;[12] Kenya, Malawi and Senegal in 1971; Sudan and Zaire in 1972; Chad, Mauritania, Nigeria, Somalia and Zambia in 1973; Ghana and Uganda in 1974; Gabon, Ivory Coast, Madagascar and Niger in 1975; and Mozambique and Seychelles in 1976. Iran's ambassadors were normally accredited in several countries. For instance, for most of the 1970s, the ambassador in Senegal was also accredited to Ivory Coast, the ambassador in Madagascar was also accredited to Mauritius, Mozambique and Seychelles, and the ambassador to Nigeria was also accredited in Ghana, Niger and Sierra Leone.

Of course, some of these relationships were stronger than others, and the closeness of ties often depended on how useful the specific country's resources or political influence could be to Iran. In a report on Iran–Africa relations submitted to the French Ministry of Foreign Affairs in 1974, the French ambassador in Tehran, Robert de Souza, observed that in spite of the 'tightening of ties with certain African countries … because of the often superficial nature of these relations, this "Iranian-African rapprochement" is nevertheless marked by a certain ambiguity'.[13] One of the reasons why Iran was apparently slow to develop substantive ties with African countries in the 1970s after the initial establishment of relations – the reason the French ambassador considered them to be superficial – was that it took time to develop the necessary expertise of Africa in Iran's Ministry of Foreign Affairs, and train diplomats who had the linguistic skills, understanding of African

[11] Shireen T. Hunter, *Iran's Foreign Policy in the Post-Soviet Era: Resisting the New International Order* (Santa Barbara, CA: Praeger), 226.

[12] Relations with South Africa were at the consular general level and remained so until the revolution.

[13] Robert de Souza to Michel Jobert, 5 March 1974, Centre des Archives Diplomatiques de Nantes (henceforth CADN) 437PO/1/55/ANL7.

affairs and willingness to relocate to Africa. For this reason, for much of the 1970s, Iran's Africa policy was to offer smart, targeted support to certain countries that could help Iran to achieve its broader economic or strategic goals, rather than give blanket support to large areas. Thus, for many countries in Africa, the establishment of relations with Iran did not bring expansive trade relations or development aid. In the mid- to late 1970s, when Iran's economy weakened and it became more difficult to invest in development projects in Africa, the Iranian government still tried to secure economic agreements with countries such as Gabon, in order to guarantee continued access to their uranium.

By examining the origins and development of Iran's expansive ties across Africa during the late Pahlavi era, this book seeks to answer several questions: What was the nature of the shah's Africa policy during this period? What strategies did the shah employ to expand its influence across the continent? Which countries or regions received special attention? How did Africa fit into the shah's broader strategic objectives? And how were these relations shaped by the two major global processes in the decades following the end of the Second World War: the Cold War and decolonisation?

The Cold War and Decolonisation

There is an important body of scholarship that has illuminated the position of the Third World in the context of the global Cold War. Correcting the Eurocentric nature of the scholarship of earlier Cold War history, modern historiography has 'helped forge a rare scholarly consensus', as Robert McMahon notes, 'that the Cold War constituted a truly global contest, in which the Third World served as a critical theatre, and that it was an event in which non-Western actors assumed a large and substantive role'.[14] Iran was on the front line of the Cold War from the very beginning in 1946, and its global interactions were

[14] Robert J. McMahon, 'Introduction', in *The Cold War in the Third World*, ed. Robert J. McMahon (Oxford: Oxford University Press, 2013), 4. Recent examples of this scholarship include: Odd Arne Westad, *The Global Cold War: Third World Interventions and the Making of Our Times* (Cambridge: Cambridge University Press, 2012); Odd Arne Westad, *The Cold War: A World History* (London: Allen Lane, 2017); and Lorenz M. Lüthi, *Cold Wars: Asia, The Middle East, Europe* (Cambridge: Cambridge University Press, 2020).

shaped and at times restricted by the great power conflict until its end.[15] Nonetheless, the shah competently and at times skilfully navigated the complex world of big power politics. As Roham Alvandi has argued, by the late 1960s/early 1970s, he had become such an important player in Cold War politics, that he was able to negotiate with the United States on his own terms, becoming one of several leaders of the Global South in this period, 'who often abetted and manipulated the superpowers in the pursuit of their own local ambitions and interests'.[16]

Iran's foreign policy went through several phases during Mohammad Reza Pahlavi's rule, as a result of international and domestic developments. The shah had come to power during the Anglo-Soviet occupation of Iran during the Second World War, so during the early years of his rule, his primary objective for Iran was 'to liquidate the consequences of the war occupation' and ensure the survival of Iran as an independent entity.[17] During the premiership of Mohammad Mosaddeq (1951–1953), Iran's government adopted a policy of negative equilibrium (*siyāsat-e movāzeneh-ye manfi*) vis-à-vis the imperial powers. The premise of this policy was that favouring neither Britain nor Russia would lead to an equilibrium, in which neither side would be able to interfere in Iran's affairs.[18] Following the ousting of Mosaddeq in August 1953, the shah embraced a policy of 'positive nationalism', which was a direct contrast to Mosaddeq's 'negative equilibrium', and essentially meant that Iran should maintain positive relations and cooperate with the great powers to ensure Iran's security in the bipolar international order. This led, in 1955, to Iran joining the pro-Western Baghdad Pact, and in 1959, its entering into a formal alliance with the United States.[19]

15 For an overview of Iran's position and role in the Cold War, and a useful summary of the historiography, see Roham Alvandi, 'Guest Editor's Introduction: Iran and the Cold War', *Iranian Studies*, vol. 47, no. 3 (2014), 373–378.

16 Roham Alvandi, *Nixon, Kissinger, and the Shah: The United States and Iran in the Cold War* (Oxford: Oxford University Press, 2014), 3.

17 Shahram Chubin and Sepehr Zabih, *The Foreign Relations of Iran: A Developing State in a Zone of Great-Power Conflict* (Berkeley: University of California Press, 1974), 36.

18 Ibid., 2.

19 Sepehr Zabih, 'Iran's International Posture: De Facto Nonalignment within a Pro-Western Alliance', *The Middle East Journal*, vol. 24, no. 3 (1970), 304.

By the early 1960s, the shah had consolidated his personal position after a tumultuous first twenty years on the throne, had launched a comprehensive set of social and political reforms, packaged as the White Revolution, and had established stable relations with the Soviet Union and the United States.[20] Consequently, he began to think more clearly about the role Iran could play in the Middle East and beyond and implemented what he termed his independent national policy (*siyāsat-e mostaqel-e melli*). The shah claimed that the reduction of the gap between rich and poor that had occurred as a result of land reform and the abolition of feudalism had contributed to a greater sense of national unity. Therefore, the shah argued, Iran was ready to initiate a new foreign policy to reflect this; a policy which was in essence both independent – in other words, not dictated by the United States or the Soviet Union – and national.[21]

The independent national policy provided the ideological basis for Iran's foreign policy from 1963 until the revolution and sought to bring about 'good relations with foreign countries ... fruitful and peaceful co-existence and cooperation irrespective of the political or economic form of other governments'.[22] From the initiation of the White Revolution in 1963 onwards, the shah was the ultimate arbiter when it came to Iran's foreign relations; deciding priorities and making all of the major – and most of the minor – decisions, to the extent that the scholar William E. Griffiths observed in 1978 that, 'The Shah *is* Iranian foreign policy, has been so since 1953, and will in all likelihood remain so as long as he reigns.'[23] In their important study on Iranian foreign relations during the Pahlavi period, Shahram Chubin and Sepehr Zabih observed several limitations and advantages of such a

[20] On the White Revolution, see Ali M. Ansari, 'The Myth of the White Revolution: Mohammad Reza Shah, "Modernization" and the Consolidation of Power', *Middle Eastern Studies*, vol. 37, no. 3 (2001), 1–24; and Rouhollah K. Ramazani, 'Iran's "White Revolution": A Study in Political Development', *International Journal of Middle East Studies*, vol. 5, no. 2 (1974), 124–139.

[21] Rouhollah K. Ramazani, *Iran's Foreign Policy, 1941–1973: A Study of Foreign Policy in Modernizing Nations* (Charlottesville: University Press of Virginia, 1975), 313.

[22] *Decade of the Revolution: Resurrection of a Nation; A Miracle of Leadership, 1963–1973* (Tehran: Central Insurance of Iran, 1973), 172.

[23] William E. Griffith, 'Iran's Foreign Policy in the Pahlavi Era', in *Iran under the Pahlavis*, ed. George Lenczowski (Stanford, CA: Hoover Institution Press, 1978), 385.

system, in which the shah was the 'sole and ultimate source of decisions affecting foreign policy, in all its manifestations'.[24]

This situation was understood fully by foreign diplomats. A 1975 British Foreign and Commonwealth Office report read, for example:

> When speaking of 'Iranian' foreign policy one is almost always speaking of the Shah's foreign policy – and *vice versa*. As in most other areas of national life here, Monarch and State are virtually synonymous – though there are certain fields, such as religion, where popular attitudes may be a constraint on the Shah's freedom of action. This imperial pre-eminence makes an analysis at once more easy and more difficult – more easy, because the Shah speaks constantly in public and in private on foreign policy issues: more difficult, because he is a complex human being whose prejudices and emotions colour his thinking. The personal invades upon the national.[25]

However, such analyses do not tell the whole story, for while the shah's central role in matters relating to foreign policy was unquestionable, one should also consider the myriad factors and individuals that influenced his decision-making. For example, Firoozeh Kashani-Sabet has explored the influence that intellectual discussions of race and social justice had on the shah's approach to the Global South.[26] Several diplomats and political figures whom the shah trusted were also able to influence him and in effect help to shape foreign policy. The shah's son-in-law and minister of foreign affairs from 1966 until 1971, Ardeshir Zāhedi, describes in detail in his memoirs the role that he played in Iran's foreign relations. In Africa, for example, Zāhedi recalls that the shah at first wanted to establish Iran's first embassy in Black Africa in Ivory Coast, but he persuaded him instead to send an ambassador to Senegal.[27] Individuals such as Zāhedi were not merely tools of the shah's autocracy, but were active participants who were able to advise and influence him.

24 Chubin and Zabih, *The Foreign Relations of Iran*, 18.

25 Anthony D. Parsons, 'Iranian Foreign Policy', 1 May 1975, 3, The National Archives, Kew, Foreign and Commonwealth Office (henceforth FCO) 8/2501.

26 See Firoozeh Kashani-Sabet, 'Colorblind or Blinded by Color? Race, Ethnicity, and Identity in Iran', in *Sites of Pluralism: Community Politics in the Middle East*, ed. Firat Oruc (Oxford: Oxford University Press, 2019), 153–180; and Firoozeh Kashani-Sabet, *Heroes to Hostages: America and Iran, 1800–1988* (Cambridge: Cambridge University Press, 2023), 241–263.

27 Ardeshir Zāhedi, *Khāterāt-e Ardeshir Zāhedi*, vol. 3 (Bethesda, MD: Ibex Publishers, 2020), 207.

Iran occupied an awkward position in the politics of the Global South. In the aftermath of the Second World War, when countries around the world gained independence from the European colonialists, Iran was generally an outsider in Third World solidarity movements. During the era of imperialism, it had not formally been colonised, but had ceded territory to the British and Russian Empires and had been forced to sign unequal treaties, which involved granting capitulatory rights to foreign merchants and selling off natural resources to enterprising foreign businessmen.[28] In short, Iran had remained a sovereign nation, but it had paid a price. Unlike the newly independent countries of the Global South, which saw Afro-Asian solidarity movements as a way to cooperate with like-minded allies to preserve their hard-fought sovereignty, Iran had no such motivation. Although the shah did send emissaries to solidarity movements, such as the Bandung Conference in 1955, Iran was a reluctant participant and did not embrace the spirit of these movements.[29] The shah did, however, join and sometimes lead movements that best suited his political agenda, such as the Islamic Conference in 1969.

Nonetheless, the global change brought about by decolonisation and the Cold War both shaped Iran's global interactions during this period, and profoundly influenced how the shah conceived Iran's position within the Global South. Although the shah was firmly on the side of the United States in the Cold War, Alvandi argues that 'the Pahlavi state sought to project an image of a resurgent Iran as an autonomous actor within the Western bloc'.[30] In the context of the changing world order that decolonisation presented, the shah attempted to 'serve as a bridge between East and West, North and South'.[31] Iran adopted a

[28] For discussion see Ali Gheissari, 'Unequal Treaties and the Question of Sovereignty in Qajar and Early Pahlavi Iran', *Durham Middle East Papers*, no. 106 (2023), 1–63.

[29] On the Bandung Conference and its legacy, see Christopher Lee, ed., *Making a World after Empire: The Bandung Moment and Its Political Afterlives* (Athens: Ohio University Press, 2019). On Iran's participation in Bandung, see Thomas Bédrède, 'Iran's Foreign Policy and the Algerian War of Independence, 1954–1962', in *Iran and Global Decolonisation: Politics and Resistance After Empire*, ed. Firoozeh Kashani-Sabet and Robert Steele (London: Gingko Library, 2023), 169–170.

[30] Roham Alvandi, 'Iran in the Age of Aryamehr', in *The Age of Aryamehr: Late Pahlavi Iran and Its Global Entanglements*, ed. Roham Alvandi (London: Gingko Library, 2018), 17.

[31] Ibid.

position of 'de facto nonalignment within the pro-Western alliance', to use Chubin and Zabih's turn of phrase, which allowed it to enjoy the benefits of alignment with the United States, while presenting itself to the decolonised Global South as a like-minded ally.[32] In some respects, the shah adopted the language of solidarity with the anti-imperialist former colonies despite his own imperial self-image.

A Pahlavi Grand Strategy?

In a recent study on Pahlavi-era foreign relations, Anoushiravan Ehteshami explores the idea that the shah developed a grand strategy, stirred by his determination to reach the Great Civilisation, and facilitated by his direct control of the state, vast increases in oil revenues, Iran's military alliance with the United States and 'an industrial and technical base able to sustain an emerging "Asian tiger" to equal Japan on the world stage'.[33] An extensive body of literature exists that examines the concept of grand strategy, and various interpretations of what it means.[34] As Clive Jones explains, 'Grand Strategy is NOT any one aspect of foreign policy; nor is it foreign policy if by foreign policy we mean the totality of state interaction with the external world, from foreign aid to the use of military force. These remain means.'[35] Rather, as Rebecca Lissner argues, '[i]t is the conceptual framework that helps nations determine where they want to go and how they

32 Chubin and Zabih, *The Foreign Relations of Iran*, 7.

33 Anoushiravan Ehteshami, 'Iran's Grand Strategy under the Pahlavis', in *Grand Strategy in the Contemporary Middle East*, ed. Tore T. Petersen and Clive Jones (Berlin: Gerlach Press, 2022), 195.

34 See, for example, Lukas Milevski, *The Evolution of Modern Grand Strategic Thought* (Oxford: Oxford University Press, 2016); John Lewis Gaddis, *On Grand Strategy* (New York: Penguin Press, 2018); Hal Brands, *The Promise and Pitfalls of Grand Strategy* (Carlisle, PA: Strategic Studies Institute, US Army War College, 2012); Williamson Murray, Richard Hart Sinnreich and James Lacey, eds., *The Shaping of Grand Strategy: Policy, Diplomacy, and War* (Cambridge: Cambridge University Press, 2011); and Paul Kennedy, ed., *Grand Strategies in War and Peace* (New Haven, CT: Yale University Press, 1991).

35 Clive Jones, 'Introduction: Grand Strategy in the Contemporary Middle East: The Concepts and Debates', in *Grand Strategy in the Contemporary Middle East: The Concepts and Debates*, ed. Tore T. Petersen and Clive Jones (Berlin: Gerlach Press, 2022), 4.

ought to get there; it is the theory, or logic, that guides leaders seeking security in a complex and insecure world'.[36]

It was during the late 1960s that Iran developed, according to Ehteshami's analysis 'the relative geopolitical space and the geo-economic advantage to build a grand strategy based on their changing role and position in the international system'.[37] This was stimulated by several important developments. First, the Six-Day War of June 1967 and the end of the Yemen civil war removed the Nasserist threat that had shaped Iran's regional security outlook since the late 1950s. Second, after the British withdrawal from the Persian Gulf in 1971, Iran emerged as the preeminent power of the region. Subsequently, the shah began to articulate a vision for the future role of Iran on the international stage, beyond the Middle East. As a result, in the words of James Goode, 'Over the next decade, the shah would pursue a grand strategy, not only in the Gulf but in the Indian Ocean.'[38]

Africa is an important area to explore the shah's grand strategy, as it developed through the 1950s, 1960s and 1970s, for several reasons. First, the eastern coastline bordered the Indian Ocean, which the shah aimed to keep free from Soviet infiltration. As the Soviets made inroads in Africa, the shah supported regimes such as Mobutu's Zaire and Barre's Somalia, as well as more stable African countries which were on the correct side of the East–West divide, such as Kenya, Senegal and South Africa. Furthermore, the security of Africa, particularly North Africa and the Horn of Africa, due to their proximity to Iran's immediate neighbourhood, could impact not only the stability of the Middle East, but also the internal security of Iran. These concerns were evident during the late 1950s and 1960s, when Nasser's Egypt was considered by the shah to be a grave threat, and to a lesser extent in the 1970s, when Qadaffi sought to take on the mantle as the leader of the Arab world after Nasser's death. In fact, the threat of Nasser in the 1960s prompted the shah to establish relations with Haile Selassie's Ethiopia, a fellow member of Israel's Policy of the Periphery, conceived in the 1950s to encourage cooperation between non-Arab states who felt threatened by Arab solidarity. As further evidence of the impact of

[36] Rebecca Friedman Lissner, 'What Is Grand Strategy? Sweeping a Conceptual Minefield', *Texas National Security Review*, vol. 2, no. 1 (2018), 56.

[37] Ehteshami, 'Iran's Grand Strategy under the Pahlavis', 198.

[38] James F. Goode, 'Assisting Our Brothers, Defending Ourselves: The Iranian Intervention in Oman, 1972–75', *Iranian Studies*, vol. 47, no. 3 (2014), 443.

Middle Eastern affairs on Iran's broader strategy, the Six-Day War of 1967 led to greater interaction between Iran and South Africa.

There was also a doctrinal aspect of Iran's grand strategy, to which Ehteshami alludes, which was based around the idea of Iran as a civilisational beacon for the world. During the 1970s, particularly after the shah's celebrations marking the 2500th anniversary of the founding of the Persian Empire in 1971, at which Haile Selassie held a prominent position, the idea of Iran as a distinct 'civilisation' became ever more popular. As Cyrus Schayegh has argued, 'Iranians believed their country had always played a role far beyond its borders. It had lost that role at the latest when Western imperialism emerged in the nineteenth century. But now, from the late 1960s, it was back: a return that many Iranians, not only the shah, saw as natural and merited given Iran's historical clout.'[39] The discourse of civilisation revealed Iran's imperial ambitions, but it was also important language that Iran employed in its interactions with countries in the Global South. For example, during her visit to Senegal in 1976, Empress Farah visited Gorée Island off the coast of Dakar, which is believed to have been a slaving post and whose colonial buildings provide a reminder of the island's sinister past.[40] Speaking of the experience to the press afterwards, the empress said:

> Paradoxically, during this overwhelming pilgrimage to this islet symbol of slavery, I felt proud of my *Iranité*. Indeed, wasn't it Cyrus the Great who, 2,500 years ago, abolished slavery in his empire, the Persian Empire, ancestor of ours ... Really, that day, I was proud to be Iranian, proud to be able to walk with head held high before the descendants of the martyrs of one of the great genocides in history.[41]

[39] Cyrus Schayegh, 'Iran's Global Long 1970s: An Empire Project, Civilisational Developmentalism, and the Crisis of the Global North', in *The Age of Aryamehr: Late Pahlavi Iran and Its Global Entanglements*, ed. Roham Alvandi (London: Gingko Library, 2018), 267.

[40] Though research has shown that Gorée Island was insignificant in the context of the Trans-Atlantic slave trade. For discussion, see Ana Lucia Araujo, *Shadows of the Slave Past: Memory, Heritage, and Slavery* (New York: Routledge, 2014), 57–65.

[41] *Bingo*, February 1976, 46. Of course, Iran had its own history of slavery, of which the empress was apparently unaware. On this history and its legacies, see Behnaz A. Mirzai, *A History of Slavery and Emancipation in Iran, 1800–1929* (Austin: University of Texas Press, 2017); and Beeta Baghoolizadeh, *The Color Black Enslavement and Erasure in Iran* (Durham, NC: Duke University Press, 2024).

Civilisational ties were a major theme of the language of Iran's diplomacy with other countries that had similarly ancient and celebrated histories, such as Egypt and Ethiopia. During the 1960s, both Iran and Ethiopia presented themselves as representing distinct Asian and African civilisations, and the discussions between the two sides were presented as discussions between two civilisations, rather than merely two sovereign nations.

Finally, there was an economic and industrial aspect to Iran's global strategy in the 1960s and 1970s, as Iran sought first to maximise oil revenues, and then strengthen its industrial base in Iran to achieve the shah's often stated goal of elevating Iran to the status of a developed country by the end of the century. Africa, like much of the world, was viewed as a market for Iranian oil, and many countries during the 1970s relied heavily on supplies of Iranian oil; the most obvious example is South Africa, which received more than 90 per cent of its crude oil from Iran in the late 1970s. This was transhipped to other countries in the region that depended on South Africa economically, including Rhodesia. Iran's long-term energy strategy involved transforming Iran into a major producer of nuclear energy. To power Iran's proposed twenty nuclear power plants, it needed a regular supply of uranium. The acquisition of uranium and investment in nuclear infrastructure thus became one of the most pressing concerns in Iran's relations with African countries in the latter half of the 1970s.

Layout and Sources

One of the challenges in researching transnational history which concerns many different countries is that source material is often spread out in libraries and archives around the world – some of which are difficult to access, and some that contain documents which have not yet been declassified. The research for this book has incorporated archival material from Canada, France, Iran, the Netherlands, the United Kingdom and the United States. Materials were sourced from state archives as well as personal papers, including those of Ardeshir Zāhedi at the Hoover Institute in Stanford, Shojāʿ al-Din Shafā at the Bibliothèque universitaire des langues et civilisations in Paris and Moshe Safdie at McGill University in Montreal. The research also draws extensively on Iranian, African, European and American newspapers. Of particular importance was the Iranian semi-official daily newspaper *Ettelā'āt*. Given the absence of a free press in Iran in the period under study, the editorial choices of the major official newspapers generally reflected the official government line. The importance of newspapers for analysis of official policy was also noted by Chubin and Zabih, who argue that the Iranian press can be 'used as an indicator of the government's views on foreign relations'.[42] Other printed sources, such as oral histories and memoirs, have formed an important part of the analysis, including those of the diplomats Jalāl 'Abdoh, Shāhrokh Firuz and Ardeshir Zāhedi.

Another difficulty in writing a history of one country's relations with an entire continent is how to set the work out in a coherent and logical manner. The book is divided into three parts chronologically, with chapters set out geographically or thematically. The first part covers the period from the 1950s until 1970, the formative years of Iran's interests in Africa, focusing particularly on the regions in which Iran had strategic, political and economic interests: North Africa, the Horn of Africa and South Africa. The second part focuses on the period from 1971 until 1975, when Iran achieved vast increases in oil revenues and, after the British withdrawal from the Persian Gulf, when Africa became an increasingly important area in the context of Iran's grand strategy. The chapters of this part explore the changing political situation in the Horn of Africa, Iran's relations with countries in West Africa, the role of Islam in Iran's Africa policy, and Iran's aid and development projects in Africa. The third part concentrates on the period of 1976 until 1979, the height of Iran's prestige in Africa, in spite of the onset of the economic crisis that would spark the revolution. Its chapters examine Iran's special relationship with Senegal, its role in the Ogaden War fought between Ethiopia and Somalia in 1977–1978, and Iran's position in southern Africa, including Iran's support of US–British initiatives to resolve the crisis in Rhodesia.

[42] Chubin and Zabih, *The Foreign Relations of Iran*, 22.

PART I

Establishing Relations (c. 1957–1970)

1 *Iran, Egypt and the Spectre of Nasserism*

During the 1950s and 1960s, Iran's regional security outlook, as well as its relations with the United States and the Soviet Union, was, to a large degree, shaped by events in North Africa, particularly in Egypt. Egypt, like Iran, had long aspired to play a leading role in regional and global politics. The marriage of the Pahlavi crown prince, Mohammad Reza Pahlavi, to Princess Fawzia Faud of Egypt in 1939 reflected both of these aspirations in different ways. For Reza Shah, who had founded his new dynasty in 1925, linking the Pahlavi royal house to an older, venerable Islamic monarchy would enhance his dynasty's legitimacy, and at the same time, against the backdrop of the Treaty of Saʿdābād, strengthen regional cooperation. For the Egyptian King Farouk, the alliance would help to validate his credentials as an important leader in the Islamic world.

While Iran had enjoyed relatively cordial relations with Egypt under King Farouk, the coup of 1952 saw the demise of the Egyptian monarchy and its replacement with a regime hostile to Iran, headed by Gamal ʿAbd al-Nasser. In the years that followed, Nasser emerged as a powerful voice within the Afro-Asian bloc, and a rallying point for revolutionary, anti-imperial movements across the Global South. This was particularly the case in the Arab world, where Nasser became the champion of the Arab cause and, to a certain extent, Islamic unity. As this chapter will show, the shah perceived Nasser as a threat not only to Iran's territorial integrity but also to Iran's internal security and to the very survival of the Pahlavi monarchy. During the Suez crisis in 1956, Iran voiced its public support for Egypt's sovereign right to nationalise the canal, partly to placate those who sympathised with the Egyptian struggle against imperialism. At the same time, however, to American and British diplomats and politicians, the shah and his ministers warned of the dangers of an Egyptian victory and encouraged their Western partners to use force if necessary. Nasser's policy of positive neutralism, which essentially meant non-alignment in, but not indifference to, world affairs, can be contrasted to the shah's policy of positive nationalism, conceived as a response to Mohammad Mosaddeq's negative or irresponsible nationalism during his premiership from 1951 to 1953. Positive nationalism, a precursor to the shah's independent national policy of the 1960s and 1970s, essentially meant that Iran pursued a nationalist agenda, but without damaging relations with the major powers.[1] Iran's relationship with Egypt perfectly captures the evolution of Iran's foreign policy during this period.

Egypt and Iran under King Farouk

On 24 February 1939, the crown prince of Iran, Mohammad Reza Pahlavi, left Tehran for Baghdad. He was accompanied by a cohort of important officials, including the speaker of the Majles, Mirzā Hasan Esfandiyāri; the minister of foreign affairs, Mozaffar Aʿlam; the minister of justice, Matin Daftari; his personal chamberlain, Dr Moʾadab Nafisi; the director general of the Ministry of Foreign Affairs, Mohammad ʿAli Moqaddam; the Majles representative, Dr Qāsem Ghani; the head of *Ettelāʿāt* newspaper, ʿAbbās Masʿudi; along with an Imperial Court minister and several adjutants.[2] This royal delegation arrived in Baghdad on 26 February, where they stayed for two nights at Zuhur Palace as guests of King Ghāzi I.[3] They then travelled onwards via Damascus to Beirut, where they boarded a ship to their final destination, Egypt. There the crown prince was to wed the sister of King Farouk, Princess Fawzia Faud.

Egypt and Iran had been allies for some time. Iran had been the first country to recognise Egypt after it achieved independence on 28 February 1922, and soon thereafter it upgraded its consulate in Cairo to an embassy. Egypt followed suit and opened an embassy in Tehran in 1925.[4] In 1928, a treaty of amity and friendship (*qarārdād-e mavaddat va dusti*) was agreed upon between Iran and Egypt – the first

[1] On the independent national policy, see *Decade of the Revolution*, 171–174.

[2] Sergei Barseghian, 'Malakeh-ye Mesri-ye Darbār-e Irān: Ezdevāj va Talāgh-e Mohammad Rezā Pahlavi va Fawziyeh', *Tarikh-e Irani*, 30 Esfand 1389. Available online: http://tarikhirani.ir/fa/news/7102/ ملکه-مصری-دربار-ایران-ازدواج-و-طلاق-محمدرضا-پهلوی-و-فوزیه.

[3] King Ghāzi died in a car accident little over a month later on 4 April 1939, aged just twenty-seven. He was succeeded by his son, Faisal II.

[4] Ahmad Bakhshi, 'Barresi-ye Tārikhi-ye Ravābet-e Khāreji-ye Irān va Qāreh-ye Āfriqā', *Tārikh-e Ravābet-e Khāreji*, vol. 35 (1387/2008), 44.

such treaty that independent Egypt had signed with an Islamic country.[5] This was followed two years later by a trade agreement, along with the establishment of an Iranian chamber of commerce in Egypt.[6]

At the same time as Iran's relations with Egypt were improving steadily, the governments of Iran, Afghanistan, Iraq and Turkey signed a treaty of non-aggression at Saʿdābād Palace in Tehran on 8 July 1937. Under the Saʿdābād Pact, the signatory governments pledged to refrain from interfering in one another's internal affairs, respect common borders, refrain from aggression towards one another and refrain from pursuing policies designed to disturb the peace between neighbouring countries.[7] Iran had sought to convince Egypt to join the pact and the Egyptian cabinet appeared keen to do so, but ultimately it refused.[8] In spite of Egypt's absence from the Saʿdābād Pact, the marriage of the two royal houses reaffirmed both Iran and Egypt's commitment to regional cooperation.[9]

Like his siblings, Mohammad Reza Pahlavi must have accepted that he would have little say in the selection of his spouse.[10] His two sisters, Shams and Ashraf, had been married in September 1936 to husbands chosen by their father. Reza Shah had decided that his son must be married to a woman of 'a great and well established line' to help legitimise the fledgling Pahlavi Dynasty as part of the global monarchical order.[11] He had considered foreign princesses, including Princess Ingrid of Sweden, as well as Iranian, such as the daughter of Ahmad Shah, the last king of the Qajar dynasty.[12] It has been

[5] Barseghian, 'Malakeh-ye Mesri-ye Darbār-e Irān'.

[6] Ibid. See also, Shahrough Akhavi, 'EGYPT vii. Political and Religious Relations with Persia in the Modern Period', *Encyclopaedia Iranica*, VIII/3 (1998), 257–262. Available online: www.iranicaonline.org/articles/egypt-vii.

[7] Laurence P. Elwell-Sutton, *Modern Iran* (London: George Routledge & Sons, 1941), 225–228.

[8] Barseghian, 'Malakeh-ye Mesri-ye Darbār-e Irān'.

[9] Also important in the context of this drive for regional cooperation is the state visit of Reza Shah to Turkey in 1934. See Afshin Marashi, 'Performing the Nation: The Shah's Official State Visit to Kemalist Turkey, June to July 1934', in *The Making of Modern Iran: State and Society under Riza Shah, 1921–1941*, ed. Stephanie Cronin (London: Routledge, 2003), 99–119.

[10] Mohammad Reza Pahlavi, *Mission for My Country* (London: Hutchinson & Co., 1961), 218.

[11] Gholam Reza Afkhami, *The Life and Times of the Shah* (Berkley: University of California Press, 2009), 40.

[12] Though the constitution stipulated that a king of Iran may not be of Qajar blood.

suggested that the idea to marry the Iranian crown prince to an Egyptian princess came from the Turkish president, Mustafa Kemal Atatürk, who relayed a message to Iran's ambassador to Iraq, Mozaffar Aʿlam, through his foreign minister, Rushdi Aras, that 'such a marriage would be in the interests of all countries in the region, especially Iran and Egypt'.[13] Iran's ambassador in Cairo, Javād Sinki, met with Princess Fawzia and sent a telegram to Reza Shah to propose a marriage between her and the crown prince.[14] Reza Shah was apparently warm to the idea, particularly as it would help to strengthen Iran's ties to the most powerful Arab state.[15]

Before this fundamentally political marriage could be agreed, it had to be debated by both the Egyptian cabinet and the Iranian Majles. The cabinet of Mostafa el-Nahas Pasha, leader of the Wadf Party, decided that it would support the marriage not only because it would strengthen the bilateral relationship with Iran but because it could play a crucial role in establishing Egypt's role in the Islamic world as the seat of a renewed Islamic caliphate.[16] At the time of the wedding, the English press reported, 'The purpose of this marriage is to revive the Islamic caliphate and choose King Farouk as the Muslim caliph.'[17]

With the approval of both governments, the engagement was announced in Cairo and Tehran on 26 May 1938 (5 Khordād 1317). This was the first time that the Iranian crown prince heard the news. In Iran, although Reza Shah had agreed to the marriage, the constitution stipulated that the parents of a shah should both be Iranian. To overcome this, Reza Shah instructed his minister of justice, Matin Daftari, to come up with a solution.[18] Daftari thus proposed a bill to

[13] Afkhami, *The Life and Times of the Shah*, 41.

[14] Barseghian, 'Malakeh-ye Mesri-ye Darbār-e Irān'.

[15] It has been suggested that it was during Reza Shah's trip to Turkey in 1934 that Atatürk first suggested to him that he marry his crown prince to the Egyptian royal family. See Barseghian, 'Malakeh-ye Mesri-ye Darbār-e Irān'.

[16] Ibid.

[17] 'Egyptian Princess Fawzia: How Her Marriage to Iran's Pahlavi Ended in Divorce', *Alarabiya*, 15 January 2019. Available online: https://english.alarabiya.net/features/2019/01/15/Egyptian-Princess-Fawzia-How-her-marriage-to-Iran-s-Pahlavi-ended-in-divorce. Just six years later, as Firoozeh Kashani-Sabet observes, some in Iran interpreted the creation of the Arab League in March 1945 as 'a modernist attempt to recast the caliphate with Egypt at its center', Firoozeh Kashani-Sabet, 'Iran on Shaky Ground: Iran between Israel and Pan-Arabism, 1930–1970s', *Middle East Studies*, vol. 59, no. 6 (2023), 953.

[18] Barseghian, 'Malakeh-ye Mesri-ye Darbār-e Irān'.

the Majles on 31 October 1938 (9 Ābān 1317), proposing that the term 'Iranian origin' in the article be interpreted to include a person who is, in the national interest, declared by imperial degree to be Iranian.[19] The bill passed on 3 November (14 Ābān).[20] In a country where the monarch traditionally married women from his own country, the significance of the future shah wedding a foreign princess was noted by foreign diplomats.[21]

The first time Mohammad Reza Pahlavi met his wife-to-be was at a banquet prepared in his honour by Princess Fawzia's mother, Queen Nazli, on 4 March 1939. The wedding was originally due to take place on 16 March but was brought forward to coincide with the birthday of Reza Shah and Egyptian Constitution Day.[22] The wedding ceremony itself was simple, according to Islamic tradition, but efforts were made to turn the marriage into a national celebration. As Qāsem Ghani recalled, 'The earth and sky were celebrating. All of Cairo was covered in flowers. The whole country participated in the celebration.'[23] One month later, on 14 April 1939, the crown prince and his bride arrived in Iran for a second wedding ceremony at Golestān Palace in Tehran.[24] The wedding triggered what Asef Bayat and Bahman Baktiari refer to as 'an outpouring of panegyric on the warm relations between Egypt and Iran'.[25] Poetry in particular referred to Iran and Egypt as 'civilisations', which were 'shining examples of an awakening East'.[26] As a result of the closer cultural ties that were forged by the union, Al-Azhar University in Cairo began to offer Persian language courses.[27]

The Anglo-Soviet invasion of Iran in August 1941 resulted in the forced abdication of Reza Shah, and his succession by Mohammad

[19] Afkhami, *The Life and Times of the Shah*, 41.
[20] Mozākerāt-e Majles-e Showrā-ye Melli, 14 Ābān 1317, Jalaseh-ye 46.
[21] Firoozeh Kashani-Sabet, *Conceiving Citizens: Women and the Politics of Motherhood in Iran* (Oxford: Oxford University Press, 2011), 71.
[22] *The Palestine Post*, 5 March 1939, 2.
[23] Qāsem Ghani cited in Barseghian, 'Malakeh-ye Mesri-ye Darbār-e Irān'.
[24] Barseghian, 'Malakeh-ye Mesri-ye Darbār-e Irān'. Princess Fawzia brought her mother, Queen Nazli, with her, along with three sisters. Apparently, they were extremely critical of the inferior jewels the Pahlavi royal family wore during the reception, which led to a dispute between her and Reza Shah.
[25] Asef Bayat and Bahman Baktiari, 'Revolutionary Iran and Egypt: Exporting Inspirations and Anxieties', in *Iran and the Surrounding World: Interactions in Culture and Cultural Politics*, ed. Nikki R. Keddie and Rudi Matthee (Seattle: University of Washington Press, 2002), 306.
[26] Ibid. [27] Ibid.

Reza Pahlavi. The invasion of Iran was met with anger in some circles in Egypt, and several Egyptian government officials resigned in disgust at the failure of their government to offer even moral support to Tehran.[28] After the death of Reza Pahlavi from a heart attack on 26 July 1944, due to the difficulties in transferring the body back to Iran at this time, it was decided to mummify the body and take it to Egypt to be transferred to Iran at a later date. The Egyptian government was helpful in issuing visas to those who would transport the body from South Africa to Egypt.[29] A funeral ceremony was held in Cairo for Reza Shah, and his body was temporarily interned at the Rifaʿi Mosque to be transferred to Iran after the completion of a mausoleum.[30]

The divorce of Mohammad Reza Pahlavi, then shah, and Princess Fawzia in 1948 caused a strain in relations between the two royal houses. Indeed, it took some diplomatic skill on behalf of Iran's ambassador in Cairo, ʿAli Dashti, to convince the Egyptians in 1950 to allow the transfer of the body of Reza Shah to Iran in an appropriately regal manner.[31] Reza Shah might have hoped that the union between the Iranian and Egyptian royal houses would lead to a closer political union, but even though relations remained warm, it is unclear whether it had the desired effect. Indeed, the marriage between Mohammad Reza Pahlavi and Princess Fawzia was ultimately an unhappy one, and the two royal families never really got along; if anything, one might conclude that the union had complicated the bilateral relationship.

Iran and Egypt under Mosaddeq and Nasser

Iran and Egypt had similar experiences with imperialism, particularly British imperialism. Although Iran had not been formally colonised by the British Empire, Britain had complete control of Iran's oil industry, just as it exercised control of the Suez Canal. While there were no attempts by Iran's political elite to challenge Britain's influence in Egypt in the nineteenth century – indeed, Naser al-Din Shah had sent a delegation to Egypt to observe the opening ceremony of the Suez

[28] Nikolay A. Kozhanov, 'The Pretexts and Reasons for the Allied Invasion of Iran in 1941', *Iranian Studies*, vol. 45, no. 4 (2012), 487.
[29] Barseghian, 'Malakeh-ye Mesri-ye Darbār-e Irān'.
[30] Afkhami, *The Life and Times of the Shah*, 84. [31] Ibid., 84–85.

Canal in 1869 – some Iranian intellectuals were involved in anti-colonial networks in Cairo.[32] For example, the famed Iranian anti-imperialist intellectual Jamāl al-Din Afghāni (1838–1897) spent some years in Egypt on a stipend provided by the Egyptian government and inspired generations of Egyptian anti-imperial intellectuals and revolutionaries, such as Mohammad Abduh.[33]

In the early 1950s, it appeared as though Egypt and Iran were following similar trajectories. The prime minister of Iran, Mohammad Mosaddeq, nationalised Iran's oil industry in March 1951. Just months later, in October, the Wadf government announced that it was abrogating the Anglo-Egyptian treaty of 1936, which allowed for the continued presence of British troops in Egypt. Throughout 1951, the process of Iran's oil nationalisation and Britain's humiliating retreat were followed closely in the Egyptian press.[34] One month later, Mosaddeq stopped in Egypt for a four-day visit on his return from New York, where he had defended Iran's case in front of the UN Security Council. Mosaddeq was received in Cairo, in the words of Lior Sternfeld, 'as a victorious leader who fearlessly faced Britain and, to British dismay, had expelled them from Iran'.[35] The Egyptian prime minister, Mostafa el-Nahas Pasha, may have hoped that by inviting Mosaddeq to Egypt at this time, he could increase popular support for his government's own struggle against British imperialism. Two years later, Mosaddeq was ousted in a coup sponsored by the British and American secret services, and the Consortium Agreement of 1954 finally settled the Iranian oil crisis.

The Free Officers' coup in July 1952 overthrew the Egyptian monarchy and precipitated the establishment of a revolutionary regime headed by Gamal ʿAbd al-Nasser. However, the coup did not

[32] Bakhshi, 'Barresi-ye Tārikhi-ye Ravābet-e Khāreji-ye Irān va Qāreh-ye Āfriqā', 44.

[33] See Rudi Matthee, 'Jamal al-Din Afghani and the Egyptian National Debate', *International Journal of Middle East Studies*, vol. 21, no. 2 (1989), 151–169. For a biography of Jamāl al-Din Afghāni, see Nikki R. Keddie, *Sayyid Jamāl ad-Dīn "al-Afghānī": A Political Biography* (Berkeley: University of California Press, 1972).

[34] On the press reaction in Egypt, see Lior Sternfeld, 'Iran Days in Egypt: Mosaddeq's Visit to Cairo in 1951', *British Journal of Middle Eastern Studies*, vol. 43, no. 1 (2016), 6–10.

[35] Ibid., 4–5.

immediately cause fundamental changes to Egypt's foreign policy. Egypt still gravitated towards the West and its primary goal was to achieve the complete withdrawal of British forces.[36] The shah was nervous about events in Egypt, as it had brought about the downfall of a regional monarchy. However, Nasser did not yet present a threat to Iran, and until the summer of 1955, the shah was evidently hopeful of developing a relationship with the Egyptian president. In April 1955, both Iran and Egypt were officially represented at the Asian–African conference in Bandung, Indonesia. Although the shah used the occasion to attempt to reach out to Nasser, in retrospect the event perfectly illustrates the different trajectories the two states took in politics of the Global South in this post–Second World War era of decolonisation. While Iran sought to take a moderate role and balance its relations with its Western allies with platitudes of solidarity with anti-colonial leaders from Asia and Africa, Nasser became ever more enticed by the possibilities of Afro-Asian solidarity. Just two and a half years after Bandung, Nasser hosted the first Afro-Asian Peoples' Solidarity Conference in Cairo.

The Bandung Conference

From 18 to 24 April 1955, representatives of twenty-nine countries attended the Asian–African Conference in Bandung, the most important gathering in the Asian–African internationalism that developed in the years following the Second World War, championed by the Indian prime minister, Jawaharlal Nehru.[37] The conference was conceived in April 1954 at a meeting of the prime ministers of Burma, Ceylon, India, Indonesia and Pakistan in Ceylon's capital, Colombo, with the goal of fostering common understanding and solidarity among members of the Afro-Asian nations, helping them to prosper as independent states.[38] Although Iran attended the conference, it was something of a reluctant participant. Indeed, until weeks before, it was not

[36] Elie Podeh, 'The Drift towards Neutrality: Egyptian Foreign Policy during the Early Nasserist Era, 1952–55', *Middle Eastern Studies*, vol. 32, no. 1 (1996), 159.

[37] On the historical background to Bandung, see Lüthi, *Cold Wars*, 266–278.

[38] Ibid., 275–276.

clear to foreign diplomats in Tehran whether Iran would agree to send a delegation at all.[39]

Iran did, ultimately, send a delegation. This delegation was led by Jalāl ʿAbdoh, the director-general of the Political Affairs Section of the Iranian Ministry of Foreign Affairs, and an experienced diplomat, having been a member of Iran's delegation to the founding conference of the United Nations in San Francisco in 1945 and having held several positions in the United Nations in the years since.[40] He was accompanied by several colleagues from the Ministry of Foreign Affairs, including Amir Aslān Afshār, who had previously spent time at the Iranian legation in The Hague. Afshār was considered by the Dutch government to be very pro-Dutch. He spoke Dutch fluently, had written a book about the Netherlands and had been granted the Officer's Cross of the Order of Orange-Nassau (Officierskruis van de Orde van Oranje-Nassau) by the Dutch government.[41] The Dutch government was concerned that the Indonesian government might use the Bandung Conference to build support for the annexation of New Guinea. Its position was that New Guinea should be able to choose its own fate and that 'the Netherlands are better equipped to fulfil the task of civilizing New Guinea and its people than Indonesia is'.[42]

In the weeks leading up to the Bandung Conference, the Dutch Foreign Ministry summoned the ambassadors to the Netherlands of Iran, Turkey, Egypt and Pakistan to implore them not to cooperate with any Indonesian initiative to discuss New Guinea.[43] Diplomats in Tehran felt that because Afshār had pro-Dutch inclinations, he 'can be

[39] Dutch Ministry of Foreign Affairs to Dutch Embassy Tehran, 22 March 1955, NA 2.05.191/470.

[40] Press Release PM/3417, 17 September 1957, UN Secretariat archive: S-0876-0001-07-00001. ʿAli Amini was originally selected to head the delegation, but he decided not to attend because of the formation of the cabinet of the new prime minister, Hoseyn ʿAlā, in which he was given the position of minister of justice. Dutch ambassador in Tehran to Ministry of Foreign Affairs, 'Iraanse delegatie ter Afro-Aziatische Conferentie', 12 April 1955, NA 2.05.191/470. Amini also decided to stay because of an upcoming visit by a representative of the oil consortium, which 'was considered more important'. Dutch ambassador in Tehran to Ministry of Foreign Affairs, 20 April 1955, NA 2.05.191/470.

[41] Dutch ambassador in Tehran to Ministry of Foreign Affairs, 12 April 1955, NA 2.05.191/470.

[42] Dutch Ministry of Foreign Affairs to ambassador in Tehran, 22 March 1955, NA 2.05.191/470.

[43] Dutch Ministry of Foreign Affairs to ambassador in Tehran, 12 April 1955, NA 2.05.191/470.

in a certain sense a "team mate" (*medespeler*)'.[44] Afshār was a keen amateur photographer, so the Dutch ambassador gave him a packet of empty colour films so that he could record his trip.[45] The day before the Iranian delegation left Iran for Bandung, the Dutch ambassador and his secretary dined with Afshār.[46] The Dutch felt convinced that the Iranian delegation would 'definitely try to have a moderating effect', however 'if push comes to shove, it will have to consider the viewpoints of other Muslim countries'.[47]

Other countries' ambassadors also briefed the Iranian delegation before it left, including those of the United States, Britain and France. The French were clearly concerned that the situation in Algeria could come under scrutiny, and the British felt that Iran, Turkey and Iraq, which would shortly after become members of the Baghdad Pact, along with Britain, would be important voices of moderation.[48] Before leaving for Bandung, ʿAbdoh had an audience with the shah, in which the shah doubted that the conference would have a positive impact, but had nonetheless decided that it was 'in the interest' of Iran to attend. 'Of course, we will refrain from taking an extreme position', he added.[49]

In his speech to the congress, ʿAbdoh articulated Iran's position of moderation. He encouraged delegates to 'avoid subjects that would bring out differences between countries', and not use the event to 'promote political ideologies'.[50] Consistent with Iran's policy not to interfere in disputes between newly independent states and their former colonisers, Iran 'expressed understanding' for the French position in North Africa, 'while recognising the legitimate aspirations of the peoples' there.[51] Upon his return to Iran, ʿAbdoh spoke positively to a small group of civil servants and foreign diplomats about the 'sense

44 J. P. B. de Graan to Willem Gevers (Dutch ambassador in Tehran), 4 April 1955, NA 2.05.191/470.

45 Ibid. 46 Gevers to de Graan, 27 April 1955, NA 2.05.191/470.

47 Gevers to Ministry of Foreign Affairs, 20 April 1955, NA 2.05.191/470.

48 Bédrède, 'Iran's Foreign Policy and the Algerian War of Independence, 1954–1962', fn. 14, 169.

49 Jalāl ʿAbdoh, *Chehel Sāl dar Sahneh-ye Qazāʾi, Siyāsi, Diplomāsi-ye Irān va Jahān: Khāterāt-e Doktor Jalāl ʿAbdoh*, vol. 1 (Tehran: Moʾassaseh-ye Khadmāt-e Farhangi-ye Rasā, 1368 [1989]), 443.

50 ʿAbdoh quoted in Bédrède, 'Iran's Foreign Policy and the Algerian War of Independence 1954–1962', 169.

51 Letter from General Ely to Antoine Pinay, Saigon, 28 April 1955. Available online: www.cvce.eu/en/obj/letter_from_general_ely_to_antoine_pinay_on_the_

of unity and interdependence between countries in spite of economic and political differences' and even claimed to have 'preferred the atmosphere and tone at Bandung over that at the assemblies of the United Nations'.[52] In the delicate diplomatic balancing act, not everyone would be pleased. In a conversation with the Dutch ambassador, ʿAbdoh expressed discomfort at having been forced to join a vote on New Guinea, against the wishes of the Netherlands.

While the Bandung Conference underlined the shah's commitment to the Western Bloc, Nasser was convinced to adopt a policy of positive neutrality and non-alignment. After returning from the conference, as Elie Podeh argues, Nasser became 'more confident in his dealings with the West', from which he had sought weapons and development aid.[53] A year before the meeting in Bandung, in April 1954, Turkey and Pakistan had signed a cooperation agreement, encouraged by the United States which intended for it to form the basis of a broader regional defence pact. Egypt feared that such a pact, if it included other Arab states such as Iraq, would undermine its negotiating position vis-à-vis the British.[54] Moreover, Nasser was concerned that 'a pact under Iraqi leadership would shift the centre of gravity in the Arab world from Cairo to Baghdad and would lead to Egypt's isolation.'[55] In February 1955, Iraq and Turkey signed the Baghdad Pact, which Nasser viewed as part of a broader Western plot to weaken Egypt's role in the region.

The presence of Egypt at the Bandung Conference two months later, represented an opportunity for Iran and Egypt to engage. At Bandung, Jalāl ʿAbdoh extended to Nasser an invitation on behalf of the shah to visit Iran. Nasser accepted the invitation in principle and even expressed a wish to spend more time in Iran in the future, since his wife, Tahia Kazem, came from an Iranian family.[56] However, the geopolitical situation changed just months later and Nasser would not build on the diplomacy started at Bandung. In September 1955, to the shock and anger of Britain, Egypt announced an arms deal with

bandung_conference_saigon_28_april_1955-en-f71582f5-0631-4b0d-a1a9-4d7a75eeffdb.html%5D%20.

52 Gevers to Ministry of Foreign Affairs, 10 May 1955, NA 2.05.191/470.

53 Podeh, 'The Drift towards Neutrality', 172. 54 Ibid., 163. 55 Ibid., 168.

56 ʿAbdoh, *Chehel Sāl dar Sahneh-ye Qazāʾi, Siyāsi, Diplomāsi-ye Irān va Jahān*, vol. 1, 475. ʿAbdoh recalls that Nasser referred to himself as a compatriot (*ham vatan*) of his.

the Soviets through Czechoslovakia. Nasser had been infuriated by the West's reluctance to supply him the arms that he wanted. During Nasser's trip to Bandung in April, he had met with the Chinese premier Chou En-Lai, who suggested that Nasser seek military aid from the Eastern Bloc.[57] Earlier in June, Nasser had warned the US ambassador, Henry Byroade, that the Soviets had offered to provide Egypt with all the arms it needed.[58] Then, in October 1955, apparently with some encouragement from the United States and Britain, the shah decided that Iran would also be joining the Baghdad Pact.[59] The shah reasoned that membership of the pact would bring guarantees of the Eisenhower administration's commitment to Iran's security.[60] Nonetheless, Nasser denounced the pact as a 'Zionist plot', perceived that Iran was backing Iraq in the battle for leadership of the Arab world, and relations between Iran and Egypt soured.[61]

The Suez Crisis

On 26 July 1956, Nasser announced the nationalisation of the Suez Canal, which had been owned and operated by the British and French since 1869. Immediately, the British and French began to draw up military plans to bring about the downfall of the Egyptian president.[62] They cooperated in these plans with Israel, which viewed Nasser as a serious threat, particularly given his acquisition of Soviet weapons. At the same time, the Eisenhower administration attempted to negotiate a peaceful settlement of the crisis. Iran's policy, according to the shah 'was thoroughly in line with that of [the] US, namely that while recognizing [the] right of Egypt to "nationalize" a purely Egyptian company, some means must be found for guaranteeing free and secure use of [the] Suez Canal as [an] international waterway'.[63] To achieve

57 Podeh, 'The Drift towards Neutrality', 171.
58 Keith Kyle, *Suez: Britain's End of Empire in the Middle East* (London: I. B. Tauris, 2011), 72.
59 Ali Rahnema, *The Rise of Modern Despotism in Iran: The Shah, the Opposition, and the US, 1953–1968* (London: Oneworld Academic, 2021), 75.
60 Alvandi, *Nixon, Kissinger, and the Shah*, 18–21.
61 Ramazani, *Iran's Foreign Policy*, 397.
62 Nasser had been elected the second president of Egypt in June 1956.
63 Telegram from the Embassy in Iran to the Department of State, Tehran, 9 August 1956, *FRUS, 1955–1957, Near East Region; Iran; Iraq, Volume XII*, doc. 362.

this, Iran ostensibly supported US-led initiatives to solve the crisis diplomatically and sent a delegation to the first Suez Canal Conference in London, held from 16 to 23 August 1956. As head of this delegation, the minister of foreign affairs, ʿAliqoli Ardalān, was 'instructed to support the American Delegation' in finding a solution.[64] Prior to the conference, President Eisenhower's secretary of state, John Foster Dulles, sent a personal message to the shah, which read: 'Your Government can, I am confident, exert an important and constructive influence, and I trust you will do so.'[65]

Iran relied heavily on the Suez Canal for the import and export of goods. In his speech to the London Conference, Ardalān told delegates that 73 per cent of Iranian exports and 76 per cent of imports were transported through the Suez Canal and that 'no less than five thousand tons of Iranian oil were transported to the western world through this waterway'.[66] The political situation in Iran was still unstable following the August 1953 coup – indeed, the prime minister, Hoseyn ʿAlā, had survived an assassination attempt just months earlier, in November 1955. Thus, a prolongation of the crisis, or a disruption in the production or delivery of Iranian oil could severely damage the Iranian economy and would, according to a US projection, 'gravely weaken the [Iranian] Government'.[67]

The Iranian position was set out by Ardalān in his speech. Iran essentially had two arguments. The first was in support of nationalisation. Ardalān said, 'It is a legal fact that the Suez Canal is an integral part of Egypt ... we believe that the action of the Egyptian Government is in conformity with her sovereign rights.' Given Iran's recent experience of oil nationalisation, public opinion was naturally sympathetic to the nationalisation of the canal, so this was as much a

64 Memorandum of a Conversation between the Iranian Ambassador (Amini) and the Under Secretary of State (Hoover), Department of State, Washington, 13 August 1956, *FRUS, 1955–1957, Near East Region; Iran; Iraq, Volume XII*, doc. 363.

65 Ibid., fn. 2.

66 United States Department of State, *The Suez Canal Problem, July 26–September 22, 1956: A Documentary Publication* (Washington, DC: The Department of State, 1956).

67 Memorandum from the Assistant Secretary of State for Near Eastern, South Asian, and African Affairs (Rountree) to the Secretary of State, Washington, 26 September 1956, *FRUS, 1955–1957, Near East Region; Iran; Iraq, Volume XII*, doc. 365.

political position as a principled one. Second, given the 'vital importance' of the Suez Canal to Iranian trade, Iran wanted continued undisturbed access to the canal. 'This is why the Government of Iran will support a form of solution or an international system that is compatible with the legitimate rights of Egypt and the guaranteed permanent freedom of navigation of the Suez', Ardalān said. 'We shall spare no effort in the achievement of this aim.'[68] Ultimately, Secretary Dulles' proposal to end the crisis, which included the provision for an international board to replace Franco-British management of the canal, received the support of eighteen out of the twenty-two nations that attended the conference.

Iran, along with Pakistan, Ethiopia and Turkey, attempted to take a leading role, by proposing, as a bloc, amendments to the proposal, which then became known as the 'Five Nation Proposal'.[69] Dulles considered the support of these nations for the proposal particularly significant, and Iran was selected by the participants of the conference as one of five nations, along with Australia, Ethiopia, Sweden and the United States, that would send representatives to Egypt to present the proposal to Nasser in person and investigate whether he would be prepared to negotiate.[70] Iran was presumably selected not only because of its enthusiastic support of the US position, but because it had experienced a similar crisis just a few years earlier, and its presence served to remind Nasser of the folly of inflexibility.

Egypt was one of the largest and most developed regional powers, with a large military, significant regional influence and historic ambitions to play a leading role in the Arab world, so Iran naturally followed events there closely. This was particularly important in light of Nasser's recent arms deal with the Soviets and his criticism of the Western-backed regional alliance, of which Iran was a member. A French report concluded that:

> Giving in to Colonel Nasser and relinquishing control of the canal to him means giving Egypt and its Arab partners an increase in influence and power such that the entire balance of power in the Middle and Near East would be

68 Department of State, *The Suez Canal Problem*, 129.

69 Editorial Note, *FRUS, 1955–1957, Suez Crisis, July 26–December 31, 1956, Volume XVI*, doc. 110.

70 Memorandum of Discussion at the 295th Meeting of the National Security Council, Washington, 30 August 1956, *FRUS, 1955–1957, Suez Crisis, July 26–December 31, 1956, Volume XVI*, doc. 149; and Kyle, *Suez*, 198.

upset; this would play into the hands of the Soviets who have ties with Egypt, and finally bring about a very serious weakening of western influence. Placed between the Russians and the Arabs, Iran would be isolated and unable to maintain its current position. An Egyptian hegemony in the Middle East would deal a fatal blow to the Baghdad Pact, from which Iraq could be led to withdraw and which Great Britain and the United States would have great difficulty in supporting.[71]

Moreover, Iran had gone through a similar nationalisation movement in 1951–1953, which had provoked a surge in anti-imperial, nationalist sentiment. A Nasser victory would represent the victory of a Muslim country in the Middle East over the colonial powers, and could potentially embolden the nationalists in Iran and weaken the authority of the shah.

Iran was keen to participate because it perceived the crisis – and Nasser – as an existential threat, and the closer the shah aligned with the West, the better he could influence their perception of the crisis. Thus, although Ardalān claimed that Iran's participation in the London conference 'was motivated by sincere conviction that international disputes can be settled by peaceful means', throughout the crisis Iran played a double game, presenting itself to the Americans as an advocate of diplomacy, while also pledging support to Britain's more hard-line approach.[72] The British secretary of state for foreign affairs, Selwyn Lloyd, argued in August 1956 that Iran would support its Security Council resolution 'because Nasser's continued success would inevitably lead to an undermining of the pro-Western Iran Government and its collapse'.[73] While the shah told the US ambassador, Selden Chapin, that he was opposed to a military solution to the Suez crisis, he also expressed his opinion that Nasser was a 'mad man', against whom he hoped the West would take a 'strong stand', and that eventually force may be necessary. The shah recognised the broader implications of the crisis, and warned the United States that 'every effort should be made to prevent [the] consolidation of "Arab

[71] Imbert de Laurens-Castelet to French Ministry of Foreign Affairs, 11 August 1956, Centre des Archives diplomatiques du ministère des Affaires étrangères, la Courneuve (henceforth CADC), 213QO/126.

[72] United States Department of State, *The Suez Canal Problem*, 127.

[73] Memorandum of a Conversation, Department of State, Washington, 30 August 1956, *FRUS, 1955–1957, Suez Crisis, July 26–December 31, 1956, Volume XVI*, doc. 152.

imperialism"'.[74] At the same time, to the British, the shah was a little more blunt, telling them that he considered 'getting rid of Nasser a very high priority'.[75]

The Break in Diplomatic Ties

In October 1956, British, French and Israeli forces invaded Egypt. The Eisenhower administration was furious and threatened severe economic sanctions should they not withdraw. Khrushchev threatened to use nuclear weapons against the belligerents. Iran, despite its distrust of Nasser, being 'bound by a certain Muslim solidarity as well as the spirit of Bandung' and fearful of an escalation of the crisis, pushed for a withdrawal.[76] The local members of the Baghdad Pact met in Tehran to coordinate their response to the crisis, and in a speech to the UN General Assembly, the Iranian diplomat Nasrollāh Entezām criticised 'the violation of Egypt's sovereignty' by Britain and France.[77] This Iranian support was noted by Nasser, who sent a note of thanks to the shah, which was read out to the Iranian parliament by Ardalān.[78]

The invaders eventually bowed to the pressure and withdrew in humiliation. The invasion became a disaster for the West, and almost led to the breakup of the NATO alliance. For Nasser it was ultimately a success, for he had, as John Lewis Gaddis writes, 'kept the canal, humiliated the colonialists, and balanced Cold War superpowers against one another, while securing his position as the undisputed leader of Arab nationalism'.[79] The implications of this were perceived with concern not only by Iran, but also other regional powers such as Iraq, Libya and Saudi Arabia. King Saud, for instance, worried that 'Nasser's ambition was to become the Napoleon of the Arabs and if he

[74] Telegram from the Embassy in Iran to the Department of State, Tehran, 9 August 1956, *FRUS, 1955–1957, Near East Region; Iran; Iraq, Volume XII*, doc. 362.

[75] Message from Prime Minister Eden to President Eisenhower, London, 6 September 1956, *FRUS, 1955–1957, Suez Crisis, July 26–December 31, 1956, Volume XVI*, doc. 181.

[76] De Laurens-Castelet to French Ministry of Foreign Affairs, 11 August 1956, CADC 213QO/126.

[77] Vincent Broustra to French Ministry of Foreign Affairs, 30 October 1956, CADC 213QO/132.

[78] Jacques-Emile Paris to French Ministry of Foreign Affairs, 17 November 1956, CADC 213QO/132.

[79] John Lewis Gaddis, *The Cold War* (London: Penguin Books, 2005), 128.

succeeded the regimes in Iraq and Saudi Arabia would be swept away'.[80] This premonition appeared to come true just two years later, when in February 1958, Egypt and Syria entered into a formal union, the United Arab Republic (UAR), which, in the words of Amin Saikal, 'was meant to increase the strength of Nasserism against the conservative forces of the region, including the Shah's regime'.[81] From the inception of the UAR, as Fawaz Gerges writes, 'Nasser inscribed pan-Arab unity as an important goal of his political discourse and action and pressured other Arab leaders to join the United Arab Republic'.[82] The shah expressed 'deep concern' at this development, which he considered to have been inspired by Moscow.[83]

Shortly after, a civil war broke out in Lebanon, which pitted pro-Nasserite against pro-Western forces. In meetings with foreign leaders, the shah continued to stress the danger that Nasser presented to regional stability and urged the United States to intervene. 'If Lebanon should fall', the shah said to President Eisenhower in a meeting on 1 July 1958, 'other states in the area would do likewise.' In this meeting, Eisenhower suggested that Nasser might not be lost to the West and could be brought 'back into the fold'. The shah gave a pessimistic assessment.

> At what price, he [the shah] asked, should Nasser be accepted as a 'new Prophet of the Arab world'? Egypt represented nothing but a few million unhappy and impoverished beggars. Nasser's ambition was to gain control of large areas in the Middle East. What would be his price for cooperating with the West? If he could be brought back with some small sacrifice, that would be all right, but not at a high price.[84]

The shah added that Nasser 'was trying to follow in the footsteps of Hitler' and was 'essentially a conspirator ... motivated by "wrong

80 Message from Prime Minister Eden to President Eisenhower, London, 6 September 1956.

81 Amin Saikal, *The Rise and Fall of the Shah: Iran from Autocracy to Religious Rule* (Princeton, NJ: Princeton University Press, 2009), 66–67.

82 Fawaz A. Gerges, *Making the Arab World: Nasser, Qutb, and the Clash that Shaped the Middle East* (Princeton, NJ: Princeton University Press, 2018), 190.

83 Henri Roux to French Ministry of Foreign Affairs, 6 February 1958, CADC 379QO/7.

84 Memorandum of Conversation between the shah and President Eisenhower, Washington, 1 July 1958, *FRUS, 1958–1960, Near East Region; Iraq; Iran; Arabian Peninsula, Volume XII*, doc. 242.

doing"'.[85] Given the danger Nasser posed, the shah told Eisenhower that it was 'essential that other countries be convinced by proof that Iran's policies were the correct policies for them to follow'. 'If they achieved good for Iran', he added, 'they would be compared favorably with the disruptive nature of communism and Nasserism in the Middle East, and would demonstrate that what happened in Syria was a poor substitute for what can happen to nations pursuing a policy of constructive nationalism, associated with other free world countries'.[86]

The shah was most concerned with the situation across the border in Iraq, where he felt 'there seemed to be even more popular support for Nasser'. He was right to be worried. On 14 July 1958, the shah's friend King Faisal II was murdered in a bloody coup and the British-backed Hashemite monarchy was abolished. Iran had lost a Baghdad Pact ally and, as Ramazani has written, 'the balance of power seemed to be tilting in favor of anti-Western Arab states'.[87] The coup left the shah 'depressed and even somewhat frightened', not only at the creation of a hostile regime on his doorstep, but also the prospect of officers in his army gaining inspiration from the Iraqi revolution and attempting a similarly bloody coup against him.[88] The shah clearly considered the new regime in Iraq to be little more than an extension of Nasserism to Iran's borders. As he said to the a US diplomat in Iran, Iraq 'means Nasser and we consider him worse than the communists'.[89] Against this backdrop, the shah signed a military pact with the United States in

[85] Comparing Nasser with Hitler had become common amongst politicians in Europe and the United States. Many examples are cited throughout Keith Kyle's *Suez: Britain's End of Empire in the Middle East.*

[86] Ibid. [87] Ramazani, *Iran's Foreign Policy*, 400.

[88] Telegram from the embassy in Iran to the department of state, 14 August 1958, *FRUS, 1958–1960, Near East Region; Iraq; Iran; Arabian Peninsula, Volume XII*, doc. 247; and Ramazani, *Iran's Foreign Policy*, 400. The shah was already aware of the dangers from within his military. In February 1958, a plot led by the commander of the Iranian army's intelligence staff, General Mohammad-Vali Qarani, was foiled and the conspirators arrested. Apparently when Qarani was arrested, officers discovered a considerable amount of literature on Nasser and the plot itself resembled the Free Officers Coup. Mark J. Gasiorowski, 'The Qarani Affair and Iranian Politics', *International Journal of Middle East Studies*, vol. 25, no. 4 (1993), fn. 16, 641.

[89] Telegram from the department of state to the embassy in Iran, 19 July 1958, *FRUS, 1958–1960, Near East Region; Iraq; Iran; Arabian Peninsula, Volume XII*, doc. 247, fn. 1.

March 1959, much to the anger of the Soviets.[90] This pact was very much in the spirit of the Eisenhower Doctrine and contained a pledge from the United States that 'In case of aggression against Iran', it would 'take such appropriate action, including the use of armed forces . . . in order to assist the Government of Iran at its request'.[91]

As Iran became more firmly entrenched in the Western camp, Nasser moved closer to the Soviets. On 26 July 1960, Egypt severed ties with Iran suddenly. In a fiery speech delivered to an audience that included Raul Castro, who was visiting Cairo to participate in the celebrations marking the fourth anniversary of the nationalisation of the Suez Canal, Nasser branded the shah's regime an opponent of the Arabs in their struggle against colonialism and Zionism, denounced Iran's membership of the Baghdad Pact and its relationship with the United States, and even called for the overthrow of the Pahlavi regime.[92] Nasser had broken off relations ostensibly because of the shah's public recognition of Israel, expressed in a press conference just three days earlier on 23 July, but the shah suspected that the break had more to do with Iran's expansion of ties with the Gulf sheikhdoms and Egyptian ambitions in the Persian Gulf.[93]

Despite the shah's insistence that there was no change in Iran's position, since it had afforded Israel *de facto* recognition since 1950, the press in Cairo and Damascus continued to lambast the shah over his relationship with Israel.[94] The shah was criticised for not showing solidarity with the Islamic world. As the proxy war in Yemen between Egypt and Saudi Arabia intensified during the 1960s, the shah became more critical of Nasser's credentials as a Muslim leader. Addressing the British press during a trip to the United Kingdom in March 1965, the

[90] For the shah's negotiations with the United States and Russia, see Ray Takeyh, *The Last Shah: America, Iran, and the Fall of the Pahlavi Dynasty* (Yale: Yale University Press, 2021), 136–140.

[91] George Lenczowski, 'United States' Support for Iran's Independence and Integrity, 1945–1959', *The Annals of the American Academy of Political and Social Science*, vol. 401 (1972), 55.

[92] Saikal, *The Rise and Fall of the Shah*, 68.

[93] Ramazani, *Iran's Foreign Policy*, 321. On Raul Castro's visit, see 'Report of the Czechoslovak Politburo Regarding Military Assistance to the Cuban Government, 16 May 1960, and CPCz Politburo Resolution, 17 May 1960', 17 May 1960, National Archives, Prague, Czech Republic. Accessed through the Wilson Centre, Digital Archive: https://digitalarchive.wilsoncenter.org/document/115140.

[94] Kashani-Sabet, 'Iran on Shaky Ground', 6.

shah, referring to the civil war in North Yemen, said that Nasser was 'pretending to be a Moslem, defender of the faith, but killing every day hundreds of people, innocent people, in that poor country, by throwing on them napalm bombs, incendiary bombs, strafing them with jet planes'.[95] In response, the Soviet-sponsored *Radio Iran Courier* (Peyk-e Irān), which was based in the Caucasus and broadcast in Persian, pledged support for Nasser's war against the regime in Yemen, which it argued was 'one of the most backward, most despotic, and most corrupt of any in the world'. The shah, 'this shameful imperialist puppet', was said to be 'shedding tears for such a shameful, criminal, and rotten regime, and [merely] expressing unhappiness for having lost such a companion'.[96]

Iran and the Algerian War of Independence

Another country that became firmly entrenched in the Nasser camp during this period was Algeria. Of the three French territories in North Africa, Morocco and Tunisia had achieved independence through peaceful means in March 1956. However, Algeria had a sizeable French population, of around one and a half million, and the three regions of Algiers, Oran and Constantine, in which the majority of these French citizens lived, were not merely colonial possessions, but were considered to be legally part of France. In November 1954, an armed rebellion of the majority Arab population broke out, led by the Front de libération nationale (FLN). This was the beginning of an eight-year civil war.[97] During the war, the FLN was backed by Nasser's Egypt, which supplied arms, training and propaganda support to the revolutionary cause.[98]

Throughout this conflict, Iran attempted to reconcile its support for the independence-seeking Muslim people of Algeria with its important relationship with France. Iran repeatedly voted in solidarity with the Afro-Asian group at the United Nations in favour of resolutions concerning Algeria, but ensured through diplomatic channels that these

95 Telegram from Foreign Office to Cairo, 3 March 1965, FO 371/183895.
96 'Comment on the shah's Interview with ITN', 3 March 1965, FO 371/183895.
97 On the beginning of the conflict, see Alistair Horne, *A Savage War of Peace: Algeria 1954–1962* (New York: New York Review Books, 2006), 83–104.
98 Kyle, *Suez*, 112.

actions would not affect Franco-Iranian relations.[99] For example, after voting in favour of a motion to put the Algerian case on the agenda in 1955, the Iranian prime minister, Hoseyn ʿAlā, assured the French ambassador in Tehran 'with warmth that Iran's attitude had no unfriendly intention towards France'.[100] ʿAlā expressed concerns that the French would retaliate against Iran and assured the ambassador that because Iran was under pressure from its co-religionists, it had no option but to vote against France on this matter. This was a line that Iran maintained throughout the conflict, and which the French understood and reluctantly accepted, despite their frustration.

Due to Egyptian support, the shah refused to recognise the Gouvernement provisoire de la République algérienne (GPRA), which had been set up in Cairo in 1958. Iran recognised the independent state of Algeria on 3 July 1962, shortly after the resolution of the war, though it did not establish political relations until after the defeat of the GPRA by Ahmed Ben Bella's Political Bureau later that year.[101] An Iranian embassy opened in Algiers on 23 September 1964.[102] But relations never really improved between Iran and Algeria until the 1970s. Algeria was in the Nasser camp, and its nationalists resented the shah's lukewarm support during their war of independence, which had extended little further than statements and votes in the United Nations. Apparently, anger against the shah for his lack of support was such that the first president of independent Algeria, Ben Bella, once said that some young Algerian revolutionaries had at one point asked for his permission to assassinate the shah on one of his trips to Europe. As much as Ben Bella resented the shah, he refused to approve this plan.[103]

*****

During the reign of King Farouk, although Iran and Egypt both harboured ambitions to play leading roles in the region, relations between the two countries were amicable. Relations also remained relatively

[99] On this see Bédrède, 'Iran's Foreign Policy and the Algerian War of Independence, 1954–1962'.
[100] French report cited ibid., 171. [101] Ibid., 192.
[102] Bakhshi, 'Barresi-ye Tārikhi-ye Ravābet-e Khāreji-ye Irān va Qāreh-ye Āfriqā', 52.
[103] Bédrède, 'Iran's Foreign Policy and the Algerian War of Independence, 1954–1962', 193.

friendly in the early years after the Egyptian Revolution of 1952 – the shah even invited Nasser to visit Iran in this period. However, in 1955, divergent Cold War allegiances caused a fracture in relations, exacerbated by the Suez crisis in 1956, and led ultimately to Nasser formally severing diplomatic ties with Iran in 1960. Nasser would remain the shah's main rival until shortly before his death in 1970. During this period, the shah had to play a careful diplomatic game; balancing support for the issues affecting the newly decolonised Global South, with the maintenance of positive relations with his Western allies. This delicate balancing act was evident not only at Bandung in 1955, but also Suez in 1956.

The Algerian civil war demonstrated to Iran the fragility of regional peace in the era of decolonisation, as well as the potential of Nasser to exacerbate crises. In his attempt to stop the spread of Nasserism, the shah sought to build relations not only with the imperial powers, but also the more conservative states in the Arab world, who were similarly threatened by Nasser's brand of Arab nationalism. These included not only Middle Eastern powers, such as Iraq (before the revolution of 1958), Jordan, Saudi Arabia and Turkey, but also states in North Africa, most importantly Morocco and Tunisia, with which Iran developed close relationships. By nurturing these alliances, the shah sought to build a separate grouping of Muslim states in the Arab world and beyond, that were not only opposed to Nasser, but which were also anti-Soviet and pro-American. One of the ways the shah and his North African allies, particularly Hassan II of Morocco, would challenge Nasser's Arab solidarity movement, was by advocating for an Islamic solidarity conference, which was eventually held in Rabat in 1969.

2 *Iran, North Africa and Islamic Solidarity*

The year 1956 was not just the year of the Suez crisis, it was also the year that Morocco and Tunisia achieved independence from French rule. Iran followed the decolonisation of North Africa with particular interest. One of the reasons for this was that the countries of this region were Muslim majority, with deep historical, cultural, linguistic and ethnic links to the Middle East. Given their new governments' potential influence on political opinion in the region, and indeed the opportunities for the shah to influence them, nurturing relationships with Morocco and Tunisia was seen as important by policy makers in Tehran. Equally important was the fact that these countries had been governed by Iran's European partners, who still maintained considerable influence there. Therefore, through stronger relations with these countries, Iran could hope to increase its influence with its allies, France and Britain in particular.

At the same time, given the break between Nasser and the Western Bloc, and the Suez crisis, which had enhanced Nasser's prestige in the region as an anti-colonial, anti-Western and pro-Arab firebrand, the shah sought allies that could moderate Egypt's influence in the Middle East and beyond. In early March 1957, an Iranian goodwill delegation was sent to the region to visit Morocco, Tunisia and Libya, led by the deputy prime minister, ʿAbdollāh Entezām, who had until recently served as Iran's minister of foreign affairs. This goodwill delegation was organised to coincide with Tunisia's Independence Day celebrations. After attending these celebrations in Tunis, Entezām visited Tripoli from 27 March until 1 April. During the visit, he dined with the Libyan prime minister, Mustafa Ben Halim, attended a reception in his honour by the minister of foreign affairs, Abdul Majid Kubar, and had an audience with King Idris. Entezām confided in the British head of chancery that he was unimpressed by any of the Libyans he had met, aside from the prime minister, Ben Halim, whom he described as 'very clever'.[1] Revealing the strategy underpinning Entezām's mission, he told the British that 'he thought it important to bring the three Maghreb States together, and encourage them to cultivate their gardens and bother less about problems further east such as Palestine'.[2] Entezām said to the French ambassador that in his conversations with the leadership of the countries he visited, he 'stressed the real danger ... of a communist infiltration concealed under the mask of Arab nationalism'.[3] Another important part of Entezām's brief was thus to attempt to win support for the Baghdad Pact and to warn North African countries of the lure of Nasser.[4]

The shah had long worried about the danger posed by radical pan-Arab movements in the Middle East, so was undoubtedly concerned at the potential of the Arab states of North Africa to become influenced by such movements. This explains the rationale behind the speed with which Iran moved to win the friendship of Libya, Tunisia and Morocco. During Entezām's visit to Libya, in spite of his low opinion of Libya's royals and politicians, he informed the British that he 'intended to recommend to his Government the appointment of a Minister to reside in Tunis and be accredited also in Rabat and Tripoli'. This should be 'a really able man', because 'there would be no point in sending a nonentity just for appearance sake'. In other words, this diplomat should be a serious political appointment. Ultimately, however, whereas Iran's relations with Morocco and Tunisia flourished, both Iran and Libya declined to pursue a bilateral relationship with any real energy. King Idris was more concerned with events in Europe and was untroubled by the prospect of a Nasserist-type revolution toppling his monarchy. The United States and Britain had oil interests and military bases in Libya, so King Idris felt certain that should any unrest threaten his throne, these foreign powers would come to his aid.[5] Of course, he was to be proven wrong, but this miscalculation led these two pro-Western conservative monarchies

[1] Walter Graham to Selwyn Lloyd, 9 April 1957, FO 371/126034. [2] Ibid.

[3] Roger Lalouette to French Ministry of Foreign Affairs, 15 March 1957, CADC 24QO/1093.

[4] Bédrède, 'Iran's Foreign Policy and the Algerian War of Independence, 1954–1962', 176.

[5] Hasan ʿAli Yāri, 'Ravābet-e Siyāsi-ye Irān va Libi dar Dowreh-ye Pahlavi-e Dovvom (Ruyārui-e Shāh va Qazāfi)', *Nāmeh-ye Tārikh Pazhuhān*, vol. 24 (1389), 133.

to remain distant acquaintances during the 1960s. Until the September 1969 military coup that overthrew the monarchy and installed its leader, Colonel Mo'ammar Qadaffi, as head of state, Iran paid little attention to Libya.

Throughout the 1960s, many countries in the Arab world, particularly those with more radical regimes, such as Egypt, South Yemen and Syria, adopted a hostile stance towards Iran, due to the Pahlavi regime's pro-Western outlook and its ties with Israel. Other countries in the region perceived Nasserism as a grave threat to their internal stability and believed that their countries were vulnerable to the types of coups that had been carried out elsewhere. In these states, the shah was seen as a moderating influence in the region and a respected non-Arab leader in the Islamic world, with strong credentials in the West, a powerful military and an emerging economy. Among the countries that gravitated towards Iran during this period were those geographically close, such as Jordan and Saudi Arabia, as well as those further away, like Morocco and Tunisia.[6] Iran's efforts to create a group of like-minded allies which could challenge the extremism of Nasser ultimately resulted in the organisation of the first Islamic Conference in Rabat in 1969.

The Shah, Habib Bourguiba and Their 'Spirit of Brotherly Understanding'

In the 1960s, Tunisia became one of the most attractive prospective partners to Iran in its efforts to contain Nasserism in North Africa. The first president of the new Republic of Tunisia was Habib Bourguiba, who had studied law and political science at the Sorbonne in Paris, and who had been engaged in the political struggle for independence since the early 1930s. As president, Bourguiba put forward a moderately progressive vision for his country: women's rights were enshrined in law; a school curriculum was designed to diminish religious influence; the number of French workers and soldiers employed in Tunisia was reduced gradually over a period of time; and although the constitution recognised Islam as the official religion of the country, it also stipulated that the political system was secular, 'based on separation of powers'.[7]

[6] Ibid., 132.

[7] 'Tunisia's Constitution of 1959 with Amendments through 2008', available online www.constituteproject.org/constitution/Tunisia_2008.pdf?lang=en.

Bourguiba was the type of leader the shah particularly liked: Western-educated, moderate in his politics and religion, and perceived as progressive by his allies in the West. He was the antithesis of Nasser and came to be considered by the shah an important ally in the Arab world.

Political relations between Iran and Tunisia were established at the time of Entezām's visit in March 1957, and in November that year Iran opened its embassy in Tunis.[8] But it took some time for a deeper relationship to develop, which is unsurprising considering the distance separating the two countries and their respective domestic and regional priorities. The son of the Tunisian president, Habib Bourguiba Jr., had served as Tunisia's ambassador to the United States at the same time as Ardeshir Zāhedi, the shah's son-in-law, served as Iran's ambassador there.[9] They were both young ambassadors, with young wives, and they developed a friendship. As Zāhedi recalled, 'We got along very well and had special gatherings.'[10] According to Zāhedi, he and Habib Bourguiba Jr. used to refer to each other as brother, and these personal ties were 'very useful in the development of relations between the two countries'.[11] In May 1961, when President Bourguiba travelled to the United States on an official visit to meet President Kennedy, Zāhedi was the only foreign ambassador whom Bourguiba invited for a private, non-ceremonial meeting. During this meeting, Bourguiba asked Zāhedi to extend an invitation to the shah to visit Tunisia.[12]

The year 1965 was a turning point in Bourguiba's relations with both Iran and the United Arab Republic. In February 1965, President Bourguiba embarked on a two-month tour of the Middle East and the Mediterranean, calling at the UAR, Saudi Arabia, Jordan, Lebanon, Kuwait, Iran, Iraq, Turkey, Yugoslavia and Greece. Bourguiba hoped that the trip would give him the opportunity 'to personally and dramatically present his views on common Arab problems' to the countries of the Arab world and those on its borders.[13] He also sought to convince the UAR and Saudi Arabia to withdraw from Yemen, and

[8] Bakhshi, 'Barresi-ye Tārikhi-ye Ravābet-e Khāreji-ye Irān va Qāreh-ye Āfriqā', 50. Tunisia's embassy did not open in Tehran until 1350.

[9] Zāhedi served his first term as his Iran's ambassador to the United States from 1960 until 1962. Habib Bourguiba Jr. was Tunisia's ambassador from 1961 until 1964.

[10] Zāhedi, *Khāterāt*, vol. 3, 212. [11] Ibid., 213. [12] Ibid., 212.

[13] Yaroslav Bilinsky, 'Moderate Realism in an Extremist Environment: Tunisia and the Palestinian Question (1965–1970)', *Revue de l'Occident Musulmane et de la Méditerranée* vols. 13–14 (1973), 109.

Iran and Turkey to adopt a harsher line towards Israel.[14] The journey began with a one-week trip to Cairo, where the Tunisian president was greeted by Nasser with full honours, driven around in an open-top car, awarded an honorary doctorate by the University of Cairo and granted the opportunity to address the Egyptian Parliament. Following an uneventful trip to Saudi Arabia, Bourguiba travelled to Jordan, where he visited the Palestinian refugee camps near Jericho. Having been affected by the plight of the Palestinians in the camp, Bourguiba declared that a 'peaceful solution' to the conflict should be found, 'in which there will be neither victor nor vanquished'.[15]

Several days later, at a press conference in Beirut, Bourguiba expressed his opposition to Nasser's proposal for an Arab boycott of West Germany should it establish diplomatic relations with Israel. Bourguiba argued that Germany has 'special circumstances because of its Nazi past', which should be considered by Arab countries. Arab countries should focus on developing good economic ties with countries in the European Common Market, and avoid taking actions 'that would harm us more than the enemy'.[16] Reiterating his conciliatory message, Bourguiba said, 'It is time to abandon demagogy. War with Israel is impossible. The great powers, guarantors of the Jewish state, would stop us.'[17]

Bourguiba's apparent call for compromise was met with anger across the Arab world. On government radios in Middle East capitals, most notably Cairo, Damascus, Baghdad, Amman and Beirut, Bourguiba was denounced as a lunatic 'who should be locked in an asylum' and a traitor to the Arab cause 'who should be immediately executed'.[18] Anti-Bourguiba protests erupted in several cities, including Cairo, where a 20,000-strong mob attempted to set fire to the Tunisian embassy. Counter-protests were organised in Tunis by the Tunisian government to demonstrate hostility towards Egypt, as well as support for Bourguiba and his calls for peace.[19] When Bourguiba

14 Ibid.
15 Gilbert Cohen-Tanugi, 'Tunisia', *The American Jewish Year Book*, vol. 67 (1966), 432.
16 *Kayhan International*, 13 March 1965.
17 Bilinsky, 'Moderate Realism in an Extremist Environment', 112.
18 'Middle East: A Man to Anger Nasser', *Time*, 7 May 1965.
19 D. C. Watt and Peter Lyon, 'Notes on the Month', *The World Today*, vol. 21, no. 6 (1965), 224.

eventually returned to Tunis on 10 April, he was met by what *The New York Times* described as 'his biggest popular reception for 10 years'.[20] The manner in which the shah of Iran had received him just less than one month earlier, in the middle of this furore, was just as emphatic.

Bourguiba arrived in Tehran on 14 March, just three days after the controversial press conference in Beirut. Tunisia was presented by Iranian state media as a modern country with a rich heritage; newspapers stressed that its capital was home to the oldest university in North Africa and had four large libraries that contained over 300,000 volumes. As well as ancient historical sites, Tunisia was a country with many tourist resorts, and a sizeable share of the population was employed in the tourism sector. In contrast to the radical Arab states such as Egypt, Iraq and Syria, the Tunisian people were said to be 'a peace-loving people, who even won independence peacefully'.[21]

Meanwhile, Bourguiba was presented in the press as a learned and honourable leader. The British ambassador in Tehran, Denis Wright, noted this in a dispatch to the Foreign Office:

> On the day of the President's arrival editorial comment and feature articles in the Iranian press were presenting him in the guise of the best sort of Arab, a man determined to serve his people, but at the same time pragmatic and realistic unlike some other current Arab leaders. The press – 'guided' as it is – seemed to carry more conviction than is usually the case on these occasions.[22]

The subheading of a biographical sketch in *Ettelāʿāt* repeated Bourguiba's oft-repeated mantra: 'Man should live for the happiness of his brothers' (*ensān bāyad barā-ye saʿādat-e barādarān-e khod zendegi konad*).[23] In this short article, the reader is informed that as a student in Paris, Bourguiba's daily diet 'did not exceed dry bread and olives' and that it was during this time that he became committed to fighting colonialism.

President Bourguiba was afforded the same reception as all honoured guests in Tehran. In a scene that was repeated many times over the following two decades, Bourguiba and his seventy-person entourage were met at the airport by the shah and shahbanu, along with all major court and government officials, including the prime

[20] *The New York Times*, 11 April 1965, 18.
[21] *Ettelāʿāt*, 23 Esfand 1343/ 14 March 1965, 5.
[22] Denis Wright report, 27 March 1965, FO 371/184053.
[23] *Ettelāʿāt*, 23 Esfand 1343/ 14 March 1965, 5.

minister, the foreign minister, the minister of court and the chief of protocol. After the customary greetings, a twenty-one-gun salute was fired and eight planes of the Imperial Air Force flew overhead. Bourguiba was driven to 24 Esfand Square where he was presented with a golden key to the city by Tehran's mayor, then proceeded by royal carriage to Golestān Palace, past crowds that thronged the streets to greet him.[24] In the afternoon, a reception was held at the Hall of Mirrors (*tālār-e āyeneh*), organised by the chief of protocol of the Imperial Court, to give all foreign ambassadors resident in Tehran the opportunity to meet and welcome President Bourguiba. Following this, Bourguiba proceeded to the tomb of Reza Shah, where he laid a wreath. In the evening, the mayor of Tehran presented a gift to Bourguiba on behalf of the citizens of Tehran; an exquisite photo album containing photos of the president and his wife from their arrival in Tehran that morning.[25]

During his speech at a banquet at Golestān Palace, the shah lavished Bourguiba with praise. 'You are not only the venerable leader of a country with which we enjoy excellent relations due to our cooperation', the shah said, 'but we regard you as a great patriot, who endured years of imprisonment and exile for the sake of the independence of his country, whom we have always looked at with respect'. The shah praised Tunisia for 'combining the ancient and noble heritage of Islamic civilisation and culture with the principles of Western democracy and respect for human rights and standards'. He then spoke of the relations between the two countries, which he traced back to the Achaemenid period, and of the continuation of ties throughout the Islamic period.[26]

Wright observed that 'there was a lot of comment about the need for an enlightened wider Moslem [sic] grouping; one or two papers put it in focus, describing the desired grouping in effect as patriotic, reasonably pro-Western, and firmly anti-Nasser'.[27] The shah clearly viewed Bourguiba as the type of respectable figure who would form a key part of this grouping. Presenting Tunisia as a model for other Muslim countries to follow, the shah said:

> Today by adopting a wise and prudent method, Tunisia is advancing on a path of material and spiritual progress. This is the situation that we sincerely

[24] *Ettelāʿāt*, 23 Esfand 1343/ 14 March 1965, 19.
[25] *Ettelāʿāt*, 24 Esfand 1343/ 15 March 1965, 13. [26] Ibid.
[27] Wright report, 27 March 1965, FO 371/184053.

wish for all Islamic nations because we believe that this is the only way to ensure the prosperity and well-being of these nations, and to give them the opportunity to play a positive and productive role in global politics for their own benefit and for the benefit of the entire Islamic world.[28]

One British diplomat observed that 'It seems pretty clear that the visit was of greater interest to the host than to the guest',[29] which is probably true, but Bourguiba was undoubtedly reassured by the shah's enthusiastic support, particularly at a time when he was being aggressively condemned by the militant Arab bloc.

At the halfway point of his two-month tour of the Middle East and the Mediterranean, Bourguiba was exhausted. The day after his arrival in Iran, the media reported that he was suffering from a cold caught in Kuwait and would not be able to complete the planned activities for the day, including trips to museums in Tehran, and subsequent trips to Isfahan and Shiraz were first postponed, then cancelled completely. Bourguiba was able to host his return banquet for the shah at the Tehran Hilton, but for the rest of the trip he was indisposed. It was widely thought that Bourguiba also wanted to remain away from the media 'to avoid being forced to repeat and confirm his anti-Egyptian stance'.[30] Finally, Bourguiba's spokesperson announced that the next leg of the trip, Iraq, would be cancelled and instead the president would remain in Iran as a private guest for four extra days before resuming the tour in Turkey. Bourguiba was certainly 'not physically at his best' as Wright observed, but this was probably not the only reason, or even the main reason for the cancellation.[31] Given the commotion caused by Bourguiba's statements on Palestine, the Iraqi government could not guarantee Bourguiba's safety, and it is unlikely that Bourguiba would have wanted to take the risk.[32] Notwithstanding

28 *Ettelā'āt*, 24 Esfand 1343/ 15 March 1965, 13.

29 M. Chevallier, handwritten response to Wright's report, 9 April 1965, FO 371/184053.

30 Dutch ambassador in Tehran, A. H. Hasselman, to Ministry of Foreign Affairs, 27 March 1965, NA 2.05.191/441.

31 Wright report, 27 March 1965, FO 371/184053.

32 Bilinsky, 'Moderate Realism in an Extremist Environment', 113. According to Denis Wright, who had spoken to the Iraqi ambassador in Tehran, the decision to cancel was taken after the Tunisian embassy in Baghdad reported anti-Tunisian demonstrations there. President Aref's claim that it was he who advised Bourguiba not to travel to Iraq because of 'the confused situation' was apparently little more than a face-saving measure after the decision had already

the huge inconvenience the extended stay caused the Iranian authorities, particularly given the size of Bourguiba's entourage and the fact that the visit coincided with the Iranian new year holidays, as the French ambassador observed, 'the hope that the front of the Arab countries will be broken by the initiatives of his guest ... obviously leads the Imperial Government to show him the greatest understanding'.[33]

During speeches and meetings, the shah and Bourguiba were able to discuss areas of common concern, and from the shah's perspective the visit was a success. Meetings between the two leaders were said by the Iranian press to have been conducted in 'a very friendly and warm environment with the spirit of brotherly understanding'.[34] In private, Bourguiba sympathised with the shah's stance on Israel and the pressure he felt as a result from the UAR. Bourguiba told the shah that he also disliked Nasser.[35] The shah later confided to the US secretary of state, Dean Rusk, that 'he had been surprised by the determination not to be pushed around by the UAR which President Bourguiba had exhibited during the recent state visit to Iran'.[36] In public, too, Bourguiba expressed agreement with the shah. In response to the shah's speech on the day he arrived, Bourguiba said:

> I fully believe that our common views on meeting the needs of our countries will harmonise our foreign policies ... We and you firmly believe that the security of our countries requires the existence of peace, and the establishment of peace in the world is not possible unless the colonial actions of any form and any kind are ended ... Fortunately, Iran has always had an anti-colonial policy.[37]

In an obvious reference to Nasser and his opposition to making peace with Israel, he said: 'Our country and yours have never fought because of malice; rather, they have fought for human dignity and human rights.'[38]

been taken by the Tunisians to cancel. See Wright report, 27 March 1965, FO 371/184053.

33 Renaud Sivan to French Ministry of Foreign Affairs, 18 March 1965, CADC 367QO59.

34 *Ettelāʿāt*, 7 Farvardin 1344/ 27 March 1965, 16.

35 Wright report, 27 March 1965, FO 371/184053.

36 Telegram from Secretary of State Rusk to the Department of State, 8 April 1965, *FRUS, 1964–1968, Volume XXII, Iran*, doc. 75.

37 *Ettelāʿāt*, 25 Esfand 1343/ 16 March 1965, 6.

38 Ibid.

The communique issued to the press at the conclusion of Bourguiba's visit gave 'the impression of a very warm, though politically outwardly cautious, relation' between Iran and Tunisia.[39] It contained the suggestion that the result of negotiations between the two sides would be drafted in the shape of a framework for cultural, commercial, economic and technological cooperation.[40] This treaty was finally signed four years later, in April 1969, as a Treaty of Amity (*'ahdnāmeh-ye mavaddat*).[41] At around the same time, an Economic and Commercial Agreement was signed (July 1968),[42] as well as a Cultural Agreement (October 1969)[43] and an agreement abolishing visa requirements for Tunisians and Iranians.[44] The signing of such agreements reflects the general trend of increasing cooperation between Iran and Tunisia in the years that followed this state visit.

The bourgeoning ties between Iran and Tunisia were certainly facilitated by the deterioration of relations between Cairo and Tunis, which continued throughout 1965. Upon his return to Tunisia, Bourguiba delivered a speech in which he set out his proposal to fix the Israel–Palestine border along the line recommended by the UN in 1948. This proposal, and his offer to mediate talks between Israel and Palestine, was rejected by both sides. In late April, violent demonstrations took place both in Cairo and Tunis.[45] Tunisia boycotted the conference of the Arab League leaders in September. Instead, Bourguiba distributed a letter to participants beforehand, in which he wrote that 'the interference of Egyptian leaders in the internal affairs of other Arab countries is unacceptable and we will refuse to cooperate with the Arab league as long as it does not show respect for the member states'. In November, Nasser retorted that Bourguiba was little more than 'the valet of the USA'.[46]

Finally, one year later, in October 1966, Tunisia severed diplomatic relations with the UAR.[47] The reasons for the break were, according to

[39] Hasselman to Dutch Ministry of Foreign Affairs, 27 March 1965, NA 2.05.191/441.
[40] *Ettelā'āt*, 7 Farvardin 1344, 16.
[41] *Asnād-e Mo'āhedāt-e do Jānebeh-ye Irān bā Sāyer-e Duval*, vol. 5 (Tehran: Daftar-e Motāle'āt-e Siyāsi va Beyn al-Melali, 1370), 303–304.
[42] Ibid., 295–298. [43] Ibid., 305–308. [44] Ibid., 309–310.
[45] Bilinsky, 'Moderate Realism in an Extremist Environment', 115.
[46] Cohen-Tanugi, 'Tunisia', 432.
[47] Bilinsky, 'Moderate Realism in an Extremist Environment', 116.

the official Tunisian announcement reported in the Iranian press, continuing 'insulting attacks of Egypt on Tunisia', and the desire of the Egyptian government 'to be the guardian of the Arab nations and [to] dominate other Arab countries with force, threat and direct intervention'.[48] As a result of Egyptian dominance, the Arab League had 'forgotten the mission that was entrusted to it ... to intensify the cooperation and mutual assistance between brotherly Arab countries, to resolve disputes through friendly negotiations, and to coordinate the efforts and activities of Arab countries'.[49] The shah must have viewed these developments with some satisfaction. As the fracture between Tunisia and Egypt widened, the shah continued to try to exploit these differences to bring other more conservative Arab states into the moderate bloc. In this mission, the shah found a kindred spirit in the king of Morocco, Hassan II.

Iran, Morocco and Islamic Solidarity

In August 1957, just months after Entezām's trip to North Africa, the Moroccan foreign minister, Ahmed Balāfrej, stopped in Tehran for a 'three-day official visit'.[50] Balāfrej was granted an audience with the shah, during which he delivered a 'message of friendship' on behalf of Sultan Mohammed, discussed the exchange of diplomatic representation between Tehran and Rabat and extended an invitation to the shah to visit Morocco.[51] The shah, whom Balāfrej found to be 'extremely well informed on North African questions', accepted this invitation.[52] In addition to this audience, Balāfrej met with the foreign minister, ʿAliqoli Ardalān, who hosted a grand reception for him, the prime minister, Manuchehr Eqbāl, and the minister of court, Hoseyn ʿAlā, as well as Entezām, whom he knew from his earlier trip. The British felt that the visit was 'a useful exercise in promoting future good relations between Iran and Morocco'.[53] Indeed, just three months later, in

[48] *Ettelāʿāt*, 12 Mehr 1345/ 4 October 1966, 4. [49] Ibid.
[50] J. W. Russell to Selwyn Lloyd, 23 August 1957, FO 371/125770.
[51] Actually, just one day before Balāfrej's arrival, on 14 August 1957, Sultan Mohammad assumed the title of king.
[52] Though he would not make an official visit until 1966.
[53] J. W. Russell to Selwyn Lloyd, 23 August 1957, FO 371/125770.

November 1957, formal diplomatic relations were established between the two countries.[54]

In November 1960, a Moroccan goodwill delegation arrived in Tehran 'to develop Irano-Moroccan relations and prepare for "political and economic" discussions between the two countries'. This seven-man delegation, led by ʿAllāl al-Fāssi, arrived on 15 November and planned to visit fourteen further countries as part of a broader mission to develop Morocco's foreign relations. Speaking to the press in Tehran shortly after the delegation's arrival, al-Fāssi said that 'Morocco, although independent, had not yet got rid of the vestiges of colonialism and could not therefore be called a free country in the true sense of the word'.[55] The delegation met with the shah and held talks with the minister of foreign affairs, during which they were assured that Iran would not take sides in any disputes between Morocco and France. At around the same time as the visit, it was announced that Mohammed V was planning to visit Iran for a seven-day trip and was due to arrive on 29 December 1960.[56] This trip was postponed due to the sudden convening of the Afro-Asian Summit in Casablanca in January 1961, and just two months after the planned visit, Mohammed V died suddenly aged fifty-one of heart failure following a minor operation.[57]

It was under Mohammed V's successor that Iran and Morocco developed a close partnership, in part due to the close personal friendship between the shah and King Hassan II. Along with King Hussein of Jordan and King Faisal of Saudi Arabia, the shah considered King Hassan to be a 'brother king', with whom he shared a deep 'understanding and friendship'.[58] The shah respected him as 'a sovereign of rare intellectual qualities', having earned a degree in law from the University of Bordeaux, as well as for his status as a descendant of the Prophet. With his educational background, coupled with his religious credentials, the shah felt that he 'perfectly combines two cultures,

[54] Bakhshi, 'Barresi-ye Tārikhi-ye Ravābet-e Khāreji-ye Irān va Qāreh-ye Āfriqā', 54.
[55] British embassy, Tehran to Foreign Office, 25 November 1960, FO 371/147121.
[56] Ibid.
[57] Pierre de Leusse to French Ministry of Foreign Affairs, 13 September 1963, CADC 367QO171.
[58] Zāhedi, *Khāterāt*, vol. 3, 216.

the European and the Koranic'.[59] The shared tradition of monarchy provided a foundation for the development of ties between Iran and Morocco, which extended not just to the monarchs themselves, but their extended families too. Ardeshir Zāhedi, husband of Princess Shahnaz and Iran's foreign minister from 1966 until 1971, recalled that at this time there began 'a kind of friendship and intimacy between the two royal families'.[60]

In order to solidify political ties, the shah paid an official visit to Morocco in June 1966. The visit had originally been planned to take place in the spring of 1965, but was postponed due to the Casablanca riots of March that year.[61] This delay, according to a British report, 'gave more context and significance to the visit than it would probably have had in 1965' because 'the delay was used for careful diplomatic spadework'.[62] Indeed, it was decided that the visit would not merely be a ceremonial affair, and that both sides would use the opportunity to cement the bilateral relationship through the signing of various agreements. In April 1966, two months before the visit was due to take place, the director of the Plan Organisation, Safi Asfiyā, led an Iranian economic delegation to Morocco. This visit was followed up in May, when the Moroccan foreign minister, Mohamed Cherkaoui, travelled to Tehran to finalise the drafts of the various agreements that would be signed in Morocco.[63] As a result of this careful planning, the British ambassador, Leonard Holliday, considered the visit to be 'of more than routine importance'.[64]

The shah arrived in Rabat on 11 June to what the newspaper *Ettelā'āt* described as an 'unparalleled welcome'. The Moroccan authorities clearly went to great lengths to ensure that the shah received an exceptional welcome in Rabat. A public holiday was declared 'so that all the people could participate in welcoming their

59 Mohammad Reza Pahlavi, *The Shah's Story* (London: Michael Joseph, 1980), 145.
60 Zāhedi, *Khāterāt*, vol. 3, 215.
61 These had begun as peaceful student protests, but gained the support of wider sections of society after a violent police crackdown. In the ensuring riots, many protestors were killed by the security forces. See Susan Gilson Miller, *A History of Modern Morocco* (Cambridge: Cambridge University Press, 2013), 168–169.
62 Leonard Holliday, 'Visit of the Shah of Iran to Morocco', 7 July 1966, FO 371/186673.
63 Charles Wiggin to Willie Morris, 26 May 1966, FO 371/190290.
64 Holliday, 'Visit of the Shah of Iran to Morocco'.

honoured guest'.[65] In order to elicit enthusiasm, the city's cinema houses screened special films about Iran, and each day during the shah's stay in Morocco, programmes were broadcast on radio and television. The streets of Rabat were decorated with effigies of the shah and flags of Iran, and loudspeakers were placed along roads so that details of the shah's arrival could be announced to the public in real time. The government's inducements appear to have had some success in bringing people onto the streets. *Ettelā'āt* reported that 'despite the intense heat in the morning', thousands had gathered. The crowd was said to be so dense that the car had to move slowly through the streets, and as a result it took an hour to reach the shah's accommodation. After arriving at the palace, where more crowds had gathered to greet the shah, a welcoming ceremony was held, during which the shah was awarded the Order of Sovereignty, Morocco's highest honour.[66] In the afternoon, the shah paid his respects at the tomb of Hassan's father, Mohammed V.

During the shah's three-day stay in Rabat, he took a day-trip to Casablanca to visit the Mohammedia refinery, where discussions took place over Moroccan purchases of Iranian oil, and potential Iranian investment in the refinery.[67] During the shah's subsequent four-day stay in Marrakesh, he travelled to Safi to tour the chemical complex there. On the basis of discussions that took place during these visits, an agreement was announced between Pars Oil Company of Iran and the Moroccan companies that owned the Mohammedia and Sidi Kacem refineries, to set up a plant at Mohammedia to produce 35,000 tons of asphalt and lubricants per year, calculated to meet all of Morocco's needs and leaving 10,000 tons for export. Crude oil for the enterprise would be imported from Iran, which in return would purchase fertilisers from the Safi chemical complex.[68] The potential for economic and technical cooperation appears to have been high on the agendas of both Morocco and the Iranian delegation, and according to the Iranian ambassador in Morocco, Mas'ud Forughi, 'what had been agreed bilaterally was considerably more important than appeared from the language of the communique'.[69] For example, the possibility was discussed of Iran sending some of its 'surplus of technicians' to

[65] *Ettelā'āt*, 22 Khordād 1345/ 12 June 1966, 13. [66] Ibid.
[67] *Ettelā'āt*, 24 Khordād 1345/ 14 June 1966, 1.
[68] Holliday, 'Visit of the Shah of Iran to Morocco', 2. [69] Ibid.

Figure 2.1 The shah and King Hassan II paying their respects at the tomb of Mohammed V. *Ettelāʿāt*, 29 Khordād 1345/ 19 June 1966, 1.

Morocco for 'employment on a large scale'. In addition, Iran would encourage private investment in Morocco in the fields of tourism and agriculture, with investments guaranteed by the Iranian National Bank.

The shah and Hassan II also visited Islamic sites. They were pictured praying at the tomb of Mohammed V, as well as at the Kutubiyya mosque in Marrakesh during Friday prayers (Figures 2.1 and 2.2). Images of these visits were printed on the front page of *Ettelāʿāt* and according to a British report, received much publicity elsewhere.[70] This presentation was deliberate, intended to emphasise that the two monarchs were not merely leaders of Muslim-majority countries, but were themselves spiritual individuals and political leaders of their faith.

The overarching theme of the visit was problems in the Middle East and how they could be solved through greater Islamic cooperation. During the state banquet in Rabat, both leaders explicitly referenced

[70] 'Programme of the Shah's Visit', 4 July 1966, FO 371/186673.

Figure 2.2 The shah and King Hassan II praying together at the Kutubiyya Mosque in Marrakesh during the shah's visit to Morocco in June 1966. Next to King Hassan are the head of *Ettelāʿāt* newspaper, Senator ʿAbbās Masʿudi, and the shah's cultural counsellor at the Imperial Court, Shojāʿ al-Din Shafā. *Ettelāʿāt*, 30 Khordād 1345/ 20 June 1966, 1.

Islam in their speeches. King Hassan said that Morocco's dedication to 'the principle of mutual respect for and non-interference in the affairs of other nations whatever their political and social systems' was inspired by Islam. 'If all nations could be equally inspired by this principle then each could work quietly and without interruption towards progress and prosperity', he declared. The shah agreed with King Hassan's comments, and argued that their countries had 'chosen the same path, guided by the precepts of Islam'. This should, he added, 'be a source of inspiration and pride to all Muslim States'.[71]

The joint communique also expressed the need for each side to express the bilateral relationship within an Islamic framework. There were no references to an Islamic summit meeting in the communique

[71] Ibid.

because, as King Hassan told the shah, he did not wish to damage the fragile Arab unity that he believed he had salvaged at the 1965 Arab League summit in Casablanca. But Hassan was pessimistic about the long-term prospects of Arab unity and felt that a formal division would eventually form between the radical states backed by the Soviets and the moderate countries. King Hassan saw Iran, Morocco and Saudi Arabia as the 'natural core of an anti-"Socialist" alliance', however Iran's reputation in the Arab world as a supporter of Israel presented some difficulty. For this reason, the Moroccans persuaded the shah to commit to describing the Palestinian problem as a Muslim problem that concerned Muslims all over the world, and to pledging his support for 'the Arab people of Palestine'.[72] References in the communique to 'spiritual values' of Islam were, according to Ambassador Forughi, supposed to convey two ideas: first, that Islam was a moral force which did not need, nor should it depend on, formal pacts; and second, that 'the essentially spiritual quality of Islam was not reconcilable with Communism or with alliances within the Communist world'.[73]

Talk of establishing a formal Islamic bloc, led by Hassan and the shah, was premature, but the shah was nonetheless asked about the prospects of such an alliance during his press conference in Rabat on 21 June. He replied:

> The Islamic states should, in my view, consult with each other and confer on various questions of the Islamic peoples and on means leading to their progress, development and prosperity. I believe that such conference should not be limited to the kings and presidents of the Islamic states, but there must be talks and consultations between Muslim ulema, workers, economists and public figures to seek ways which can ensure the progress of the Islamic world so that it can remain always in the vanguard and keep up with the caravan of human civilisation.[74]

Although King Hassan was reluctant formally to endorse the creation of an Islamic bloc at this time, the language of the communique and the shah's words at the press conference were an indication of things to come. Indeed, the British ambassador felt that as a result of the visit 'in [the] case of [the] conflict between the Pan Arab and Pan Islamic concepts Morocco is now committed to the latter'.[75]

[72] Holliday, 'Visit of the Shah of Iran to Morocco', 3. [73] Ibid.
[74] 'The Shah's Press Conference in Rabat', 21 June 1966, FO 371/186673.
[75] Holliday telegram to the Foreign Office, 23 June 1966, FO 371/186673.

To the shah this was not just about Islam. Islam provided him with an alternative philosophy to help Arab states like Morocco realise that they did not have to follow Nasser's lead and that there was another path; a moderate path that the shah's Iran represented. 'Iran has always supported Arab countries', the shah said during the press conference, '[. . .] but one cannot say that there is any reciprocity in the position of the Arab countries regarding Iran'. The shah expressed his hope that Morocco, 'a brotherly Arab country, will serve as an example to other countries henceforth. We ourselves are ready for excellent relations with the Arab world.'[76] According to the British, the visit of the shah served as a warning to Nasser that 'Morocco is not in so isolated a position as she recently appeared to occupy'.[77]

In the years that followed, Iran appeared ready to utilise its relationship with Morocco to strengthen its ties with other Arab states. In April 1968, two years after the shah's visit to Morocco, King Hassan travelled to Iran for an eight-day official visit.[78] During a meeting between King Hassan and Iran's foreign minister, Zāhedi, and prime minister, Amir ʿAbbās Hoveydā, King Hassan offered to act as a mediator in solving a recent disagreement between Saudi Arabia and Iran.[79] He ordered his foreign minister to travel to Riyadh forthwith and to resolve the problem, 'so that our Egyptian comrades, whom we know well, do not take advantage of this issue'.[80] King Hassan was apparently successful in reconciling Iran and Saudi Arabia on this occasion. Asadollāh ʿAlam later recorded in his diary: 'It was King Hassan who made peace between us and King Faisal. We are very grateful to him.'[81]

[76] Holliday, 'Visit of the Shah of Iran to Morocco', 4. [77] Ibid.

[78] *Gāhnāmeh-ye Panjāh Sāleh-ye Shāhanshāhi-ye Pahlavi*, vol. 4 (Paris: Soheil Publishers, 1985), 1,723.

[79] Relations between Iran and Saudi Arabia had been strained after the Saudis had invited the Sheikh of Bahrain as head of state just one week before the shah's intended visit to Riyadh. The shah cancelled his trip and for some time after relations were tense. *Yāddāsht-hā-ye ʿAlam*, vol. 1, 139, fn. 1. For context, see Banafsheh Keynoush, *Saudi Arabia and Iran: Friends or Foes?* (New York: Palgrave Macmillan, 2016), 93–96. In his meeting with the shah, Hassan also raised Arab concerns that the shah planned to seize Bahrain, and received assurances from Zāhedi and Hoveydā that Iran would not make such a move.

[80] Report of a meeting between the King of Morocco and the prime minister and foreign minister, 29 Farvardin 1347/ 18 April 1968, Zāhedi Archives, box 8, folder 14.

[81] Diary entry 12 Esfand 1347/ 3 March 1969, *Yāddāsht-hā-ye ʿAlam*, vol. 1, 139.

Hassan began the meeting by referring to the 'fraternal and friendly relations between the two governments' and observing that, 'Relations between the two countries are developing well based on a policy that is in line with a spirit of intimacy and brotherhood, and we must work hard to strengthen and expand them.'[82] He proposed that economic and technical bilateral commissions be formed, which should meet twice a year (once in Tehran and once in Rabat) to 'propose new ideas and plans'. Turning to the international arena, King Hassan argued that 'in terms of foreign affairs and the problems facing the world, the roles of Iran and Morocco are extremely important'. Despite their geographical distance, he said, 'due to their sincere ties to each other' they could play an 'effective role politically'.[83]

The idea of Islamic solidarity was a major theme of the speeches delivered during this visit. During his speech at the banquet in honour of King Hassan, the shah connected the bilateral relationship to wider issues within the Islamic world.

> Now, the foundations of vast economic and cultural cooperation between our two countries have been laid, which will surely develop more day by day. I am sure that this cooperation will not only benefit both of our countries, but at the same time, it will benefit the Islamic world and the whole human society.[84]

In his response, King Hassan advised that the Islamic world 'should take a lesson from the prophet of Islam by re-establishing the conditions that brought about the unity of the Muslim population at the height of its civilisation'. The hardships Muslims faced in the world were caused ultimately by Muslims deviating from the 'right path', he argued. On the third day of the visit, King Hassan addressed the Iranian senate, in which he argued that 'the understanding and cooperation of Muslim nations will remove the roots of malaise and disagreements'.[85] It is clear that the idea of Islamic solidarity was gaining momentum and that the shah and King Hassan would seek to play a leading role in such an initiative (Figure 2.3).

[82] Report of a meeting between the King of Morocco and the prime minister and foreign minister, 29 Farvardin 1347/ 18 April 1968, Zāhedi Archives, box 8, folder 14.

[83] Ibid. [84] *Ettelā'āt*, 24 Farvardin 1347/ 13 April 1968, 4.

[85] *Ettelā'āt*, 25 Farvardin 1347/ 14 April 1968, 25.

Figure 2.3 The shah kissing King Hassan goodbye at Mehrābād Airport, printed on the front page of *Ettelā'āt*, 31 Farvardin 1347/ 20 April 1968, 1.

Just two months after this visit, the shah stopped in Morocco for a short five-day trip on his return to Iran from Europe. The fact that this visit took place so soon after King Hassan's trip to Iran demonstrates both the friendly relationship that had developed between the two monarchs, but also the alliance that was forming between the two conservative states. During the visit, which gained comparatively little media attention in Iran due to the visit there of the Iraqi prime minister, Taher Yahya,[86] 'important talks' were said to have taken place between King Hassan and the shah, 'not only about relations between Iran and Morocco, but also the Arab and Islamic world'.[87] Having spent much time discussing the potential for Islamic solidarity, all that

[86] Prime Minister Taher Yahya visited Iran from 24 to 29 June. This story dominated front pages because it was the first visit of an Iraqi prime minister to Iran in a decade. See Farzad Sharifi-Yazdi, *Arab-Iranian Rivalry in the Persian Gulf: Territorial Disputes and the Balance of Power in the Middle East* (London: I. B. Tauris, 2015), 225.

[87] *Ettelā'āt*, 2 Tir 1347/ 23 June 1968, 21.

was needed was a spark, a major event that would galvanise the Islamic world and allow the two monarchs to present their vision to the world. That would come little over one year later.

The First Islamic Summit Conference, 22–25 September 1969

On 21 August 1969, in occupied Jerusalem, the Al Aqsa mosque, one of the holiest shrines in Islam, was set on fire by a lone arsonist. The fire raged for some three hours, causing extensive damage, including to the famous Minbar (pulpit) of Saladin.[88] King Faisal had earlier suggested the creation of an Islamic pact, which had been supported by the shah, but rejected by Nasser as an imperialist scheme to control the Middle East.[89] The shock, anger and revulsion at the burning of the Al-Aqsa mosque in Israeli-occupied Jerusalem renewed the call for greater Islamic solidarity. Thus, the first Islamic Summit Conference took place in Rabat one month after the fire, from 22 to 25 September. The conference was attended by the heads of state or their representatives of twenty-five Muslim-majority countries, many of which disagreed on central political issues. Iraq declined to attend the conference because Turkey and Iran refused to sever relations with Israel. Syria cited its lack of diplomatic relations with Morocco as a reason not to attend. Nasser was ill, so Egypt was represented by its vice-president, Anwar Sadat.

Iran was the driving force behind the organisation of the conference, and Iran's foreign minister, Zāhedi, played a central role in bringing the various groups together.[90] When it came to the politics of the Islamic world, the shah held an awkward position, particularly among the Arab states, due not only to his refusal to join the oil embargo in 1967, but his benefitting from it, and Iran's continuing relationship with Israel. The conference, therefore, represented an opportunity for him to re-establish his credentials as an Islamic ruler, and in the process deflect criticism of Iran's support of Israel, as well as other problematic regimes, such as South Africa. Reflecting his importance to the proceedings, the shah was the second leader to enter the conference hall, behind the host, King Hassan II. He also delivered the first speech of

88 'The Burning of Al Aqsa', *Time*, 29 August 1969.

89 Shameem Akhtar, 'The Rabat Summit Conference', *Pakistan Horizon*, vol. 22, no. 4 (1969), 337.

90 Zāhedi, *Khāterāt*, vol. 3, 166–177.

the conference after King Hassan's opening remarks. In it he spoke in general terms about the 'philosophy of Islam' and the need for Islamic solidarity:

> We are gathered here to get to know each other more and better, to love one another more, to coordinate our actions, and to discuss all the issues that contribute to the advancement of the great and lofty goals of Islam. I think that all the delegates will share in the excitement that the convening of this great conference has created, because the convening of this conference is, in fact, the greatest event that has taken place in the history of Muslim countries. This should be pursued with passion and perseverance, and this community should not be our first and last community. Such conferences should continue in order to increase understanding and increase feelings of brotherhood among Muslims.[91]

Although the event was held against the backdrop of the burning of the Al-Aqsa mosque, the shah made no mention of this, nor of Israel, in his speech. To the shah, this was not about uniting the Islamic world against colonial oppression or Zionism; it was about shaping Islam in his image, and providing a strong, alternative discourse to that offered by Nasserism.

The conference was limited in what it could achieve, not least because it was hastily convened, leaving little time to put together a comprehensive agenda, and because of the refusal to attend of several important Muslim countries.[92] As a result, the declaration signed at the end of the conference was particularly vague and weak. In it, all participants pledged support for Palestine, to appeal to the great powers to ensure the withdrawal of Israeli forces from areas occupied during the Six-Day War, and to 'consult together with a view to promoting between themselves close co-operation and mutual assistance in the economic, scientific, cultural and spiritual fields, inspired by the immortal teachings of Islam'.[93] However, the conference was significant, insofar as it laid the groundwork for future cooperation. At the first Islamic States' Foreign Ministers' Conference, held in Jeddah in March 1970, a permanent secretariat was established as

[91] *Ettelā'āt*, 1 Mehr 1348/ 23 September 1969, 4.
[92] Mehrunnisa Ali, 'The Second Islamic Summit Conference', *Pakistan Horizon*, vol. 27, no. 1 (1974), 29.
[93] 'Islamic Summit: A Historical Perspective', *The Pakistan Times*, 2 February 1974.

the Organisation of Islamic Cooperation, 'to act as liaison between the participating states' with its headquarters at Jeddah. Three further Foreign Ministers' Conferences were held, in Karachi (December 1970), Jeddah (March 1972) and Benghazi (March 1973), which resulted in the setting up of an Islamic Development Bank. At the Karachi conference, too, the foreign ministers for the first time turned their attention to a non-Arab Muslim issue, by denouncing the Portuguese attack on Guinea in West Africa.[94] The second Islamic Summit Conference was held in Lahore in 1974.

*****

The Islamic Summit in 1969 was an important moment in the context of Iran's engagement with Afro-Asian solidarity, and in that of the decline of Nasserism. In 1955, Nasser had returned from the Bandung Conference a hero, welcomed by adoring crowds, whereas the Iranian delegation's return was barely noticed in the Iranian press.[95] Fourteen years later, times had changed. While the shah delivered his speech to the Islamic leaders who had gathered from across Asia and Africa, Nasser stayed in Egypt. His vice-president, Sadat, quoted lines of the Persian poets Saʿdi and Hafez to the shah. 'Plant a sapling of friendship that will fill your heart with joy', he said. 'Cut down the tree of enmity that brings endless suffering.'[96] During the conference, also, the shah had the opportunity to meet and form a 'close acquaintance' with the president of Algeria, Houari Boumédiène, which ultimately brought to an end the long period of disharmony between the two countries.[97] But the shah did not have an essentially Islamic motive, nor did his idea of Islamic unity share similar aspirations to other Afro-Asian solidarity initiatives, such as that articulated at Bandung, though he borrowed some of their language. The shah's adoption of Islam was motivated by practical concerns and strategic calculations.

Nasser had been significantly weakened by his failure in Yemen and the catastrophe of the Six-Day War. But at the same time, the shah had

94 Ibid.
95 De Gezant to Dutch minister of foreign affairs, 10 May 1955, NA 2.05.191/470.
96 Zāhedi, *Khāterāt*, vol. 3, 177.
درخت دشمنی برکن که رنج بیشمار آرد نهال دوستی بنشان که کام دل به بار آرد
97 Ibid., 174.

been successful in building a coalition of allies who shared his fears of Nasser's influence spreading further across the Middle East and North Africa, where Nasser remained until his death an extremely popular figure. Tunisia and Morocco were led by the types of cosmopolitan, well-educated, and moderate leaders that the shah enjoyed working with – the antitheses of the unpredictable and rash Egyptian president. But Nasserism was not only perceived as a threat to the stability of Muslim states, but non-Muslim majority countries, too. One of these was Ethiopia, which the shah identified as another potential partner in his anti-Nasser alliance.

3 'Creating Influence and Dialogue with the African Continent' (1960–1968)

The years 1960 to 1968 marked the formative period of Iran's policy in sub-Saharan Africa. Although it was not until the 1970s that Iran actually developed expansive relationships across the continent, during the 1960s it identified areas of strategic, economic and political importance, and formed coherent policies to achieve its broader strategic goals. This was a very slow process. Until 1960, Iran had had very little contact with sub-Saharan African countries, and the establishment of these ties took some time fully to materialise. This was largely due to two factors. First, Iran's Ministry of Foreign Affairs lacked in-depth knowledge of these countries. Second, the vast majority of African countries were, during this period, emerging from long periods of colonial rule. In many cases, former colonial powers maintained control over sectors of their economies and strongly influenced politics, which left limited room to manoeuvre for faraway countries like Iran. Moreover, during the 1960s, Iran was itself a developing nation that could not compete with the likes of the United States, the Soviet Union, France and the United Kingdom, to which many newly independent African countries turned for financial support. Nonetheless, connections were made with some countries, such as Cameroon, Nigeria and Ghana.

As Iran sought to make inroads into sub-Saharan Africa, Ethiopia emerged as a natural early partner, for several reasons. First, Ethiopia had not been colonised, so had more freedom and experience in its foreign relations than other countries in Africa, which maintained close connections to their former colonisers. Second, the Horn of Africa was geographically close to Iran's sphere of influence, and as a result Ethiopia and Iran had common interests and concerns. Third, both Ethiopia and Iran were monarchies in a region, and world, in which monarchies were increasingly threatened by revolutionary ideologies. As demonstrated in Chapter 2, the shah established close ties with King Hassan II of Morocco for similar reasons, and organised the Islamic

Summit Conference in 1969 in order to engender solidarity among the more conservative leaders of the region in response to revolutionary regimes established in Algeria, Egypt, Iraq and Syria.

Fourth and finally, there were remarkable similarities between the shah and Haile Selassie as rulers, and their perceptions of global politics. Both were rulers of emerging states in the Global South, whose countries had been important regional powers in the past, and who aspired to assert greater regional influence in the future. They both presented their countries and cultures as thousands of years old and based their legitimacy on the longevity of their monarchical traditions. Haile Selassie held the official title of *Negusa Nagast* and Mohammad Reza Pahlavi that of *Shāhanshāh*; both mean 'King of Kings'. In spite of the ancientness of their monarchical institutions, each ruler also cultivated the image of himself as a moderniser. They had each suffered the ignominy of imperial aggression – Haile Selassie in 1936 at the hands of the Italians and the shah in 1941, when his father was overthrown and his country occupied by Russia and Britain – and they had each subsequently pursued close alignment with the United States. It is perhaps unsurprising that they should be drawn together so closely during this period.

Decolonisation and Early Iran–Africa Connections

The 1950s and 1960s formed a transformative period in Africa, as a wave of independence movements swept across the continent. From Ghana (1957) to Sudan (1956), Nigeria (1960), Algeria (1962) and Kenya (1963), European colonies were replaced with sovereign nations. Whereas in 1950, there had been only four independent nations in the whole of Africa, by the end of the 1960s, there were over forty. The Iranian government watched these developments closely. As each new country declared independence, Iran made sure to send messages of recognition and congratulations, though as shown in Chapter 2 with Algeria, it was careful not to damage relations with its European allies in the process. The government also sought the advice of the former colonial governments to ensure that its messages were properly addressed.[1] This message to Mali is a typical example:

[1] For example, the Ministry of Foreign Affairs asked the British to advise them on to whom they should address their formal recognition of Guinea in 1959. Geoffrey Harrison telegram, 8 January 1959, FO 371/138814.

On the occasion of the proclamation of the independence of the Federation of Mali, I ask your Excellency to kindly convey to the authorities of the new state my warmest congratulations and the best wishes that I form for the progress and prosperity of the Malian nation. Abbas Aram, Minister of Foreign Affairs.[2]

It was not only Iran that had begun to think about the opportunities that independent Africa could present in the pursuit of its interests, but African countries also began to reach out to Iran, largely a result of connections established through the United Nations.

In March 1959, Jalāl ʿAbdoh, at that point Iran's permanent representative at the UN, was elected to serve as UN plebiscite commissioner to oversee the plebiscites that would be held in Cameroon under British administration. ʿAbdoh was one of Iran's most senior diplomats. He had served as Iran's deputy permanent representative at the UN from 1949 until 1953, and permanent representative from 1955 until 1959, when he became for a short time the Iranian minister of foreign affairs.[3] During this time, ʿAbdoh developed a reputation for 'his ability in reconciling opposing factions' and his 'genial and even-tempered' manner.[4] As part of this mission, ʿAbdoh spent some time in the region, particularly in Cameroon, but also Nigeria, where he was able to meet with political leaders. After his mission had ended, ʿAbdoh represented Iran at Nigeria's Independence Day celebrations on 1 October 1960. Nigeria had only decided to invite African countries, the five permanent members of the UN Security Council, British Commonwealth countries, countries that had consulates in Nigeria and countries that had expressed an interest in establishing an embassy in Lagos. Iran did not meet any of these criteria, but when the Nigerian prime minister found out that Iran had expressed interest in attending, he ordered that Iran's representative be given the same treatment as all other representatives.[5]

2 ʿAbbās Āram telegram, 26 June 1960, CADN 184PO/1/417.
3 'Biographical Note: Ambassador Djalal Abdoh of Iran', 28 September 1959, Press Release BIO/24/Rev.1, UN Secretariat S-0876-0001-07-00001.
4 'Iranian Conciliator' [undated newspaper cutout], UN Secretariat S-0876-0001-07-00001.
5 ʿAbdoh, *Chehel Sāl dar Sahneh-ye Qazāʾi, Siyāsi, Diplomāsi-ye Irān va Jahān*, vol. 1, 610.

Figure 3.1 The prime minister of Eastern Nigeria, Michael Okpara, with the prime minister of Iran, ʿAli Amini. *Ettelāʿāt*, 1 Tir 1340/ 21 June 1961, 24.

Emboldened by these early connections, political figures from Nigeria and Cameroon travelled to Iran to attempt to deepen ties. On 22 June 1961, the prime minister of Eastern Nigeria, Michael Okpara, travelled to Iran on a one-day unofficial visit (Figure 3.1).[6] During the trip, Okpara held talks with the Iranian prime minister, ʿAli Amini, and the minister of foreign affairs, Hoseyn Qods-Nakhaʿi.[7] At a press conference, Okpara confidently declared his intention to 'establish political and trade relations with Iran'. Okpara was standing up while introducing himself, but then sat down and said: 'I would like to sit down before speaking because this is a friendly and familial gathering.' For the benefit of his Iranian audience, Okpara introduced his country; its land mass, population size, the three regions that made

[6] After independence in 1960, the Nigerian state was made up of the federal government, headed by the prime minister, Sir Abubakar Tafawa Balewa, and the three regional administrations of the northern, eastern and western provinces.

[7] *Ettelāʿāt*, 1 Tir 1340/ 22 June 1961, 24.

up the federal state, the major political parties and Nigeria's main exports.[8] He mentioned that three-quarters of Nigerians were Muslim, and that he was the first Nigerian head of government to visit Iran. He was not only drawn to Iran because it was a fellow Muslim nation, he said, but also because of its 'vast and modern oil industry'. As Nigeria looked to expand its own oil industry, he sought to explore ways in which Nigeria could learn from Iran. Continuing his charm offensive, Okpara said that 'the extraordinary love and hospitality' he received during his visit, 'aroused in me a strange passion and I am confident that we can have a deep friendship'.[9]

Just ten days after this trip, the prime minister of Northern Nigeria, Ahmadu Bello, arrived in Tehran for a four-day visit. Like Okpara, Bello held meetings with government officials, including Prime Minister Amini, but he also had time to travel further afield, to Isfahan, where he was invited to inaugurate the *nāz* vegetable oil factory and visit historical sites. He was even granted an audience with the shah at Saʿdābād Palace in Tehran.[10] Like Okpara before him, Bello drew attention to Islam as the basis of relations between Iran and Nigeria. In a letter to Amini, Bello wrote that the visit had given him 'a golden opportunity of building a firm foundation for our direct personal contact, thereby strengthening the brotherly relations which have already been established between us by our common religion'.[11] Amini responded that he was 'confident' that the personal contacts would 'further cement the religious ties already existing between the people of Iran and the people of Nigeria'.[12]

That these two trips from Nigerian politicians occurred so close together probably reflects the competition between the regional administrations in Nigeria at the time, and the fears of one region achieving dominance over the others, which, according to historians Toyin Falola and Matthew Heaton, 'clouded any sense of national unity in Nigeria in the 1960s'.[13] In Iran, the two trips were said by the French embassy in Tehran to have been successful in highlighting this part of

[8] *Ettelāʿāt*, 4 Tir 1340/ 25 June 1961, 5.
[9] *Ettelāʿāt*, 4 Tir 1340/ 25 June 1961, 20.
[10] *Ettelāʿāt*, 13 Tir 1340/ 4 July 1961, 20; and 14 Tir 1340/ 5 July 1961, 14.
[11] Ahmadu Bello to ʿAli Amini, 6 July 1961, NLAI 230/040698.
[12] Amini to Bello, 18 July 1961, NLAI 230/040698.
[13] Toyin Falola and Matthew M. Heaton, *A History of Nigeria* (Cambridge: Cambridge University Press, 2014), 165.

the world to the Iranian government, and accordingly the visits were given considerable attention in the Iranian press. Subsequently, as a result of these visits, in August 1961, the Iranian Ministry of Foreign Affairs expressed its intention to open diplomatic missions in Ethiopia, Ghana, Libya, Nigeria and Sudan.[14]

Just over one year later, from 7 until 10 October 1962, a five-man goodwill delegation visited Iran from Cameroon, headed by the deputy foreign minister, Nzo Ekangaki.[15] Jalāl ʿAbdoh met with the Cameroonian delegation during the visit, and his work on the plebiscite in Cameroon was praised by Ekangaki in a speech at a reception at the *Ettelāʿāt* headquarters.[16] At the same reception, the head of the newspaper, ʿAbbās Masʿudi, assured the Cameroonian delegation of the 'complete interest of the Iranian people in the independence of ... the newly independent countries that have been living under colonial conditions until now'.[17] While the work of ʿAbdoh had clearly helped to improve goodwill between Iran and Cameroon, the Cameroonian delegation had also hoped to conduct trade negotiations. The delegation spokesperson told the press that the Cameroonians would hope to trade oil for bananas,[18] and together with Iranian officials drew up three draft agreements relating to cultural relations, commercial relations, and technical and economic assistance.[19]

The shah himself became curious about Africa during this period, as is evident in the remarkable travelogue of the Nigerian traveller and writer Olabisi Ajala, who visited Iran in 1960 as part of his 'one-man Odyssey around the world'.[20] While in Iran, Ajala was granted an audience with the shah at Saʿdābād Palace, arranged by the court minister, Hoseyn ʿAlā, during which they strolled around the palace garden and spoke about a variety of topics.[21] The shah, whom Ajala describes as 'cool, reserved and simple ... aflame with intelligence and

[14] French Ministry of Foreign Affairs to the French ambassador in Dakar, 20 August 1961, CADN 184PO/1/417.
[15] *Ettelāʿāt*, 16 Mehr 1341/ 8 October 1962, 1.
[16] *Ettelāʿāt*, 17 Mehr 1341/ 9 October 1962, 13. [17] Ibid.
[18] *Ettelāʿāt*, 16 Mehr 1341/ 8 October 1962, 20.
[19] *Echo of Iran*, 11 October 1962.
[20] Olabisi Ajala, *An African Abroad* (London: Jarrolds, 1963), 14.
[21] Ajala recalled fondly that, 'Without the kindly guidance of the Shah's Minister of Court, Mr Alah, a short, quietly shrewd and conservative man, my chances of ever being received by the Shah would have been nil.' Ibid., 107.

alertness', was particularly interested in learning about Africa. Ajala writes:

> Unlike most of the statesmen and leaders I have met, the Shah did not profess to know everything about Africa. While he was not talking particularly about politics, he was very keen to know about African nationalism and the social and educational advancement of the continent.
>
> Regrettably and shamefully on my part, I could not answer most of the searching questions he posed: 'What is the average life-span among Africans? Is it in the region of eighty years? What is the anthropological origin of Africans? Have there ever been traces of manuscripts, and, if so, what type of letters and methods of communication were used by Africans in the ancient days?'
>
> Such unexpected questions revealed to me the hidden sharpness of the Shah. He was very interested in the welfare and progress of the newly independent African countries and expressed a desire to visit the African continent at a future date.[22]

Ajala was clearly impressed by the shah, who appeared to him 'simple and kindly in his thoughts, words and actions'.[23] Ajala was also struck by the shah's inquisitiveness, which reflects his growing interest in African affairs.

The Congress of African Unity and the Shah's Goodwill Delegation

As countries across Africa gained independence towards the end of the 1950s and into the early 1960s, international political movements emerged throughout the continent to support liberation, rid Africa of the vestiges of European colonialism and engineer some sense of African unity. Two main groups appeared at this time: the Casablanca Bloc and the Monrovia Bloc, named after gatherings held in those cities. The Casablanca Bloc, consisting of Algeria, Egypt, Ghana, Guinea, Morocco, Mali and Libya, called for the unification of African states into a single political entity. The Ghanaian prime minister, Kwame Nkrumah, who was one of the central figures in this bloc and had established the All African Peoples' Congress in Accra in December 1958, spoke of abolishing the old borders created by the

[22] Ajala, *An African Abroad*, 109. [23] Ibid., 101.

colonialists and creating an African federal state.[24] The Monrovia Bloc, on the other hand, which was comprised of Nigeria and most of francophone Africa, sought a political union, but one in which states would maintain their sovereignty and existing borders.[25]

In order to try and bridge the differences between these differing visions of African unity, a conference was held in Addis Ababa in 1963, the Summit Conference of Independent African States. Despite the revolutionary fervour of the time, the conference host, Emperor Haile Selassie, was still respected throughout Africa as a symbol of liberation and the anti-colonial struggle, and was regarded by many of the younger leaders, even the more radical ones, with paternal reverence.[26] Thirty-two heads of African states attended the conference and each was personally greeted by the emperor upon their arrival at the airport in Addis Ababa. Although Nkrumah used his platform to argue forcefully for a deep political union, Haile Selassie, in his role as conference chair, argued for moderation and succeeded in securing the unanimous support for the charter of the Organisation of African Unity (OAU), in which member states pledged to respect the old borders established by the colonialists.[27] Whereas the period before the conference had been marked by discord, the gathering successfully demonstrated unity among African states in their shared desire to work together to remove the remnants of colonialism, challenge imperialism and racism, and oppose minority regimes.

The message received by countries like Iran was that Africa was open for business, and they felt emboldened to reach out and try to make a mark in this part of the world. A detailed report of the conference was written by Iran's Ministry of Foreign Affairs and submitted to the prime minister's office.[28] Shortly thereafter, the Imperial Court commissioned another report authored by deputy court minister and the shah's cultural advisor, Shojāʿ al-Din Shafā, who

24 See Kwame Nkrumah, *Africa Must Unite* (London: Heinemann, 1963).

25 On the differences between these two positions see Adom Getachew, *Worldmaking after Empire: The Rise and Fall of Self-Determination* (Princeton, NJ: Princeton University Press, 2019), 131–138.

26 See, for example, Nelson Mandela's description of him in *Long Walk to Freedom* (London: Little, Brown and Company, 1994), 293–294.

27 See K. Mathews, 'The Organization of African Unity', *India Quarterly: A Journal of International Affairs* vol. 33, no. 3 (1977), 310–312.

28 Report by the Sixth Political Bureau of the Ministry of Foreign Affairs, 7 Khordād 1342/ 28 May 1963, NLAI 230/29553.

outlined the potential opportunities on offer in Africa, politically, culturally and economically, and argued that Iran should pursue closer relations with the continent as a matter of urgency:

> In this situation, to further their own interests, both politically and economically, all non-African governments need to find a position for themselves in this vast continent. In this competition, any country that has on the one hand the necessary conditions and potential to bring investment [to Africa] and on the other [the ability to] do so sooner and better, will naturally get the most privileged position.[29]

The report, which goes into detail on the history, culture and geography of each country in Africa, was to be made available to all the economic, political and cultural organs of the state, so that they might explore the possibilities independent Africa presented. Shafā concluded the report by putting forward suggestions as to how Iran could assert its influence in sub-Saharan Africa, which included: establishing two Iranian offices, one in West and one in East Africa, to serve as points of contact; sending trade missions to study the opportunities for establishing trade and business relations; establishing scholarships for African students to study at Iranian universities; facilitating travel by Iranian technicians and engineers to Africa; and establishing a Centre of Excellence in African Studies at the University of Tehran, to provide the necessary research on aspects of African history, politics, geography, culture, economy and religion.[30]

At around the same time, the Ministry of Economy carried out studies to support the implementation of Iran's export development programme, which concluded that African and Southeast-Asian countries would be suitable trade partners. It concluded that a high-level goodwill delegation should be sent to tour these regions to explore in more detail opportunities there.[31] A former deputy at the Ministry of Commerce, Hushang Ansāri, was selected to head the delegation, and 'to gain more respect for the delegation and the possibly of conducting the negotiations at a high level', he was granted the title of *safir-e kabir*

[29] Shojāʿ al-Din Shafā, 'Gozāresh-e Mokhtasar Marbut beh Afriqā', 1964(?), 2, Shojāʿ al-Din Shafā Archives, carton 11, Bibliothèque universitaire des langues et civilisations, Paris.
[30] Ibid., 17.
[31] Minister of economy to minister of foreign affairs, 28 Esfand 1352/ 18 March 1964, NLAI 240/056015.

(grand ambassador).[32] Ansāri was accompanied on the mission by three senior officials at the Ministry of Economy: Mehdi Bahremand, the director general of information and public relations; Mostafā Derakhshesh, the head of the international organisations office; and Abu al-Hasan Bakhtiyāri, deputy of the office of economic affairs.[33] This delegation, which travelled in August 1964, visited seven African countries – Ethiopia, Kenya, Uganda, Tanganyika (Tanzania), Ghana, Nigeria and Ivory Coast.[34]

In discussions with senior government officials and heads of state, the Iranian delegation apparently made a strong impression. In a one-hour meeting with the delegation, the Nigerian prime minister, Sir Abubakar Tafawa Balewa, praised the shah for the economic and social development of Iran, and reiterated his country's hope to learn from Iran's oil industry. Ansāri explained to Balewa the goods that Iran could export, including cement and chemical fertilizers, and also that Iran was one of the largest import markets in the Middle East, so 'can be a good buyer of Nigeria's export products'. Balewa 'expressed his hope that the countries will be able to establish political agencies and develop commercial and cultural relations in the near future' and accepted 'with great pleasure' Ansāri's invitation to visit Iran.[35]

Based on Ansāri's final report of his goodwill mission, some officials strongly encouraged the government to pursue closer economic ties with Africa. One official, Malekpur Maleki, wrote to the prime ministerial advisor, Javād Mansur, about Ghana. He argued that since Ghana had developed good political and economic relations with Pakistan and some Middle Eastern countries, due to its sizeable Muslim population, it would be relatively easy for Iran to develop similar relations. The fact that it was 'free from the political entanglements' of Israel, the United States and the Eastern Bloc was also considered favourable to Iran. Maleki argued that a deal be struck for the export of cotton, oil and chemical products, and there were

32 Minister of economy to prime minister, 5 Ordibehesht 1343/ 25 April 1964, NLAI 240/056015.

33 Minister of economy to Ministry of Foreign Affairs, 4 Mordad 1343/ 26 July 1964, NLAI 240/056015.

34 Renaud Sivan to minister of foreign affairs, 19 September 1964, CADC 367QO59.

35 Hushang Ansari to minister of foreign affairs, 14 Shahrivar 1343/ 5 September 1964, NLAI 240/056015.

possibilities to cooperate in the fields of health and culture. He concluded his letter: 'Fortunately, with the warm welcome and positive attention that the high officials of the government of Ghana have given to the Iranian goodwill delegation, there seems to be great prospects for future economic, political and cultural relations between the two countries, should political and economic representatives be established and exchanged.'[36]

As Shafā made clear in his report, deepening ties with Africa was not merely about establishing economic relations and opening new trade routes, but there were political advantages too. Reflecting on the political importance of the continent in his *Towards the Great Civilisation*, published in the late 1970s, the shah observed: 'Black Africa, which up to the end of the Second World War held no significant place in the world equation, now controls one third of the votes of the United Nations.'[37] The potential importance of African nations as allies on whose votes Iran could depend was reiterated by Ardeshir Zāhedi, who wrote in his memoir, 'their envoys voted at the United Nations and other international forums, and these votes could have been needed'.[38]

In his report, Shafā recognised in particular the political importance of Ethiopia within Africa. He wrote, 'from a political perspective, after holding the international conference of Africa in Addis Ababa, the country has found a special and privileged position on this continent'.[39] Addis Ababa was already home to the United Nations Economic Commission for Africa, but the establishment of the permanent headquarters of the Organisation of African Unity cemented its status as the diplomatic capital of the continent. There were certainly opportunities for economic cooperation, but given Ethiopia's political importance within Africa, establishing relations with Ethiopia was perceived, as Zāhedi recalled, as 'a way of creating influence and dialogue with the African continent'.[40] Moreover, Haile Selassie had gained a reputation as a statesman of impeccable standing who

[36] Malekpur Maleki to Javād Mansur, 15 Farvardin 1344/ 4 April 1965, NLAI 230/030339.
[37] Mohammad Reza Pahlavi, *Besu-ye Tamaddon-e Bozorg* (Tehran: Pahlavi Library, 2536/1977), 22.
[38] Zāhedi, *Khāterāt*, vol. 3, 206.
[39] Shafā, 'Gozāresh-e Mokhtasar Marbut beh Afriqā', 10.
[40] Zāhedi, *Khāterāt*, vol. 3, 221.

commanded respect everywhere he went, not just in Africa, but in Asia, Europe and America, too. One article in the Iranian semi-official daily *Ettelāʿāt* read that his speech at the 1963 conference 'had a profound effect on the young leaders of Africa and placed the emperor in their hearts as a wise father and leader'.[41] In a report in December 1966, the British ambassador to Ethiopia wrote: 'By any account Emperor Haile Selassie is the most eminent figure in Africa today ... As a world figure of real class and proven durability, Haile Selassie stands on his own.'[42] For this reason, as Iran sought to gain a foothold in Africa, Ethiopia – and Haile Selassie – received special attention.

Iran, Ethiopia and Haile Selassie's 1964 Visit

In the late 1950s and into the 1960s, as countries across Africa achieved independence from the European colonial powers, Ethiopia found itself in an awkward position. Although it had been occupied by the Italians from 1935 until 1941, it had not been formally colonised in the same way that most other areas of Africa had been. Therefore, in this period of rapid decolonisation, it was not the imperialists that threatened Haile Selassie's Solomonic kingdom, but the radical revolutionary movements in its newly independent neighbours. From the mid-1950s, Nasser had attempted to incite the Islamic minority populations Eritrea and supported Somalia's claims to the Ogaden region.[43] On the irredentist ideology of independent Somalia, Haile Selassie said, 'The Somalis would not have dreamt of such an idea without being incited by Nasser.'[44] The threat from regional movements was brought home to Haile Selassie in December 1960, when the Imperial Bodyguard, dissatisfied with the backwardness of Ethiopia in relation to the seemingly more progressive developments taking place across the continent, attempted a coup d'état to replace the emperor with his son.[45] In his

[41] *Ettelāʿāt*, 12 Khordād 1347/ 2 June 1968, 7.
[42] Haggai Erlich, *Haile Selassie: His Rise, His Fall* (Boulder, CO: Lynne Reinner Publishers, 2019), 129.
[43] Howard A. Patten, *Israel and the Cold War: Diplomacy, Strategy and the Policy of the Periphery at the United Nations* (London: I. B. Tauris, 2013), 31.
[44] Ibid., 118.
[45] Christopher Clapham, *The Horn of Africa: State Formation and Decay* (Oxford: Oxford University Press, 2017), 41–42.

memoir, Ardeshir Zāhedi notes that the shah made a concerted effort to support Haile Selassie after this failed coup.[46]

In 1950, Iran had appointed an Extraordinary Envoy and Minister Plenipotentiary to the Court of Haile Selassie. This first representative was ʿAbbās Khalili, who also served as Iran's representative to Yemen.[47] Khalili recalled that during his first meeting with Haile Selassie, the emperor gave him a pair of young lions to present to 'my brother' the shah.[48] The relationship remained at this ceremonial level until 1960, when, during this period of turmoil, Iran and Ethiopia decided to establish a formal political relationship at the ambassadorial level. It is significant that Israel, which had pursued good relations with both Iran and Ethiopia as part of its Policy of the Periphery opened an embassy at around the same time, in 1961.[49] Like Iran, Israel viewed the preservation of Haile Selassie's Solomonic kingdom as essential to prevent the spread of Nasserism and other radical Islamic regimes in the Horn of Africa. In 1961, the shah's envoy to Haile Selassie's court left his post and ʿAbdolhoseyn Meykadeh arrived in Addis Ababa as Iran's first ambassador to Ethiopia. However, Meykadeh returned to Iran after the embassy closed abruptly one year later, apparently as a cost-saving measure.[50] A report from the Imperial Court merely states that 'the government of Iran has tried to establish agencies in this country [Ethiopia], but then it stopped'.[51] It appears that at this stage, although each country faced similar threats, there was no strategic or economic imperative strong enough to drive either side to pursue the relationship with any real vigour. This changed in 1964 when Haile Selassie paid a much-publicised trip to Iran.

[46] Zāhedi, *Khāterāt*, vol. 3, 221–222.

[47] Mohammad Gelban, ed., *Dar Āyneh-ye Tārikh: Khāterāt-e Siyāsi-ye ʿAbbās Khalili (Modir-e Ruznāmeh-ye Eqdām)* (Tehran: Anusheh, [1380] 2001), 19. Until the establishment of full diplomatic relations, the shah's representative in Addis Ababa served as ambassador elsewhere. In 1957, Iran's ambassador to Saudi Arabia, Mahmud Salāhi, also served as representative to the court of Haile Selassie. Jean Sauvagnargues to French Ministry of Foreign Affairs, 15 April 1957, CADC 367QO/3.

[48] Apparently, the female died during transportation by sea from Ethiopia to Iran, but the male arrived safely in Iran. *Ettelāʿāt*, 21 Shahrivar 1343/ 12 September 1964, 6.

[49] Patten, *Israel and the Cold War*, 120–121.

[50] Giraudon letter, 25 August 1964, CADC 367QO/59.

[51] Shafā, 'Gozāresh-e Mokhtasar Marbut beh Afriqā', 10.

Haile Selassie had first been invited to Iran in 1961, at the opening of the Iranian embassy in Addis Ababa, but although he had accepted the invitation, the idea was apparently abandoned after the closure of the embassy.[52] Three years later, in August 1964, Hushang Ansāri's goodwill delegation arrived in Ethiopia, the first stop on its tour, and, during an audience with Haile Selassie, Ansāri extended to the emperor an invitation to visit Iran. According to Dutch reports, 'Haile Selassie understood this polite platitude as a real invitation for a state visit ... declared he would gladly accept the invitation and immediately set a date'.[53] This date was around three weeks later, which gave Iran very little time to prepare.[54]

Organising the visit at such short notice 'caused many problems', not least because the Ethiopian representative to Iran was based in New Delhi and had not visited Iran in years. Iran had no ambassador in Ethiopia either, so attempts were made to arrange the trip 'through direct exchange of telegrams' between the two royal courts. Since this strategy 'delivered insufficiently concrete results', the British ambassador to Iran, Denis Wright, who had previously served in Ethiopia and had maintained a good relationship with Haile Selassie, was called upon to help arrange the visit.[55] Ansāri, who was still away from Iran on his goodwill mission in Africa, had intended to wait until his return before submitting his report on Ethiopia, but now considered it necessary to send the report 'without delay', to be used in any potential trade negotiations in Tehran.[56]

One week before Haile Selassie's arrival, articles appeared about him in the Iranian press, which stressed the important historical role he had played as a leader on the African continent. Iran's former representative in Ethiopia, ʿAbbās Khalili, published a series of six

[52] Giraudon letter, 25 August 1964, CADC 367QO/59; and Renaud Sivan letter, 6 July 1962, CADC 367QO/59.

[53] Dutch ambassador in Tehran to Dutch Ministry of Foreign Affairs, 28 September 1964, Nationaal Archief (henceforth NA) 2.05.191, The Hague.

[54] Although the timing was not perfect, it did provide the shah with a welcome excuse not to have to travel to Athens for the wedding of King Constantine II. Iran had strongly supported Turkey over the crisis in Cyprus, and it was felt that an imperial visit to Greece would undermine this stance.

[55] Dutch ambassador in Tehran to Dutch Ministry of Foreign Affairs, 28 September 1964, NA 2.05.191.

[56] Ansāri to minister of economy, 3 Shahrivar 1343/ 25 August 1964, NLAI 230/ 030339.

articles in *Ettelāʿāt*, introducing readers to the geography, culture and history of Ethiopia, and the character of Haile Selassie. The emperor was widely presented not only as an eminent statesman in the modern world, but also a proud monarch of an ancient and romantic kingdom. One journalist referred to Haile Selassie as a 'distinguished guest from the legendary land of Sheba' and stated that 'the arrival of such a figure to our ancient nation gives us much pride'.[57] Attention was also drawn to the ancientness of the relations between the two countries, which could be dated to the Achaemenid king Cambyses' campaign on Egypt, after which Abyssinia became a satrapy in the Persian Empire.[58] In his report, the French ambassador in Tehran remarked wryly that the press had 'done so much juggling with the centuries during these four days that it is difficult to know where one is'.[59] By drawing on these ancient connections, both the relations between Iran and Ethiopia and Iran's role in the region were declared to have been as old as the tradition of monarchy in each country.

During Haile Selassie's visit, the local press also reflected Iran's antipathy towards Nasser and other actors supporting liberation movements in Africa, such as China. One newspaper read that 'with the exception of the "Pharaoh of Egypt" [Nasser], all leaders of Middle Eastern countries seek to maintain friendly relations with the countries of Africa. Without the intrigues of Gamal ʿAbd al-Nasser, the Middle East and Africa would be able to successfully resist the activities of the agents of Peking and collaborate to exploit their resources.'[60] Some foreign diplomats in Tehran suspected that one of the main reasons Haile Selassie had been received in Tehran with such pomp was to demonstrate the unity of these two powerful countries in opposition to Nasser. The chargé d'affaires of the Soviet Union told the French ambassador that he felt that the shah was perhaps 'above all concerned with, in a more immediate and direct way, using the influence of the Negus to counteract that of Nasser and in particular to get him to slow down his action in the direction of the Persian Gulf'.[61]

57 *Ettelāʿāt*, 23 Shahrivar 1343/ 14 September 1964, 2. 58 Ibid.

59 Renaud Sivan to minister of foreign affairs, 19 September 1964, CADC 367QO/ 59.

60 Renaud Sivan to the minister of foreign affairs in Paris, 19 September 1964, CADC 367QO/59.

61 Renaud Sivan to the Ministry of Foreign Affairs in Paris, 18 September 1964, CADC 367QO/59.

Haile Selassie was viewed by Iran as a particularly important ally in its defence against the 'Pharaoh of Egypt' because of his lofty status. An article in *Tehran Mossavar* judged that his visit to Iran would elevate him even further 'in Africa and above all within the independent bloc that Haile Selassie has founded on the black continent'. It continues, 'Haile Selassie has refused to bow to the influence of Nasser and that is the reason for which he has created a group of African states that has gained considerable importance in the eyes of the occidental world and even of the communist bloc ... The efforts of this bloc have joined those of Iran'.[62] The French ambassador believed that the claim of an 'independent bloc' centred around Haile Selassie was 'without doubt a little premature', but that the visit of the emperor to Iran, Iran's efforts to reach out to countries across Africa and Haile Selassie's analogous moves into the Middle East indicated that the two sides were indeed working together to counter the threat from radical regimes. A French source in the Ministry of Foreign Affairs confirmed that the article in *Tehran Mossavar* represented the opinion of Iran's minister of foreign affairs, ʿAbbās Ārām.[63]

High-level negotiations took place during the visit between the shah and Haile Selassie, and between the Iranian prime minister, Hasan ʿAli Mansur, and the foreign minister, ʿAbbās Ārām, and the Ethiopian emperor.[64] Inspired by the language of Afro-Asian solidarity, the talks were framed by the two sides as discussions not merely between two sovereign nations, but between the continents of Asia and Africa. An official statement on the negotiations released to the press read:

> The leaders of the two countries have stated with full confidence that the historical interests between the two ancient Asian and African countries should be further strengthened for the good of the two nations. Their majesties acknowledged the full understanding in the negotiations as another clear sign of the unity of purpose that unites the nations of Africa and Asia in their efforts to achieve a better life for their citizens and the establishment of justice and freedom.

The statement further confirmed that the negotiations took place in a 'cordial and fraternal environment' and that there was 'complete understanding and agreement' on all issues.[65] It concluded, '[T]he

[62] Renaud Sivan to the minister of foreign affairs, 19 September 1964, CADC 367QO/59.
[63] Ibid. [64] *Ettelāʿāt*, 26 Shahrivar 1343/ 17 September 1964, 17. [65] Ibid.

results of the negotiations in Tehran are a sign of the understanding between the nations of Africa and Asia.'[66]

During the final banquet on 16 September, the shah and Haile Selassie delivered speeches. Haile Selassie stressed the importance of the countries of the Global South working together '[to] be able better to face the challenges of humanity'. He cited his role in creating the Organisation of African Unity as evidence of the importance of unity and argued that this should be a guiding principle not just for Africa, but for the whole of mankind. Turning to the shah, the emperor praised his White Revolution reforms and said: 'You have done these great things in a way that reminds one of the stories of the Bible and of this wise saying: "Do unto others as you would have them do unto you." You put into practice the true meaning and wisdom of these biblical words.'

The shah then spoke: 'Your Majesty, the warm words you have spoken about me sit heavy on my heart because they were uttered by someone who, during his reign, practically embodied the concepts of patriotism, pride, realism and national devotion.' The shah then spoke of their shared experiences of foreign invasion and how this influenced how they perceived their roles in the world and the way they approached the imperial powers. He referred to Haile Selassie as 'a shining torch of national resistance' (*mash'al-e derakhshān-e moqāvemat-e melli*) for his role in ridding his country of Mussolini's Fascist forces. The shah recalled that as a student in Switzerland he read about the Italian invasion of Ethiopia:

> Shortly afterwards, the country of me and my father suffered a similar fate [and] I once again remembered the events that had befallen you. We also fought to preserve the freedom of our nation because our country was occupied by foreigners ... Today, with the help of almighty god, I meet with the representative of an ancient and gentle nation who, like me, longs for independence and freedom. We meet as free men who each care about the fate of their nations. I salute you, [a king] who is a brave warrior and a peaceful politician and who wishes peace for his own and all the nations of the world.[67]

This illuminating passage reveals the shah's views on the similarities of their struggles with European imperialism and his admiration for

[66] *Ettelā'āt*, 26 Shahrivar 1343/ 17 September 1964, 1.
[67] *Ettelā'āt*, 26 Shahrivar 1343/ 17 September 1964, 17.

fellow monarchs like Haile Selassie, who had overcome challenges to their nations from colonial forces and to their thrones from domestic opposition, and had prospered.

Though one should perhaps not expect to find obvious foreign policy pronouncements in such banquet speeches, as they are in large part intended to flatter, these two speeches do express a strong alignment of interests, a clear mutual respect and a willingness to cooperate. The shah often spoke at international forums about the need to work together to solve pressing international problems, and in his *White Revolution*, published around the time of Haile Selassie's visit, he outlined Iran's foreign policy principles: '[W]e seek peace, co-existence, and better understanding between other nations, whatever their ideologies may be; we will assist efforts in bridging the gap between the rich and poor nations of the world; we will support any plans for international co-operation, campaigns against illiteracy, poverty, disease, and other contemporary ills.'[68] He spoke also of 'convert[ing] peaceful co-existence into international co-operation and understanding', and in Haile Selassie he found a kindred spirit.[69] While revolutionary regimes such as those in Egypt, Iraq and Syria encouraged conflict and disorder, Mohammad Reza Pahlavi and Haile Selassie cultivated images of themselves as paragons of peace and stability, partly, of course, to ensure the continued military and diplomatic support of the United States.

Most importantly, Ethiopia and Iran viewed closer cooperation as key to enhancing their regional influence and asserting a moderating influence over the Afro-Asian community. As the French ambassador writes:

> It is perhaps in fact, beyond the similarities between the regimes – that common desire for non-engagement and for a certain independence with regards to the great powers, though it is a measured independence and limited by the need for assistance – that could constitute the most solid link between these two nations that are aware of their superiority in terms of their traditions, their stability and a certain wisdom, over the majority of developing countries, and that have the impression that they will be able to, if they support each other, to a certain extent control the evolution of the

[68] Mohammad Reza Pahlavi, *The White Revolution* (Tehran: Pahlavi Library, 1967), 165.
[69] Ibid., 173.

Afro-Asian world and even, by joining their efforts with those of countries like Yugoslavia, play a moderating role in global politics.[70]

Based on the speeches delivered and conversations with members of Iran's Ministry of Foreign Affairs, ambassadors, such as the French, concluded that this visit served a greater purpose than merely the strengthening of a bilateral relationship. It was intended 'to examine the means of mutual support to reinforce their position in the modern Afro-Asian world'.[71]

This first three-day visit laid the groundwork for the subsequent intensification of ties between Iran and Ethiopia and contributed to the shah's strategic objective to gain a foothold in Africa. One Iranian newspaper article read that it was hoped that the visit would have 'a profound impact on the relations between our country and Ethiopia in particular and the community of African countries in general ... we hope that the visit can be the key to effective cooperation between Iran and the community of African countries'.[72] In evidence of the significance of the visit in establishing a political dialogue, one month after the visit, in Mehr 1343 (September/October 1964), the Iranian embassy in Addis Ababa reopened, two years after it had been closed.[73] At the end of Haile Selassie's three-day trip, he invited the shah to visit him in Addis Ababa, an invitation which the shah accepted.

The Shah's State Visit to Ethiopia (3–9 June 1968)

Four years had passed since Haile Selassie's visit to Iran in 1964, and by 1968, on the surface, it did not appear that Iran had made a great deal of progress in its diplomatic push into Africa; it had still only established diplomatic relations with five countries on the whole

[70] Renaud Sivan to minister of foreign affairs, 19 September 1964, CADC 367QO59.
[71] Ibid. [72] *Ettelā'āt*, 28 Shahrivar 1343/ 19 September 1964, 2.
[73] Mohammad Rezā Tārtār, 'Negāhi beh Tārikhcheh-ye Ravābet-e Irān va Etiyupi', Report by the Cultural Counsellor of the Embassy of the Islamic Republic of Iran, Addis Ababa. Available online: http://icro.ir/index.aspx?pageid=32738&p=10&showitem=15370. For economic reasons, Ethiopia did not establish an embassy in Tehran, and its representative remained in India. Bakhshi, 'Barresi-ye Tārikhi-ye Ravābet-e Khāreji-ye Irān va Qāreh-ye Āfriqā', 19.

continent.[74] One of the reasons for this was that Iran still lacked diplomats who were knowledgeable in African affairs. Of course, Shafā had earlier noted the importance of establishing a centre of African studies at the University of Tehran. Another problem, as Zāhedi noted, was that Africa was not a popular destination among diplomats at Iran's Ministry of Foreign Affairs. 'They all wanted to go on missions to the so-called advanced countries', he wrote, '[where] they knew they would have comfort, medical and recreational facilities, and their children would be able to go to proper schools'.[75] Nonetheless, the shah remained determined to deepen ties with the continent, and a visit to Ethiopia was seen as an ideal opportunity. Indeed, throughout his trip, the shah sought to underline its significance by drawing attention to Addis Ababa's status as the political capital of Africa.

The shah's visit to Ethiopia had been planned for an earlier date, but had been delayed several times, apparently due to the nervousness of the ambassador, Mohammad Qavām, who 'was not looking forward to having to assume responsibility for this imperial stay'.[76] It was first put on hold following demonstrations organised by students at the University of Addis Ababa in opposition to measures taken by the Iranian government during student unrest in Tehran in 1965.[77] The ambassador was then recalled in November 1966. Plans for the visit were revived in February 1967, after the visit to Addis Ababa of the shah's brother, Prince ʿAbdolrezā Pahlavi, and the appointment of a new ambassador, Manuchehr Eʿtemād Moqaddam, in April.[78]

The significance the regime attached to this visit is reflected in the size of the shah's retinue, which included high-level court, government and military officials.[79] This enthusiasm was certainly reciprocated, and the Solomonic Kingdom ensured that its imperial guests were treated with great honour. *Ettelāʿāt* reported that the shah and Empress Farah were welcomed 'with dazzling beauty and impressive

[74] They were Algeria, Ethiopia, Morocco, Libya and Tunisia. *Ettelāʿāt*, 16 Khordād 1347/ 6 June 1968, 4.
[75] Zāhedi, *Khāterāt*, vol. 3, 206.
[76] Jean-Pierre Bénard to Michel Debré, 18 June 1968, CADN 9PO/1998003/116/ Mo-7.
[77] For some background to this period of unrest in Iran, see Rahnema, *The Rise of Modern Despotism in Iran*, 432–447.
[78] Ibid. [79] *Ettelāʿāt*, 12 Khordād 1347/ 2 June 1968, 4.

Figure 3.2 Stamp commemorating the visit of the shah to Ethiopia in June 1968. Author's collection.

glory',[80] and *The Ethiopian Herald* that they were 'given a rousingly spontaneous and warm welcome'.[81] Thousands gathered along the roads of Addis Ababa, which had been decorated with flags of the two nations, to cheer Haile Selassie and his guests as they made their way from the airport through the city towards Jubilee Palace in a royal carriage escorted by the Imperial Guard. A huge arch displaying words of welcome was erected along the way on Africa Avenue, and life-size portraits of the shah and Haile Selassie 'appear[ed] majestically framed near the Jubilee Palace'.[82] As the royal carriage approached Jubilee Palace, it was met with a guard of honour and the national anthems of the two countries.[83] Shops sold miniature commemorative statues of the shah and shahbanu, and a special commemorative stamp was commissioned to mark the visit (Figure 3.2).

As during Haile Selassie's visit to Iran four years earlier, the Ethiopian press spoke about the historicity of the relations between the countries. One article, for example, stated that 'Friendly relations

[80] *Ettelāʿāt*, 14 Khordād 1347/ 4 June 1968, 1.
[81] *The Ethiopian Herald*, 4 June 1968, 1.
[82] *The Ethiopian Herald*, 2 June 1968, 1.
[83] *The Ethiopian Herald*, 4 June 1968, 3.

between Iran and Ethiopia date back to the fifth century B.C.'[84] An editorial in *The Ethiopian Herald* spoke of the 'old ties of friendship between the two sister countries' and the fact that 'from time immemorial, relations between Iran and Ethiopia have been characterised by mutual respect and co-operation'.[85] The media spoke in glowing terms about the Pahlavis, and the Iranian royals made a strong an impression. The French ambassador appears to have been caught up in the excitement, reporting that 'the two sovereigns seduced all those who could approach them, the Emperor by his poise, and the young Empress by her charm'.[86] This enthusiasm seems to have been genuine. As Asfa-Wossen Asserate, an eyewitness to the visit, recalls, '[W]e literally fell over ourselves trying to get close to the enchanting empress as often and for as long as we could.'[87]

On the evening of 13 Khordād 1347 (3 June 1968), a special dinner was held at Menelik Palace in honour of the shah and Empress Farah, at which were present members of the Ethiopian royal family, including the crown prince, as well as the prime minister, members of parliament and the senate, high ranking military officers, and foreign ambassadors and their wives.[88] In a laudatory welcoming speech, Haile Selassie said:

It gives us great happiness to welcome our dear friend, His Imperial Majesty the Shahanshah of Iran and Her Highness Shahbanu Farah Pahlavi. The whole of Ethiopia has been eagerly awaiting the trip of Your Imperial Majesties and on behalf of ourselves and our nation, we welcome you on this trip.

When we visited Iran a few years ago, the warmth of the welcome the great nation gave us, and the sundry examples of respect and love towards us that we observed in the Iranian capital, affected us deeply. We have preserved the memories of those days like a precious treasure, and we believe that by reciprocating the feelings of friendship and brotherhood that were bestowed on us in Tehran, during their stay in Ethiopia, Their Majesties have become

[84] *The Ethiopian Herald*, 6 June 1968, 2.
[85] *The Ethiopian Herald*, 4 June 1968, 2.
[86] Benard to Debré, 18 June 1968, CADN 9PO/1998003/116/Mo-7.
[87] Asfa-Wossen Asserate, *King of Kings: The Triumph and Tragedy of Emperor Haile Selassie I of Ethiopia* (London: Haus Publishing Ltd., 2017), 241.
[88] 'Gozāresh-e Safar-e Shāhanshāh Āryāmehr va ʿOlyāhazrat Shahbānu-ye Irān', Ziyāfat-e Shām beh Eftekhār-e Aʿlāhazratayn, 14 Khordād 1347, NLAI 264/27596.

aware of the depth of the respect that we hold for the nation and country of Iran.[89]

As the shah did during Haile Selassie's visit to Iran four years earlier, the emperor drew attention to the ancientness of Iran and its rich cultural heritage, and its achievements as a 'prosperous and independent nation that has accelerated with its brilliant industrial and agricultural life, and is on a continuous path of economic and social development'.[90]

In the shah's response, he praised Ethiopia for having 'one of the longest histories in the world'. The re-established relations were considered by the shah to represent 'a renewal of a covenant between two histories of several thousands of years'.[91] However, although in his introductory and concluding remarks, the shah employed such rhetoric on the ancient ties between Iran and Ethiopia, for the vast majority of the speech, the shah spoke not about Ethiopia specifically, but about Africa more generally.

The shah began by noting that at the time Ethiopia joined the United Nations, there were only 'two or three' independent nations in the whole of Africa. Now there were around fifty.[92] While earlier, according to the shah, Africa had 'virtually no influence on world politics, the votes of the continent are now a very important weight in the United Nations and in international politics'.[93] The shah praised those African nations that 'are not only independent and sovereign', but had embarked on 'positive and optimistic activity in various economic, social and cultural fields, which promises a very bright future for this vast, rich and young continent'. He also stated that he was impressed by the eagerness of the African delegates who attended the UNESCO World Conference of Ministers on the Eradication of Illiteracy, held in Tehran in 1965, for their tenacity in trying to 'make the most of the opinions and advice' of the experts present. He continued, 'We have seen the same interest from the representatives of African countries in the World Congress of Human Rights, which was recently convened in Tehran, so we are sure that despite the

[89] Ibid. [90] Ibid.
[91] 'Sokhanān-e Shāhanshāh dar Ziyāfat-e Shām-e Kākh-e Menelik dar Pāsokh-e Bayānāt-e Emperātur-e Etiyupi', Ziyāfat-e Shām beh Eftekhār-e Aʿlāhazratayn, 14 Khordād 1347, NLAI 264/27596.
[92] The shah was incorrect – there were forty-two. [93] Ibid.

problems and issues that exist in the wider world, more and more material and spiritual progress will be made by African nations.'[94]

Turning to the struggles of majority black populations for their rights in South Africa and Rhodesia, the shah argued that 'one of the most serious problems facing Africa is the issue of racial discrimination'. Iran had, he said, 'always supported the legitimate struggle of African nations', had 'deep sympathy' for them, and 'wholeheartedly endorse[d] any attempt to combat racial discrimination'. Moreover, he said,

> Obviously, our country, as an old friend, will certainly not shy away from any sincere cooperation that may be possible for the progress of African nations. Not only have we voted for the interests of African nations throughout the life of the United Nations, but we have also been ready for practical cooperation with African countries. We are confident that in the future, these [current] connections and other cultural and economic relations will develop gradually, and the tradition of cooperation and long-standing friendship between Iran and Africa will continue to grow stronger.[95]

The shah ended his speech by stressing the important role that Haile Selassie and his 'spiritual dignity' could play in the progress of Africa, but it is clear that he was not the only, or even the primary, audience of this speech. The shah was making a pitch to Africa's political leaders on African soil, in a city that he understood to be the diplomatic capital of the continent.

Indeed, throughout the whole trip, the shah made an effort to appear sympathetic to the struggles and values of Africa. On the day following the banquet, he visited the Economic Commission for Africa in Africa Hall, and held a meeting with the secretary general of the OAU, Boubacar Diallo Telli. During the shah's meeting with Telli, echoing themes expressed in his speech to Haile Selassie, he again referred to the International Conference on Human Rights held the previous month in Tehran as evidence of Iran's 'commitment to combat the remnants of colonialism and apartheid, which we strongly condemn'. Telli presented the charter of the OAU to the shah and, responding positively to his overtures, said: 'We are aware of the important role of Iran and the role he [the shah] himself plays in the great family of Asia and Africa and we know that Iran has never raised its voice against

94 Ibid. 95 Ibid.

Africa in international affairs.'[96] Following this, the royal couple visited a school for the blind, where Empress Farah made a donation of teaching equipment, said to be worth $25,000.[97] Just weeks later, the local press reported that the empress had made a further donation of equipment to the school worth $12,000.[98] This philanthropy served to demonstrate the Pahlavis' commitment to the development of Africa.

The Iranian royals also visited the cities of Lalibela in northern Ethiopia, and Asmara, the capital of Eritrea, following the same itinerary as Queen Elizabeth II of Great Britain one year earlier. The act of bringing foreign visitors to Asmara served to legitimise Ethiopia's claims to Eritrea, which it had annexed in 1962.[99] But there was a greater significance to the shah's visit there, since, unlike Queen Elizabeth II, the shah was the ruler of an Islamic country. As the French ambassador noted: 'That a Mohammedan ruler should have agreed to go to visit this Islamic part of the Empire, where rebellion and repression arouse so much criticism and hostility from the Muslim world, is a success from which the government of Addis Ababa derives great satisfaction, as Mr Ketema Yifru, minister of foreign affairs, told me.'[100] During meetings with the shah, Haile Selassie and his foreign minister asked for the shah's help to appease the regional Islamic powers that were fiercely critical of him. The shah had faced the resentment of the same Arab rulers for his ties to Israel, and the way in which he had benefited from the Six-Day War by refusing to join the Arab oil boycott. The shah's visit to this site, then, was intended to demonstrate his solidarity with conservative rulers like himself, who had the courage to resist outside pressure, particularly from radical Muslim countries.

96 *Ettelā'āt*, 14 Khordād 1347/ 4 June 1968, 20.
97 *The Ethiopian Herald*, 5 June 1968, 3.
98 *The Ethiopian Herald*, 28 June 1968, 1.
99 Haile Selassie's annexation of the territory violated the UN General Assembly Resolution 390-A(V) of 2 December 1950, which granted full autonomy to Eritrea in domestic affairs and the creation of a democratic government as part of a federation with Ethiopia. Haile Selassie had repeatedly defiled the resolution throughout the federation and the annexation in 1962 was the final violation. See Semere Haile, 'The Origins and Demise of the Ethiopia-Eritrea Federation', *Issue: A Journal of Opinion*, 15 (1987), 9–17.
100 Benard to Debré, 18 June 1968, CADN 9PO/1998003/116/Mo-7.

During a private meeting between the shah and Haile Selassie, the emperor spoke of their shared values and objectives. He said, 'I know that Iran's policy is similar to ours, and there is a consensus among [our] governments on important principles of foreign policy, such as peaceful coexistence – the peaceful settlement of international disputes, and finally national progress and development.'[101] In this context, the emperor spoke about his recent trips to Asia, where he had sought to 'build more cooperation between the two continents' since 'Asian and African countries cannot do their duty to their nations and humanity if they do not work together.'[102] They must, he asserted 'form a united front against the great states'. He envisioned something akin to the Organisation of African Unity, but on a cross-continental scale; 'a wider community of Asian and African countries that may be formed in my country [and] will provide waves of greater cooperation and collaboration between the two continents'.[103]

Haile Selassie's most pressing problem, for which he sought the shah's assistance, was the Arab–Israeli conflict. Haile Selassie had maintained relations with both Israel and the Arabs, and had supported a peaceful resolution of the Six-Day War of June 1967. The emperor complained to the shah that this policy 'has drawn the hostility of some Arab countries towards us' and that specifically Egypt, Iraq, Saudi Arabia and Syria had since been trying to destabilise his country. Recognising the shah's influence as the head of an Islamic country and a fellow non-Arab regional power, Haile Selassie said to the shah: 'In general, our most important issue is maintaining peace in the region, and for this purpose, joint action by Iran and Ethiopia can be fruitful.'[104] The shah agreed with Haile Selassie and said:

> Israel has existed as a result of a UN resolution since 1948. And whether the Arabs want it or not the state [of Israel] exists[. . .] Our policy in this regard is similar to Ethiopia. We agree with the November 1967 resolution [242] of the Security Council and in no way agree to the occupation of territories by force, but at the same time we believe that a peaceful and just solution must be found, and in our opinion, it is the best authority of the United Nations; that is, the desired solution must be sought within the organisation.

[101] 'Mozākerāt Beyn-e A'lāhazrat Shāhanshāh Āryāmehr va A'lāhazrat Hāil Selāsi', 14 Khordād 1346/ 4 June 1968, Zāhedi Archives, box 9, folder 19.
[102] Ibid. [103] Ibid. [104] Ibid.

He spoke frankly about the 'belligerence' and 'spirit of adventure' of the Arab nations, in particular Egypt and Syria, which 'must not be allowed to continue, otherwise there will never be lasting peace'.[105]

During a follow-up meeting, the two countries' foreign ministers, Ketema Yifru and Ardeshir Zāhedi, elaborated on Ethiopia's problems with the Arab states and discussed what the Iranians could do practically to help. Yifru said:

> There is danger for us from the north and the Red Sea. Soviet weapons go to the Persian Gulf, Yemen and South Yemen. We need to work together to see how we can prevent this danger. As His Majesty said, we must rely on ourselves. Of course, your country is more loved by nature than us and you have more facilities. Unfortunately, Saudi Arabia is located in that part of the Red Sea and we have a lot of problems with them[. . .] In addition to Saudi Arabia, Sudan does not treat us well. These two countries are provoking our country. Some of the weapons that flow into Syria from the Soviet Union, Bulgaria and Czechoslovakia go to Khartoum and from there to Ethiopia to be distributed to insurgents and rioters. Saudi Arabia provides financial assistance[. . .] You have security considerations in the Persian Gulf, and we in the Red Sea and our purposes are common and close to each other. If we have more contact and cooperation with Saudi Arabia, peace and security in the region will be ensured.[106]

Given Iran's position as a wealthy regional power which had good relations with both Israel and Saudi Arabia, it was thought that closer alignment between Iran and Ethiopia would help to take some of the pressure off Ethiopia. Iran's status as an Islamic nation was important in this regard, too, since one of Saudi Arabia's major grievances with Ethiopia was its treatment of its minority Islamic population. Yifru said, 'His Majesty the Shāhanshāh can bring us closer together and Iran can generally play an important role in our relations with Saudi Arabia', to which Zāhedi responded, 'we have a relationship with Saudi Arabia and we are willing to help you in this regard'.[107]

During the shah's visit, a treaty of amity was signed between Zāhedi and Yifru, based on the 'desire to expand and develop long term interests . . . [and] with mutual faith in the need for closer cooperation

105 Ibid.
106 'Mozākerāt Beyn-e Jenāb Āqā-ye Ardeshir Zāhedi Vazir-e Omur-e Khārejeh va Jenāb Āqā-ye Katama Yifru Vazir-e Omur-e Khārejeh-ye Etiyupi', 16 Khordād 1347/ 6 June 1968, Zāhedi Archives, box 9, folder 19.
107 Ibid.

between the two countries in the field of international relations based on peace and justice and the principles of the UN Charter'.[108] In a joint declaration released to the press, echoing the discussions held in private, the two sides pledged support for the efforts of the United Nations and 'peace-loving nations' to bring about a settlement of the Arab–Israeli conflict. They agreed that 'the withdrawal of troops from the occupied territories is an essential step for ensuring lasting peace and stability in the region', and 'reiterated their adherence to the Security Council's resolution of November 22, 1967'.[109] The two states also agreed to expand further their cultural and economic relations and commence negotiations on a trade deal.[110] This never materialised and the treaty of amity remained the only formal treaty signed by Iran and Ethiopia.[111]

The Iranian delegation spoke to the press about the opportunities the African continent presented as a market for Iranian goods, and the potential for Iran to provide its expertise to the newly independent nations' development programmes.[112] The press announced that the Iranian government planned to have political representation in four additional countries by the end of 1968; Kenya and Tanzania in the east, and Ivory Coast and Nigeria in the west.[113] This was broadly in line with the recommendations contained in the report published by the Imperial Court four years earlier, which suggests that Iran's Ministry of Foreign Affairs was following a clearly defined strategy in its push into Africa.[114]

*****

In his Harvard Oral History interview, Denis Wright, who had served as British ambassador in both Ethiopia under Haile Selassie and Iran under the shah, was asked: 'Were there any similarities at all, as far as the Court and the Shah – the two kings, were concerned?' Wright responded that there were clear differences. For example, the Ethiopian court was 'much more medieval', the levels of corruption in Iran were much more profound, Ethiopia lacked the 'highly-trained

108 *Asnād-e Mo'āhedāt-e do Jānebeh-ye Irān bā Sāyer-e Duval*, vol. 2, 519–520.
109 'Ethio-Iranian Joint Communique', 9 June 1968, NA 2.05.174/100.
110 *Ettelā'āt*, 19 Khordād 1347/ 9 June 1968, 21.
111 Dutch embassy in Addis Ababa to Ministry of Foreign Affairs, 13 June 1968, NA 2.05.174/100.
112 *Ettelā'āt*, 16 Khordād 1347/ 6 June 1968, 4. 113 Ibid.
114 Shafā, 'Gozāresh-e Mokhtasar Marbut beh Afriqā', 17.

sort of people as there were in Iran', and, important for the ambassador's role, 'there was no mystique about the British power there [in Ethiopia] that there was in Iran'. On the other hand, Wright noted that both rulers were 'shrewd operators' and each served as his own foreign minister, meaning 'if you had any serious business, you had to deal with the Emperor, and nobody but the Emperor'.[115]

One of the reasons this relationship endured throughout this period was precisely because the shah and Haile Selassie had full control of foreign policy and saw eye-to-eye on many issues. Thus, it was not necessarily the relationship between Iran and Ethiopia that was positive, but rather the relationship between the shah and Haile Selassie. They were remarkably similar rulers, who shared equivalent worldviews, ideologies, as well as an understanding of their countries' historical position and a sense of imperial grandeur. They were also both monarchs in an age when the monarchy as a global institution was under threat from revolutionary movements and modern political ideologies. To the shah, monarchy was a worldwide fraternity, as evidenced by the manner in which its members were regaled at Persepolis in 1971. As one of the last remaining rulers to hold the title 'emperor', Haile Selassie was an honoured member of his international order and a symbol of its endurance.

Iran–Ethiopia relations were also profoundly shaped by mutual fears of radical movements in this time of profound global upheaval. Importantly, both countries were closely allied to the West, though Ethiopia was a member of the non-aligned movement. This common position shaped their regional and global interactions and fear of revolutionary regimes supported by the Soviets. But the shah's efforts should also be seen in the broader context of Iran's increasing interest in Africa in the 1960s. Although Haile Selassie had invited the shah to visit Ethiopia to strengthen the bilateral relationship, the shah saw the trip as a way to reach out to the rest of the continent by meeting with the chairman of the Organisation of African Unity and during his speeches making pronouncements against racial discrimination. It is curious, therefore, that the next country Iran would establish relations with in Africa would not be Kenya, Tanzania, Ivory Coast or Nigeria, as suggested by Iran's media, but the apartheid regime of South Africa.

[115] Denis Wright, in an interview with Habib Ladjevardi, Aylesbury, UK, 10 and 11 October 1984, Iranian Oral History Collection, Harvard University, transcript 7, 40–41.

4 *Establishing Ties with Apartheid South Africa*

From 22 April until 13 May 1968, Iran hosted the United Nations-sponsored Human Rights Conference. The conference, which was compared – in the Iranian press, at least – to the Bandung Conference thirteen years earlier, gathered states from around the world

> to promote further the principles contained in the Universal Declaration of Human Rights, to develop and guarantee political, civil, economic, social and cultural rights and to end all discrimination and denial of human rights and fundamental freedoms on grounds of race, colour, sex, language or religion, and in particular, to permit the elimination of *apartheid*.[1]

Speeches delivered by delegates covered all of the major issues of the day, including the Vietnam War, famine, and uneven economic development, but another major theme of the conference was global racial struggles.[2] South Africa was a particular focus, and delegates from across Africa, including Ghana, Tanzania and Mali, as well as the representative of the OAU, decried the horrors of apartheid and demanded that the conference take action.[3]

During the conference, Iran was praised as a progressive nation, notably by the US representative, Roy Wilkins, who noted the success of the shah's White Revolution.[4] In June 1968, just weeks after the closing of the conference, the shah embarked on his much-publicised trip to Ethiopia. During this trip, the shah was presented as an ally of the independent nations of Africa, and a champion of the right of majority black populations to self-determination. During speeches

[1] United Nations, *Final Act of the International Conference on Human Rights: Tehran, 22 April to 13 May 1968* (New York: United Nations, 1968), 1.
[2] See Firoozeh Kashani-Sabet, 'Global Civil Rights in Iran: Race, Gender, and Poverty', in *Iran and Global Decolonisation: Politics and Resistance After Empire*, ed. Firoozeh Kashani-Sabet and Robert Steele (London: Gingko Library, 2023), 283.
[3] Ibid., 287–290. [4] Ibid., 283.

and conversations with officials, the shah frequently referenced the 1968 conference on human rights held in Tehran as evidence of Iran's tolerance as well as its opposition to racism, prejudice and imperialism. However, even as the shah was in Ethiopia expressing solidarity with the rights of black Africans, his ministers were exploring the possibilities of establishing ties with apartheid South Africa.

Zāhedi wrote in his memoir that in spite of Iran's rejection of South Africa's policy of racism, 'in foreign policy, one must be realistic [*dar siyāsat-e khāreji bāyad vāqeʿ bin bud*]. South Africa was the largest economic power on the continent; it was a developed nation, with military power and a sizeable industry.'[5] This perhaps reveals something of Iran's goals on the continent and the methods it employed to achieve them. Solidarity was a language the shah adopted to garner support, but in reality, Iran was motivated by practical concerns. As the British embassy observed at the time, 'Iranians are keenly aware of the importance of South Africa not only as a market for Iranian goods, but also because of the Cape Route, which is crucial for Iranian oil exports.'[6] This route became even more vital after the closure of the Suez Canal in 1967.

At the same time, Iran was outwardly an outspoken critic of the apartheid regime during this period. In 1968, an Iranian, Manuchehr Ganji, was hired as the UN's Commission on Human Rights' Special Rapporteur, to conduct what became the *Study of Apartheid and Racial Discrimination in Southern Africa*. Ganji describes the purpose of his study as drawing attention to the 'evils of apartheid and racial discrimination', and providing suggestions 'to combat these evils' by various means, including through propaganda and collective action by member states.[7] The tone of Ganji's report invited complaints by some foreign diplomats friendly to South Africa, including the US ambassador in Tehran, and although Ganji was reprimanded by the shah, the fact that he was allowed to remain in his position is significant.[8]

[5] Zāhedi, *Khāterāt*, vol. 3, 208.

[6] C. D. S. Drace-Francis to P. A. E. Stanbridge, 15 June 1970, FCO 45/637.

[7] Manouchehr Ganji, *Study of Apartheid and Racial Discrimination in Southern Africa: Report of the Special Rapporteur* (New York: United Nations Economic and Social Council, 1968).

[8] H. E. Chehabi, 'South Africa and Iran in the Apartheid Era', *Journal of Southern African Studies*, vol. 42, no. 4 (2016), 690.

Indeed, Iran made it clear to South Africa from the outset, that the establishment of political relations between the two countries would not prevent Iran from criticising apartheid at international forums.

During the 1970s, Iranian embassies, particularly those in countries in which Iran had strong political and economic interests, were famous for their magnificent banquets, where guests were regaled with expensive wines and copious amounts of caviar. The embassy in Washington is the most well-documented example, but there were others. For example, Iran's ambassador to Venezuela called the Iranian embassy in Caracas 'one of the most glamorous embassies in town'.[9] But, beyond this caviar diplomacy, Iranian missions were also places where Pahlavi Iran could demonstrate its values and principles. The consulate in Johannesburg was no different and although Iran did not overtly contravene apartheid laws and regulations, it did offer some subtle resistance. This chapter examines the early years of Iran–South Africa cooperation in the late 1960s and early 1970s, including Iran's economic and strategic motivations to pursue the relationship in spite of expected criticism from the international community, and how Iran tried to circumvent that criticism by downplaying the significance of its relationship with South Africa.

Reza Shah's South African Exile

The first connections between Iran and South Africa were forged during the Second World War, in a time of crisis for Iran. In August 1941, Iran had been invaded by Britain and the Soviet Union, and as a result Reza Shah had been forced to abdicate, hand the throne to his son, and leave Iran to live the rest of his life in exile.[10] Reza Pahlavi believed, and had apparently been told, that he would be sent to South America, but as his ship arrived outside the port of Bombay, his British captors informed him that he would instead proceed to Mauritius.[11] The exiled shah and his entourage arrived on the

[9] Manucher Farmanfarmaian, *Blood and Oil: Memoirs of a Persian Prince* (London: Random House, 1997), 430.

[10] Yann Richard, *Iran: A Social and Political History since the Qajars* (Cambridge: Cambridge University Press, 2019), 222.

[11] Shaul Bakhash, *The Fall of Reza Shah: The Abdication, Exile, and Death of Modern Iran's Founder* (London: I.B. Tauris, 2021), 67

island on 18 October.[12] However, Reza Shah despised life on Mauritius; he and his family were constantly monitored by the British and he felt that he was a prisoner. 'To us this existence is unreal – a sort of death in life', he said to the British governor of Mauritius.[13] His declining health and intense displeasure prompted the British to find him a new home. They had planned to send him to Canada, but upon arrival in South Africa and in recognition of his ailing health, it was decided that he would stay put. Besides, Reza Shah disliked travel by boat, and had no appetite for such a long voyage by sea.[14]

It was a result of this somewhat accidental series of events that the founder of the Pahlavi dynasty, Reza Shah, spent the final two years of his life – from April 1942 until his death on 26 July 1944 – in Johannesburg. There were some fears from the British that the Pahlavi family might be made to feel uncomfortable due to the deeply engrained racism in South African society. One British diplomat wrote that this was almost inevitable since 'Unfortunately, they are a rather dark-skinned family.'[15] The Iranians do not seem to have experienced any racist incidents, but the racial segregation did not escape their attention. For example, Princess Ashraf, who briefly visited her father in Johannesburg, recalled in her memoir that although Johannesburg was attractive, 'the beauty of the city was marred by the cruel and highly visible signs of segregation. Theatres, restaurants, parks, beaches, and even sidewalks were segregated.' The princess wrote that this experience 'made a deep and lasting impression', and that as a result, in her first speech at the Human Rights Commission at the United Nations, she addressed the issue of racial discrimination in South Africa.[16]

The British did, however, face some problems in finding suitable housing for the exiled shah due to their racial status. For the first few weeks in Johannesburg, Reza Shah and his family stayed in the Langham Hotel, after which they were moved into two small houses.[17] These houses were considered by the Iranians to be inadequate for a

[12] On Reza Shah's stay in Mauritius, see H. E. Chehabi, 'Royal Exile in the Indian Ocean: Reza Shah's Sojourn in Mauritius', in *Iran and Persianate Culture in the Indian Ocean World* ed. A.C.S. Peacock (London: Bloomsbury, 2025 [forthcoming]).

[13] Bakhash, *The Fall of Reza Shah*, 81. [14] Ibid., 92. [15] Ibid., 95.

[16] Ashraf Pahlavi, *Faces in a Mirror: Memoirs from Exile* (Englewood Cliffs, NJ: Prentice-Hall, 1980), 62.

[17] Chehabi, 'South Africa and Iran', 688.

large family, and Reza Shah resented the landlord for not carrying out repairs, for which he had paid, in a timely manner.[18] To solve the housing problem, the British decided to search for a property that Reza Shah could purchase. There were obstacles to this, not least the colour bar, which denied non-whites certain rights that were enjoyed by the minority white population, for example entering bars and restaurants. Reza Shah would not entertain the prospect of living outside of the city centre or its environs, but the Gold Law prohibited the sale or rent of property in reserved areas, which included most of Johannesburg, to 'Asiatics'.[19] The British were unable to circumvent this law, even by purchasing a property on behalf of the former shah.

Eventually, the British did find a property large enough to house Reza Shah and his entourage, in a district of Johannesburg not covered by the Gold Law. However, the title deeds to the house, on 41 Young Avenue, Mountain View, forbade the granting of leases to 'Coolies, Asiatics or Coloured Persons'. If a tenant who fell into either of these categories was found to be living in the property, then any complaint by a local resident would result in their eviction.[20] The British attempted to receive assurances from the authorities that the former shah would not be evicted, but these requests fell on deaf ears, and the British were told that all racial clauses would apply to the Iranians. No complaints were made against Reza Shah, and he was able to live in the property for the last year of his life, until his death in the early morning of 26 July 1944. Shortly thereafter, his body was transferred to Egypt for burial.

The Purchase of the Reza Shah House

In the fifteen or so years that followed the death of Reza Shah, there was little communication between Iran and South Africa, and South African interests in Iran were looked after by the British embassy.[21] This began to change in the early 1960s, largely by chance. It so happened that the embassies of Iran and South Africa in Washington, DC, were located directly next to one another on Massachusetts Avenue, which facilitated some dialogue between the

[18] Bakhash, *The Fall of Reza Shah*, 97. [19] Ibid. [20] Ibid., 98.
[21] D. F. Murray to M. H. Morgan, 17 November 1970, FCO 45/637.

two missions.[22] Ardeshir Zāhedi had served as Iran's ambassador in the United States from 1960 to 1962, before being transferred to London, where he came into contact with the South African ambassador there, Dr Hilgard Muller. Zāhedi described Muller as an 'honourable man', with whom he got along very well. Zāhedi recalled that during their conversations, Muller repeatedly discussed the subject of Reza Shah's residence in Johannesburg. Coincidentally, like Zāhedi, Muller left his post to become his country's foreign minister, so that at that time the foreign ministers of Iran and South Africa were well acquainted with one another.[23] In 1968, Muller suggested to Zāhedi that Reza Shah's former residence in Johannesburg be donated to the Iranian government by the government of South Africa so that it may be turned into a museum. Although Zāhedi was keen on the idea, he argued that the Iranian government should instead purchase the house in its own name.[24]

In October 1968, the chairman of the National Iranian Oil Company, Manuchehr Eqbāl, was invited to South Africa as the guest of celebrated heart surgeon Christian Barnard, who had visited Iran earlier that year. According to the British ambassador, Denis Wright, Eqbāl 'returned full of enthusiasm for South Africa and has clearly been thoroughly brain-washed on the apartheid issue. He had broadcast his views to all and sundry, including the Shah.'[25] Eqbāl told the ambassador that after speaking with him, the shah had taken the decision to purchase the house of Reza Shah in Johannesburg. Shortly thereafter, Iran's ambassador to Sweden, Khosrow Khosravāni, was sent to South Africa along with junior diplomat Ahmad Tehrāni to negotiate the sale of the house.[26]

[22] Chehabi, 'South Africa and Iran', 689. In fact, as Zāhedi recalls, when he arrived in Washington, there was a plot of land separating the two embassies, which both governments were interested in purchasing in order to build a separate ambassadors' residence outside the embassy premises. Iran won the bid and on the land a residence was constructed in traditional Persian style. In its domed hall, called the Persian Room, Zāhedi would regale the elite of American politics, business and culture during his second spell as ambassador. Zāhedi, *Khāterāt*, vol. 3, 209.

[23] Zahedi was foreign minister from 1966 to 71, Muller from 1964 to 1977.

[24] Zāhedi, *Khāterāt*, vol. 3, 209.

[25] Denis Wright to A. R. Moore, 4 November 1968, FCO/45/243.

[26] Ahmad Tehrāni (1928–2012) was born to a wealthy family in Kerman and had close connections to the Zāhedi family, having married the niece of Fazlollāh Zāhedi. He became first secretary at the Iranian embassy in London during the

Frikkie Botha, undersecretary in the South African Ministry of Foreign Affairs, was asked by Muller to facilitate the sale of the Reza Shah house from the South African side.[27] In his memoir, Zāhedi claims that the house was valued at one and a half million dollars, but that the owner of the house, a retired colonel named Jack Scott, agreed to sell the property for much less, 'in honour of Reza Shah and in honour of the [current] shah and nation of Iran'.[28] In fact, as the historian Houchang Chehabi has shown, the matter was a little more complicated. Khosravāni and Tehrāni found Colonel Scott to be rather unaccommodating and most reluctant to sell the property to the Iranians. The initial reason he gave for his unwillingness to accommodate the request was that his wife had died in the property, but later it transpired that he there were two further reasons. First, Scott was 'incensed' by Manuchehr Ganji's report to the UN, which had been reported in the South African press.[29] Second, the title deeds to the property stipulated that it could not be transferred to certain non-white racial groups. In the end, Scott was persuaded to sell by Khosravāni, who assured him that Ganji had not acted on behalf of the Iranian government – 'Ganji is a pain in our own neck!' he said – and Botha, who convinced him that the sale of the property to the Iranians would serve the national interest.[30]

Before completing the sale, the racial clause was removed through a law passed in the House Assembly, ostensibly because Botha did not want a clause forbidding the sale of the property to 'Asiatics' to appear in the Iranian press.[31] The South African government proved far more

ambassadorship of Ardeshir Zāhedi from 1962 until 1966. When Ardeshir Zāhedi became foreign minister, Tehrāni was appointed superintendent of the minister's private secretariat and subsequently became head of the Far East section of the Foreign Ministry in April 1969. The British Foreign Office describes him as being 'very much a Zahedi man, and destine[d] for important posts, as long as Mr. Zahedi is in power'. This certainly proved to be the case. See, Biography of Ahmad Tehrani, FCO/45/637.

27 Frikkie Botha, 'The Iran Incident' [unpublished note]. I am grateful to Houchang Chehabi for giving me a copy of this document.

28 Zāhedi, *Khāterāt*, vol. 3, 209. Zāhedi's account very closely resembles Tehrāni's, recorded in Nurmohammad Asgari, *Qol'eh-hā-ye Qodrat dar du Daheh-ye Pāyāni-ye Dudemān-e Pahlavi (Shāh, Amir 'Abbās Hoveydā, Ardeshir Zāhedi)* (Beh Āfarin, 1394), 172–190. They contain the same anecdotes, descriptions and errors.

29 Chehabi, 'South Africa and Iran', 689.

30 Botha, 'The Iran Incident'.

31 Ibid.

accommodating than they had been in 1943, when they had flatly refused to grant any legal exception to the exiled Reza Shah. Much had changed in the intervening years. Iran was no longer an occupied country, a victim of foreign aggression, but rather an emerging player in global politics, with a growing economy and vast oil reserves. South Africa, meanwhile, had become increasingly ostracised by the international community for its policies of apartheid and racial discrimination. United Nations General Assembly Resolution 1761 of 6 November 1962, requested, among other things, that member states 'enact legislation prohibiting their ships from entering South African ports'.[32] Meanwhile, the 1967 Arab oil blockade in response to Western support of Israel in the Six-Day War demonstrated to South Africa the dangers of disruptions to oil markets, particularly if they became the target of a blockade. Establishing and maintaining ties with an influential oil-producing nation, particularly one like Iran, which had resisted pressure to join the Arab blockade, was important to ensure the continuing flow of oil into the country.

There had already been some cooperation between Iran and South Africa in the oil sector; indeed, the British understood there to have been a secret oil agreement in place between the two countries since 1966, through which the National Iranian Oil Company (NIOC) had supplied crude oil for the South African stockpiling project and acquired a 17.5 per cent equity in the Sasolburg refinery.[33] Between the Iranian years 1345 (1965/1966) and 1346 (1966/1967), the value of exports of Iranian oil products to South Africa doubled from $40 to $80 million.[34] By the summer of 1970, there were some 285 Iranians working at the Sasolburg refinery, including welders, pipe fitters and electricians. They were housed on site, together with local South African, German and Irish workers. In September 1970, the NIOC announced that it would be sending a second group of skilled workers to make a total of 515 Iranians working on the site. This second group

32 Resolution 1761: 'The Policies of Apartheid of the Government of the Republic of South Africa', United Nations General Assembly, Seventeenth Session, 6 November 1962.

33 M. S. Berthoud to J. E. C. Macrae, 7 July 1970, FCO 45/637.

34 The value of imports of South African products also more than doubled during this period, which seems to suggest that a trade deal was, indeed, in place. 'Ravābet-e Bāzargāni-e Irān bā Keshvar-e Āfriqā-ye Jonubi', Vezārat-e Eqtesād, 1969[?], NLAI 245/004425.

appear not to have been deterred by a reported 'successful punch up' that the first had had 'with the Irish workers sharing their quarters'.[35]

In addition to acquiring Iran's oil, South Africa also had some interest in assisting in the exploitation of an £80 million open-cast copper mine that was soon to be established near Kerman. A South African expert was reported to have been based in Iran for eleven months, 'drawing up plans, including necessary legislation, to provide for the orderly exploitation of Iran's mineral resources'. There was some more technical cooperation, too. Two Iranians had completed Master of Science degrees in mining engineering at the University of Witwatersrand in Johannesburg, and in return Iran had offered two scholarships in Iranian history and culture, 'which would probably be taken up by cadets in the Department of Foreign Affairs'.[36] In view of the growing cooperation between the two countries, the two sides began to explore the possibilities of establishing formal diplomatic ties.

Establishment of Political Relations

Even during the first Iranian visit to South Africa to secure the sale of the Reza Shah house, some British observers who spoke with Tehrāni felt that he was 'plainly here with a much wider brief' and that the purchase of the house was 'meant to be the beginning of a closer relationship'. During his stay in South Africa, Tehrāni held meetings with several officials at the Department of Foreign Affairs, including Botha, and a first secretary, Neil Peter van Heerden.[37] Shortly after the sale of the house, in late 1969, Botha took a detour to Tehran during a trip to Israel to examine the possibilities of building on the earlier contact established through the sale of the Reza Shah house.[38] Botha was met at the airport by a member of the Ministry of Foreign Affairs, and told by Tehrāni that, on the shah's orders, he was to be treated as a guest of the government.[39] The Iranians pointed out to Botha the

35 D. F. Murray to M. H. Morgan, 17 November 1970, FCO 45/637. Zāhedi recalled that the Irish technicians and engineers caused many problems because they considered themselves irreplaceable, and probably resented the increasing numbers of Iranians arriving to replace them. Zāhedi, *Khāterāt*, vol. 3, 210.

36 Murray to Morgan, 17 November 1970, FCO 45/637.

37 R. A. Farquharson Report to Southern African Department, 11 February 1969, FCO 45/243.

38 Botha, 'The Iran Incident'.

39 Ibid.

similarities between their countries' economic situations, in the sense that they were both dependent on a dwindling resource – oil and gold – so Iran could learn from South Africa's approach to tackling this problem.[40]

Several months later, in June 1970, Khosravāni and Tehrāni again came to South Africa to hold meetings with the South African Department of Foreign Affairs, this time with the express purpose of negotiating the imminent exchange of representatives.[41] Although United Nations Resolution 1761 had urged member states to break off existing diplomatic relations with South Africa and to refrain from establishing new relations, and Iran did not wish to be seen as diverging from global consensus on such a delicate matter, it nevertheless viewed South Africa as a potentially important strategic and economic partner.

Establishing relations with the apartheid regime was therefore a complicated affair and had to be handled discreetly. To discover the types of arrangements other countries had with South Africa, Tehrāni held meetings with the British, French, Japanese, Lebanese and US missions.[42] The Japanese told him that they had a consul-general in Johannesburg, who was accredited as ambassador to Botswana, Lesotho and Swaziland, and thus held ambassadorial rank.[43] The purpose of this arrangement was to avoid criticism in the rest of Africa and internationally on the basis that the establishment of full diplomatic relations could be construed as condonement of apartheid. Lebanon, the only Arab country to have a diplomatic presence in South Africa, had a similar arrangement. In the end, although South Africa's undersecretary concerned with Middle Eastern affairs, Paul Lindhorst, confided to the British that 'the South Africans would have liked an exchange of ambassadors', the Iranians decided to follow the Japanese and Lebanese model.[44]

Having taken this decision, Tehrāni travelled to Lesotho, Swaziland and Botswana to gain the approval of their governments. According to Tehrāni, although Swaziland and Lesotho were enthusiastic about the

[40] Letter from British embassy in Pretoria, 3 November 1969, FCO 45/243.
[41] Martin Berthoud to John Macrae, 9 June 1970, FCO 45/637.
[42] Asgari, *Qol'eh-hā-ye Qodrat dar du Daheh-ye Pāyāni-ye Dudemān-e Pahlavi*, 175.
[43] Chehabi, 'South Africa and Iran', 692.
[44] Berthoud to Macrae, 9 June 1970, FCO 45/637.

idea, Botswana declined, due to its rather complicated relationship with South Africa.[45] Besides providing the rank of ambassador to the consul-general, establishing relations with these smaller countries was a way of branching out further in Africa, and gaining potential votes at the United Nations.[46] Having ambassadors accredited in more than one country was a practice that would be replicated elsewhere in Africa. In April 1971, for example, Iran established diplomatic relations with Malawi, with Iran's ambassador in Addis Ababa, Kāzem Niyāmir, given accreditation in Lilongwe.[47] Iran also enjoyed good relations with the two kingdoms of Lesotho and Swaziland because they belonged to the global monarchical fraternity, which the shah greatly valued. Indeed, both Lesotho and Swaziland were represented at the celebrations held in 1971 to commemorate the founding of the Persian Empire by Cyrus the Great. Tehrāni apparently enjoyed a good relationship with King Moshoeshoe II, and during his regular visits to Lesotho once he became Iran's ambassador, he would sometimes invite the king back to his residence in Johannesburg as a guest.[48] Over the course of the following decade, in addition to pledging aid to development projects, Iran also sent a police officer, one Colonel Fereydun Madani, to head the police force of Lesotho, a position he held for several years.[49]

Although Iran–South Africa relations were only at the consul-general level, other missions in South Africa understood that it was more significant than this official designation suggested. The Dutch ambassador in South Africa, for example, wrote, 'In name these will be consuls general, though in practice the concerned officials will be treated as diplomatic representatives; they will be viewed as such, according to the explanation one of my staff received from the relevant

45 Tehrāni interviewed by Chehabi, 'South Africa and Iran', 692. In this period, Botswana sought to replace its dependency on South Africa, a remnant of the colonial era, with a relationship of independence and mutual respect, which explains its reluctance to join this arrangement. See Willie Henderson, 'Independent Botswana: A Reappraisal of Foreign Policy Options', *African Affairs*, vol. 73, no. 290 (1974), 37–49.

46 Zāhedi, *Khāterāt*, vol. 3, 206.

47 *Ettelā'āt*, 17 Farvardin 1350/ 6 April 1971, 13.

48 Tehrāni to Zāhedi, 5 Ordibehesht 1353/ 25 April 1974, Zāhedi Archives, box 128, folder 6.

49 Zāhedi, *Khāterāt*, vol. 3, 210.

Figure 4.1 Ahmad Tehrāni, introduced in the press as Iran's first consul-general in South Africa. *Ettelāʿāt*, 24 Ābān 1349/ 15 November 1970, 13.

civil servant in the Ministry of Foreign Affairs here.'[50] Due to the personal connections he had developed with figures in South Africa, and his familial ties to Iran's foreign minister, Zāhedi, Ahmad Tehrāni was appointed Iran's first consul-general in South Africa in November 1970 (Figure 4.1). He had apparently been very keen on the role for some time and according to one British diplomat, Charles Drace-Francis, had been going 'out of his way to be hospitable to South Africans who pass through Tehran'. Drace-Francis said that he had once been present at a gathering at which Tehrāni had 'shown great interest in a South African lady ... and he was telling her in effusive terms how right and proper the South African Government's policy of apartheid was – unfortunately without realising that she was a rabid anti-apartheid Liberal'.[51]

50 Dutch ambassador in South Africa, E. J. Baron Lewe van Aduard, to minister of foreign affairs, 22 October 1970, NA 2.05.191/451.

51 Drace-Francis to Stanbridge, 15 June 1970, FCO 45/637.

Tehrāni had established close relationships with several members of the political elite of South Africa by the time he became consul-general in 1970. He confided in the British that each time he travelled to South Africa, he made sure to pay a visit to the minister of foreign affairs, Hilgard Muller, whom he knew well from his time in London during Zāhedi's ambassadorship.[52] Having already developed these connections, Tehrāni was able quickly to establish a strong position for himself as consul-general. The Dutch ambassador noted this in a report to his Foreign Ministry in May 1974, when he wrote: 'The Consul-General has managed to acquire an exceptional position. He maintains close ties with the Central Government in Pretoria and is, as far as I know, a frequent guest at several ministries.'[53]

Paul Lindhorst, the undersecretary who had led the discussions with the Iranians over the establishment of diplomatic relations, had hoped to assume the position of South Africa's consul general in Iran himself, but he had since been appointed South Africa's ambassador to Greece.[54] Instead, John Oxley, another undersecretary in the Department of Foreign Affairs, was appointed and arrived in Tehran on 2 November 1970. He was met by a first secretary, Neil Peter van Heerden, who had been involved in the negotiations over the establishment of diplomatic relations, and whose role was to help establish the mission before returning to South Africa.[55] Oxley was also joined by a vice-consul and two trade assistants.[56] Oxley was an English-speaker from Natal, who had held positions in Congo and London, and had served as South Africa's consul-general in Wellington. According to the British high commission in Pretoria, he was a known philanderer,[57] but was knowledgeable and forthright when discussing government policy. He was described as old fashioned, 'with a fondness for blazers and bow ties', and 'a pleasant, if rather light-weight colleague'.[58]

Despite the clear warmth of these ties, Iran was still cautious about announcing them to the press. Indeed, shortly after Oxley's arrival in

52 Ibid.
53 Dutch ambassador in South Africa, A. H. Hasselman, to Ministry of Foreign Affairs, 10 May 1974, NA 2.05.191/433.
54 M. H. Morgan to D. F. Murray, 27 October 1970, FCO 45/637.
55 Ibid.
56 Murray to Morgan, 17 November 1970, FCO 45/637.
57 This British report reads, 'his love life has become something of a legend in his Department, and affairs are reported to have included one with the first wife of the present South African Secretary of Foreign Affairs'.
58 Morgan to Murray, 27 October 1970, FCO 45/637.

Tehran, the Iranian Ministry of Foreign Affairs released a statement to deny rumours, apparently started in London, that Iran and South Africa were on the verge of establishing full diplomatic relations.[59] It was not until nearly two weeks later, on 15 November, that the Iranian Ministry of Foreign Affairs finally made an official announcement. *Ettelāʿāt* justified the delay on the grounds that 'the sudden death of General de Gaulle [on 9 November] has overshadowed all domestic and foreign political issues over the past few days', but the announcement could in fact have been made before this date.[60] Indeed, the arrival of the first Burmese ambassador in Tehran had been reported in the same newspaper on 3 November; the day after Oxley's arrival in Tehran.[61] It appears that there was some hesitation from the Iranian side as to how exactly the establishment of ties with South Africa should be communicated, given the widespread condemnation of the apartheid regime across the Middle East, and the rumours that the move essentially represented the establishment of full diplomatic relations. Stressing Iran's continuing opposition to the apartheid regime, the announcement was careful to refer to the new partner as '*dowlat-e nezhād parast-e Āfriqā-ye Jonubi*' – *the* racist government of South Africa.

In the article, an official from Iran's Ministry of Foreign Affairs downplayed the significance of the relationship. It stressed that 'the relations that have been established between the two countries at the consular level do not have diplomatic characteristics and Iran has taken this step solely to protect the interests of Iranians living in South Africa, whose number is constantly increasing'.[62] No other reason for the establishment of ties was given. However, attempts to play down the formation of relations should not merely be seen as an Iranian endeavour. The Dutch ambassador in Pretoria said that he had been informed by the Foreign Ministry that the news would be given 'as little publicity as possible'. The ambassador added that this was part of the South African government's 'low-key diplomacy', which aimed, so far as possible, to elude the attention of elements abroad who opposed South Africa.[63]

[59] Murray to Morgan, 17 November 1970, FCO 45/637.
[60] *Ettelāʿāt*, 24 Ābān 1349/ 15 November 1970, 13.
[61] *Ettelāʿāt*, 12 Ābān 1349/ 3 November 1970, 4.
[62] *Ettelāʿāt*, 24 Ābān 1349/ 15 November 1970, 13.
[63] E. J. Baron Lewe van Aduard, 22 October 1970, NA 2.05.191/451.

Iran's new representative in South Africa did not appear to have received this instruction and spoke enthusiastically to the press about the prospects of increased trade between the two countries. An article that appeared in one of South Africa's main daily newspapers, *The Star*, on 16 November, just one day after the report in Iran, reported Tehrāni as saying, 'We are exporting oil, fertilizers and handicrafts to South Africa, and our Persian carpets are in great demand here ... From South Africa we import machinery. With our two countries making increasing trade contact, we will see what else Iran can import from South Africa.'[64] It was even suggested that Iran could export cement to South Africa to help alleviate a shortage of building materials. Tehrāni's words reflected the true nature of the relationship. He was not there merely to look after the interests of oil workers, but to oversee and stimulate the expansion of cooperation between the two countries in various fields.

In Iran, too, although Oxley assumed his role with significantly less fanfare, his appearance was said by the British embassy to have 'excited a good deal of interests and we have received numerous enquiries from people wishing to get in touch with him'. As he later recalled, he was treated by the Iranians with much respect, had close contact with the Iranian Ministry of Foreign Affairs, and on occasion would be invited to dinner with the shah and the imperial family.[65] Clearly undeterred by the Iranian government's public rejection of the notion that full diplomatic relations would be established, Oxley told the British ambassador during their first meeting in 1970 that he intended to turn his consulate-general into an embassy, 'although he realised that he would have to go slowly'.[66] Even though Iran presented the establishment of relations with South Africa as undesirable but necessary, and continued to criticise South Africa in public, it is clear that in private the two sides maintained a strong relationship, which lasted until the revolution in 1979.

Iran and Apartheid

Prior to the establishment of political relations, Iran had been a constant critic of South Africa's apartheid regime at international forums.

64 *The Star*, 16 November 1970, newspaper cut-out in FCO 45/637.
65 Chehabi, 'South Africa and Iran', 693.
66 Murray to Morgan, 17 November 1970, FCO 45/637.

For example, in a speech to the United Nations General Assembly on 2 October 1969, Ardeshir Zāhedi said:

> Blended with racism and the denial of human rights, colonial domination in southern Africa has created a situation that poses not only a challenge to the authority and prestige of our Organization, but also a threat to world peace and stability. We continue to condemn the policies of *apartheid*, suppression and exploitation of colonial Territories and peoples. We continue to endorse their legitimate struggle to restore their fundamental rights, freedom and independence...[67]

When discussing the establishment of diplomatic ties, Iran's representatives made it clear to South Africa that any relationship would have no effect on Iran's stance vis-à-vis the apartheid regime at the United Nations and other international forums.[68] Iran's opposition to South Africa's racist policies was not merely optics, and in private, too, some Iranians expressed their unease. From the outset, to avoid any embarrassment, the South African government deliberately avoided defining the racial status of Iranians. Indeed, when asked in the House of Assembly on 29 September 1970 to racially classify Iranian workers at the Sasolburg refinery, the South African minister of the interior, Marais Viljoen, replied that 'temporary residents of the Republic are not subject to the provisions of the Population Registration Act of 1950 and are, accordingly, not classified in terms of the Act'.[69]

Although such a distinction was not legally made, and on occasion Iranians were counted as 'honorary whites',[70] social interactions with the local populations were difficult because, as Chehabi notes, Iranians' 'physical characteristics vary widely and cover all the four official apartheid-designated population groups in South Africa'.[71] The South African government accepted the Iranians' view of themselves as Aryan and thus white, but in society at large, the situation was a little more complicated. A newspaper article in October 1970, for instance, referred to Iranian engineers arriving to work at the Sasolburg refinery

[67] United Nations General Assembly, Twenty-Fourth Session, 1776th Plenary Meeting, New York, 2 October 1969, 15, A/PV.1776, UN Archives.
[68] Martin Berthoud to John Macrae, 9 June 1970, FCO 45/637.
[69] Stanbridge to R. C. G. Harrison, 12 October 1970, FCO 45/637.
[70] Drace-Francis to Stanbridge, 15 June 1970, FCO 45/637. This letter refers to a tennis tournament in which Iranians were categorised as 'honorary whites'.
[71] Chehabi, 'South Africa and Iran', 702.

as 'dark skinned Iranians'.[72] Many Iranians, therefore, struggled to assimilate. A report from the South African press in 1970 announced that forty-five '"lonely" Iranian technicians were flying back to Iran while some of the remaining 196 commented that they were having trouble finding girl friends [sic]'. Apparently, one white local girl who was interviewed by the newspaper commented that 'she would not mind an Iranian escort – but it would cause gossip if she was seen with him in Sasolburg'.[73] The Iranian consulate sometimes arranged bus trips for the workers to go to Swaziland, where there was no racial segregation, to socialize.[74] Some Iranians visiting the country short-term, though they were light-skinned enough to be considered white, were deeply uncomfortable with racial segregation. On one occasion in 1970, an Iranian officer who was part of the crew of the destroyer *Artemiz*, was stopped by police in Cape Town while walking in the street with 'a Coloured girl'. According to the report, he was 'warned off', and later told the press that he 'could not understand the laws of South Africa and had much preferred Mombasa [in Kenya] to South African ports'.[75]

At the diplomatic level, not only did the Iranian government continue to oppose the apartheid regime at international forums, it also insisted that increased trade relations did not mean that it approved of, or would even adhere to, South Africa's racist policies. Indeed, as Zāhedi recalled, during functions at the Iranian consulate, 'our delegation was instructed to disregard the rules of racial discrimination'.[76] South Africa's official policy was that if non-whites attended official receptions organised by foreign missions, then government officials were forbidden from attending. Iran made it clear that if its diplomats could not invite whoever they wanted to the Iranian consulate, then in return officials from Iran's foreign ministry would not be permitted to attend events organised by South Africa's consulate-general in Tehran either.[77] As a result of Iran's insistence, Zāhedi continued, 'guests of all colours and races were invited [to the consulate] and participated.

72 Stanbridge to Harrison, 12 October 1970, FCO 45/637.
73 Stanbridge to Drace-Francis, 3 December 1970, FCO 45/637.
74 Chehabi, 'South Africa and Iran', 702.
75 Berthoud to Macrae, 7 July 1970, FCO 45/637.
76 Zāhedi, *Khāterāt*, vol. 3, 210.
77 Tehrāni interviewed by Chehabi, 'South Africa and Iran', 701.

We broke the barrier that created herds. But that was Iran's policy.'[78] This decision was not merely political and Firoozeh Kashani-Sabet has shown that in the 1960s and 1970s, even as the state built a strong national identity around the Aryan race, intellectuals and state actors were aware of and sympathetic to anti-racist, anti-colonial struggles around the world.[79]

During one of his early meetings with the British delegation in South Africa, Tehrāni informed them that he believed that Iran 'could have a beneficial and "eye-opening" effect on South Africa'. According to the same report, Tehrāni 'seemed to have got it into his head that the South Africans have already modified some housing law or regulation as a result of Iranian influence'.[80] Tehrāni's optimism was perhaps not entirely misplaced. On one occasion, when the local Indian community was denied permission to hold a reception in the new luxury Carlton Hotel in Johannesburg due to segregation regulations, they turned to Tehrāni for support. Tehrāni sought the help of Frikkie Botha,[81] who granted permission for the event to take place, providing Tehrāni attended and gave a guest lecture, which he agreed to, as long as the South African government also sent representatives. Thus, as Chehabi writes, 'this was the first time that white officials were present at a 200–300-person reception given by Indians'.[82] Chehabi adds that after the closure of the Lebanese consulate-general in 1976, the Lebanese community would also on occasion turn to the Iranian embassy for support.

South Africa's Muslim population is predominantly Sunni, but because Iran, though Shia, was the only Muslim-majority country represented in South Africa, relations developed between Iran and South Africa's Muslims. In 1969, prior to the establishment of relations, Iran was asked by the Muslim community to assist in arranging

[78] Zāhedi, *Khāterāt*, vol. 3, 210.
[79] Kashani-Sabet, 'Colorblind or Blinded by Color?', 153–180.
[80] Berthoud to Macrae, 7 July 1970, FCO 45/637. Tehrāni was most probably referring to the law that was changed for the purchase of the Reza Shah house.
[81] At the time of the opening of the hotel in 1972, Botha was South Africa's ambassador to the United States (1971–1975), so it is interesting that he was still used by Iran as a link to the South African administration. It is worth pointing out, too, that Zāhedi was Iran's ambassador in Washington at around the same time (1973–1979). Botha later recalled that Zāhedi 'gave the South Africans more caviar than they cared to consume'. Chehabi, 'South Africa and Iran', 702.
[82] Chehabi, 'South Africa and Iran', 693.

an Islamic art exhibition in South Africa.[83] On later occasions, the consul-general was invited to an Eid celebration, and Empress Farah made a 15,000 rand (approximately $21,000) donation to support the establishment of a mosque and community centre near Johannesburg.[84] Because of the absence of clear cultural and historical links between Iran and South Africa, until the 1970s, Persian language and Iranian history were not taught at any university in South Africa, aside from some courses on ancient history and archaeology.[85] This began to change in the 1970s, when the University of Durban-Westville (formerly the University College for Indians), whose Orient Islamic School had been teaching Arabic since 1963, announced its intention to begin offering Persian classes, too. In May 1975, the head of the school, Harold Spencer, wrote to Shojāʿ al-Din Shafā to inform him about 'the studies in Persian which I am trying to establish here at the University of Durban Westville' and to request that he 'provide us with some of the publications which are published under the aegis of your Ministry for use in our Library'.[86] As a result of Spencer's efforts, the name of the department was changed to Arabic, Urdu and Persian.[87]

Security Relations

One of the reasons Iran was so keen to develop a closer relationship with South Africa was the increased significance of the Cape of Good Hope given the closure of the Suez Canal at the beginning of the Six-Day War in June 1967. Tehrāni had discovered quite early on that South Africa had an intelligence sharing deal with the United States, whereby South Africa would take aerial photographs of ships travelling around the Cape and provide the United States with copies. Tehrāni informed the shah about this arrangement. The shah responded that he, too, would like to know of the ships that entered

83 Daoud S. Mall to H. Davoudi, head of the cultural department of the Ministry of Foreign Affairs, 19 February 1969, NLAI 250/018333.
84 Chehabi, 'South Africa and Iran', 693.
85 'Afriqā-ye Jonubi', Shafā Archives, box 11, file: South Africa.
86 Harold Spencer to Shojāʿ al-Din Shafā, 3 May 1975, Shafā Archives. It is not clear whether or not this request was granted, but the note was translated into Persian and distributed within the Pahlavi Library.
87 Ebrahim Mahomed Mahida, *History of Muslims in South Africa: A Chronology* (Durban: Arabic Study Circle, 1993).

the Persian Gulf containing military cargo, what type of military equipment they contained, and their port of destination in Iraq. He thus asked Tehrāni to request that the South African government also share these photographs with Iran, which they did.[88] In a diary entry in November 1972, the shah's court minister, Asadollāh ʿAlam, wrote that Iran was 'currently benefitting enormously from the South Africans' willingness to pass on information about every Soviet ship that rounds the Cape of Good Hope en route to Iraq', which allowed Iranian intelligence to 'build up a picture of the sort of equipment the Soviets are supplying'.[89] Security relations between the two countries continued to expand during the 1970s.

In June 1970, shortly before the formal establishment of political relations between Iran and South Africa, the Iranian destroyer *Artemiz* called at Durban; the first time an Iranian warship had done so.[90] Two years later, in June 1972, the commander of the Imperial Iranian Navy, Admiral Farajollāh Rasāʾi, paid a goodwill visit to South Africa, along with two Iranian frigates, *Sām* and *Zāl*.[91] During talks between Rasāʾi and South Africa's naval chief, Vice Admiral James Johnson, an agreement was signed whereby each navy would have a permanent representative stationed in the other's country.[92] A Dutch report written two years later stated that 'close ties exist between the navies of both countries' and that since the signing of the agreement, 'Iranian warships visit Simonstad from time to time for reparations and maintenance'.[93] It was expected that as Iran's naval presence in the Indian Ocean increased towards the late 1970s and into the 1980s, the use of South African ports would become 'increasingly important'.[94]

[88] Asgari, *Qolʿeh-hā-ye Qodrat dar du Daheh-ye Pāyāni-ye Dudemān-e Pahlavi*, 177.
[89] Diary entry 28 November 1972, Asadollah Alam, *The Shah and I: Confidential Diary of Iran's Royal Court, 1969–1977*, ed. by Alinaghi Alikhani (London: I. B. Tauris, 1991), 261.
[90] Berthoud to Macrae, 9 June 1970, FCO 45/637.
[91] F. R. Metrowich, *South Africa's New Frontiers* (Sandton: Valiant, 1977), 130.
[92] Chehabi, 'South Africa and Iran', 699.
[93] A. H. Hasselman to minister of foreign affairs, 6 April 1974, NA 2.05.191/433. Also noted by the British. See R. J. Alston to J. M. O. Snodgrass, 28 April 1975, FCO 8/2501. The destroyer *Artemiz*, for example, visited South Africa again in 1974 for maintenance at Table Bay in Cape Town, while twenty-four of its sailors took a course in Simonstad. See Chehabi, 'South Africa and Iran', 699.
[94] Alston to Snodgrass, 28 April 1975, FCO 8/2501.

In 1973, a senior military commander, General Charles 'Pop' Fraser, replaced John Oxley as South Africa's consul-general in Tehran, an appointment he held until the revolution. Fraser was known to the shah, as he had been received with honours and granted an audience with the shah on a prior trip to Iran in 1969, during which he apparently 'charmed the Shah with his dapper demeanour of an English officer'.[95] The appointment of such a senior military figure as South Africa's representative in Iran indicates the strategic importance of the relationship in the view of both countries.[96]

*****

The relationship that developed between Iran and South Africa at the end of the 1960s and into the early 1970s was significant for both sides. The shah was uneasy about apartheid, but he was beginning to develop a strategy in Africa and relations with South Africa, as the largest economy and most powerful military on the continent, were key to furthering it. Moreover, Iran recognised the geographical significance of South Africa in light of the closure of the Suez Canal. In the context of the shah's strategic goals, the benefits of dealing with South Africa outweighed the potential costs. Interestingly, although Iran occasionally drew criticism from the members of the OAU and the UN for its ties to South Africa, on the whole these ties did not prevent it from establishing friendly relationships with countries across the continent throughout the 1970s.

Iran–South Africa relations attained a greater significance to both sides over the course of the 1970s, particularly after the Yom Kippur War in 1973, when South Africa became increasingly dependent on Iran as a source of oil. Similarly, as the price of oil increased dramatically at this time, Iran was able to invest heavily in infrastructure and industry. In both respects, South Africa was a useful partner, since it exported huge volumes of concrete to feed Iran's construction boom, and cooperated with Iran in the development of its industrial plants. But this was not a relationship of equals, for although South Africa sent valuable resources to Iran, South Africa was, by the mid-1970s, almost completely reliant on Iran for its supply of oil. By some estimates, by 1978 Iran was supplying as much as 96 per cent of South

95 Chehabi, 'South Africa and Iran', 691.
96 Metrowich, *South Africa's New Frontiers*, 130.

Africa's annual crude oil imports. At the same time, Iran was able to use its influence with South Africa to force it to encourage the Ian Smith government in Rhodesia to accept UK–US proposals to resolve the crisis there.

By the end of the 1960s, Iran had established relationships with Morocco and Tunisia in North Africa, Ethiopia in the Horn of Africa, and South Africa, but beyond those four countries, its interactions across the rest of the continent were minimal. However, considerable groundwork had been laid, and within the first two years of the 1970s, the first formal political relationships were established with the newly decolonised countries of sub-Saharan Africa. The following four chapters examine these developments.

PART II

Forming an Africa Policy (1971–1975)

5 *North Africa, Islam and the Great Civilisation*

During the 1970s, Iran's relationships with Africa flourished, both in terms of the number of ambassadors accredited to African countries, and in terms of volume of trade and extent of political dialogue. At the beginning of the decade, Iran had diplomatic relations with just five countries in the whole of Africa – Algeria, Ethiopia, Libya, Morocco and Tunisia. By the time of the revolution, this number had increased to over thirty-five. It had been with Ethiopia and Morocco, and to a lesser extent Tunisia, that the shah had pursued his first special relationships in Africa, but as the 1970s developed, more and more countries sought to nurture friendly ties with Iran.

The rapid expansion of Iran's ties across Africa was precipitated by two important developments. First, the Arab defeat in the Six-Day War of June 1967, which had severely weakened Nasser, and ultimately led to a rapprochement between Iran and Egypt in 1970. Nasser's revolutionary rhetoric and the instability he brought to the region had preoccupied the shah for the past fifteen years. Nasser died in 1970 and was succeeded as president by Anwar Sadat, who would become one of the shah's closest allies. For the remainder of the 1970s, bilateral relations between the two countries flourished and they cooperated closely on many regional issues. This was a remarkable turn of events considering the hatred that had existed between the leadership of the two countries throughout the 1960s. Moreover, the removal of Nasser enhanced to a certain extent the shah's credibility as a leader in the Islamic world, and through connections established during the Islamic unity conferences, Iran came to be perceived as a potentially important ally to the Muslim countries of Africa.

Second, Iran's revenues from oil saw extraordinary growth in the 1970s, increasing from $555 million in 1963–1964 to $1.2 billion in 1970–1971, then, as a result of price increases forced through OPEC, to

$5 billion in 1973–1974 and $20 billion in 1975–1976.[1] These increased revenues gave the shah the status of a major economic player in the Global South, and it also allowed him to invest in industrial projects in Africa and purchase not only raw materials to satisfy Iran's construction boom, but also strategic resources such as uranium and phosphates. However, despite this extraordinary newfound wealth, and in spite of its avowed intentions, as will be shown in Chapter 8, Iran was unable – and unwilling – to distribute large amounts of aid to developing countries.

The following four chapters explore aspects of Iran's strategy in Africa from the beginning to the middle of the 1970s. They question why the independent states of Africa found Iran and the shah appealing, and what strategies the Pahlavi regime employed to project an image of Iran as a historically important global power and a civilising force in the world, which aspired to continue to influence world affairs in a positive way. The shah presented Iran as a member of the emerging alliance of the Global South, a fellow victim of imperialism who sympathised with the struggles of the former colonised world. Yet, underneath the veneer of solidarity, the shah harboured greater aspirations and sought to create a position for himself on the continent in line with broader strategic objectives. Iran was not just a member of the Global South, but had historic claims to be an important leader of the Global South. These imperial impulses became more urgent following the withdrawal of the British from the Persian Gulf in 1971 and vast increases in oil revenues after 1973.

Rapprochement with Egypt

Iran's rapprochement with Egypt was one of the major events in the context of Iran's regional policy during the late Pahlavi period. As was shown in earlier chapters, Nasserism was seen as an existential threat to the Iranian regime during the early 1960s. Because the shah was forced to focus much of his efforts on containing this threat locally, the resources he was able to commit to building relations with the rest of the world, including Africa, were limited. Nasser's power had diminished considerably following his defeat in the Six-Day War of June 1967, which had forced him to withdraw his forces from

[1] Michael Axworthy, *Revolutionary Iran: A History of the Islamic Republic* (London: Penguin Books, 2009), 71–72.

Yemen and cease propaganda activities in the Arabian Peninsula.[2] Furthermore, the emergence of the Baʿathist regime in Iraq in 1968 represented a new threat to both Iran and Egypt, and contributed to the decision to re-establish relations in 1970.[3]

On 29 August 1970 (7 Shahrivar 1349), less than one month before the death of Nasser, the re-establishment of relations between Iran and Egypt and the imminent exchange of ambassadors was officially announced. Minutes after the official announcement, a new plaque was unveiled at the embassy of Afghanistan in Tehran in the presence of the Afghan ambassador and the Egyptian charge d'affaires. At this ceremony, photos of which appeared on the front page of *Ettelāʿāt*, the old plaque, which indicated that the Afghan embassy had been looking after Egyptian interests in Tehran, was replaced with one that read 'Embassy of the United Arab Republic' (Figure 5.1).[4] Egypt announced that it would be sending a senior diplomat to take charge of the embassy in Tehran, a gesture which Iran pledged to reciprocate.

Iran–Egypt rapprochement was 'welcomed with happiness' in diplomatic circles in Tehran. The ambassador of Pakistan said that it was 'extremely gratifying to hear this long-awaited news', while the ambassador of Jordan said 'this joyful development will have a positive effect on the efforts made to establish peace and security in the Middle East'.[5] Many pointed to the significance of the victory of Suleiman Frangieh in the Lebanese elections one week earlier, on 17 August, in improving Iran's relations with the Arab world. Iran had broken off relations with Lebanon on 2 April 1969 due to the presence there of Teymur Bakhtiār, who was wanted in Iran on charges of treason.[6] With the election of a new government headed by Frangieh, declared by the press to be 'a friend of Iran', it was felt that the re-establishment of relations with Lebanon was imminent.[7] The Indonesian ambassador said that the

[2] For a study of these events and Nasser's decline in this period, see Jesse Ferris, *Nasser's Gamble: How Intervention in Yemen Caused the Six-Day War and the Decline of Egyptian Power* (Princeton, NJ: Princeton University Press, 2012).
[3] Seyed Mohammad Houshisadat, *Iran's Regional Relations: A History from Antiquity to the Islamic Republic* (London: Routledge, 2021), 143.
[4] *Ettelāʿāt*, 8 Shahrivar 1349/ 30 August 1970, 1. [5] Ibid., 4.
[6] Abbas William Samii, 'The Shah's Lebanon Policy: The Role of SAVAK', *Middle Eastern Studies*, vol. 33, no. 1 (1997), 80.
[7] *Ettelāʿāt*, 8 Shahrivar 1349/ 26 August 1970, 4.

اعلامیه مشترک ایران و جمهوری-
متحده عرب در تهران و قاهره
انتشار یافت

مناسبات
ایران و مصر
رسماً تجدید شد

میان تهران و قاهره تا ده روز دیگر
سفیر مبادله میشود

Figure 5.1 Ceremony reinstating the embassy of the United Arab Republic in Tehran. *Ettelā'āt*, 8 Shahrivar 1349/ 30 August 1970, 1.

development would insert 'new blood in the veins of Islamic unity',[8] and many other Muslim country leaders expressed similar hopes.

The new Egyptian ambassador to Iran, Mohammad Sami' Anwar, arrived in Tehran four months after the plaque unveiling ceremony, on

[8] Ibid.

29 December 1970, and pledged to 'spare no effort in developing relations and cooperation between the two countries'.[9] Anwar was met at Mehrābād Airport by Iran's new ambassador to Egypt, Khosrow Khosravāni, the career diplomat who had recently played a role in the establishment of ties between Iran and South Africa and who had previously served as Iran's ambassador to Turkey and the United States. Upon his arrival in Cairo several days later, Khosravāni said to reporters:

> Regarding the relations between Iran and Egypt, we believe that our relations are now at the perfect level, each of us understands the other well. Have faith that this is not just a diplomatic expression, but that the interests between the two countries are the interests of civilisation and culture. It is historical interests, or deep roots, that facilitate understanding between us.[10]

Considering the animosity between Iran and Egypt during the 1960s, the sudden transformation was remarkable. Not only had a major threat to Iran been removed, but Iran had gained an ally with which it could cooperate on security matters.

This reconciliation between Iran and Egypt coincided with the death of Nasser on 28 September 1970 and his much-publicised funeral on 1 October, which was attended by the Iranian prime minister, Amir ʿAbbās Hoveydā. Though past personal grievances between Nasser and the shah appear not to have impeded either country's commitment to re-establish relations, as Rouhollah Ramazani observed, Nasser's death did help to speed up this rapprochement.[11] Nasser's successor, Anwar Sadat, focused on reviving Egypt's economy and attempting to convince the United States to pressure Israel to leave the Egyptian territories it had occupied during the Six-Day War.[12] He felt that to achieve these goals, it was vital to reduce Egypt's dependency on the Soviet Union and seek rapprochement with conservative Arab states, in particular Saudi Arabia. This was essentially an adherence to foreign policy decisions taken during the final months of Nasser's rule, but Sadat was able to enact this new policy much more quickly and

[9] *Ettelāʿāt*, 9 Dey 1349/ 30 December 1970, 17.
[10] Bakhshi, 'Barresi-ye Tārikhi-ye Ravābet-e Khāreji-ye Irān va Qāreh-ye Āfriqā', 45.
[11] Rouhollah K. Ramazani, 'Iran and the Arab-Israeli Conflict', *Middle East Journal*, vol. 32, no. 4 (1978), 419.
[12] William E. Griffith, 'Iran's Foreign Policy in the Pahlavi Era', in *Iran under the Pahlavis*, ed. George Lenczowski (Stanford, CA: Hoover Institution Press, 1978), 377.

Figure 5.2 Anwar Sadat greeting Ardeshir Zāhedi at the Presidential Palace on his trip to Cairo in May 1970. *Ettelā'āt*, 23 Ordibehesht 1350/ 13 May 1970, 1.

effectively because, although he had been vice president under Nasser, he lacked the baggage of Nasser and was thus able to sell Egypt's new moderate policy more convincingly.

Ardeshir Zāhedi had spoken with his Egyptian counterpart, Mahmud Riaz, several times on the sidelines of the UN General Assembly about further deepening relations between the two countries and each had invited the other to visit his capital; first Riaz visited Tehran, then shortly after Zāhedi travelled to Cairo.[13] Zāhedi's visit took place in May 1971, just five months after the official installation of diplomatic representatives. A smiling Zāhedi and Sadat were pictured shaking hands on the front page of *Ettelā'āt*, each exuding warmth and friendliness (Figure 5.2). During this visit, Zāhedi held a three-hour meeting with Sadat, in which he assured the Egyptian president of Iran's commitment to securing peace in the Middle

[13] Zāhedi, *Khāterāt*, vol. 3, 165.

Figure 5.3 The shah greeting Anwar Sadat at Mehrābād Airport in October 1971, as Iran prepared for the beginning of the imperial celebrations. *Ettelā'āt*, 19 Mehr 1350/ 11 October 1971, 1.

East and of the shah's support of 'the wise policy of Egypt' in this regard.[14] Zāhedi was presented with Egypt's highest honour, the Order of the Nile, and addressed by Riaz in a speech as 'my dear brother Ardeshir'. In response to this speech, Zāhedi joked: 'I thought you Egyptians loved me, but now I see that you are causing me problems, because when I return to Tehran, the shah may have me imprisoned.'[15]

On 11 October 1971, the shah prepared to receive the world's elite in Iran to celebrate the 2500th anniversary of the founding of the Persian Empire by Cyrus the Great. Anwar Sadat had decided not to attend the celebrations – along with most Arab heads of state – but he chose this moment, the day before the celebrations began, to pay his first visit to Iran as president. Sadat's visit was just a brief two-hour stop on his way from Kuwait to Moscow, but it was highly publicised and as a result, on the eve of 'the most magnificent party in the history of Iran', the shah was pictured on the front page of Iran's main newspaper greeting Anwar Sadat (Figure 5.3). Sadat presumably wished to reassure the shah of his commitment to the development of Iran–Egypt relations in spite of his decision not to attend the celebrations in person.

[14] *Ettelā'āt*, 23 Ordibehesht 1350/ 13 May 1971, 29.
[15] Zāhedi, *Khāterāt*, vol. 3, 165.

President Sadat emerged from the plane and descended the stairs 'with a cheerful look, a burnt face and a friendly smile'.[16] Grasping the hand of the shah who met him at the bottom of the stairs, he said, 'Shāhanshāh, as a brother I applaud your efforts to uphold the rights of the Arabs.' Sadat was received with full honours and was welcomed by important political, court and military figures, after which negotiations took place in a special hall of Mehrābād Airport. Upon receiving the Order of the Nile, which President Sadat presented to the shah after the negotiations, the shah said, 'It is a pleasure to receive this honour from you, the president of a friendly brother country.' The shah then presented to Sadat the Order of Pahlavi (Neshān-e Pahlavi), along with the Order of the Pleiades (Neshān-e Haft Peykar) for the first lady, Jehan Sadat.

Before leaving Iran, Sadat gave a message to the shah in Persian, which was printed in newspapers. This emphatic note began by expressing the 'feelings of love and brotherhood' that the Egyptian people felt for the Iranians.[17] Referring to the upcoming celebrations, he said that the people of Egypt 'will celebrate with you on this occasion, because your ancient civilisation is the civilisation of the East, that is, our civilisation, so your celebration is in fact a celebration of the ancient civilisation of the East'. Referring to Iran's support for Egypt's peace proposals, Sadat said that Egyptians would 'never forget your support for us in times of crisis, because you have proven that you are our kind and sincere friend'. He then quoted the poet Sa'di, saying 'A kind friend and companion, everybody loves, and so do I'.[18] The shah appears to have been charmed by Sadat, and the visit, brief though it was, set the tone for future engagement. Nonetheless, it was not until after the 1973 Arab–Israeli conflict that Egypt and Iran drew much closer, and Sadat became one of the shah's closest allies. For now, on 11 October 1971 at 12:40, the shah said goodbye to Sadat at the steps to his aeroplane. Sadat continued his journey on to Moscow, while the shah took a helicopter to Niyāvarān Palace to prepare for his journey to Shiraz later that day for the start of his imperial celebrations.

[16] The description of this visit is taken from *Ettelā'āt*, 19 Mehr 1350/ 11 October 1971, 4.

[17] *Ettelā'āt*, 19 Mehr 1350/ 11 October 1971, 4.

[18] رفیق مهربان و یار همدم   همه کس دوست می‌دارند و من هم

The 2500th Anniversary Celebrations

The celebration marking the 2500th anniversary of the founding of the Persian Empire by Cyrus the Great in 1971 is often remembered more for who did not attend than for who did, and the absence of several important Western leaders, such as Queen Elizabeth II of the United Kingdom, President Pompidou of France, President Heinemann of Germany and President Nixon of the United States, is sometimes used to ridicule the shah. According to an article published in *Newsweek*, for instance, the shah 'invited virtually everybody who was anybody – but mostly nobodies showed up'.[19] An article published at the time by an opposition newspaper referred to the guests as 'third rate plenipotentiaries'.[20] The celebrations were also ridiculed for their extravagance, and even compared to the meeting held between King Henry VIII of England and King Francis I of France in 1520, known for its opulence as the Field of Cloth and Gold. In fact, the event might better be compared to the Bandung Conference in 1955 because, though it may have appeared less serious, the presence in Iran of the leaders of the recently newly independent nations, who received the same honours as every other leader, served to legitimise their existence and their struggles. During the shah's speeches at the celebrations, he delivered messages of unity, of all the nations of the world solving the problems of humanity together. The shah even tried to mediate talks between India and Pakistan over the conflict in West Pakistan (Bangladesh).[21]

In the context of the shah's desire to present himself as a leader of the Global South, the attendance of the countries of Asia and Africa was as important, if not more so, as the representation of the United States and Western European countries, with which Iran already had long-established relationships. Indeed, the shah used the celebrations at Persepolis to court states from around the world and they in turn sought to ingratiate themselves with the Pahlavi regime. No fewer than twelve African heads of state or their representatives attended the celebrations at Persepolis, including: the emperor of Ethiopia, Haile Selassie; the king of Lesotho, Moshoeshoe II; the president of Senegal,

[19] *Newsweek*, 14 October 1974, 27.
[20] *Iran Free Press*, vol. 1, no. 2 (October 1971), 6.
[21] See Robert Steele, 'Pahlavi Iran on the Global Stage: The Shah's 1971 Persepolis Celebrations', in *The Age of Aryamehr: Late Pahlavi Iran and Its Global Entanglements*, ed. Roham Alvandi (London: Gingko Library, 2018), 135–136.

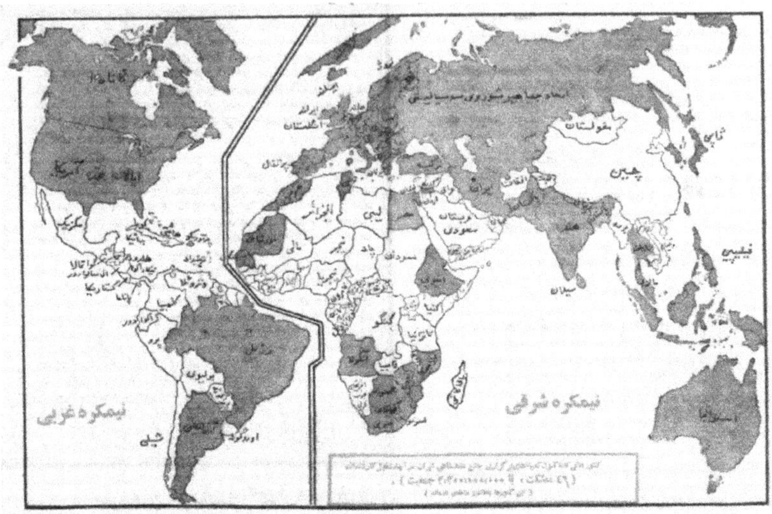

Figure 5.4 Map showing the various Cyrus the Great Committees that had been set up around the world. *Ruznāmeh-ye Jashn-e Shāhanshāhi-ye Irān*, 25 Shahrivar 1350/ 16 September 1971, 8.

Léopold Sédar Senghor; the president of South Africa, Jacobus Johannes Fouché; the president of Dahomey, Hubert Maga; the president of Mauritania, Moktar Ould Daddah; Prince Moulay Abdallah and Princess Lamia of Morocco; the vice president of Egypt, Hussein el-Shafei; the son of the president of Tunisia, Habib Bourguiba Jr; the prime minister of Swaziland, Prince Makhosini; the speaker of the house of representatives of Liberia, Richard Henries; and an advisor to the president of Algeria, Mustafa al-Ashraf.[22] Most of the invited sub-Saharan countries sent their heads of state, while the countries of the Arab north sent lower-level representatives, presumably having agreed this with most other Arab rulers.[23]

Most of these countries had also established special committees in their own countries, which were charged with ensuring that their country made a marked contribution to the celebrations at home (Figure 5.4). These committees were each made up of high-level political and cultural figures. The committee of Tunisia, for instance, had

22 *Kayhan International*, 23 October 1971, 3.
23 With the exception of King Hussein of Jordan and President Suleiman Frangieh of Lebanon.

over eighty members, with the president, Habib Bourguiba, at the head. It counted among its members heads of newspapers, cultural institutes and television and radio stations, along with government ministers, including the minister of foreign affairs, Mohamed Masmoudi, the minister of information and cultural affairs, and the minister of education.[24] Although the president decided not to attend, the attendance of his son in his place was perceived by the French as a sign of the 'excellent relations' between Iran and Tunisia.[25] Habib Bourguiba Jr had served as foreign minister from 1964 until 1970, and had developed close personal relations with members of the Pahlavi elite – he even attended the wedding of the shah's nephew, Prince Shahram in August 1966. As part of the Tunisian contribution to the celebrations, the school of literature at the University of Tunis established an independent chair for Persian language, and there were no fewer than seven books published, with titles including *Historical Relations between Iran and Tunisia* and *Tunisia and Iran: Centuries of Cross-Cultural Fertilisation*.[26]

Other countries in North Africa that had not been represented at the highest level in Persepolis made an effort at home, too. In Morocco, Rabat's institute of music organised a programme of traditional Iranian music and dancing, and Egypt's programme included an art exhibition, an exhibition of Persian manuscripts, events at universities, and the publication of four books.[27] The countries of sub-Saharan Africa also arranged a notable programme of events. Included in the programme organised by the committee of Ethiopia was a series of talks at the Haile Selassie I University, several publications about Iran, and the naming of a street in Addis Ababa 'Iran'.[28] Organising such events and, more importantly, ensuring that the Pahlavi court knew about it, was an important way in which countries demonstrated their friendly attitude towards Iran.

[24] *Gāhnāmeh-ye Panjāh Sāleh-ye Shāhanshāhi-ye Pahlavi*, vol. 5, 2056; *Ruznāmeh-ye Jashn-e Shāhanshāhi-ye Irān*, 11 Mordād 1350/ 2 August 1971, 8.
[25] Georges Gaucher to French Ministry of Foreign Affairs, 13 December 1971, CADC 367QO/171.
[26] For details on these publications, see Yahyā Dustdār and Hoseyn Tayyebāti, *Ketābshenāsi-ye Jashn-e Shāhanshāhi-ye Irān* (Tehran: Showrā-ye Markazi-ye Jashnhā-ye Shāhanshāhi-ye Irān, 1351).
[27] *Gāhnāmeh-ye Panjāh Sāleh-ye Shāhanshāhi-ye Pahlavi*, vol. 5, 2038.
[28] *Ruznāmeh-ye Jashn-e Shāhanshāhi-ye Irān*, 12 Mehr 1350/ 4 October 1971, 4.

The participation of South Africa in the celebrations was also significant. Although the state president, Jacobus Johannes Fouché, agreed to serve as the head of the South African committee, in the months leading up to the celebrations, it was still unclear whether he would accept the invitation to travel to Iran for the ceremonies. Iran's representative in Tehran was informed by South Africa's Foreign Ministry that Fouché generally did not travel abroad, and that they would not wish to accept the invitation in principle if it might later transpire that he would be unable to attend.[29] In the end, he was convinced to go and as H.E. Chehabi has noted, his presence was 'interpreted ... as a departure from the international ostracism to which the country was increasingly subjected'.[30] Indeed, it was particularly noted that Fouché and his wife were given the same personal welcome by the shah and Empress Farah upon their arrival as all other guests.[31]

The Iranian Ministry of Foreign Affairs felt it was important that South Africa put together a programme of events because of the presence of the Reza Shah house in Johannesburg.[32] In South Africa itself, exhibitions were held in Johannesburg, Durban and Cape Town on Iranian art, and the pianist Novin Afruz performed ten concerts across the country, which King Moshoeshoe II and President Fouché attended.[33] At the same time, the house that Reza Shah lived in while exiled in Johannesburg, was inaugurated as a museum.[34] The chief Rabbi gave a special sermon in the Great Synagogue in Johannesburg on 10 October, in which he spoke about Cyrus the Great's profound influence on Jewish history. 'May God's blessing be bestowed upon the Persian nation that has shown itself versed in the gentle arts of peace', he said. 'May the good-neighbourliness that has endured between our

[29] Tehrāni to Zāhedi, 5 Esfand 1349/ 24 February 1971, NLAI 263/027197.
[30] Chehabi, 'South Africa and Iran', 694.
[31] Metrowich, *South Africa's New Frontiers*, 130.
[32] Ministry of Foreign Affairs to Shojāʿ al-Din Shafā, 27 Āzar 1349/ 18 December 1970, NLAI 265/02197.
[33] Tehrāni to Zāhedi, 5 Ordibehesht 1353/ 25 April 1974, Zāhedi Archives, box 128, folder 6.
[34] Ibid., 3. The eighteen-member South African 'Committee of Cyrus the Great' was chaired by the state president, Jacobus Fouché, and included others familiar with Iran such as the minister of foreign affairs, Hilgard Muller, and the heart surgeon Dr Christian Barnard. The purpose of the committee was, according to a press report, to 'ensure that the event is accorded due prominence in the Republic'. 'Today's News', 14 October 1971, 5, FCO 45/921.

peoples for 2,500 years blossom into a full and fruitful alliance stamped with the brave hallmark of Cyrus of old.'[35] Details of these events were passed on to Shojā' al-Din Shafā, who was in charge of overseeing the activities of these international committees, and many of them received mentions in the Iranian press.[36]

The most honoured guest during the celebrations was the shah's friend Haile Selassie. The emperor had recently travelled to China and was referred to by *The New York Times* as 'the most sought-after person in town'. Among those who visited his tented residence were King Constantine of Greece, King Moshoeshoe II of Lesotho, President Senghor of Senegal, President Kai-Uwe von Hassel of the West German Bundestag and President Tito of Yugoslavia.[37] He held a prominent position throughout the celebrations as the only other emperor present,[38] was seated next to the shah at all the major events and frequently pictured walking beside him. Haile Selassie even had the honour of responding to the shah's banquet speech to the gathered guests from around the world on 14 October. In a speech delivered in Amharic, he declared, with typical aggrandisement, 'under the wise and far-sighted leadership of Your Imperial Majesty Iran has undergone a spiritual and material renaissance ... When the history of Iran of today comes to be written, Your Imperial Majesty will no doubt find an equally prominent place [as Cyrus the Great] for having revitalised your nation to face up to the challenges of modernisation.'[39]

Supporting the shah's presentation of himself as a facilitator in international relations within the Afro-Asian bloc, the prime minister of Swaziland, Prince Makhosini, stated that he had used the opportunity to hold meetings with other leaders at Persepolis. 'The formation of such a large community of heads of state in Iran', he said,

[35] 'Excerpt from Sermon by Chief Rabbi Casper in the Great Synagogue, Johannesburg, in honour of the 2500th Anniversary of the Founding of the Persian Empire', 10 October 1971, NLAI 264/027197.

[36] For details of the activities of these committees elsewhere in the world, see Robert Steele, *The Shah's Imperial Celebrations of 1971: Nationalism, Culture and Politics in Late Pahlavi Iran* (London: I. B. Tauris, 2020), 93–107; and the file NLAI 264/028628.

[37] *The New York Times*, 16 October 1971.

[38] Emperor Hirohito of Japan decided not to attend and was represented by his brother Prince Mikasa.

[39] 'Reply of His Imperial Majesty Haile Selassie I at Iran banquet', NA 2.05.191/554.

'demonstrates the need for such meetings in today's turbulent world ... because nothing is more effective and important than direct contact between the leaders and politicians of the world.'[40] Other leaders were said to have enjoyed the fraternal atmosphere of the celebrations, and the many opportunities to engage with other leaders. President Fouché, for example, had been invited to join the Indonesians for a cocktail and had himself invited, among others, the King of Lesotho for a similar occasion.[41]

During his trip to Ethiopia in 1968, the shah had presented himself as an ally to the independent countries of Africa, and the celebrations at Persepolis reinforced this image of solidarity. It was particularly significant that President Moktar Ould Daddah of Mauritania was present at the ceremonies, since he also served as the chairperson of the Organisation of African Unity at the time. Indeed, it is likely that he was invited precisely because he held this position. In a message to the shah, President Daddah described Iran as a 'beautiful country', declared his 'honour' to attend the celebrations, and expressed gratitude for the 'warm reception and generous hospitality' extended to him during his stay.[42] It seems that the events at Persepolis had done much to endear the shah to the leaders of Africa and reinforce messages he delivered during his state visit to Ethiopia three years earlier. Although Iran was criticised from time to time for its economic relations with South Africa, from the time of the celebrations until 1978, the shah was perceived as a friendly ally to many of the countries of sub-Saharan Africa. In the years that followed, a constant stream of African leaders visited Tehran, seeking the support of the shah for various projects and initiatives.

The Persian Gulf and Libyan Hostility

In December 1971, not long after the dust had settled on the ceremonies at Persepolis, the British completed the withdrawal of its forces from the Persian Gulf, marking the end of over 100 years of British hegemony in the region.[43] The government of the Labour prime

40 *Ruznāmeh-ye Jashn-e Shāhanshāhi-ye Irān*, 24 Ābān 1350, 7.
41 H. A. Hoogendoorn to Dutch Minister of Foreign Affairs, 21 October 1971, NA 2.05.191/554.
42 *Ruznāmeh-ye Jashn-e Shāhanshāhi-ye Irān*, 18 Ābān 1350, 8.
43 On the nature of the British protectorate, see James Onley, 'Britain and the Gulf Shaikhdoms, 1820–1971: The Politics of Protection', Center for International

minister, Harold Wilson,[44] had announced its intention to retreat from the region in January 1968; a prospect that presented Iran with opportunities as well as challenges, for although there was a danger that Arab states would try to assert control over the Persian Gulf, Iran also had the chance to take a leadership role in the region, in line with its Independent National Policy.[45] During negotiations with the British, Iran relinquished its long-standing claims to Bahrain, but claimed the islands of Abu Musa and the Greater and Lesser Tunbs. The shah's decision to abandon Bahrain also contributed to the improvement of ties between Iran and Egypt in 1969–1970, because it demonstrated that the shah was willing to temper his ambitions.[46] But although the shah's relations with Egypt improved at this time, he gained an enemy across the border.

In September 1969, Colonel Moʿammar Mohammad Qadaffi came to power in Libya following a military coup, overthrowing the pro-Western monarchy and establishing a pro-Soviet, Arab-Socialist regime. Qadaffi was a fervent follower of Nasser and quickly got to work replicating his model. He adopted Nasser's slogan, 'Freedom, Socialism and Solidarity', copied the basic law of Egypt, dissolved all political parties in favour of one Arab socialist party, and pledged to join the Palestinian struggle against Israel.[47] Shortly after, on 27 December 1969, the Tripoli Charter was signed by Nasser, Qadaffi and President Jaʿfar Nimeiry of Sudan to bring about greater Arab unity. Just eleven months later, the Syrian coup of November 1970 brought to power Hafez Assad, who declared his intention to join the new alliance.[48]

and Regional Studies, Georgetown University School of Foreign Service in Qatar, Occasional Paper No. 4 (2009).

44 Harold Wilson (1916–1995), was the prime minister of the United Kingdom from February 1963 to October 1964, and again from June 1970 to March 1974.

45 Roham Alvandi, 'Muhammad Reza Pahlavi and the Bahrain Question, 1968–1970', *British Journal of Middle Eastern Studies*, vol. 37, no. 2 (2010), 161–162.

46 Ibid., 176.

47 Ronald Bruce St John, 'The Ideology of Muammar al-Qadhdhafi: Theory and Practice', *International Journal of Middle East Studies*, vol. 15, no. 4 (1983), 473.

48 See Peter K. Bechtold, 'New Attempts at Arab Cooperation: The Federation of Arab Republics, 1971–?', *Middle East Journal*, vol. 27, no. 2 (1973), 152–172.

These developments were met with concern in Iran. Just days after the September 1969 coup in Libya, the shah's court minister, Asadollāh ʿAlam, held a meeting with the Moroccan ambassador in Tehran, who was 'very panicked' by events in Libya, not only out of concern for his own country and king, but for moderate countries everywhere.[49] The ambassador expressed his fears that once Bourguiba died, Tunisia might fall to a similar revolutionary movement, at which point Morocco would be the only remaining moderate country in North Africa. In private, the shah, too, was growing increasingly concerned by events in Libya, and he was particularly anxious at hearing news that the crowds gathered in Libya to greet Nasser during his first visit to the country were so vast that it took him four hours to reach Benghazi from the city's airport.[50]

In spite of the shah's misgivings, in the early years after the revolution, Iran maintained relations with Libya. Between November 1970 and February 1971, the Iranian ambassador to Tunisia, who was accredited in Libya, visited Libya and met with Qadaffi, and the Libyan minister of oil also visited Iran during this period.[51] The danger Qadaffi posed lay in the financial muscle he added to Nasser's populism. But given the decline of Nasser's standing after the Six-Day War and his rapprochement with Iran, the shah did not perceive Qadaffi as an immediate threat. Two events changed this assessment; the death of Nasser in 1970 and the British withdrawal from the Persian Gulf in November 1971.

Qadaffi would often declare that 'We are following the path of Nasser, the path of Arab Revolution', indicating that he was ready to assume the mantle of leader of the Arab world after Nasser.[52] Still, he had to wait for a chance to cement his credentials. This opportunity came in 1971, when on 30 November, after the British withdrawal from the Persian Gulf, Iran occupied the islands of Abu Musa and the Greater and Lesser Tunbs. Egypt's reaction was notably subdued. It did call for Iran to withdraw its forces and for the Arab character of the islands to be preserved, however, it did not join Algeria, Iraq, Libya and South Yemen in unequivocal condemnation and in referring

[49] Diary entry 16 Shahrivar 1348/ 7 September 1969, *Yāddāsht-hā-ye ʿAlam*, vol. 1, 260.
[50] Diary entry 8 Dey 1348/ 29 December 1969, *Yāddāsht-hā-ye ʿAlam*, vol. 1, 341.
[51] Yāri, 'Ravābet-e Siyāsi-ye Irān va Libi', 137. [52] Ibid.

Iran to the UN Security Council.[53] Egypt's position was not a surprise, since the Iranians had solicited Egypt's support for their Persian Gulf policy since the resumption of diplomatic ties in 1970. At Nasser's funeral in October 1970, Prime Minister Hoveydā had spoken to Egyptian leaders about the Persian Gulf, and Iran's Persian Gulf policy was at the top of the agenda when Iran's foreign minister, ʿAbbās ʿAli Khalʿatbari, visited Egypt in May 1971.[54] Sadat's friendly visit to Iran a little more than a month before Iran's occupation of the islands and the general warming of relations between the two countries contributed to Egypt's relative reserve.

Given Egypt's failure to lead the Arab campaign against Iran, Qadaffi's Libya took up this torch. Qadaffi's position was recognised by the leader of Ras Al Khaimah, Sheikh Saqr bin Mohammed al-Qasimi, who immediately contacted Qadaffi to elicit his support.[55] Qadaffi assured Sheikh Qasimi of his intention to send squadrons of paratroopers to secure the islands. Shortly thereafter, Major General ʿAbdol Salām Jalud was dispatched to Kuwait to see what could be done, but in a press conference announced that while it had been Libya's plan to send paratroopers to the islands, this plan had been abandoned because there were no bases from which to launch the attack.[56] Days later, on 8 December, Iranian newspapers reported that Qadaffi had come 'suddenly to the Persian Gulf' to hold in-person talks with the leader of Ras Al Khaimah about the actions of Iran.[57] Qadaffi's options were limited, but this confrontational move was designed to maintain pressure on Iran and demonstrate to the Arab world that he was playing a personal role in the movement against Iran. At the same time, on 7 December, Qadaffi nationalised British oil interests in Libya to protest British collusion with Iran and its failure to uphold its obligations to the Arab emirates.[58]

Iranian newspapers reacted to Qadaffi's threats with anger and scorn. The front page of *Ettelāʿāt* printed the words of Iran's representative to the United Nations Security Council, who said 'Iran will not allow the encroachment of a single inch of its territory'.[59] In a meeting

[53] Ramazani, *Iran's Foreign Policy, 1941–1973*, 425. [54] Ibid., 422–423.
[55] Yāri, 'Ravābet-e Siyāsi-ye Irān va Libi', 139. [56] Ibid., 139–140.
[57] *Ettelāʿāt*, 17 Āzar 1350/ 8 December 1971, 1. See also, *Ettelāʿāt*, 18 Āzar 1350/ 9 December 1971, 4.
[58] Ramazani, *Iran's Foreign Policy, 1941–1973*, 425.
[59] *Ettelāʿāt*, 20 Āzar 1350/ 11 December 1971, 1.

of the Iranian Senate on 11 December 1971, Iranian sovereignty over the three islands and Libya's threats were on the agenda. Senator Jamshid A'lam said with incredulity, 'Libya has a population of two million and wants to send paratroopers to Iran. If [any] people of our country die, the Libyan paratroopers will be blown away!'[60] Iran did not take Qadaffi's threats seriously and it is unlikely that Qadaffi genuinely intended to attack Iran. Qadaffi surely knew that the Arab states that had joined him in condemning Iran lacked the means to intervene, but by raising tensions and doggedly championing the Arab cause, he became, in the eyes of many, Nasser's successor.[61] Qaddafi's ability to draw the support of radical Arab states was more dangerous in the long term than his paratroopers were in the immediate term.

In January 1972, Libya along with Iraq, Algeria and South Yemen, lodged a complaint at the UN Security Council over Iran's seizure of Abu Musa and the Greater and Lesser Tunbs. Their complaint was unsuccessful, but relations between Iran and Libya continued to decline. When the mission of Iran's first ambassador to Libya ended in December 1972, Iran declined to send a replacement. Over the next few years, Qadaffi became one of the shah's main adversaries, who challenged Iran's role as a leader in the Islamic world, provoked instability in regions under the shah's sphere of influence, and even strained some of the shah's relationships with allies. These tensions are best exemplified by the Second Islamic Summit Conference.

The Second Islamic Summit Conference, Lahore, 20–24 February 1974

The Second Islamic Summit Conference took place in 1974, some five years after the first. It was proposed by the secretary-general of the Organisation of the Islamic Conference, Tunku Abdul Rahman, to consolidate Islamic unity in the aftermath of the Yom Kippur War of October 1973. The conference, he suggested, might be held in Pakistan. Prime Minister Bhutto quickly assumed a leadership role in the initiative and began what one British diplomat referred to as 'an intense lobbying campaign within the Islamic world'.[62] The hosting of

[60] Ibid., 4. [61] Yāri, 'Ravābet-e Siyāsi-ye Irān va Libi', 140.
[62] 'Islamic Summit Conference at Lahore: 20–24 February, 1974', 6 March 1974, 2, FCO 160/160/31.

such a gathering would allow Bhutto to flaunt his Islamic credentials and boost his status within the Islamic world. It would also serve as a pretext to bring about recognition of Bangladesh. Given that this event took place against the backdrop of the latest Arab–Israeli conflict, the conference 'was naturally expected to take a hawkish line on Middle East questions', a prospect that slightly perturbed 'the traditional fence-sitters', Iran and Turkey.[63] With the addition of Qadaffi, the tone was expected to be more radical than past conferences.

In a meeting with the US ambassador, Richard Helms, in December 1973, Hoveydā said that he felt 'strongly that the whole idea is a silly one' and that Bhutto was organising the summit 'for his own self-aggrandisement'. Hoveydā saw no 'good coming out of such a conference' and feared that 'some counterproductive resolution might get adopted which would in no sense advance the Islamic cause'. He further noted that 'serious effort' was being made to convince the shah to attend, but that he was 'strongly counselling the shah against this'.[64] With the conference scheduled to take place in the middle of January 1974, the shah, in an attempt to get out of attending, told Bhutto that he would not be free until February, and that it might be prudent to reschedule the conference anyway so that it would not clash with the Arab–Israel conference in Geneva.[65] Bhutto called the shah's bluff and postponed the conference until the middle of February.

By early February, according to Asadollāh ʿAlam, the shah had still not decided what to do. Although he would have liked to support an initiative headed by Bhutto, with whom he was on friendly terms, 'he had very serious reservations about attending any conference at which Ghaddafi [sic] of Libya would also be present'. The shah, ʿAlam said, 'did not at all relish the prospect of attending a conference from which he might be obliged to walk out.'[66] Summarising the shah's feelings about Qadaffi, ʿAlam said, citing a Persian proverb, that 'it was best

[63] Ibid., 2–3.

[64] Richard Helms telegram, 10 December 1973, WikiLeaks Cable 1973TEHRAN08692_b.

[65] Nicholas Browne to Peter Williams, 9 January 1974, FCO 37/1504; Helms telegram, 7 January 1974, WikiLeaks Cable 1974TEHRAN00130_b. The Geneva Conference was held on 22 December 1973 to try to bring lasting peace after the Yom Kippur War. Although an agreement was not signed in Geneva, the discussions formed the basis of an agreement signed in January 1974.

[66] Richard Ellingworth to George Chalmers, 7 February 1974, FCO 37/1504.

not to embrace a fool nor to allow a fool to embrace you'.[67] Finally, on 13 February, the press confirmed that the shah had decided not to attend due to the presence of 'certain individuals whose conduct run counter to the spirit of Islamic morality'.[68] Iran's minister of foreign affairs, Khalʿatbari, would instead represent Iran at the conference. Although the attendance of Qadaffi was cited as the main reason for the shah's refusal to attend, the shah informed the US ambassador 'in utmost confidence, his principal reason for not attending was that he did not want to become involved or participate in the inflammatory rhetoric which he anticipates will take place'.[69]

The shah had played a key role in the Rabat conference in 1969, but the Lahore conference, which took place from 22 to 24 February, was dominated by Bhutto. While the militant leaders, Yasser Arafat and Qadaffi, were the 'crowd-pleasers', King Faisal of Saudi Arabia, President Sadat and Houari Boumédiène, the chairman of the Revolutionary Council of Algeria, asserted a calm control over the conference and, according to the US report, had the 'most significant impact on [the] final outcome'.[70] Nevertheless, Qadaffi did cause a stir when he used his speech to put forward a proposal for three-tiered oil pricing. Khalʿatbari, who it was said 'could hardly conceal his disdain for [the] motley group around him', used his speech to put forward another solution to lessen the impact that increasing oil prices would have on the economies of the Global South. Khalʿatbari, answering calls from previous speakers from Uganda, Niger and Gambia, announced the shah's proposal to make available 'at least one billion dollars' in aid to developing countries, which would be channelled through the World Bank and the IMF.[71] After Arafat and Ugandan president Idi Amin expressed their distrust of such international organisations, Khalʿatbari insisted that the fund would be administered by an independent governing committee.[72]

Article ten of the Final Declaration and Resolutions of the conference called on member states to 'continue their support of African causes and their struggle against colonialism and racist regimes,

[67] Ibid.
[68] Nicholas Browne to George Chalmers, 14 February 1974, FCO 37/1504.
[69] Helms telegram, 13 February 1974, WikiLeaks Cable 1974TEHRAN01229_b.
[70] King telegram, 26 February 1974, WikiLeaks Cable 1974LAHORE00326_b.
[71] *Kayhan International*, 12 March 1974, 1.
[72] King telegram, 24 February 1974, WikiLeaks Cable 1974LAHORE00306_b.

particularly in Rhodesia, South Africa and the Portuguese colonies, and to put an end to all forms of cooperation and dealing with these regimes, in particular to stop all shipments of oil and to prevent any derogation to that rule.'[73] Iran did sign the declaration, but stipulated that its acceptance was 'subject to their international commitments'.[74] Because Iran had long-term deals in place with South Africa, its support of this article was little more than show.

Many sub-Saharan African countries were represented at the conference, including Gabon, Gambia, Guinea, Guinea Bissau, Chad, Mali, Mauritania, Niger, Senegal, Somalia, Sudan and Uganda.[75] Although Khalʿatbari 'maintained [a] low profile throughout', presumably on orders from Tehran, Iran's participation, and Khalʿatbari's proposal, was significant in terms of Iran's African diplomacy. Idi Amin met with Khalʿatbari on the sidelines of the conference, and both sides agreed to establish diplomatic relations and open embassies in each other's capitals. Amin told reporters that he had always harboured 'indescribable feelings of friendship and love for Iran' and hoped to visit Tehran in the near future.[76] Following his impromptu trip to Iran just months after the conference (Figure 5.5), in May, relations were officially established in October.[77] Visits to Iran from African representatives on their way home from Pakistan were common during this period. For example, the Guinean delegate to the Second Islamic Foreign Minister's Conference in Karachi, in December 1970, stopped in Tehran on his journey home to bring a goodwill message from President Sékou Touré.[78] In it, Touré thanked the shah for Iran's condemnation of the Portuguese aggression against Guinea through the Organisation of the Islamic Conference. This led directly to the establishment of diplomatic relations between the two countries in April 1971.[79]

[73] 'Islamic Summit Conference at Lahore: 20–24 February, 1974', 6 March 1974, 13, FCO 160/160/31.

[74] C. H. Seaward to C. R. Reynolds, 5 April 1974, FCO 37/1504.

[75] Two of these – Chad and Uganda – were not actually Muslim-majority countries.

[76] *Ettelāʿāt*, 7 Esfand 1352/ 26 February 1974, 4.

[77] See Introduction to this book.

[78] Dutch ambassador in Tehran to Dutch Ministry of Foreign Affairs, 21 January 1971, NA 2.05.191/392.

[79] Letter to Dutch Ministry of Foreign Affairs, 28 April 1971, NA 2.05.191/392.

Figure 5.5 Amir ʿAbbas Hoveydā greeting Ugandan president Idi Amin on his impromptu visit to Iran in May 1974. *Ettelāʿāt* 18 Ordibehesht 1353/ 8 May 1974, 1.

Following the Lahore conference in February 1974, the president of Sudan, Jaʿfar Nimeiry, travelled directly to Tehran for a six-day visit. The focus of discussions during this trip was Islam and Africa. The newspaper *Ettelāʿāt* drew attention to the fact that Nimeiry would also be visiting the Imam Reza shrine in Mashhad, Iran's holiest site.[80] The headline in *Kayhan International*'s report of Nimeiry's visit read, quoting the shah's banquet speech to the Sudanese president: 'Unity – Key to Islamic Glory'.[81] In his speech, the shah said that 'only in unity

[80] *Ettelāʿāt*, 6 Esfand 1352/ 25 February 1974, 1.
[81] *Kayhan International*, 2 March 1974, 2.

can the Islamic World regain the material and spiritual glory of its past'. In this regard, the visit of Nimeiry was 'a good omen' for the expansion of Islamic ties.[82] At the same time, the importance of Sudan as not only an Islamic country, but an African Islamic country, was emphasised. One article in *Ettelāʿāt* on Sudan's role in Africa referred to the country as the 'key to Africa'.[83] The Dutch ambassador in Tehran noted that such visits from African politicians and the friendliness with which they were received, reflected the shah's 'ambition to advance and expand relations with Black Africa and non-Arab Muslim countries as much as possible'.[84]

Algerian Rapprochement

Although Qadaffi emerged as the shah's most despised adversary during the 1970s, his influence in the rest of North Africa proved to be weaker than Nasser's had been. While Iran developed stronger ties with Egypt, particularly in the aftermath of the Yom Kippur War in 1973, and continued its good relations with Morocco and Tunisia, it also made an effort to improve relations with Algeria. Iran had maintained an embassy in Algeria since 1964 and the two countries signed a cultural treaty in August 1968, but otherwise interaction between Iran and Algeria remained limited.[85] Relations became strained in 1971 when Iran occupied the islands in the Persian Gulf, and Iran recalled the Iranian ambassador to Algeria in 1973 after President Boumédiène's public criticism of 'Iranian imperialism'.[86] 'I do not have to take this kind of talk', said the shah, 'and have no intention of doing so'.[87]

However, little over one year later, both the shah and Boumédiène saw fit to put aside their dislike of one another and to rebuild the bilateral relationship. In February 1975, commenting on the rapid rapprochement between Iran and Algeria, the British ambassador to Algeria observed that Boumédiène was 'prepared to swallow his

[82] Ibid. [83] *Ettelāʿāt*, 6 Esfand 1352/ 25 February 1974, 6.
[84] Dutch ambassador in Tehran to Dutch minister of foreign affairs, 13 March 1974, NA 2.05.191/433.
[85] *Asnād-e Moʿāhedāt-e do Jānebeh-ye Irān bā Sāyer-e Duval*, vol. 3, 181–184.
[86] Bakhshi, 'Barresi-ye Tārikhi-ye Ravābet-e Khāreji-ye Irān va Qāreh-ye Āfriqā', 53.
[87] Helms telegram, 2 October 1973, WikiLeaks Cable 1973TEHRAN06996_b.

principles in dealing with the shah.' He added, 'He seems to be swallowing hard. Only nine months ago he described the shah, confidentially, as America's agent in the Middle East.'[88] In an interview at around the same time, Boumédiène said that, 'The prospects for cooperation between Iran and Algeria are enormous and we are convinced of the need to widen them further.'[89] He added, 'We are of Iran and Iran is of us. Our historical and cultural ties bind us inextricably.'[90] What was the reason for this sudden reversal? The answer is oil and leverage in OPEC. The British ambassador to Algeria noted wryly that, 'Boumediene would ally himself with the devil if it could help him to sell his oil at a higher price. I was left wondering whether the same might not be true of the shah.'[91]

Both the shah and Boumédiène had ambitious development plans which relied on an uninterrupted flow of oil revenue. Both agreed that having fought to achieve price increases, the OPEC countries should maintain a united front against increasing insistence, and threats, from the West that prices should be reduced. Boumédiène agreed with the shah that the price of oil should be indexed against other commodities, particularly industrial products. 'If the Western countries continue to demand a drop in oil prices this would have to apply equally to the other products which we need', Boumédiène said. 'The problem lies in the search for harmonisation between our interests and those of the industrial countries.' Expressing solidarity with the shah, Boumédiène argued that criticism of Iran should be considered an attack on all members of OPEC.[92] In an interview with the Algerian newspaper *Revolution Africaine*, Iran's minister of the interior, Jamshid Āmuzegār, argued that Iran's economic policy was 'identical with that of Algeria'.[93]

Iran's goal in seeking closer ties with Algeria was to gain an OPEC ally within the Arab world. If the shah put a proposal to the Gulf Arab states alone then he might not be taken seriously, but his arguments could be more persuasive with Algerian backing. In late 1974, Algeria sent an ambassador to Iran for the first time, and subsequently an

[88] Robinson telegram (no. 52), 7 February 1975, FCO 8/2501.
[89] Robinson telegram (no. 54), 7 February 1975, FCO 8/2501.
[90] *Kayhan International*, 15 February 1975, 3.
[91] Robinson to Anthony Parsons, 3 February 1975, FCO 8/2501.
[92] Robinson telegram (no. 54), 7 February 1975, FCO 8/2501.
[93] Robinson telegram (no. 53), 7 February 1975, FCO 8/2501.

Iranian ambassador arrived in Algiers to what the British ambassador described as an 'exceptionally warm welcome'.[94] This ambassador was Asad Sadri, a career diplomat who had been born in Karbala and whose Arabic was said to be better than his Persian. He had previously served as Iran's ambassador to the International Commission of Control and Supervision (ICCS) in Vietnam.[95] The British ambassador in Tehran, who was an 'old friend' of Sadri, reasoned that Sadri had been chosen for this role 'because he was the kind of man who would be able to make an intelligent judgement as to whether Iranian participation in the ICCS was worth while or not. Perhaps he has been sent to Algiers with the same kind of brief ie to see whether anything can be made of a relationship with Boumedienne [sic].'[96] Having spoken to Sadri at length upon his arrival in Algiers, the British ambassador to Algeria reached the same conclusion.

Shortly after, in March 1975, Boumédiène played a key role in securing an agreement between the shah and Saddam Hussein at the first OPEC summit, held in Algiers in March 1975, over long-standing disputes concerning the delineation of the border in the Shatt al-Arab waterway. Such a meeting between the leaders of Iran and Iraq would have been difficult in the presence of Qadaffi, so Boumédiène made it clear to the Libyan leader that he was not welcome at the summit.[97] When the shah arrived in Algiers, he found a determined Boumédiène, who 'pushed hard and showed great interest in bringing me together with Saddam'.[98] Boumédiène's interest in mediating between Iran and Iraq can be dated to the Arab League summit that had taken place in Rabat in October the previous year, when Hussein had asked for help in convincing the shah to cease his support of the Iraqi Kurds. Boumédiène spoke to the Iranian ambassador in Algiers in December, who explained Iran's concerns, and subsequently the shah agreed to talks with Saddam Hussein at the OPEC summit. The shah

[94] Robinson telegram (no. 52), 7 February 1975, FCO 8/2501.
[95] The ICCS was an international monitoring force, formed after the Paris Peace Accords in January 1973. On Iran's mission to the ICCS, see Arash Azizi, 'Iranians and the Vietnam War: Cold Warrior Enmities or Anti-colonial Solidarities?', in *Iran and Global Decolonisation: Politics and Resistance After Empire*, ed. Firoozeh Kashani-Sabet and Robert Steele (London: Gingko Library, 2023), 217–221.
[96] Parsons to Robinson, 13 February 1975, FCO 8/2501.
[97] Yāri, 'Ravābet-e Siyāsi-ye Irān va Libi', 146.
[98] Helms telegram, 10 March 1975, WikiLeaks Cable 1975TEHRAN02237_b.

felt that he was 'taking a major gamble', so 'insisted that Boumediene be present during all the discussions with Saddam in order to have witness and to provide added assurance regarding Iraqi performance'.[99]

Following the successful meeting between the shah and Saddam Hussein in Algiers, the Algerian foreign minister, Abdelaziz Bouteflika, was invited by the shah to continue Algeria's mediating role, by taking part in discussions between the Iranian minister of foreign affairs, Khalʿatbari, and his Iraqi counterpart, Saadun Hamadi. In Tehran, Bouteflika declared to the press, 'I can say with confidence that the Iran-Iraq talks will be successful.'[100] Given the mistrust between the Iranians and Iraqis, the role of Algeria as arbitrator was crucial to securing the Algiers Agreement. Boumédiène was not motivated solely by a selfless desire to secure peace between Iran and Iraq; he hoped to increase his prestige and secure concessions. Indeed, a US intelligence summary stated that: 'Though far from the front lines, President Boumediene undoubtedly expects to receive some financial aid and political support for his proposals for a new economic order as a fallout from his part in arranging the Algiers agreement.'[101]

Cultural Relations

While shared Islamic identity provided opportunities for Iran to initiate interactions with African states, political relationships did not always follow. One country with which Iran did not establish political relations, yet maintained some ties due to historical connections and a shared Islamic heritage, was Tanzania. During the Sasanian period, particularly after the Iranian conquest of Yemen in the sixth century AD, some networks were established connecting East Africa to the Sasanian Empire, given its relative proximity. As a result of these connections, when the Arabs invaded Iran in the seventh century, some Iranians migrated to the east coast of Africa.[102] From around the tenth

[99] Parker telegram, 19 March 1975, WikiLeaks Cable 1975ALGIER00738_b.
[100] *The New York Times*, 16 March 1975, 17.
[101] Paper Prepared in the Office of Current Intelligence, Central Intelligence Agency, Washington, 1 May 1975, *FRUS, 1969–1976, Volume XXVII, Iran; Iraq, 1973–1976*, doc. 286.
[102] 'Āfriqā-ye Sharqi: Tānzāniyā (Zanzebār va Tāngānikā)', Shafā Archives, carton 11, East Africa.

century, Shirazi settlers colonised areas along the coast, particularly Zanzibar, an island just off the Swahili coast, and parts of mainland Tanzania.[103] The name of Zanzibar itself derives from the Persian Zangbār, meaning black (zang) coast (bār). The integration of the Shirazi population in the region was such that the term Shirazi was once interchangeable with Swahili, the language spoken in the region, which is a mixture of Bantu, Arabic and Persian.[104]

Several schools existed in Zanzibar that served its Khoja Shia Ithna-Asheri community, and some of these schools had connections to Iran in the 1960s and 1970s.[105] One such institute was the Faize Ithna-Asheri, which had been established in the 1920s to care for the community, and which included a night school that provided not only religious classes to the boys of Zanzibar, but Persian classes too. In December 1963, the headmaster of the Faize Ithna-Asheri Night School, Mohammed Ebrahim Jivraj, wrote directly to the shah's cultural counsellor, Shojāʿ al-Din Shafā, to request that he send some Persian language books for the school. He also informed Shafā that often he could not get good enough reception to listen to Radio Iran, so requested assistance in providing better bandwidth. Finally, Jivraj thanked Shafā for the medical attention he and his sister had received from Iran's medical team in Mecca while on the Haj.[106]

Given the historic and cultural links between Iran and the Shia communities of East Africa, it is perhaps unsurprising that in 1964, when the Iranian goodwill delegation toured sub-Saharan Africa, one of the seven countries it visited was Tanzania. This visit was followed up by an economic delegation, which arrived in Tanzania in February 1968.[107] In spite of these early connections between the two countries, Iran was hesitant to establish a more formal political partnership, first

[103] See Neville Chittick, 'The "Shirazi" Colonization of East Africa', *The Journal of African History*, vol. 6, no. 3 (1965), 275–294.

[104] Kitula King'ei and Paul Musau, 'The Shirazi Influence on Swahili Language', *Papers Presented during the First Conference on the Historical Role of Iranians (Shirazis) in the East African Coast: 2nd–3rd February 2001* (Nairobi: Cultural Council of the Embassy of I. R. Iran, 2001), 85.

[105] On the Khoja community of Tanzania, see Iqbal Akhtar, *The Khōjā of Tanzania Discontinuities of a Postcolonial Religious Identity* (Leiden: Brill, 2016).

[106] Mohammed Ebrahim Jivraj to Shojāʿ al-Din Shafā, 20 December 1963, Shafā Archives, carton 11, East Africa.

[107] 'Ravābet bā Irān', *Afran*, www.afran.ir/modules/publisher/item.php?itemid=345.

due to the shah's mistrust of Tanzania's regime, which was one of the more radical ones in East Africa, and later also due to his personal dislike of Tanzania's president, Julius Nyerere, who had failed to come to the aid of Zanzibar's Iranian community in 1970.

The independent Arab government of Zanzibar had been overthrown in January 1964, and in April 1964, the Zanzibar Revolutionary Council and the Tanganyika Parliament created a single sovereign state. Zanzibar was to be governed according to the Tanganyika constitution, which was modified to grant a separate legislature to Zanzibar, as well as an executive with authority over certain matters, including defence, internal security and foreign affairs. Its president, Abeid Karume, served as the head of the Revolutionary Government of Zanzibar, as well as first vice president of the union. The autonomy it enjoyed within the federal state meant that Zanzibar was a law unto itself, and there was little the government in Dar es Salaam could do to exert its authority there.[108] A British diplomat reporting on the situation in Zanzibar in 1970 wrote that 'there is no question but that in the years since 1964 the Union here has simply been used by "Sheikh" Karume and his Revolutionary Council as a respectable background against which to tighten their dictatorial grip on Zanzibar until it has become a police state'.[109] As the Revolutionary Council introduced more repressive measures and violated the rights of its people with impunity, Nyerere was so anxious to avoid a confrontation with Karume and not overstep the mark, that he was, the report continues, 'apparently prepared to condone the breach of equally basic principles of justice and the freedom of speech and action'.[110]

In 1966, the Revolutionary Government introduced a law that made it illegal for Zanzibari parents to withhold consent for their daughters to marry. Karume insisted that the law would help bring about greater racial cohesion, but minority populations felt that it was designed to make their daughters more easily obtainable by Karume and his cronies.[111] In 1970, Karume himself attempted to marry four young

108 George W. Triplett, 'Zanzibar: The Politics of Revolutionary Inequality', *The Journal of Modern African Studies*, vol. 9, no. 4 (1971), 615–616.

109 Horace Phillips, 'Zanzibar, 1970', 9 April 1970, FCO 160/113/18.

110 Ibid.

111 William Edgett Smith, *We Must Run While They Walk: A Portrait of Africa's Julius Nyerere* (London: Victor Gollancz, 1971), 133.

Persian girls of the Khoja Shia Ithna-Asheri sect. When they refused, he ordered the arrest of their male relatives and pledged to deport Zanzibar's entire Khoja Shia Ithna-Asheri population. Karome was persuaded by Nyerere to drop the charges.[112] Just months later, in September 1970, four Persian girls, aged between fourteen and twenty, were forced to marry senior members of the government, two of whom served on the Revolutionary Council.[113] Another member of the Council performed the ceremony.[114] Eleven of the girls' male relatives were imprisoned and received lashes for protesting the marriages. At the sentencing, the judge accused the men of 'sowing the seeds of racism'.[115]

Despite protests from across East Africa, petitions from other nations, including Britain and Iran, and appeals from government officials on the mainland, Karume refused to back down, arguing that such unions were important to bring about racial equality.[116] Nyerere was undoubtedly embarrassed by the international attention this episode attracted, and his inability to stand up to Karume undermined his position in Africa as a leading opponent of Rhodesia and South Africa. As one of his allies put it, 'How can we talk about human rights when this is going on?'[117] The episode also strained relations between Iran and Tanzania until after the fall of the shah in 1979. As Iran established relations with countries across the continent in the years following the 1971 imperial celebrations, Tanzania was ignored, despite recognition from the Iranian Ministry of Foreign Affairs in the mid-1970s that it needed an additional embassy in East Africa, since it was becoming difficult for its embassy in Nairobi to cover Iran's interests in the entire region.[118] Later, in 1977, the US ambassador, William Sullivan, asked Khalʿatbari whether Iran might be interested

112 Ibid.
113 Triplett, 'Zanzibar: The Politics of Revolutionary Inequality', 616.
114 Andrew Coulson, *Tanzania: A Political Economy* (Oxford: Oxford University Press, 2013), 267.
115 Smith, *We Must Run While They Walk*, 133. This episode had, in the words of Iqbal Akhtar 'a profound psychological impact on the Khoja in communicating the level of personal insecurity in revolutionary Zanzibar' and convinced many in the community to resettle on the mainland throughout the 1970s. Akhtar, *The Khōjā of Tanzania*, 182.
116 *The New York Times*, 9 April 1972, 14.
117 Smith, *We Must Run While They Walk*, 134.
118 Helms telegram, 17 July 1974, WikiLeaks Cable 1974TEHRAN05900_b.

in opening an embassy in Dar es Salaam. Khalʿatbari responded that 'although he appreciated [the] value of Tanzania, he was not sure [the] shah would approve of opening an embassy there because [the] shah does not entirely approve of Nyerere'. Khalʿatbari told Sullivan that the shah's attitude dated back to Nyerere's refusal to intercede in the forced marriages in Zanzibar after direct appeals from Iran.[119]

Although the shah could be quite forgiving of those he disagreed with, he was not quick to forget when he felt he had been insulted, or shown inadequate deference. For example, as a result of President Pompidou's declining to attend the 2,500th anniversary celebrations, economic and political relations between Iran and France were strained for some time.[120] The shah was especially sensitive when affronted by leaders of smaller countries, such as Nyerere in 1970 and, as will be shown in Chapter 11, President Jomo Kenyatta of Kenya in 1978.

*****

Egypt had been Iran's main adversary and the biggest threat to Iran's regional aspirations for ten years. In the early 1970s, the settlement of this long-standing rivalry and the friendliness of relations between Iran and the new government headed by Anwar Sadat allowed the shah to focus resources on pursuing Iran's interests in other parts of the world. In a perfect reflection of the impact of Egypt–Iran rapprochement on Iran's international relations, in the same *Ettelāʿāt* article that reported the meeting between Sadat and Zāhedi in May 1971, it was also reported that Iran had recently established relations with Guinea and that Zāhedi would shortly be travelling to Senegal to initiate relations there too.[121] Meanwhile, the imperial celebrations held at Persepolis in 1971, and the attendance there of several African countries, helped to advance the reputation of Iran and the shah across the Global South, including Africa.

The coup in Libya in 1969 and the subsequent emergence of Qadaffi as the leader of the radical Arab bloc in 1971 presented a new set of challenges to the shah. Qadaffi was indeed similar to Nasser in his

119 Sullivan telegram, 30 October 1977, WikiLeaks Cable 1977TEHRAN09552_c.
120 See Steele, *The Shah's Imperial Celebrations of 1971*, 64.
121 *Ettelāʿāt*, 25 Ordibehesht 1350/ 15 May 1971, 4.

charisma and revolutionary rhetoric, but although he became increasingly popular during the 1970s among other Muslim leaders, including Iran's allies, such as Pakistan, he did not present the same threat to Iran as Nasser had in the 1960s. Qadaffi undermined the shah's role in the Islamic bloc and the shah loathed him, but Libya was a less powerful country than Egypt, with a much smaller population, and where Soviet influence was limited, so Qadaffi was perceived as little more than a rabble-rouser. While the Egypt–Iran rapprochement gave the shah greater flexibility in his foreign policy, the withdrawal of the British from the Persian Gulf gave him an opportunity to establish Iranian supremacy over the Persian Gulf region. After the shah had achieved this, his security interests expanded beyond his immediate neighbourhood to include parts of East and Southern Africa.

6 *Trouble in the Horn and Soviet Encroachment*

The shah often expressed his belief that the Persian Gulf was one of the most strategically important areas of the world, due to the vast amounts of oil transported through its waters. The British withdrawal from the Persian Gulf in 1971 gave the shah a chance to assert Iran's control over the region and articulate a vision for Iran's future global strategy. But it also gave him the responsibility to police it. To protect the Persian Gulf and the traffic passing through it, the shah needed to increase Iran's military capabilities to defend not only the Gulf itself, but also the Strait of Hormuz and the Gulf of Oman, which connect it to the Indian Ocean. And his ambitions did not end there; the shah's Indian Ocean policy, which developed after 1971, was essentially an extension of his Persian Gulf policy in the late 1960s–early 1970s; a policy whose superseding principle was, as Ramazani writes, 'that great powers should keep out of the area'.[1] The security of the Indian Ocean should, the shah often argued, be a concern for the countries of the Indian Ocean, not the likes of the big powers, in particular the Soviet Union.[2]

Iran's push into the Indian Ocean was also motivated by political developments on its eastern border. The Pahlavi state enjoyed friendly relations with both of its eastern neighbours; Afghanistan and Pakistan. Afghanistan had a close relationship to the Soviet Union, and had been a recipient of Soviet economic, technical and military aid since the 1950s. As a result, the Soviets supported Afghanistan during border disputes with Pakistan and the issue of the self-determination of Pashtuns in Pakistan, whose region the Afghans referred to as Pashtunistan.[3] The shah suspected that the Soviets supported

[1] Rouhollah K. Ramazani, 'Iran's Search for Regional Cooperation', *Middle East Journal*, vol. 30, no. 2 (1976), 180.
[2] R. K. Karanjia, *The Mind of a Monarch* (London: George Allen & Unwin, 1977), 234.
[3] Saikal, *The Rise and Fall of the Shah*, 143.

Afghanistan in the hope of weakening Pakistan and ultimately securing direct access to the Indian Ocean. The signing of the Indo-Soviet Treaty of Friendship and Cooperation in 1971 and the Indo-Pakistani War in the same year, which resulted in the independence of Bangladesh, prompted the shah to strengthen his support for Pakistan. The signing of the Treaty of Friendship and Cooperation between the Soviet Union and Iraq in April 1972 increased the shah's fears of Soviet encirclement.

In light of these developments, the shah spoke with increasing urgency about his aspiration to create an economic and military union for the countries bordering the Indian Ocean, from Australia and Singapore to India, Iran and South Africa. In pursuit of this Indian Ocean policy, the shah sought to develop ties with countries across the Indian Ocean, and he paid official visits to many of them throughout the 1970s, including Australia (1974), New Zealand (1974) and Pakistan (1975). Although the shah did not visit East or Southern Africa during this period, these areas were vital to Iran's broader security strategy, and the shah established a strong diplomatic presence there. Part of this strategy in Africa was to bolster anti-Soviet regimes, and attempt to induce states that had received Soviet support to seek instead the cooperation of neutral countries, such as Iran. One of the regions that received particular attention during this period was the Horn of Africa.

Africa and the Indian Ocean Initiative

In a meeting between the shah and Henry Kissinger in Washington on 27 July 1973, just ten days after a coup had taken place in Afghanistan which saw the abolition of its monarchy and its replacement with a republic, the security of Pakistan was one of the issues at the top of the agenda. On tensions between India and Pakistan, Kissinger said to the shah: 'Pakistan is best protected if the Indians know that an attack on Pakistan would involve Iran. We will strengthen Iran to help Pakistan.'[4] The shah replied:

> I agree. I have told the Indians I would go to the aid of Pakistan if Pakistan is attacked. They know I could not tolerate the disintegration of Pakistan.

[4] Memorandum of Conversation, Washington, 27 July 1973, *FRUS, 1969–1976, Volume XXVII, Iran; Iraq, 1973–1976*, doc. 30.

I have also said this to the Russians. We could not close our eyes to active Afghan-Soviet pressures in Pushtunistan. On border problems, we will cooperate with Pakistan.

To demonstrate his growing security concerns on Iran's south-eastern border, the shah discussed his plans for the naval and air base at Chābahār, on the Arabian Sea, close to the border with Pakistan, on which construction had begun in 1972. 'We are going to build a road from there to the Pakistani border', the shah said. 'We will also extend the railroad. We will eventually have three armored brigades in that region. Eventually there will be an armored division in Kerman. We have to watch both the Afghan and Pakistani borders.'[5]

The shah's fears over a 'Moscow-Kabul-New Delhi-Baghdad axis' prompted him to expand his immediate strategic objectives and, in the words of the historian Amin Saikal, 'to redefine the Iranian region of security and interests'.[6] The British had previously maintained peace in the Persian Gulf region and ensured the continued flow of oil through the area. The shah was happy to take over this role from the British and assert Iran's dominance over the region. But, even though the shah expanded his security interests further to the Gulf of Oman and ultimately into the Indian Ocean, this was often justified in the context of the need to maintain the security of the Persian Gulf. For example, in an interview with the Egyptian journalist Mohamed Heikal in September 1975, the shah justified Iran's military build-up by saying:

The situation in the Persian Gulf warrants concern. The superpowers maintain war fleets in the Indian Ocean and their ships sometimes enter Persian Gulf waters. Three medium powers exist in the Persian Gulf – Iran, Iraq and Saudi Arabia ... What worries me is that the superpowers have a specified strategy each. Behind these strategies are determined decision-makers. Iran enjoys a united will, while the seven Arab states along the Persian Gulf littoral think along divergent, if not hostile, lines. We are worried about ourselves especially in view of the fact – if you agree with me – that the Persian Gulf has become a seat of tensions and will be so for at least twenty years more. This is precisely the reason behind our military build-up. I want Iran to be determined and prepared at every juncture.

And the Indian Ocean, he argued, was the natural extension of the Persian Gulf.

[5] Ibid. [6] Saikal, *The Rise and Fall of the Shah*, 145.

In the same interview, the shah said: 'There is a power vacuum in the Indian Ocean. We do not claim to be able to fill the void entirely on our own. We believe that the area's countries must maintain a naval presence in the ocean, especially close to the straits of the Persian Gulf, which provide access to the heart of Iran.'[7] In spite of the shah's insistence that Iran did not want to 'fill the void' on its own, it became increasingly clear by the middle of the 1970s that the shah intended to be the dominant power in any regional alliance. A US State Department report from 1975 noted that 'The Shah wants to be the leading – if not the dominant – power in the Indian Ocean . . . Over the longer term, the Shah will work for the elimination of both Soviet and US military presence in the Indian Ocean.'[8]

During conversations with foreign heads of state and in joint communiques, the need to keep the Indian Ocean free from big power competition was often stressed. For example, addressing the thirtieth session of the UN General Assembly in September 1975, Iran's minister of foreign affairs, ʿAbbās ʿAli Khalʿatbari, outlined Iran's plans 'to establish a zone of peace in the region' and its proposal for a 'Conference of Littoral and Hinterland States of the Indian Ocean'. This idea had not originated in Tehran, however, but in Lusaka. The declaration of the Third Conference of Non-Aligned Countries, held there in September 1970, called on all states to 'consider and respect the Indian Ocean as a zone of peace from which great Power rivalries and competition as well as bases conceived in the context of such rivalries and competition should be excluded'.[9] One year later, in December 1971, the United Nations General Assembly proposed its own 'Declaration of the Indian Ocean as a Zone of Peace'. This declaration noted the 'determination of the peoples of the littoral and hinterland States of the Indian Ocean to preserve their independence, sovereignty and territorial integrity, and to resolve their political, economic and social problems under conditions of peace and tranquillity'. The littoral and hinterland countries of the Indian Ocean should,

[7] 'Highlights of Mohammad Heikal's Exclusive Interview', September 1975, FCO/8/2501.

[8] 'National Intelligence Estimate', Washington, 9 May 1975, *FRUS, 1969–1976, Volume XXVII, Iran; Iraq, 1973–1976*, doc. 121.

[9] 'Resolution 2832: Declaration of the Indian Ocean as a Zone of Peace', United Nations General Assembly, Twenty-Sixth Session, 2022nd Plenary Meeting, 15 December 1971.

through 'regional and other co-operation' establish a 'system of universal collective security'.[10]

With the oil boom of the early 1970s, Iran was able to invest heavily in expanding its military capabilities. While between 1949 and 1972, Iranian imported arms worth $1.2 billion, in the six years from 1972 until 1978, Iran spent $10.4 billion on military equipment. This included the most sophisticated weaponry from the United States and Britain.[11] In the short period from 1974 to 1978, the budget for military personnel increased from $812 million to $2.5 billion. With 300,000 active military personnel, in the Middle East, Iran was rivalled only by Egypt in terms of the size of its military.[12] In the context of the shah's plan to establish Iran as the preeminent power of the Indian Ocean and to enforce his belief that the Indian Ocean should be a zone free of imperial competition, an integral focus of this military spending was building a powerful navy.

Investment in the Imperial Iranian Navy increased over 200-fold from the third to fifth development plans, from $5.5 million in the third plan (1963–1968), to $55 million in the fourth plan (1968–1973) and $1.2 billion in the fifth plan (1973–1978).[13] A French report from February 1974 notes that.

> While the Imperial Navy regularly reinforces its potential in fast escorts – even in 'combatant II' speedboats of which it has just purchased six from us – it is moving towards the constitution of a real naval tool and envisages, in addition to the purchase a cruiser in Great Britain to perhaps acquire an aircraft carrier, more likely two helicopter carriers and finally submarines which we are beginning to hear we could be the suppliers of.[14]

While Iran took the time to build its naval capabilities, it kept a close eye on developments in the region and was critical of its allies who deviated from its principle of non-big power-intervention. For

[10] Ibid. The declaration was unanimously approved the following year, on 16 December 1972. See 'Resolution 2992: Declaration of the Indian Ocean as a Zone of Peace', United Nations General Assembly, Twenty-Seventh Session, 2111th Plenary Meeting, 15 December 1972.

[11] Ehteshami, 'Iran's Grand Strategy under the Pahlavis', 204. [12] Ibid.

[13] Kim C. Beazley, 'The October War, the 1973–1974 Arab Oil Embargo, and U.S. Policy on the Indian Ocean', in *The Indian Ocean in Global Politics*, ed. Larry W. Bowman and Ian Clark (Boulder, CO: Westview Press, 1981), 116.

[14] French ambassador in Iran, Robert de Souza, to minister of foreign affairs, Michel Jobert, 27 February 1974, CADN, 43PO/1/55/ANL7.

example, Bahrain was a particular target of Iran's criticism, 'although discreet', for allowing the United States to build a base there, since this decision had merely prompted Iraq to grant identical facilities to the Soviets at Umm al-Qasr.[15]

Iran identified South Africa as the key strategic country in the western Indian Ocean and as noted in Chapter 4, a naval agreement was concluded, whereby Iranian warships were able to stop at the naval base of Simonstad in the Western Cape for repairs and maintenance, and from 1972, an Iranian navy representative was permanently based in South Africa.[16] Iran had interest in concluding naval agreements with other Southern African countries, including with Mauritius. These relations were initiated in early August 1972, when Iran's ambassador to Pakistan, the scholar Mohammad Hoseyn Mashāyekh Faridani, travelled to Mauritius.[17] The two countries had already agreed to establish diplomatic relations, and the primary purpose of this trip was to conclude the purchase by the government of Iran of the Valory Chateau in Moka, in which Reza Shah had lived during his Mauritian exile (October 1941–April 1942). Like Reza Shah's house in Johannesburg, Iran intended to turn the Valory Chateau into a museum.[18] The secondary purpose of Faridani's trip was to invite the prime minister of Mauritius, Seewoosagur Ramgoolam, to pay an official visit to Iran. Ramgoolam, who according to the British high commissioner 'never refuses an invitation and a chance to travel', eagerly accepted the invitation.[19]

In the days prior to the arrival of Ramgoolam in December 1972, articles were published about the visit in the local press, framing it as the first in a series by 'leaders from the Indian Ocean'.[20] During his four-day trip, the prime minister was granted a sixty-minute audience with the shah and was entertained at a banquet in his honour by Hoveydā, with whom he also had extensive talks. Ramgoolam and his accompanying minister were said by the British diplomat Hugh James

15 Ibid. 16 Chehabi, 'South Africa and Iran', 699.

17 J. L. Pumphrey to Iain Sutherland, 26 July 1972, FCO 31/1229.

18 Renovation work began in the late 1970s, and Princess Shams visited as part of her tour of Southern and East Africa in 1976, but by the time of the revolution, it remained incomplete. Chehabi, 'Royal Exile in the Indian Ocean'. See also the file NLAI 264/026051.

19 P. A. Carter to J. L. Pumphrey, 28 August 1972, FCO 31/1229.

20 P. A. E. Renardel de Lavalette to Ministry of Foreign Affairs, 6 December 1972, NA 2.05.191/416.

Arbuthnott to have 'made a good impression . . . although the Iranians were puzzled by the Mauritian insistence on long periods of sleep'.[21] The purpose of the visit, from the Iranian side, was to ensure cooperation on the Indian Ocean, which is reflected in the joint communique, in which both sides 'stressed their interest in the preservation of stability and peace in the Indian Ocean area and agreed that the security of navigation through its waterways is in the interests not only of Iran and Mauritius but also of the international trade and the world peace'. They further expressed a desire that the Indian Ocean would 'become free from the rivalries of the great powers'.[22]

One of the issues discussed during the visit was the possibility of Iran constructing Iranian port and communication facilities in Mauritius.[23] Ramgoolam told the press that although these were only preliminary discussions, Mauritius did not have the capacity by itself to keep the area free from imperial powers, so it could be open to allowing countries bordering the Indian Ocean to construct such facilities in the future.[24] Although the local press took the prime minister's gesture to mean that this was a done deal – one headline read, for example, 'Iran getting Indian Ocean port facilities' – it appears that no such deal was struck. The Dutch ambassador believed that Mauritius had 'undoubtedly been promised satisfactory compensation by Iran in exchange for the commitment', in the form of Iranian support for Mauritian 'socio-economic development projects'.[25]

Iran did not build its port facilities on Mauritius, but remained cautious about Soviet encroachment in the area. For example, when reports reached the Iranian Ministry of Foreign Affairs that Ramgoolam was about to sign a deal with the Soviets in 1975, the US Deputy Chief of Mission in Tehran, Jack Miklos, was asked by the Iranians to find out exactly what was going on.[26] Miklos reported that the government of Iran was 'suspicious of Soviet intentions in Indian Ocean Area' and would appreciate 'occasional up-dating on their

[21] Arbuthnott to B. Smith, 15 December 1972, FCO 31/1229.

[22] Joint communique, Iran-Mauritius, 6 December 1972, NA 2.05.191/416.

[23] *Kayhan International*, 5 December 1972, 1.

[24] Peter Ramsbotham telegram, 15 December 1972, FCO 31/1229.

[25] P. A. E. Renardel de Lavalette to Ministry of Foreign Affairs, 6 December 1972, NA 2.05.191/416.

[26] Jack Miklos telegram, 7 July 1975, WikiLeaks Cable 1975TEHRAN06478_b.

significant activities on Mauritius, as well as any signs of a shift in GOM's [Government of Mauritius] political orientation'.[27]

Towards the middle of the 1970s, the Iranian government became increasingly concerned with making sure that Iran was properly represented in countries bordering the ocean. In 1975, for instance, the Ministry of Foreign Affairs announced that it would establish embassies in Sri Lanka and Madagascar, since they were both at the time served by the ambassador resident in Islamabad. This upgrade in representation was said to represent the shah's desire to establish 'closer cooperation with Indian Ocean countries in political, security and economic areas'.[28] The ambassador sent to Madagascar, one Amir Malek-Madani, said to be an 'aristocrat of some influence', though based in Antananarivo, was also accredited to Mauritius, Mozambique and Seychelles.[29] Incidentally, Iran established ties with Seychelles in 1976, the same year it achieved independence, which illustrates that Iran was eager to move quickly to secure some influence with newly independent states.[30] Reporting on conversations with US officials and the Iranian Ministry of Foreign Affairs' chief of African Affairs, ʿAli Akbar Shahbāzi, in April 1975, about the imminent independence of Comoros, the Americans found Shahbāzi 'surprisingly well informed about [the] island's situation and prospects'. He had, they added, 'already prepared two reports on [the] subject for his superiors'.[31]

[27] Miklos telegram, 8 July 1975, WikiLeaks Cable 1975TEHRAN06543_b.

[28] Richard Helms telegram, 28 December 1975, WikiLeaks Cable 1975TEHRAN12234_b.

[29] Marshall telegram, 30 July 1976, WikiLeaks Cable 1976NAIROB08023_b.

[30] One year before this, in late 1975, the son of Princess Ashraf, Prince Shahram, purchased an island of the Seychelles, D'Arros, which the preliminary planning application stated would be 'a holiday centre for members of the Iranian royal family including the shah'. See file FCO 40/681. Personal relations between the Pahlavi royal house and the Seychelles government during the early period of independence must have been fairly close, because in June 1977, the shah received a telegram from a close associate of the president of the Seychelles, who had recently been ousted in a coup. The associate, perhaps playing to the shah's hatred of Qaddafi, said that 'the coup was engineered by the Libyans and has no popular support'. He added that he was 'confident that he [the president] can restore the situation and wants the shah to provide "suitable transport" to get him back to the Seychelles immediately'. The shah doubted that he would be able to help, but nonetheless, asked the British ambassador to bring him an assessment of the situation. Anthony Parsons to Foreign Office, 5 June 1977, FCO 8/2986.

[31] Helms telegram, 17 April 1975, WikiLeaks Cable 1975TEHRAN03581_b. ʿAli Akbar Shahbāzi held a PhD in political science from the University of Tehran,

The Ethiopian Revolution and the Shah's Strategy in the Horn of Africa

Another area that gained importance to the shah during the 1970s was the Horn of Africa, particularly after the fall of his close ally, Haile Selassie. Throughout the post–Second World War period, Haile Selassie had been a key ally of the West in the Horn of Africa and had gained much strength from these relations. But towards the end of the 1960s, the power dynamics in East Africa shifted and Haile Selassie was faced with a new set of challenges. In May 1969, Colonel Jaʿfar Mohammad Nimeiry seized power in Sudan in a military coup and installed a pro-Nasser military regime, which received arms from the Soviets. As a result, the Eritrean Liberation Front (ELF) was able to operate across the border in Sudan with impunity, a major advantage in its separatist struggle.[32] In the north of Africa, Qadaffi's revolutionary rhetoric posed a new challenge to both Haile Selassie's Solomonic kingdom and his personal position as the leading political figure in Africa. Qadaffi also supported the ELF and declared an Islamic holy war against Ethiopia. While Haile Selassie's pro-Israeli, pro-Western position had generally served him well in the post-war period, it was now becoming increasingly problematic. The ELF gained the support of other liberation groups, such as the Palestinian Liberation Organisation, and the Eritrean struggle became part of the global fight against Zionism and imperialism. Eritrean fighters were trained in Palestinian camps and Libya and Palestine sent military equipment to support the fight against Haile Selassie through South Yemen, across the Red Sea.[33] By 1970, the ELF could call upon as many as 10,000 regular and irregular forces.[34]

In October 1969, another military coup established a Marxist-Leninist military regime in Somalia, under the presidency of Major General Siad Barre. One of the key goals of Barre's Somali nationalism

and was a career diplomat, having joined the Ministry of Foreign Affairs in 1957. He had worked at several embassies, including in Morocco, and according to a biographical note had published 'articles on Iranian foreign policy and imperialistic policies in African Countries'. *Iran Who's Who* (Tehran: Echo of Iran, 1976), 518.

32 Erlich, *Haile Selassie*, 145. 33 Ibid.

34 Jeffrey A. Lefebvre, 'Middle East Conflicts and Middle Level Power Intervention in the Horn of Africa', *Middle East Journal*, vol. 50, no. 3 (1996), 393.

was to reclaim Somali-populated territories in bordering Kenya and Ethiopia, which required a significant strengthening of his army. This he achieved with the support of the Soviets, who had begun to attribute greater strategic significance to the Horn of Africa after their expulsion from Egypt by President Sadat in 1972.[35] As a result of this support, the Somali army grew from 4,000 to 17,000 men, 3,600 Soviet advisors were sent to Somalia, two Soviet bases were established, and the Somalis began to foment uprisings in Ethiopia against Haile Selassie.[36] Regional issues also exacerbated domestic problems. For example, the closure of the Suez Canal from 1967 had a hugely damaging impact on Ethiopia's already struggling economy.[37] By 1972, life expectancy in the country had decreased to thirty, 60 per cent of children did not survive their first twelve months, and from 1970 a devastating draught led to famine, which resulted in the deaths of as many as 200,000 Ethiopians by 1974.[38]

As shown in Chapter 3, during the 1960s and early 1970s, Iran maintained a close relationship with Ethiopia. The two sides were drawn together partly due to shared concerns about revolutionary ideologies such as Nasserism, and partly due to the respect the two leaders shared for one another as representatives of ancient monarchical traditions. However, with the British withdrawal from the Persian Gulf in 1971 and the establishment of Iranian supremacy in the Persian Gulf, the Horn of Africa gained strategic significance in the context of the shah's Indian Ocean initiative. As early as 1972, the shah's policy in the region was increasingly viewed in the context of Indian Ocean security. In a meeting with President Nixon and Henry Kissinger in May that year, he told them that 'Iran had established relations with Ethiopia and Africa to make sure that there was a common policy in the Indian Ocean'.[39] The shah was particularly concerned that should the Russians gain a foothold in the Horn of Africa and maintain a strong presence in the Red Sea, this would

[35] Clapham, *The Horn of Africa*, 56–57.

[36] Ibid., 57; David D. Laitin, 'The War in the Ogaden: Implications for Siyaad's Role in Somali History', *The Journal of Modern African Studies*, vol. 17, no. 1 (1979), 99.

[37] Erlich, *Haile Selassie*, 141.

[38] Peter Koehn, 'Ethiopia: Famine, Food Production, and Changes in the Legal Order', *African Studies Review*, vol. 22, no. 1 (1979), 51.

[39] Memorandum of conversation, Tehran, 31 May 1972, *FRUS, 1969–1976, Volume E–4, Documents on Iran and Iraq, 1969–1972*, doc. 201.

threaten Iranian aspirations to be the dominant power across the Indian Ocean.

In a meeting between the shah and the US secretary of defence in July 1973, the shah said

> They [the Soviets] moved into Egypt, almost got the Suez, and are now in Aden, Somalia (Djibouti) and the island of Socotra. We can not shut our eyes to the in-roads the Russians have made. By beefing up their efforts in Somalia and Socotra, the Russians clearly threaten Ethiopia, and once Haile Selassie is gone, Ethiopia will be in grave danger, as his son is ineffective.[40]

The shah saw the security of Ethiopia as essential to minimising Soviet infiltration in the Middle East and East Africa, and on occasion petitioned his allies to support Haile Selassie. For instance, in a meeting between Israeli and US officials in Washington in May 1973, the Israeli minister of foreign affairs, Abba Eban, recorded a conversation he had had with the shah: 'He [the shah] sees a triangle – Israel, Ethiopia, and Iran – which if buttressed by US support will be a stabilizing influence. We exchanged information with respect to the internal stability, and the problem about Ethiopia. We hope he [Haile Selassie] gets strong support here [in the US].'[41] The fact that the shah lobbied for US support in the region is evidence that by the early 1970s, he considered it part of Iran's wider sphere of influence. Ethiopia was no longer a bridge to the rest of the continent, or merely a friendly monarchical regime, or even a counterweight to radical political movements; it now played a key strategic part in Iran's regional foreign policy.

But there are indications that despite this, the shah's personal enthusiasm for Ethiopia had waned. Indeed, in October 1972, just one year after the shah had flaunted Haile Selassie during the 2,500th anniversary celebrations, the shah told the British that although he was 'toying with the idea of closer links in particular with Ethiopia ... he was doubtful in view of the Emperor's age and the country's backwardness and isolation'.[42] As another sign of his growing unease with Ethiopia, the shah had sent a destroyer in 1971 to the annual Massawa Navy Days,

[40] Meeting between the Shah of Iran and the Secretary of Defense Washington, 24 July 1973, *FRUS, 1969–1976, Volume XXVII, Iran; Iraq, 1973–1976*, doc. 26.

[41] Memorandum of conversation, Washington, 12 May 1973, *FRUS, 1969–1976, Volume XXV, Arab-Israeli Crisis and War, 1973*, doc. 166.

[42] Hugh Arbuthnott to D. G. Allen, 5 October 1972, FCO 31/1126.

but did not repeat this gesture in 1972.[43] At this stage, however, Iran's embassy in Addis Ababa did still have 'an Ambassador of some seniority', and thus the British stated that 'for a country with no specific interests in Ethiopia, Iran is therefore relatively well represented'. The British concluded that although 'the Emperor would no doubt be flattered by any new attentions paid to him by the Shah ... the scope for increased economic relations between Iran and Ethiopia was small'.[44]

The aged emperor and his government became progressively less able to solve any of the problems facing the country and the results of a decade of financial mismanagement, poor government and corruption finally came to the surface. During 1974, unrest spread through the military and society. On 12 January, two discontented military contingents in the southern towns of Dolo and Negale mutinied over living conditions and poor pay, detaining not only their officers, but also the special envoy sent by the emperor to meet the mutineers. Haile Selassie acquiesced to the demands of the mutineers, thereby setting a precedent and an expectation that not only would such disobedience go unpunished, but that it could achieve positive results.[45] Another revolt over pay took place on 10 February, this time at an air base closer to the capital.[46] This was followed on 18 February by a strike of the Ethiopian Teachers' Association, whose 18,000-strong membership demanded salary increases and reforms to the educational system. But as Teferra Haile-Selassie has noted, unlike those of the mutinying soldiers, the demands of the striking teachers 'cut across the society' and reflected more widespread grievances.[47] Additional demands by the teachers included, for example, the introductions of a national minimum wage and industrial pension scheme, a

[43] Richard Dorman to Brian Birkmyre, 9 November 1972, FCO 31/1126. The Iranian destroyer that visited Ethiopia in February 1971 was Artemiz. From 13 to 17 October 1971, H. M. S. Ethiopia was invited by the Imperial Navy to visit Iranian ports in the Persian Gulf. 'Ravābet-e Irān bā Keshvar-hā-ye Āfriqā-ye Siyāh', darbār-e shāhanshāhi, markaz-e omur-e farhangi va matbuʿāti, 2, NLAI 264/025388.

[44] Birkmayre to I. R. Murray, 12 October 1972, FCO 31/1126.

[45] Teferra Haile-Selassie, *The Ethiopian Revolution, 1974–91: From a Monarchical Autocracy to a Military Oligarchy* (London: Kegan Paul International, 1997), 87.

[46] Fred Halliday and Maxine Molyneux, *The Ethiopian Revolution* (London: Verso, 1981), 84.

[47] Haile-Selassie, *The Ethiopian Revolution, 1974–91*, 88.

review of labour laws, and rights for employees in the civil sector to form trade unions.[48] University students joined the teachers' demonstrations, as too did the taxi drivers of Addis Ababa.[49]

Again, the emperor offered a conciliatory message to solve this immediate crisis, without realising that the grievances of the protestors 'were caused by years of neglect'.[50] On 25 February 1974, the Second Division in Asmara, which made up one-third of the total ground force of the Ethiopian army, mutinied, arrested all officers, the mayor of the city, and occupied the radio station. Among their demands, in addition to salary increases, were the right to form political parties, land reform and the arrests of corrupt officials. The emperor again capitulated, offering more concessions and salary increases. On 27 February, the cabinet resigned and Endelkachew Makonnen replaced Aklilu Habte-Wold as prime minister.[51] Makonnen, however, failed to resolve the demands of the protestors and in March and April more strikes and protests followed, deepening the crisis.

The shah was entertaining the president of Zaire, Mobutu Sese Seko, and the president of Sudan, Ja'far Nimeiry, in Tehran on 27 February, when the cabinet of Aklilu Habte-Wold resigned. The shah was undoubtedly disturbed at the rapidly deteriorating situation in Ethiopia and feared what would happen in the event of Haile Selassie's fall. In March, the shah relayed a message to Haile Selassie through President Nimeiry, asking whether he could help the emperor in his present situation. The emperor responded that he was 'most grateful [for the] shah's offer but needed no assistance at this time'.[52] In April 1974, the shah had confided in Sudan's minister of defence, Lieutenant General Awad Khalafalla, that Iran would be willing to assist Sudan in helping to alleviate food shortages in Ethiopia 'since he did not wish [to] see "communism" spreading in Africa'.[53] In July, Iran received Ethiopia's foreign minister, Zewde Gabre-Selassie, who wished to acquire financial assistance and military equipment to tackle threats from Eritrea and Somalia.[54] The shah rejected these requests

[48] Ibid. [49] Ibid., 89. [50] Ibid., 91.

[51] Halliday and Molyneux, *The Ethiopian Revolution*, 84.

[52] US ambassador to Sudan, William Dodd Brewer, telegram, 14 March 1974, WikiLeaks Cable 1974KHARTO00575_b.

[53] Brewer telegram, 27 April 1974, WikiLeaks Cable 1974KHARTO00910_b.

[54] Deputy Head of US Mission to Ethiopia, Parker D. Wyman, telegram, 5 July 1974, WikiLeaks Cable 1974ADDIS07814_b.

because although at this stage the Somalis were a greater threat to the security of the region given the backing of the Soviets, while the unrest in Ethiopia continued, he did not wish to provide equipment which might later 'fall into the hands of dissidents within the country'.[55] The shah was right to be cautious.

The period between June and September 1974 in Ethiopia is often referred to as a 'creeping coup', as a military committee, the Derg, gradually appropriated power in the country.[56] This coordinating committee was set up in June and elected as its chairman Major Mengistu Haile Mariam of the Third Army Division.[57] Aristocrats, officials and political figures were arrested on various charges, including corruption and covering up the famine.[58] In July, the Derg forced the resignation of Prime Minister Makonnen and replaced him with Lij Michael Imru, who was a relative of Haile Selassie with socialist sympathies. Having succeeded in dissolving imperial institutions and confiscating properties owned by the emperor and the royal family, in August, the Derg 'stepped up its propaganda of vilification against the person of the emperor'.[59] Finally, on 12 September, a group of soldiers came to Jubilee Palace, read out a message informing the emperor that his rule was over, led him out of the palace and pushed him unceremoniously into a Volkswagen Beetle that was waiting outside. He was taken first to the Fourth Division headquarters for several weeks of questioning, then to Menelik Palace, where he lived his final year under house arrest.[60]

The shah was sad to see the fall of Haile Selassie, not least because, as foreign minister Khalʿatbari said, 'whatever else may happen, the institution of the monarchy still provides an essential unifying force in countries such as Ethiopia'.[61] The shah's court minister, Asadollāh ʿAlam, was disconcerted at hearing the news of the demise of a king who had achieved so much in his early years, but whose record had been blemished during his final years.[62] The shah was as conscious of Haile Selassie's decline as his court minister.

55 Miklos telegram, 12 July 1974, WikiLeaks Cable 1974TEHRAN05718_b.
56 Halliday and Molyneux, *The Ethiopian Revolution*, 87.
57 Haile-Selassie, *The Ethiopian Revolution, 1974–91*, 121. 58 Ibid.
59 Ibid., 126. 60 Ibid., 176–178.
61 Helms telegram, 12 September 1974, WikiLeaks Cable 1974TEHRAN07673_b.
62 ʿAlam, diary entry 22 Shahrivar 1353 / 13 Sept 1974, *Yāddāsht-hā-ye ʿAlam*, vol. 4, 237–238.

Newspapers in Iran decried the treatment of Haile Selassie at the hands of the army, and predicted that the emperor's supporters would come to his aid.[63] Although Iran's official reaction to the fall of Haile Selassie was rather muted and there was no question of Iranian military intervention, the development did impact Iran's cooperation with the United States in Ethiopia. The United States had been Ethiopia's main arms supplier for the past twenty years, and was concerned that 'an end to [the] flow of American equipment might cause [the] regime to turn to [the] communist world as Nasser did in 1955 when Washington rejected his arms demands'.[64] The United States had expected to send some second-hand F-5A aircraft from Iran, but shortly after the fall of Haile Selassie, considered that the scheme was 'in serious question ... since the Shah is even more interested in the fate of the former emperor than the U.S.'.[65] As well as honouring his friendship with the emperor, the shah was thinking practically. Ethiopia's foreign minister, Zewde Gabre-Selassie, felt that under normal circumstances, the shah would be open to selling second-hand aircraft to Ethiopia, but that ultimately 'the shah wanted to know who he would be arming: friends or possible enemies'.[66]

In May 1975, Iran eventually agreed to release its surplus aircraft, which included eight F-5As and two F-5Bs, directly to the United States. 'If [the] USG [United States Government] wished to transfer [the] aircraft to Ethiopia', said Iran's military procurements officer, General Hasan Tufāniān, 'that was not Iran's concern'.[67] However, Saudi Arabia, which had, like Iran, quickly developed a distaste for the Derg regime, refused to allow the aircraft to reach Ethiopia through its airspace. Responding to a suggestion that Iran might help transfer the aircraft, ambassador Helms reiterated that, 'Iranians want neither responsibility nor involvement in our transfer of F-5s to Ethiopia. General Toufanian was quite definitive in asserting that [the] movement of aircraft to Ethiopia was strictly [a] USG affair. We should not consider asking GOI [for] assistance in moving [this] aircraft.'[68]

63 See, for example, *Ettelā'āt*, 23 Shahrivar 1353/ 14 September 1974, 1.
64 Kissinger telegram, 9 December 1974, WikiLeaks Cable 1974STATE269868_b.
65 Ibid.
66 Kissinger telegram, 25 September 1974, WikiLeaks Cable 1974STATE211322_b.
67 Helms telegram, 28 May 1975, WikiLeaks Cable 1975TEHRAN04974_b.
68 Helms telegram, 4 June 1975, WikiLeaks Cable 1975TEHRAN05189_b.

Knowing that the aircraft would be transferred to Ethiopia, Iran could have blocked the sale. The fact that they did not do so indicates that in spite of the fall of a fellow monarch, the shah was convinced to a certain degree by the US position; that in order to stop Ethiopia turning to the Soviets for military support, weapons must be supplied to them by non-communist countries.

Sudan

The situation in Ethiopia and the fear of Soviet infiltration in the region had convinced the shah to reach out to other powers in the region. The president of Sudan, Jaʿfar Nimeiry, who had come to power through a military coup in May 1969, was inspired by Nasser and his pan-Arab socialist revolution; his type of military rule was modelled on that of Nasser's Egypt and in matters of policy, Sudan followed Egypt's lead.[69] Therefore, with the rapprochement between Iran and Egypt in 1970, Iran came to look on Sudan as a potential ally in the region. Nonetheless, it still received military aid from the Soviets. The situation changed in July 1971, when a communist coup was attempted against Nimeiry, which might have succeeded were it not for the swift intervention of Sadat and Qadaffi.[70] The attempted coup had a significant impact on big power competition in the Horn of Africa since Nimeiry, suspecting Soviet involvement, broke relations with Moscow and sought an alliance instead with Washington.[71]

The newspaper *Keyhān* reported that 'the political milieu of Tehran have welcomed with satisfaction the failure of the coup in Sudan, and the re-establishment of the authority of Nimeiry'.[72] Although the Iranian press was generally critical of the summary executions of suspected communist coup-plotters without judicial process, as the French ambassador observed 'the Iranians could not help but be pleased with the failure of an attempt to bring to power an extremist

[69] Robert O. Collins, *A History of Modern Sudan* (Cambridge: Cambridge University Press, 2008), 95; Jeffrey A. Lefebvre, 'Globalism and Regionalism: U.S. Arms Transfers to Sudan', vol. 17, no. 2 (1991), 216.

[70] Collins, *A History of Modern Sudan*, 101.

[71] Veronica Nmoma, 'The Shift in United States-Sudan Relations: A Troubled Relationship and the Need for Mutual Cooperation', *The Journal of Conflict Studies*, vol. 26, no. 2 (2006), 50.

[72] François Charles-Roux to French minister of foreign affairs, 29 July 1971, CADC 367QO/171.

government in the region'.[73] Just one year later, in 1972, Iran and Sudan established formal diplomatic relations at the ambassador level. From this period onwards, Nimeiry became one of the shah's closest allies in the region, and a partner in halting Soviet advances in the Horn of Africa.

Nimeiry paid a six-day visit to Iran in February 1974, during which he received the 'red carpet treatment'. Meetings between the two heads of state and their officials resulted in the signing of a joint communique, calling for the 'consolidation and expansion of mutual ties'.[74] Two months later, Sudan's minister of defence, General Khalafalla, visited Iran for five days as the guest of the chief of staff of Iran's armed forces, General Gholām Rezā Azhāri. During the trip, he was taken to inspect various military installations throughout the country, and he held talks with General Tufāniān about the potential transfer of arms to Sudan.[75] One of the problems Iran faced in dealing with requests from countries like Sudan was that much of Iran's military equipment came from the United States and third-country transfers required US approval. In September 1974, the United States turned down a request from Iran to allow the transfer of 1,000 US-provided rocket launchers to Sudan.[76] Shortly after, in January 1975, at a ceremony at Sudan's main port, in the presence of President Nimeiry and Iran's ambassador in Khartoum, six Iranian patrol craft were presented to Sudan.[77] It later transpired that four of these craft had been manufactured in the United States and that their transfer, because prior approval had not been sought, contravened US regulations. Given that the only other option was to demand that Iran recall the boats, which would be embarrassing for Iran and would potentially damage Iran-Sudan relations, the United States decided retroactively to approve the transfer.[78]

In line with their common strategic interests, Iran and Sudan also concluded some financial agreements. After the increase in the price of oil from January 1974, Iran concluded agreements with several countries in the region to help alleviate the financial impacts on their

[73] Ibid.
[74] Lehfeldt telegram, 9 March 1974, WikiLeaks Cable 1974TEHRAN01901_b.
[75] Helms telegram, 19 April 1974, WikiLeaks Cable 1974TEHRAN03055_b.
[76] Helms telegram, 19 September 1974, WikiLeaks Cable 1974TEHRAN07931_b.
[77] Brewer telegram, 17 January 1975, WikiLeaks Cable 1975KHARTO00155_b.
[78] Helms telegram, 20 March 1975, WikiLeaks Cable 1975TEHRAN02642_b.

economies. In April 1974, as a follow-up to Nimeiry's visit in February, Sudan's minister of economic affairs travelled to Iran. Upon his return home, the minister said that Iran's approaches 'were well beyond our hopes and expectations'.[79] On 27 April 1974, Iran agreed to loan Sudan $54 million, at a 5 per cent interest rate, with payment commencing five years later, to cover the costs of oil imports for one year.[80]

Zaire and Angola

As part of Iran's drive to achieve regional supremacy following the departure of the British in 1971, the shah became more willing to assist his regional allies, providing materiel support and, on occasion, military intervention. The clearest example is Iran's support for Sultan Qābus of Oman in his fight against the Dhofar rebels (1963–1976).[81] The shah had first offered to provide military support to Sultan Qābus at Persepolis in 1971, during the 2,500th anniversary celebrations. The sultan refused to accept at this stage, given Iran's imminent occupation of the Persian Gulf islands.[82] It did not take him long to change his mind, and by the end of 1972, 150 Iranian special forces arrived in Oman. Another 1,500-strong Imperial Iranian Battle Group arrived in late 1973, followed by 2,900 more in December 1974.[83] These soldiers came well-armed, and were supported by the Imperial Iranian Air Force, which provided transportation of supplies and troops, as well as air defence against potential attacks from South Yemen.[84] Iran's participation was, as the historian James Goode writes, 'crucial in bringing the war to a relatively quick and successful conclusion'.[85]

[79] P. A. E. Renardel de Lavalette to minister of foreign affairs, 6 April 1974, NA 2.05.191/433.

[80] Helms telegram, 16 September 1974, WikiLeaks Cable 1974TEHRAN07769_b.

[81] On this conflict, see Abdel Razzaq Takriti, *Monsoon Revolution: Republicans, Sultans, and Empires in Oman, 1965–1976* (Oxford: Oxford University Press, 2013).

[82] James F. Goode, 'Assisting Our Brothers, Defending Ourselves: The Iranian Intervention in Oman, 1972–75', *Iranian Studies*, vol. 47, no. 3 (2014), 447.

[83] Takriti, *Monsoon Revolution*, 295–297.

[84] Goode, 'The Iranian Intervention in Oman, 1972–75', 451; Takriti, *Monsoon Revolution*, 296.

[85] Goode, 'The Iranian Intervention in Oman, 1972–75', 453.

The shah was concerned about other areas that were vulnerable to Soviet encroachment, including parts of Central and Southern Africa. Soviet-backed rebel activity in Angola during its struggle for independence was viewed with particular apprehension in Iran. The headline of an article in February 1974 in *Ettelāʿāt* read: 'God Save Africa.'[86] It warned of the dangers facing Africa, of endless wars, and of a new kind of colonial interference bringing instability throughout the continent. It claimed that 'the ongoing war in Africa [specifically Angola] is greater than the war in Vietnam' and that 'Hitler's collaborators are seizing and mutilating the independence-seeking people of Africa'.[87]

While Iran became more concerned about the Soviet expansion across Africa in the mid-1970s, greater congressional oversight made it increasingly difficult for the United States directly to arm their allies on the continent. The weakness of the United States in Southern Africa was exposed during the Angolan Civil War in 1975–1976. In this conflict, the United States supported the Frente Nacional de Libertação de Angola (FNLA) as a counter to the Soviet-backed Movimento Popular de Libertação de Angola (MPLA). Washington viewed Soviet involvement in the conflict as a violation of détente, but scarred by its humiliating withdrawal from Vietnam, was unwilling to provide the necessary support to the FNLA.[88] Then the Tunney Amendment of 20 December 1975 prohibited the United States from supporting covert military operations in Angola for the remainder of the fiscal year, and the Clark Amendment, passed on 10 February 1976, made the ban unequivocal and permanent.[89] During a meeting on the situation in Angola and the possibilities of war spreading into Zaire, an exasperated Kissinger said:

> I know that we are most moral – to a degree not rivalled by anyone in history, but to tell me that the U.S. would declare in a bill of lading that we were delivering arms to Zaire! Now really! What are we going to do when we really want to ship arms to Zaire? And this is something that could come

[86] The publication of this article coincided with the state visits of the president of Zaire, Mobutu Sese Seko, and the president of Sudan, Jaʿfar Nimeiry.

[87] *Ettelāʿāt*, 9 Esfand 1352/ 28 February 1974, 5.

[88] Arthur J. Klinghoffer, 'US-Soviet Relations and Angola', *Harvard International Review*, vol. 8, no. 3 (1986), 16.

[89] *The Washington Post*, 20 December 1975, 1; Mahmood Mamdani, *Good Muslim, Bad Muslim: America, the Cold War, and the Roots of Terror* (New York: Pantheon, 2004), 82.

up in six months or so. If we allow something like this to stop us then we are going to have a monumental problem. What can we tell Zaire – that we have these arms but cannot deliver them? Now are you trying to tell me that we cannot deliver arms?[90]

The answer to his question was that as far as arms deliveries were concerned, the administration was hamstrung. Kissinger blasted the Tunney Amendment as 'a national disgrace ... the worst American foreign policy disaster that I can remember'.[91]

Kissinger sent messages to Riyadh and Tehran, to convince his allies that 'we are not out of business, and that the Executive Branch is resolved to pursue the Angola matter vigorously and with full determination. We do not intend to sit idly by in the face of Soviet intervention.' Given the problems arising as a result of the Tunney Amendment, Kissinger urged the shah 'to make available funds to Zaire for additional equipment and arms which would help preserve the kind of military position for the non-communist forces which is essential if a negotiated settlement is to be achieved'.[92] Kissinger added that the transfer of US-made weapons was out of the question because of the difficulties in Congress, but that he was exploring other ways that Iran and Saudi Arabia could contribute 'directly through Zaire to a strengthening of the non-communist forces in Angola'.[93] In response to this letter, the shah said that he would give the required funds to Zaire, but would not ask the government of Zaire what it did with the money. Although the shah would inform the US ambassador, Richard Helms, what had been done, 'he would keep such notification entirely private', to avoid Congress finding out.[94]

Iran enjoyed fairly good relations with Zaire, having established formal diplomatic ties in 1973. President Mobutu visited Iran for the first time in February 1974, and during a banquet in his honour, spoke of the trip as an opportunity 'for the cooperation between our two

90 Memorandum for the Record, 12 March 1976, *FRUS, 1969–1976, Volume XXVIII, Southern Africa*, doc. 182.

91 Cited in Nancy Mitchell, *Jimmy Carter in Africa: Race and the Cold War* (Washington, DC: Woodrow Wilson Center Press, 2016), 32.

92 Kissinger to Helms, 20 December 1975, *FRUS, 1969–1976, Volume XXVIII, Southern Africa*, doc. 159.

93 Ibid.

94 Backchannel Message from the Ambassador to Iran (Helms) to Secretary of State Kissinger, Tehran, 21 December 1975, *FRUS, 1969–1976, Volume XXVII, Iran; Iraq, 1973–1976*, doc. 151.

countries to become more tangible and fruitful from now on'.[95] He expressed hope that the shah would continue his support for Africa, and that the efforts of the two leaders 'would be effective in bringing about equilibrium and justice in the international community'.[96] The shah, during his banquet speech, in words that were printed on the front page of *Ettelāʿāt*, said that 'Iran is ready for all types of help to Africa' (Figure 6.1).[97] On 19 May 1974, during a two-hour speech to commemorate the seventh anniversary of the founding of the ruling party of Zaire, the Popular Movement of the Revolution (Mouvement Populaire de la Révolution), Mobutu decried the recent increases in the price of oil globally, but applauded Iran for being the only country to sell oil to Zaire at an affordable price.[98] One month later, an Iranian economic delegation travelled to Zaire, headed by the head of Iran's Plan and Budget Organisation, ʿAbdol-Majid Majidi, followed shortly after in November by a visit to Iran of a Zairian delegation.[99] For Iran, the purpose of building an economic relationship was to help strengthen Zaire in the face of regional instability. Iran's ultimate aim was, in line with that of the United States, to halt the spread of communism in Africa.

Given the temporary paralysis of the Executive in the United States, Iran, Saudi Arabia and Egypt assumed a greater role in the region. But, although they were encouraged by the United States, it would be erroneous to view them merely as American proxies; they were state actors pursuing their own interests, which happened to align partially with the interests of Washington. For example, the director of the Saudi intelligence service, Kamal Adham, kept Kissinger abreast of the activities of Saudi Arabia and its allies in Angola. According to a report sent to Kissinger in December 1975, Egypt had sent a group of military advisors to Angola to assess the type of support needed, the results of which would be relayed to Iran and Saudi Arabia. The troika would then decide how much aid to send and how it would be delivered. Adham sent a message directly to the shah suggesting that

95 *Ettelāʿāt*, 5 Esfand 1352/ 24 February 1974, 13. 96 Ibid. 97 Ibid., 1.
98 US Embassy in Zaire, 20 May 1974, WikiLeaks Cable 1974KINSHA04356_b.
99 'Ravābet-e Irān bā Keshvar-hā-ye Āfriqā-ye Siyāh', darbār-e shāhanshāhi, markaz-e omur-e farhangi va matbuʿāti, 6, NLAI 264/025388. A formal agreement on economic, technical, scientific and cultural cooperation was finally agreed in September 1978. *Asnād-e Moʿāhedāt-e do Jānebeh-ye Irān bā Sāyer-e Duval*, vol. 6, 689–692.

Figure 6.1 The shah and shahbanu pictured with Zairian president Mobutu and his wife. The headline reads: 'Iran is ready for all types of help to Africa.' *Ettelā'āt*, 5 Esfand 1352/ 24 February 1974, 1.

he 'channel Iranian aid through South Africa, with which the Shah maintains good relations but with which neither Saudi Arabia nor Egypt has any contact'.[100] In response to US offers to deliberate on the ways in which this aid might best be transferred, Adham responded 'definitively that he would rather deal with the problem in direct coordination with Sadat and the Shah'.[101]

[100] US Embassy in Saudi Arabia to Kissinger, 21 December 1975, *FRUS, 1969–1976, Volume XXVIII, Southern Africa*, doc. 162.
[101] Ibid.

In September 1976, a covert intelligence alliance was set up by the heads of the secret services of Egypt, France, Iran, Morocco and Saudi Arabia, called the Safari Club. It is often said that this alliance was conceived by the director of the French Service de Documentation Extérieure et de Contre-Espionnage, Comte Claude Alexandre de Marenches, but Egypt, Iran and Saudi Arabia were already cooperating in Africa before this time.[102] Therefore, it appears as though the group represented the modest formalisation and expansion of intelligence ties that were already in operation. According to a document cited by the journalist Mohamed Heikal, an operational headquarters was set up in Cairo, which would 'evaluate what was going on in Africa, identify the danger spots, and make recommendations for dealing with them'.[103] The historian Farid Boussaid has cautioned that despite the regular communications between members of the club, 'one needs to keep in mind that this alliance was relatively informal in nature and doubt exists in how much it has really functioned as a mechanism through which actions were coordinated'.[104] In practical terms, the Safari Club was probably inconsequential, and in the two major conflicts in which its members were involved – the Shaba crises of 1977 and 1978 and the Ogaden War of 1977–1978 – it is difficult to detect sophisticated coordination.[105] This can be explained partly by the short period of time the alliance was in operation, given the shah's fall in 1979. Notwithstanding its limitations, the Safari Club is evidence that at this time its members recognised waning US influence in Africa, and felt compelled to fill this vacuum to counter the spread of communism.

The Shaba crisis of 1977, which began in March when Congolese rebels crossed into Zaire's Katanga (Shaba) province, and the general

[102] Rachel Bronson, *Thicker than Oil: America's Uneasy Partnership with Saudi Arabia* (Oxford: Oxford University Press, 2006), 132.

[103] Mohamed Heikal, *Iran: The Untold Story: An Insider's Account, from the Rise of the Shah to the Reign of the Ayatollah* (New York: Pantheon, 1982), 113.

[104] Farid Boussaid, 'Brothers in Arms: Morocco's Military Intervention in Support of Mobutu of Zaire during the 1977 and 1978 Shaba Crises', *The International History* Review, vol. 43, no. 1 (2021), 195.

[105] On the Shaba wars, see Piero Gleijeses, 'Truth or Credibility: Castro, Carter, and the Invasions of Shaba', *The International History Review*, vol. 18, no. 1 (1996), 70–103; Miles Larmer, 'Local Conflicts in a Transnational War: The Katangese Gendarmes and the Shaba Wars of 1977–78', *Cold War History*, vol. 13, no. 1 (2013), 89–108; and Boussaid, 'Brothers in Arms'.

Soviet penetration of Africa were viewed with alarm in Tehran. To illustrate this, every day in Farvardin 1356 (March–April 1977), articles appeared in Iran's main daily newspaper *Ettelāʿāt*, closely following developments in Zaire and reporting on the tour of the Chairman of the Presidium of the Supreme Soviet, Nikolai Podgorny, in Africa. One article was headlined 'Africa is becoming Red: What do the Soviets and Cuba want in Africa?' and warned that 'the Red danger severely threatens Black Africa'. It claimed that Nikolai Podgorny and Fidel Castro's tours of Africa, which occurred at around the same time, represented a 'carefully planned diplomatic attack', which ultimately sought to create Socialist regimes across the continent. It is no coincidence, it argued, that at the same time as these tours took place, gendarmes from Angola attacked Katanga in Zaire.[106] Other articles repeated concerns that Africa was the 'scene of a diplomatic attack from the Reds'[107] and warned that Zaire was 'becoming the new Vietnam'.[108] These articles provided justification for the intensification of Iran's involvement in Africa. The ultimate manifestation of this was Iran's support for Somalia in its war against Ethiopia which began later that year, and will be explored in greater detail in Chapter 11.

*****

While in the 1950s and 1960s, the regional security situation shaped the shah's approach to the Global South, by the 1970s, having achieved a position of relative stability in the Middle East, the shah could consider the potential role Iran could play on the global stage. The central aspect of his vision was to establish Iran as the preeminent naval power of the Indian Ocean and to prevent non-Indian Ocean powers from challenging Iran in this endeavour. In the early to mid-1970s, Iran developed a strategy to deal with the increasing Soviet presence in the west Indian Ocean, including East and Southern Africa,

106 *Ettelāʿāt*, 9 Farvardin 1356/ 29 March 1977, 8. This point was made by the Moroccan ambassador to the United States, Abdelhadi Boutaleb, who said in a meeting with secretary of state, Cyrus Vance, that 'Morocco sees Katangan invasion of Zaire developing within framework built by African tours of Soviet President Podgorny and Cuban Premier Castro'. Telegram from the Department of State to the Embassy in Morocco, 17 April 1977, *FRUS, 1977–1980, Volume 17, part 3, North Africa*, doc. 150.

107 *Ettelāʿāt*, 18 Farvardin 1356/ 7 April 1977, 8.

108 *Ettelāʿāt*, 7 Farvardin 1356/ 27 March 1977, 8.

which included building security alliances with its allies, supporting friendly regimes, expanding its diplomatic presence in the region, beefing up its naval presence in the Indian Ocean, and working with the United States on security issues.

In this period, Iran was firmly on the side of the United States in the Cold War – it received military backing from the United States and strove to stop the spread of communism. However, Iran had its own priorities and pursued them with increasing confidence, finding its own path in the Cold War. As revolution and war threatened Iran's grand strategy in the Indian Ocean, the shah took on a bolder, more proactive role in East Africa, committing resources and engaging in diplomacy to tackle these threats. But Iran did not focus only on geographical areas that were vulnerable to Soviet incursions, or areas with which Iran had strong cultural ties; it also developed relations with West Africa.

7 *Iran and West Africa*

Iran's interests and priorities in West Africa were quite different to those in North, East and Southern Africa, for two key reasons. First, Iran had no clear historical ties to West African countries, and second, they were far away, and in contrast to the countries of East and Southern Africa, did not directly impact Iran's Persian Gulf or Indian Ocean policies. But in spite of this, Iran saw many economic opportunities in the region, particularly in the sale of oil and investment in petroleum infrastructure, and they had resources that Iran required, most important of which, in the latter half of the 1970s, was uranium. In addition, many of the countries of West Africa have Muslim-majority populations, so shared Islamic ties could form the basis for political relations. Equally importantly, many countries of West Africa were French-speaking, which appealed to the Francophile predispositions of the Pahlavi political elite.

This chapter explores Iran's interests in West Africa, focusing particularly on two of the most politically and economically important powers in the region, Senegal and Nigeria. Iran's relationships with these two countries were completely different. While Nigeria was viewed primarily as an economic partner, relations with which were a necessity given Nigeria's status as the largest economic power in West Africa and a fellow oil-producing nation, with Senegal Iran developed a particularly friendly relationship. This was due to the skilful diplomacy of Senegal's poet-president, Léopold Sédar Senghor, as well as the investment opportunities Senegal offered. Moreover, Iran desired a close relationship with a country in Black Africa that could help to deflect criticism of its increasingly close ties to South Africa. As the former capital of French Africa, Senegal was an appealing prospect.

Iran and Senegal

Under French colonial rule, Senegal had enjoyed a prominent position due, in part, to its strategic location on the western tip of the African continent – offering the shortest route from Africa to South America, a convenient route from sub-Saharan Africa to Europe and an ideal stopping point for ships travelling around the Cape of Good Hope.[1] Dakar became the capital of French West Africa (*Afrique Occidentale Française*) in the early twentieth century, when, in the words of Sheldon Gellar, it was, 'transformed into an imperial city containing the most advanced administrative and social services in French Black Africa'.[2] As a mark of its importance to the French, Senegal was the only colony in which assimilationist policies were applied. For instance, full French citizenship rights were granted to Africans born in the urban communities of Dakar, Gorée, Rufisque and Saint-Louis.[3] One student to take advantage of this was the future president of independent Senegal, who won a scholarship to attend university in Paris and, when filling in his name and nationality on forms, wrote: 'Léopold Sédar Senghor, French.'[4] Even after Senegal gained independence, first as part of the Mali Federation in June 1960, and then as an independent state two months later, the country remained strongly influenced by French language and culture. Within the community of French-speaking nations, Senegal took a privileged position and President Senghor became a leading proponent of the establishment of a formal federation of French-speaking countries, *la francophonie*.

In the decade following Senegal's independence, France continued to have a strong hold on its economy. Ninety-five per cent of all investment in the country, for example, came from French capital.[5] Furthermore, 80 per cent of all its trade was with France, all peanut exports were bought by France at subsidised rates, France provided two-thirds of Senegal's development capital, as well as technical assistance, and the French treasury covered Senegal's trade deficits.[6] As Mohamed Mbodji has written, 'Senegal's independence in 1960 did not affect a complete separation from France, but rather gave

[1] W. A. E. Skurnik, *The Foreign Policy of Senegal* (Evanston, IL: Northwestern University Press, 1971), 3.

[2] Sheldon Gellar, *Senegal: An African Nation between Islam and the West* (Boulder, CO: Westview Press, 1982), 10.

[3] Ibid., 9.

[4] Janet G. Vaillant, *Black, French, and African: A Life of Léopold Sédar Senghor* (Cambridge, MA: Harvard University Press, 1990), 67.

[5] Catherine Boone, *Merchant Capital and the Roots of State Power in Senegal 1930–1985* (Cambridge: Cambridge University Press, 1992), 113.

[6] Gellar, *Senegal*, 51.

way to the continuation or even the reinforcement of the 300-year-old political and economic relationship.'[7] Under the colonial regime, peanut farming and exports had been such an important sector for the colony's economy that by 1966, the peanut sector still accounted for 80 per cent of employment.[8] Through the 1960s, Senegal's non-agricultural exports became more significant, for example fish products, phosphates, fertilisers and petroleum products (it had established an oil refinery, the Société africaine de raffinage, in 1961).[9] However, peanut products still counted for more than 50 per cent of exports, and the knock-on effects of occasional poor yields, caused for example by reduced rainfall, meant that economic growth fluctuated. When France eventually decided to end subsidies on peanuts and to henceforth purchase peanuts at global market prices, the consequences were dire for the already struggling Senegalese farmers.[10] Not just investment, therefore, but also some diversification of the economy was necessary for Senegal's economic development, and Senegal began to look further afield for partners to support both goals.

Ardeshir Zāhedi recalled in his memoir that at the time he became foreign minister in 1966, the shah was considering establishing one Iranian embassy in West Africa, and that he had promised Ivory Coast it would be located in Abidjan. However, Zāhedi had spoken to the Senegalese foreign minister, Amadou Karim Gaye, during preparations for the Islamic Conference in 1969, and the two had met again at the Second Islamic Conference of Foreign Ministers held in Karachi in December 1970.[11] As a result of these exchanges, according to a French report, 'despite everything that separates them, strong bonds of friendship were established between the two men'.[12] Zāhedi thus

[7] Mohamed Mbodji, 'The Politics of Independence: 1960–1986', in *The Political Economy of Senegal under Structural Adjustment*, ed. Christopher L. Delgado and Sidi Jammeh (New York: Praeger, 1991), 119.

[8] Ibid., 120.

[9] François Boye, 'A Retrospective Analysis of the Senegalese Economy', The Center for Economic Research on Africa, Montclair State University (1990), 5.

[10] Philippe Bonnefond and Philippe Couty, 'Agricultural Crisis: Past and Future', in *The Political Economy of Senegal under Structural Adjustment*, ed. Christopher L. Delgado and Sidi Jammeh (New York: Praeger, 1991), 38.

[11] Zāhedi, *Khāterāt*, vol. 3, 168.

[12] Jean Meadmore, French embassy, Dakar, to Maurice Schumann, Head of African Affairs at the French Foreign Ministry, 8 June 1971, CADN 1840PO/1/531.

asked the shah to reconsider Ivory Coast as the location of Iran's first embassy in West Africa.

For me, from a political perspective and in terms of budget, this [Ivory Coast] was not a priority. Senegal was a more important country. It cooperated with us on international issues, particularly the holding of the Islamic Conference, and was of greater importance from a cultural, religious and economic perspective.[13]

According to Zāhedi, the shah was convinced by his arguments and decided to focus on nurturing links with Senegal instead.

Shortly after this decision had been taken, Zāhedi travelled to Dakar for talks with his counterpart, Amadou Karim Gaye, President Senghor and Prime Minister Abdou Diouf, during which, as well as discussing cooperation on security in the Middle East, preliminary discussions were held on the potential for establishing comprehensive economic ties.[14] Zāhedi's visit to Dakar was the first stop on a three-nation trip, which also included Nigeria and Kenya. According to a French diplomatic report, the fact that Senegal had been chosen as the first capital that Iran's foreign minister visited

brought President Senghor and the Senegalese leaders the satisfaction of prestige; satisfaction that is all the greater since, according to the information collected here, it is to two English-speaking countries, Nigeria and Kenya, that Mr Ardeshir Zahedi will then go. Senegal is thus assigned a preeminent role among the French-speaking states.[15]

Indeed, Dakar did come to occupy a special place in the eyes of Iranian policymakers at this time. *Ettelā'āt* reported at this time that 'Iran has identified Dakar as its first base for large-scale efforts and constructive cooperation in Sub-Saharan Africa.'[16]

Senegal's former prominent position in the French Empire marked it as an appealing prospect symbolically for Iran, and its location en route from sub-Saharan Africa to both Europe and the Americas, would be strategically important for extending Iran's global reach. Senegal was also a country possessing, in the words of Peter J. Schraeder, 'a profoundly nationalist spirit', largely because of the

[13] Zāhedi, *Khāterāt*, vol. 3, 207.
[14] *Ettelā'āt*, 11 Khordād 1350/ 1 June 1971, 21.
[15] Meadmore to Schumann, 8 June 1971, CADN 1840PO/1/531.
[16] *Ettelā'āt*, 11 Khordād 1350/ 1 June 1971, 21.

position it had held in the French Empire.[17] Senegal's historical status as a regional power formed the basis of its claims to regional authority, a position comparable to that of Iran. In addition to strategic considerations, from the very beginning, personal relationships played an important role in the development of this bilateral relationship. In his memoir, Zāhedi referred to Senghor as an 'exceptional character', with whom he developed a 'very friendly and trusting relationship', and recalled that his trip in 1971 'marked the beginning of a lasting friendship between the two countries, as well as between the President and His Majesty'.[18]

Zāhedi's trip ended with the official announcement of the decision taken by both countries to establish full diplomatic relations, with residence of ambassadors in Dakar and Tehran. Iran's first ambassador was Morteẓā ʿAdl Tabātabāʾi, who presented his credentials to President Senghor on 30 September 1971.[19] In a relatively brief message, Tabātabāʾi conveyed to the president the shah's 'strong desire to see amicable relations between our two countries develop further'.[20] Senghor was more exuberant in his response: 'You are, I believe', he said, 'the first [Iranian] ambassador to be accredited in a francophone country in this part of the continent. But for us, His Imperial Majesty, the Shahinshah Aryamehr, is not a stranger, nor your country a terra ignota.' Senghor stressed his admiration for the efforts of the shah in modernising Iran, and his respect for Ancient Persia, particularly Cyrus the Great, whose exploits Senghor had read about during his university studies. 'What struck me then, as the young humanist that I tried to be', he said, 'was the new spirit that Cyrus the Great introduced to Asia'. This new spirit meant 'putting man above all else' and respecting the 'freedom of their political and philosophical opinions, as well as their

[17] Peter J. Schraeder, 'Senegal's Foreign Policy: Challenges of Democratization and Marginalization', *African Affairs*, vol. 96 (1997), 485–508.

[18] Zāhedi, *Khāterāt*, vol. 3, 211–212.

[19] Hubert Argod, French ambassador to Senegal, to Maurice Schumann, 29 December 1972, CADN 1840PO/1/531. Senegal's first ambassador to Iran, Massamba Sarre, was appointed several months later, in June 1972. Sarre was resident in Tehran, but was also accredited in Pakistan and Turkey. He had previously been Senegal's ambassador to Morocco.

[20] 'Presentation des lettres de creance de Son Excellence Monsieur Monteza[sic] Adl Tabatabai, Ambassadeur impérial d'Iran', 30 September 1971, CADN 1840PO/1/531.

روزنامه

جشن شاهنشاهی ایران

شماره هشتادو نهم ـ شنبه پانزدهم آبان‌ماه ۱۳۵۰

ایران گهواره تمدن قرون و کانون زنده افکار
بشردوستانه معاصر است

سدار سنگور رئیس جمهوری سنگال

Figure 7.1 A section of Senghor's farewell letter printed on the front page of the official daily newspaper of the imperial celebrations, which reads: 'Iran is the cradle of centuries of civilisation and a living centre of contemporary humanitarian thought.' *Ruznāmeh-ye Jashn-e Shāhanshāhi-ye Irān*, 15 Ābān 1350/ 6 November 1971, 1.

moral and religious ideas'.[21] Senghor congratulated the shah and his people for celebrating Cyrus the Great and for their 'intent to proclaim, in front of the world, their fidelity to the spirit of Cyrus'. Senghor clearly had one eye on Persepolis, for he had been invited to attend these celebrations which began less than two weeks later.

Senghor's visit to attend the celebrations was his first trip to Iran and was important not only in deepening the relationship between the two rulers, but in shaping Senghor's approach to the Pahlavi regime. As a poet, Senghor understood the power of words, and the effectiveness of using the right language to communicate with leaders such as the shah, who wielded near total control over his country's foreign policy. Senghor articulated an affinity and respect for Iran and the ideology expressed through the celebrations during a farewell message to the shah (Figure 7.1). In it, Senghor wrote,

If Iran has been able to show the world the glorious reflection of its destiny, it is because of its attachment to the values that have always made it great.

[21] 'Reponse de Monsieur le President de la Republique', ibid.

Today to the foreign visitor Iran also represents a civilisation that is admired all over the world. Iran is the cradle of this civilisation that has flourished over the centuries, and also, as a living centre of contemporary humanitarian thought, will nurture its spiritual values and a means to strengthen unity and as the essence of its progress.[22]

Senghor also praised the shah and his father, Reza Shah, for their role in 'transforming the face of contemporary Iran' and for their 'unparalleled courage' in striving to achieve economic, social and cultural progress.

Senghor then wrote about the bilateral relationship between Iran and Senegal, and stressed the significant role that Iran played at the United Nations, which 'will undoubtedly help contribute to a close affinity with Africa, in particular Senegal'. Senghor referenced a private meeting he had held with the shah during the imperial celebrations, which had convinced him of the importance of developing close ties with Iran. He wrote, 'I am convinced that the diplomatic relations that have been established between our two countries will open the prospects for joyful and fruitful cooperation based on a shared consensus on the issues of the current world, and our diplomacy will be a source of happiness for our nation.' The message ended with Senghor imploring the shah 'to accept my greatest respect'.[23] Senghor's eloquent endorsement of the shah had the desired effect, as over the following months and years Iran pledged large amounts of money to development projects in Senegal, and economic cooperation between the two sides developed significantly.

Iran–Senegal Cooperation in the 1970s

On 9 July 1972, not long after the establishment of relations between the two countries and Senghor's successful visit to Iran during the 1971 imperial celebrations, a team of experts from Iran visited Senegal 'to develop commercial cooperation between Iran and Senegal'. Upon their return to Iran, this team of experts submitted a report detailing the projects that Iranian financial aid would support, including rice and forest cultivation projects, rural expansion, and

22 *Ruznāmeh-ye Jashn-e Shāhanshāhi-ye Irān*, 15 Ābān 1350/ 6 November 1971, 3.
23 Ibid.

initiatives to generate water supply to pastures.[24] These types of projects were examined in greater depth over the following months, and exchanges of technical experts continued. On 18 July 1973, Iran signed an agreement to provide Senegal with loans of over $2.4 million for two development projects – to provide drinking water in rural areas and develop an audio-visual educational programme.[25] In the years after, economic relations between the two countries intensified and even greater sums were pledged following several high-level visits between the political elite of the two countries.

The shah had planned to undertake a tour of Senegal and Kenya early 1974. The trip had been announced, but just a few weeks before the shah was due to embark, it was 'postponed'.[26] In the weeks leading up to visit, there were major security concerns. Asadollāh ʿAlam had spoken to officials in Senegal in December 1973 to seek assurances that the Senegalese security services would be able to protect the shah throughout his stay. ʿAlam explained that the shah had suffered many attempts on his life and had to be provided with high-level protection. ʿAlam was not reassured by the response. He wrote in his diary, 'I am extremely worried' (*man bi andāzeh negarān hastam*).[27] To assuage these concerns, the Iranians requested that Senegal approach the French police to handle the shah's security arrangements.[28] Senghor appeared relieved not to have to take on this responsibility, and 'much preferred that the maximum precautions be taken during his [the shah's] visit to Dakar'.[29]

Although security was a genuine concern, the real reasons for postponing the trip were political. The Iranian ambassador in Kenya claimed that the shah was unwilling to be away from his capital at a time in which Iran was preparing for important negotiations on the oil

24 'Gozāresh-e Vazʿ-e Hamkāri-ye Eqtesādi-ye Dowlat-e Shāhanshāhi-ye Irān bā Jomhuri-ye Senegāl', Sāzmān-e Barnāmeh va Budjeh, 29 Bahman 1954/ 18 February 1976, NLAI 220/4571.

25 Ambassador P. A. E. Renardel de Lavalette to His Excellency the Minister without Portfolio charged with Development Cooperation, 24 July 1973, NA 2.05.191/239.

26 Richard Helms telegram, 28 January 1974, WikiLeaks cable 1974TEHRAN00718_b.

27 ʿAlam, diary entry 14 Āzar 1352/ 5 December 1973, *Yāddāsht-hā-ye ʿAlam*, vol. 3, 281.

28 Xavier de la Chavalerle to Phillippe Rebeyrol, 9 January 1974, CADN 180PO/1/ 531.

29 Ibid.

crisis.[30] Another issue was the Islamic Conference in Lahore, to which the shah had been invited, but which he did not wish to attend. Had the shah given an excuse not to attend the Lahore Conference, but then embarked on a foreign visit at around the same time, this could have offended (further) the host of the conference, the prime minister of Pakistan, Zulfikar Ali Bhutto. Officials in Iran said that although the shah's calendar would allow him to maintain the trip to Senegal, but not to Kenya, the shah 'did not want to appear to discriminate against this single country and preferred to cancel his two trips to Africa'.[31] The decision to cancel this trip was not taken lightly, but it was perhaps made a little easier by Iran's concerns over the security situation, particularly in Senegal.

Iran was eager to 'make it clear that this postponement should not be interpreted as a discourteous gesture towards President Senghor', so had offered to send Empress Farah to visit alone, but 'by mutual agreement' it was decided that it was preferable to postpone the royal visit until a later date, when the shah could come too. An official visit to Senegal (though not Kenya) still took place on the planned dates, but Prime Minister Hoveydā was sent 'in lieu of ... the shah'.[32] According to a report from the US ambassador in Dakar, '[the] Iranians pulled out all [the] stops to make their visit exceptional'.[33] They set up a photography exhibition on the evolution of Iran, organised in Dakar by the Iranian Ministry of Information and installed by Iranian technicians in the Dakar Chamber of Commerce, which was intended as an introduction to Iran for the people of Senegal.[34] They also threw a 'lavish, large reception' for the Senegalese political elite.

According to the US ambassador, '[the] Senegalese too did their best to put on [an] impressive show, according Hoveyda [the] attention normally only reserved for [the] chief of state'.[35] The president and prime minister each held banquets in honour of their Iranian guest, and during a meeting with President Senghor, Hoveydā was awarded Senegal's highest honour. When Hoveydā was not attending receptions or accompanying his hosts to visit cultural sites and development

[30] Anthony D. Marshall telegram, 29 January 1974, WikiLeaks Cable 1974NAIROB00794_b.

[31] Report du Voyage du Chah au Senegal, 28 January 1974, CADN 180PO/1/531.

[32] Aggrey telegram, 13 February 1974, WikiLeaks Cable 1974DAKAR00771_b.

[33] Ibid. [34] *Ettelā'āt*, 21 Bahman 1352/ 10 February 1974, 16.

[35] Aggrey telegram, 13 February 1974, WikiLeaks Cable 1974DAKAR00771_b.

projects, he was engaged in discussions with his counterpart, Abdou Diouf. During these meetings, which, according to the Tehran press, 'took place in an atmosphere of cordiality and prefect comprehension', Hoveydā and Diouf 'found a wide agreement of views on all the problems discussed'.[36] These various issues of common understanding, including the Arab–Israeli conflict, the 'sovereign right of each state to freely dispose of its national resources', a condemnation of racial discrimination and colonialism, and a commitment to the principles of the UN Charter, were outlined in a joint communique.[37]

The visit was said by *Ettelā'āt* to come at a time when 'Iran's increasing economic power, and its ability to support the economic development of African countries has increased, [therefore] Iran's assistance can be provided through joint agricultural and cultural projects'.[38] To this end, Hoveydā expressed Iran's readiness to participate in Senegalese development projects, and an agreement establishing a framework for cultural, scientific and technical cooperation was signed by both prime ministers.[39] During the visit, a total of eleven projects were discussed, including Iranian cooperation in the construction of an oil refinery.[40] Shortly after, a Senegalese delegation headed by the minister of industrial development, Louis Alexandre, travelled to Tehran to explore these projects in greater detail with the Iranian government, and subsequently, 'Abdol-Majid Majidi, the head of the Plan Organisation, travelled to Senegal as head of an Iranian delegation of technicians to look into the projects, in particular the prospective oil refinery.[41]

At the end of his 1974 trip, Hoveydā had invited Diouf to pay a return visit to Iran. This trip took place just a few months later, from 6 to 12 July 1974. Travelling with Diouf on this occasion were the minister of higher education, the minister of industry and development, and a team of ten Senegalese technicians. Diouf was afforded a warm welcome on his visit and was presented with a medal by Court

[36] *Le Journal de Téhéran*, 12 February 1974, 1.
[37] 'Communique conjoint Irano-Senegalais', 11 February 1974, NA 2.05.191/432.
[38] *Ettelā'āt*, 20 Bahman 1352/9 February 1974, 4.
[39] 'Accord de coopération culturelle, scientifique et technique entre le gouvernement Impérial de l'Iran et le gouvernement de la République du Sénégal', 11 February 1974, NA 2.05.191/239.
[40] *Kayhan International*, 16 February 1974, 3.
[41] *Ettelā'āt*, 15 Tir 1353/ 6 July 1974, 20.

Minister ʿAlam, reciprocating the award received by Hoveydā.[42] The director of African affairs in Iran's Ministry of Foreign Affairs, ʿAli Akbar Shahbāzi, said that the visit went 'like clockwork' because most of the details of the agreements had been worked out earlier so 'Diouf's trip was merely to sign'.[43] During this visit, Iran and Senegal signed several deals. Iran pledged a further $8.5 million for projects in Senegal, including $4 million towards the Delta dam, $1.5 million towards irrigation and $3 million towards the creation of a free industrial zone (*Zone Franche Industrielle*) in Dakar.[44]

An agreement on tourism cooperation was also signed at the same time by the Iranian minister for information and tourism, Gholāmrezā Kiyānpur, and Senegal's ambassador in Tehran, Massamba Sarre. The deal stated that, 'considering the importance of tourism for their two countries both in terms of the economy and as a factor in the understanding between the peoples', they would take measures 'with a view to promoting and intensifying the exchange of tourists between their countries and to encourage visits by tourists from third countries'. The two sides agreed to meet regularly to discuss how they could ensure the most 'effective exploitation of its potential'.[45] Iran focused much attention on developing its tourism sector during the 1960s and especially the 1970s, and signed many similar cooperation agreements with allies to, for example, abolish visas and ensure mutual technical assistance.[46] Diouf said to the press that he hoped Iran could assist in the construction of hotels and the training of hospitality staff.[47]

Most importantly, a protocol agreement was signed concerning a $400 million joint venture to create an industrial complex comprising an oil refinery and petrochemical facilities, as well as to exploit and develop of Senegal's phosphate reserves.[48] Curiously, this deal did not

[42] *Ettelāʿāt*, 18 Tir 1353/ 9 July 1974, 20.

[43] Helms telegram, 18 July 1974, WikiLeaks Cable 1974TEHRAN05923_b.

[44] *Ettelāʿāt*, 19 Tir 1353/ 10 July 1974, 17. This industrial free trade zone was designed to attract export-oriented assembly firms to Senegal. See Boone, *Merchant Capital and the Roots of State Power*, 175.

[45] 'Accord de coopération touristique entre le gouvernement Imperial de l'Iran et le gouvernement de la République du Sénégal', 9 July 1974, NA 2.05.191/239.

[46] On this subject, see Robert Steele, 'Iran's Golden Age of Tourism: The Development of the Travel Industry in the Late Pahlavi Period (c. 1960–1979)', *Journal of Tourism History*, vol. 14, no. 3 (2022), 256–257.

[47] *Kayhan International*, 13 July 1974, 3.

[48] Ambassador P. A. E. Renardel de Lavalette to minister of foreign affairs, 24 July 1974, NA 2.05.191/239.

receive as much attention in the Iranian press as other similar deals struck with France, Germany and Italy, among many others. When asked by the US ambassador why this was the case, a deputy at the Iranian Ministry of Foreign Affairs responded that 'four or five other African governments had wanted Iranian help in building refineries and petrochemical plants, but GOI [Government of Iran] had decided to concentrate its efforts in one country and did not want to offend others by rubbing it in'.[49] Senegal was chosen partly because it was one of the first to request Iran's assistance, but chiefly because Iran had already identified it as a country with which it wished to develop a close partnership.

On the final day of the July 1974 visit, Hoveydā and Diouf issued a joint communique, in which, in addition to stressing their desire to strengthen economic and cultural relations, they made some comments on regional security. Iran pledged its support for the liberation of African countries, while Senegal agreed that the security of the Persian Gulf should be managed solely by Gulf countries. They also jointly stressed the importance of maintaining peace and stability in the Indian Ocean and, given its importance for global trade, avoiding big power competition there.[50] Signalling his understanding of Iran's desire to expand its influence internationally, Diouf said, 'Not only will I be the goodwill ambassador of Iran in my country, but I will also be the goodwill ambassador of the *Shāhanshāh Āryāmehr* everywhere I am.'[51]

It would be no exaggeration to say that between 1971 until 1974, all of Iran's efforts in West Africa were focused on Senegal. Iran was comparatively slow to establish diplomatic relations with the other major economic powers in the region – for example, Nigeria in 1973, Ghana in 1974 and Ivory Coast in 1975 – and few additional embassies were established. Iran's ambassador to Ivory Coast, for instance, was based in Dakar, while the ambassador resident in Lagos was accredited also to Ghana, Niger and Sierra Leone, and also dealt with issues in smaller countries in which Iran had no official representation. Even towards the end of the 1970s, when deals were signed between Iran and other countries in West Africa, Senegal

49 Helms telegram, 18 July 1974, WikiLeaks Cable 1974TEHRAN05923_b.
50 *Ettelā'āt*, 22 Tir 1353/ 13 July 1974, 16.
51 *Ettelā'āt*, 18 Tir 1353/ 9 July 1974, 40.

remained a special case. The development of this special relationship in the last half of the 1970s will be explored in greater detail in Chapter 9.

Iran and Nigeria

Shortly after Nigeria had achieved independence from Great Britain in October 1960, there had been some attempts to establish relations with Iran. As discussed in Chapter 3, the prime ministers of Northern and Eastern Nigeria travelled to Iran in early summer 1961 to initiate a dialogue and to explore what each side could gain from cooperation. In 1963, Nigeria became a republic, replacing the British monarch with a Nigerian president as the head of state. In the spring of 1964, Hushang Ansāri's goodwill delegation visited Nigeria, and in the years that followed, the value of Iranian oil products exported to Nigeria saw a more than twenty-fold increase.[52] In January 1966, a military coup took place in Nigeria. Several senior politicians were murdered, including the federal prime minister, Tafawa Balewa, and the prime minister of the Western Region, Ahmadu Bello, who had travelled to Iran in 1961.[53] Nigeria was then plunged into civil war in May 1967, when the military governor of the Eastern Region, Lieutenant Colonel Ojukwu, declared the independence of the Eastern Region and renamed it the Republic of Biafra.[54] This devastating war ended two and a half years later, in January 1970, having left between one and three million people dead.[55]

Although the civil war had prevented Iran and Nigeria from developing close political relations during this period, each side of the civil war sought both Iran's support and assurances that it would not support the other side. In March 1967, before the civil war began, Ojukwu sent a long letter to Hoveydā, giving his perspective on the situation. A military blockade on Eastern Nigeria imposed by the central government 'can only be effective if it received the assistance of foreign governments ... I have no doubt that I can count on your

[52] The total value of Iranian oil products exported to Nigeria increased from $125,000 in 1343 (1964/65) to: $457,000 in 1344 (1965/66); $1.9 million in 1345 (1966/67); reaching $2.9 million in 1347 (1968/69). 'Vazʿ-e Mobādelāt-e Bāzargāni-ye Irān bā Keshvar-e Nijeriyeh', Vezārat-e Eqtesād, 1969[?], NLAI 245/004425.

[53] Falola and Heaton, *A History of Nigeria*, 172.

[54] Ibid., 174–175.

[55] Ibid., 180.

country's sympathy and understanding in our struggle for security and freedom'.[56] His next letter came on 30 May 1967, the day Ojukwu had announced the independence of Biafra. In the letter, he summarised the situation, outlined the prospects for co-operation between Iran and the newly independent nation, and looked 'forward to the development of mutual and beneficial relations between our two governments and peoples'.[57] Two weeks later, a letter arrived from the head of the Federal Military Government, Major-General Yakubu Gowon, informing Hoveydā that the breakaway state was 'illegal and unconstitutional' and 'should be recognised by all friends of Nigeria as an act of rebellion'. Gowon warned Hoveydā that 'any attempt at recognition of the rebellious group as a sovereign state will be regarded as an unfriendly act' and advised him against taking 'such [an] ill-advised step'.[58] Hoveydā responded that he was 'deeply grieved' by the situation in Nigeria and urged Gowon to bring a peaceful resolution to the conflict, so that 'construction and development might replace destruction and ruin'.[59]

As Nigeria emerged from the civil war, which ended in 1970 with the defeat of the breakaway Biafra state, oil came to have a more significant role in Nigeria's economy. Prior to the civil war, agriculture had accounted for 80 per cent of Nigeria's exports by value, but by the mid-1970s, oil accounted for over 90 per cent of its exports.[60] Nigeria joined OPEC in 1971 and thus, as a fellow member state with an economy based on petroleum, it provided many opportunities for cooperation in the oil sector. Nigeria was one of the most outspoken critics of South Africa's apartheid system in the whole of Africa, and because of its size – it was home to around 25 per cent of the total population of Africa – and increasing economic muscle, sought to play an important role in bringing an end to minority rule in Southern Africa.[61] Moreover, the oil price hikes of 1971 and 1973 had provided

[56] Odumegwu Ojukwu to Hoveydā, 16 March 1967, NLAI 230/031218.
[57] Ojukwu to Hoveydā, 30 May 1967, NLAI 230/031218.
[58] Major General Yakubu Gowon to Hoveydā, 14 June 1967, NLAI 230/031218.
[59] Hoveydā to Gowon, 11 October 1967, NLAI 230/031218.
[60] Paul Lubeck, 'Nigeria: A Political Economy', *Africa Today*, vol. 24, no. 4 (1977), 6.
[61] See Nicholas J. Spiliotes, 'Nigerian Foreign Policy and Southern Africa: A Choice for the West', *Issue: A Journal of Opinion*, vol. 11, no. 1/2 (1981), 41–45.

the Nigerian state with vast revenue increases, which presented opportunities to diversify the economy. This in turn provided states like Iran with good openings to cooperate in oil, industrial and agricultural development projects, but also to gain influence with an emerging, ambitious regional power – not too dissimilar to itself.

Iran began to cooperate with Nigeria on development projects in the early 1970s. On 28 February 1973, the Ministry of Agriculture and Natural Resources announced that, following a request from the Nigerian government, it would cooperate with Nigeria in the field of sheep breeding and livestock research. In October 1974, the manager of the water and power organisation of Azerbaijan travelled to Nigeria to visit its irrigation networks, and in November, a delegation headed by Nigeria's minister of agriculture visited Iran to negotiate with Iranian authorities. The following month, on 8 December 1974, Nigeria's first ambassador to Iran arrived in Tehran, and in April 1975, Shāhrokh Firuz was appointed Iran's first ambassador to Nigeria.[62] Nigeria's ambassador to Iran, George T. Kurubo (Figure 7.2), was an experienced diplomat, who had previously served as Nigeria's ambassador to the Soviet Union, but Shāhrokh Firuz, who had no previous diplomatic experience, was a curious choice to head the Iranian embassy. So, why was he chosen for this position?

Shāhrokh Firuz and the Iranian Embassy in Lagos

Shāhrokh Firuz was the son of Firuz Nosrat al-Dowleh III, who was the eldest son of ʿAbdolhoseyn Mirzā Farmān Farmā and the grandson on his maternal side of the Qajar shah Mozaffar al-Din (r. 1896–1907). During the 1960s and 1970s, Firuz was a private citizen and did not have any political position, but because of his family and influence, he would often be invited to embassies around the world during his travels.[63] As Firuz narrates in his memoir, one day, he went horse riding with the former British ambassador, Denis Wright, in the Nowruz-Ābād equestrian centre in Tehran, owned by his cousin Narsy

[62] 'Ravābet-e Irān bā Keshvar-hā-ye Āfriqā-ye Siyāh', darbār-e shāhanshāhi, markaz-e omur-e farhangi va matbuʿāti, 22–23, NLAI 264/025388; *Kayhan International*, 27 April 1974.

[63] Shāhrokh Firuz, *Zir-e Sāyeh-ye Alborz* (Washington, DC: Mage Publishers, 2011), 745.

Figure 7.2 Nigeria's first ambassador to Iran, George T. Kurubo, presenting his credentials to the shah at Niyāvarān Palace, 7 Dey 1353. This image was printed on the front page of *Ettelā'āt*, 8 Dey 1353/ 29 December 1974, 1.

Firuz.[64] While riding, the two spoke primarily about horses.[65] A few days later, Firuz was visited by a SAVAK agent, who asked him to explain the nature of his conversation with the former British ambassador.

Shortly after, Asadollāh ʿAlam summoned Firuz to a meeting. Firuz believed that the shah had been informed of his meeting with Wright by the head of the special office of the imperial inspectorate, Hoseyn Fardust.[66] Firuz implicitly trusted ʿAlam, and spoke candidly about his feelings about the political situation in Iran. He told ʿAlam that he felt the government had become too separated from the people, and that while the shah in Iran had historically served also as the head of the Shia faith, the Pahlavi monarchy appeared to have lost that characteristic.[67] Firuz was also asked to explain the nature of his visits outside of Iran. At the end of the meeting, ʿAlam told him that he had been appointed Iran's ambassador to Nigeria. 'The ambassador is in reality the representative of the king', ʿAlam said, 'so you should be very proud of this!'[68] When Firuz told him that he needed to discuss the issue with his wife first, ʿAlam responded, 'I am waiting for your positive response.'[69] Firuz ultimately accepted the appointment. Indeed, he felt that it was an order rather than a request, and in his memoir implied that he had been sent out of the country because he was viewed as a potential trouble causer.[70]

Firuz's early months in Nigeria were spent establishing his mission and finding a suitable embassy and accommodation – he lived for a while on the top floor of the Federal Palace Hotel, which was normally

[64] Ibid., 747.
[65] Firuz offered Wright his curious theory that the Arab Horse was descended from the Persian Horse, because according to him, when the Arabs invaded Iran, they rode on camels, not horses.
[66] Ibid., 748. [67] Ibid., 745. [68] Ibid., 748. [69] Ibid.
[70] His elder brother, Mozaffar Firuz, lived in exile and was a self-proclaimed enemy of the Pahlavi regime. In 1971, as the shah was preparing to celebrate the 2,500th anniversary of the Persian Empire, Firuz published an attack on the shah and the historical narrative the celebrations promoted, in his *L'Iran face à l'imposture de l'histoire*. According to the historian Cyrus Ghani, he was known to desire the fall of the Pahlavi dynasty. See Cyrus Ghani, *Iran and the West: A Critical Bibliography* (London: Kegan Paul International, 1987), 131–132. Of course, we cannot discount the possibility that Firuz's account of his nomination is incorrect, and that (as one anonymous diplomat from the era told me) he instead actively sought out such an appointment, using his wealth and connections as leverage.

reserved for visiting heads of state.[71] But the setting up of his mission coincided with the revolution in Ethiopia, which saw the dethronement of the shah's friend Haile Selassie. As shown in Chapter 6, the shah's response to these events was relatively muted, as Iran followed the restraint shown by the United States. However, the Nigerians apparently received some intelligence that Iran had set in motion a plan to rescue Haile Selassie.[72] Firuz was informed by the Nigerian Foreign Ministry that as a result of the shah's interference, the Iranian ambassador had been declared a persona non grata, and that he had just twenty-four hours to leave the country. Firuz recalled that he held a meeting with the president, Murtala Ramat Muhammed, who informed him, quite apologetically, that the OAU was unequivocal in its demand that foreign states should not interfere in African affairs. As a result, his hands were tied; Firuz must leave. Firuz sent frantic cables to the Iranian Ministry of Foreign Affairs to ask them what he should do, but he received no response. Eventually, after Firuz had booked a ticket to Switzerland and was ready to leave, he received word from Nigeria that the situation had been resolved and he could stay.[73] Notwithstanding potential inconsistencies in Firuz's account, it does demonstrate that although Iran was a potential economic partner to Nigeria, the latter was fully prepared to break these relations in the service of African unity. Iran was a rich ally, but it still had to navigate African politics with some diplomacy.

Unsurprisingly, Iran's relationship with South Africa caused some difficulties in its relations with Nigeria, particularly as Nigeria emerged as one of Africa's most powerful and vociferous critics of apartheid. At a UN Security Council meeting on 25 March 1977, stressing Nigeria's hard-line approach to those states who continued to trade with South Africa, its foreign minister, Brigadier Joseph Garba, said: 'Some countries are reluctant to act because of their investments in South Africa. But they also have investments in black Africa.

[71] Firuz, *Zir-e Sāyeh-ye Alborz*, 752.

[72] It is unclear to what Firuz is referring here. Haile Selassie had been arrested in September 1974 and was murdered on 27 August 1975. General Murtala Mohammed, who informed Firuz that he must leave, was president of Nigeria from 29 July 1975 until 13 February 1976. It is possible that Firuz remembered incorrectly and the president was actually Murtala Mohammed's predecessor Yakubu Gowon. Either way, it appears that Nigeria's response was perhaps a knee-jerk reaction to faulty intelligence, or press reports in Iran.

[73] Firuz, *Zir-e Sāyeh-ye Alborz*, 761–766.

We would not hesitate to take retaliatory economic action, if necessary.'[74] Given this stance, Nigeria's growing ties with the Iranians, whose close ties with South Africa were a very open secret, must have caused some internal tensions. At a United Nations meeting in New York in October 1974, just months after Firuz had arrived in Lagos as Iran's ambassador, the Nigerian permanent representative and chairman of the Special Commission Regarding Apartheid, Edwin Ogebe Ogbu, reproached Iran for its 'growing trade relations' with the apartheid regime.[75]

One of the problems Firuz faced, particularly in the first two years of his appointment, was that he believed his embassy was not considered particularly important by policymakers in Tehran. In his memoir, Firuz notes that during the 1970s, there was competition between the various foreign embassies in Lagos, particularly those of Western European countries, to set up radio broadcasts in their own languages, and report on news and events in their home countries.[76] On one occasion during a visit to Tehran, Firuz was invited for lunch by the foreign minister, ʿAbbās ʿAli Khalʿatbari, along with the head of Iranian National Television and Radio and Empress Farah's cousin, Rezā Qotbi. During the lunch, Firuz suggested to Qotbi that Iran also broadcast in West Africa for the Iranian population living there. This could be very useful, he argued, and would be relatively cheap because the infrastructure already existed in Lagos. Qotbi responded in 'a rude and sarcastic manner':

> How many listeners do you think you have in Africa?! We have to adapt to the modern advanced countries, so as not to lag behind them. Do you think West Africa is very important for Iran?! Maybe you are attaching importance to this issue in order to inflate your own position and post![77]

Firuz did not take kindly to Qotbi's retort, and after a vicious exchange of words, Qotbi stormed out of the lunch.

Firuz was a proud man, who had an almost quixotic aspect to his character, and he perceived the lack of interest in his initiatives as personal slights. Even the US ambassador in Tehran, Richard Helms, who was well acquainted with Firuz, commented that he was 'well

[74] *Anti-Apartheid News*, May 1977, 4.
[75] Dutch permanent representative to the United Nations, New York, to Dutch Ministry of Foreign Affairs, 7 Oct 1974, NA 2.05.191/451.
[76] Firuz, *Zir-e Sāyeh-ye Alborz*, 777. [77] Ibid., 778.

known for his easily damaged dignity'.[78] For example, in September 1975, Firuz was summoned to Libreville by President Bongo to present his credentials as Iran's non-resident ambassador to Gabon. This visit coincided with that of the shah's half-brother, Prince Gholāmrezā.[79] However, after four days, Firuz left, frustrated that no one, not even the foreign minister, had asked to see him. Firuz was immediately asked to return and was finally able to hand copies of his credentials to the foreign minister, but he was unable to secure a meeting to present the originals to Bongo in person. In response, Firuz refused to attend the dinner Bongo held for the visiting prince, and returned to Lagos 'very upset about [the] treatment accorded him', 'with credentials still in hand' and a vow 'that he will not come again to Libreville without [a] firm appointment for credentials ceremony'.[80] President Bongo was due to arrive in Tehran just weeks later, so from Lagos, Firuz reported his ill-treatment to his superiors in the hope it would 'induce GOI to dampen [the] reception planned for Bongo in Iran'. Firuz never forgot Bongo's snub. Over two years later, in January 1978, in conversation with the US ambassador to Nigeria, Firuz referred to Bongo contemptuously as 'Gigolo' in response to the criticism of the OAU, of which Bongo was at the time president, of the shah's pronouncements on the war between Ethiopia and Somalia.[81]

The exact details and wording of his disagreement with Qotbi might have been embellished by Firuz, who was prone to exaggeration, or remembered inaccurately, not least because he wrote about the event in his memoirs some forty years later. However, other evidence attests to the difficulties Firuz faced in convincing authorities in Iran of the importance of West Africa. Firuz was energetic, full of ideas and eager to make his mark, but his ambition was matched neither by the Ministry of Foreign Affairs nor the shah himself. Firuz was also particularly unfortunate that his arrival in Lagos coincided with the

78 Helms telegram, 29 September 1975, WikiLeaks Cable 1975TEHRAN09543_b.

79 See Chapter 8.

80 Steigman telegram, 26 September 1975, WikiLeaks Cable 1975LIBREV01545_b. According to US reports: 'Firuz initially fell victim to Gabonese bureaucratic fumbling, with fonmin [sic] evidently uninformed of convocation arranged by presidency, but subsequently ran more seriously afoul of Bongo's growing reluctance to accept non-resident ambassadors.'

81 US ambassador to Nigeria, Donald B. Easum, telegram, 26 January 1978, WikiLeaks Cable 1978LAGOS01095_d.

imposition of new budgetary restraints as a result of the downturn in oil revenues.[82]

In July 1974, shortly after he had arrived in Lagos, Firuz returned to Tehran to present a proposal to the shah to set up an Iranian foreign assistance programme for West Africa. The idea was that a fund of around $250 million would be established, to be administered by the embassy in Lagos, which would be used for joint investment in infrastructure projects and for soft loans, to assist five countries: Dahomey, Togo, Niger, Chad and Cameroon. These countries would first be required to undertake feasibility studies, which would then have to be verified by the World Bank, and would finally be sent to Tehran for approval.[83]

Despite Firuz's enthusiasm for the project, he reported to Helms, that 'the shah was not receptive to his proposals'.[84] Firuz felt, perhaps optimistically, that although the shah turned him down, he 'gained [the] impression [the] shah might reconsider [the] matter later on'.[85] Firuz's request perhaps came at the wrong time. The shah had recently proposed the establishment of an aid and development fund through the International Bank for Reconstruction and Development (IBRD) and the International Monetary Fund (IMF), so he likely preferred to wait for the outcome of that proposal before initiating a similar scheme. One year later, in December 1975, Helms reported that Firuz, with a 'well-established penchant for indulging in wishful thinking and overstating his case', still maintained hope that the fund in West Africa might materialise.[86] Helms believed that Firuz was 'out of touch with the change in the GOI attitude towards foreign assistance'. Furthermore, he felt that 'West Africa does not rate high enough on the scale of political importance to override Iran's current and foreseeable economic squeeze'.[87]

Firuz also devised a hugely ambitious plan to construct a railway line connecting the countries of West Africa, from Gabon to Senegal. On a trip to Accra, he discussed the project with Shirley Temple Black, who

[82] These will be discussed in Chapter 8.
[83] John Reinhardt telegram, 24 July 1974, WikiLeaks Cable 1974STATE161180_b.
[84] Helms telegram, 24 July 1974, WikiLeaks Cable 1974TEHRAN06123_b.
[85] Helms telegram, 26 August 1976, WikiLeaks Cable 1974TEHRAN07194_b.
[86] Helms telegram, 16 December 1975, WikiLeaks Cable 1975TEHRAN12148_b.
[87] Ibid.

was then the ambassador of the United States to Ghana, who agreed with him that such an enterprise would benefit not only the countries of West Africa, but would also be highly profitable for whichever companies invested in the project.[88] Each agreed to confer with their respective governments. Firuz wrote directly to both the Ministry of Foreign Affairs and the Imperial Court about the matter, but received no response from either, and the proposal came to nothing. On another occasion, Firuz asked the Ministry of Foreign Affairs in Tehran to send him copies of the Quran to distribute to Nigeria's Muslim population. He again received no answer.[89]

Firuz wrote to ʿAlam to express his frustration at the situation. He felt that certain individuals in the Ministry of Foreign Affairs ignored many of the reports and requests he submitted because they were jealous of him and disapproved of his position.[90] Whether or not this was the case, it appears that the Ministry of Foreign Affairs was not amenable to projects or initiatives in West Africa that extended beyond its rather rigid set of policy goals. Indeed, Firuz explained that around 80 per cent of his work was related to issues that were the ultimate responsibility of the shah; most notably oil and securing contracts for resources such as uranium – areas which allowed for little flexibility. Beyond this, only 'around twenty percent or less' of his work directly concerned the Ministry of Foreign Affairs.

The volume of trade between Iran and Nigeria remained modest throughout this period. According to statistics in the Ministry of Commerce, in 1355 (1976/77), the value of Iranian exports to Nigeria was just $31,000. This fell to below $500 in the first nine months of 1356 (March–December 1977). In those first nine months, the total value of Iranian exports to Africa was $19.6 million. Considering a quarter of the population of the continent lived in Nigeria, these figures are surprising and indicate that the relationship was based almost entirely on technical cooperation and politics.[91] Nigeria was in a similar position to Iran in the sense that its economy was heavily reliant on oil revenues, so sought to cooperate with OPEC members to maintain control of prices in the face of pressure from the

[88] Firuz, *Zir-e Sāyeh-ye Alborz*, 801–809. [89] Ibid., 773. [90] Ibid., 816.

[91] Vezārat-e Bāzargāni, 'Mobādelāt-e Bāzargāni-ye Irān bā Keshvar-hā-ye Qāreh-ye Āfriqā', 1977[?], NLAI 245/003909. The only agreement between Iran and Nigeria was an agreement on cultural, scientific and technical cooperation. See NLAI 297/053679.

Iran and Guinea to expand relations —Hoveyda

PRIME Minister Amir Abbas Hoveyda and Guinea counterpart Lansana Beavogui pledged efforts to expand friendship and cooperation between Iran and Guinea this week.

The statements of the two premiers came at a dinner given by Hoveyda in honour of his guest.

Hoveyda stressed the amicable ties between the two countries and cited fields for mutually beneficial cooperation.

Beavogui spoke at length about Iran's development achievements and expressed desire for diversified cooperation and trade and cultural exchanges between the two countries.

Earlier, Hoveyda and Beavogui, accompanied by their aides, held talks on prospects for expanded trade and economic relations.

They probed possibilities for cooperation in fields where the two countries' resources could complement each other.

Hoveyda was assisted by Minister of Economics and Finance Hushang Ansary, Minister of State and Plan and Budget Organisation director Abdol Majid Majidi, Minister of Commerce Fereidun Mahdavi, Minister of Industry and Mines Farrokh Najmabadi, and Deputy Foreign Minister Gholam Reza Tajbakhsh.

Informed sources said that possibilities for financial and technical assistance by Iran to Guinea and joint investment in natural resource development were reviewed.

PREMIERS MEET — Prime Minister Hoveyda exchanges views with Guinea's Lansana Beavogui at Mehrabad Airport's VIP pavilion after greeting him on arrival in Tehran last weekend.

Figure 7.3 Prime Minister Hoveydā with his Guinean counterpart, Lansana Beavogui. *Kayhan International*, 10 May 1975, 3.

West. Nigeria was also the major regional powerhouse, so the embassy in Lagos was a perfect base for Iran to explore relations with other countries in the region.

Other Areas of West Africa

Throughout the 1970s, Iran's relations with other countries in West Africa expanded. These countries often sought development aid, which will be discussed in Chapter 8, but some also recognised Iran as a powerful ally and a potentially important trading partner. As a result, many African leaders or high-level representatives visited Iran during the 1970s, normally with a trade delegation in tow. For example, in May 1975, the prime minister of Guinea, Lansana Beavogui, visited Iran and held talks with the prime minister and other senior government ministers (Figure 7.3).[92] The express purpose of the trip and these

[92] *Kayhan International*, 10 May 1975, 3.

discussions was to explore possibilities for increasing trade and economic relations.

Iran had for some time considered establishing relations with Ivory Coast, as it was one of the largest economies in West Africa. Hushang Ansāri's goodwill delegation had visited in 1964 and some modest trade had taken place between the two countries. Indeed, as noted earlier, the shah had long considered opening Iran's first embassy in West Africa there before deciding to open it in Senegal instead. In August 1975, just a few months after the visit of the Guinean prime minister, a trade delegation from Ivory Coast arrived in Tehran, headed by the finance minister, Henri Konan Bédié, for a ten-day visit.[93] At the end of the visit, a trade deal was announced, according to which Iran would import agricultural products from Ivory Coast, including cocoa, and Iran would examine the possibilities of engaging in joint investment projects in several industries in Ivory Coast, including iron ore, paper pulp and sugar cane.[94] Iran's minister of industries and mines, Farrokh Najmābādi, was invited to travel to Ivory Coast 'to continue negotiations aimed at expanding trade and industrial relations between the two countries'.[95]

Shortly after this visit, on 2 October 1975, the formal establishment of diplomatic relations between Ivory Coast and Iran was announced.[96] Two years later, from 24 until 28 May 1977, the president of Ivory Coast, Félix Houphouët-Boigny, paid an official visit to Iran. During this visit, Houphouët-Boigny was afforded the same red-carpet treatment as other heads of state. He was met at the airport by the shah and was greeted with military honours, before being driven to the Shahyād Tower, where he was given a golden key to Tehran by the mayor of the city, Gholāmrezā Nikpey. In addition to the expected state banquet hosted by the shah, Houphouët-Boigny had lunch with Prime Minister Hoveydā, met with Princess Ashraf, who had visited Ivory Coast the year before, and travelled to Isfahan and Shiraz.

According to *Ettelā'āt*, this five-day visit should be seen in the context of Iran's continuing diplomatic push into Africa, and this

[93] *Kayhan International*, 9 August 1975, 7.
[94] *Kayhan International*, 16 August 1975, 6. [95] Ibid.
[96] Bakhshi, 'Barresi-ye Tārikhi-ye Ravābet-e Khāreji-ye Irān va Qāreh-ye Āfriqā', 89. This formal document was signed by Iran's permanent representative to the United Nations, Fereydun Hoveydā and his Ivorian counterpart Siméon Aké.

was a theme that was repeated in other newspapers.[97] The American embassy noted, for example that the 'background theme to [the] visit was GOI['s] perception that Houphouet-Boigny is one of the outstanding leaders of a continent with which Iran is developing strong ties and with which Iranians must take increasing interest'.[98] During the banquet in his honour, for example, the shah hailed his guest as 'not only the head of state of a friendly country, but one of the continent's most prominent leaders'.[99]

In a press release at the end of the trip, the two leaders announced their intention to establish embassies in each capital, since Iran's representative in Abidjan had until then been based in Dakar, as well as the establishment of a joint economic commission for economic and technical cooperation at the ministerial level.[100] On the day Houphouët-Boigny left Iran, he invited the shah to pay a return visit to Ivory Coast, which the shah accepted. Of course, the shah was unable to go, and the shah's trip to Ethiopia in 1968 would remain his only trip to sub-Saharan Africa during his reign. However, the shah had received so many invitations to visit sub-Saharan Africa and had been so close to travelling in 1974, that one imagines that a tour would have happened at some point.

The shah also presented himself to Houphouët-Boigny as a champion of Africa's rights to self-determination. At the banquet in Houphouët-Boigny's honour, the shah stated his belief that 'all traces of imperialism in Africa must be eliminated', and that 'majority rule should be established in all African countries' (Figure 7.4).[101] Especially when establishing new ties with African countries, the shah and his diplomats made great efforts to present Iran as anti-imperialist and a fellow member of the Global South. For example, when presenting his credentials to the president of Cameroon, Ahmadou Ahidjo, Iran's first ambassador there, Hoseyn Montazem, said that his country was 'imbued with a fervent desire for peace', and believed in 'the principle of territorial integrity; national sovereignty of all states; peaceful co-existence; [and] non-interference in the internal affairs of

[97] *Ettelā'āt*, 3 Khordād 1356/ 24 May 1977, 28.
[98] Miklos telegram, 31 May 1977, WikiLeaks Cable 1977TEHRAN04777_c.
[99] *Ettelā'āt*, 4 Khordād 1356/ 25 May 1977, 28.
[100] Miklos telegram, 31 May 1977, WikiLeaks Cable 1977TEHRAN04777_c.
[101] *Ettelā'āt*, 4 Khordād 1356/ 25 May 1977, 1 and 28.

Figure 7.4 The shah with the president of Ivory Coast, Félix Houphouët-Boigny, on his trip to Iran in May 1977. The shah: 'Majority rule should be established in all African countries.'

other countries'.[102] Responding to these remarks, President Ahidjo added that the two states also shared 'common ideas and aspirations ... because they both belong to the Third World and to the Afro-Asiatic community'.[103]

The effective delivery of these messages was most important, given the continuation and intensification of Iran's relationship with South Africa in the from the mid-1970s onwards. Iran was so successful at avoiding severe condemnation of its ties with South Africa, despite them being an open secret, partly due to its expansive ties across the continent and care to nurture relationships with even the comparatively smaller economies, and partly due to the effectiveness of the anti-imperial messages that the Pahlavi regime espoused. There is some evidence that by the late 1970s, even as Iran supplied over 90 per cent of South Africa's crude oil imports, governments across the continent became more accepting of Iran's position, even Nigeria, which due to its desire to play a political role on the continent, had previously been particularly critical of Iran. In April 1978, Firuz informed the US

[102] Hoseyn Montazem was a career diplomat, who had joined the Ministry of Foreign Affairs in 1955 and had worked at several embassies in Europe, including the Hague, Rome and Prague. *Iran Who's Who* (Tehran: Echo of Iran, 1972), 259.

[103] *Nouvelles Du Cameroun* (Washington, DC: Press and Information Service of Cameroon Embassy), 30 October 1978, 11–12.

ambassador of a meeting he had held with the Nigerian president's chief of staff, Shehu Musa Yar'Adua, who had recently returned from a trip to Iran. Firuz believed that Yar'Adua 'had learned a lot in Tehran' and 'was no longer outspokenly critical of Iran's crude oil trade with South Africa'.[104] The American ambassador believed that the shah had managed to convince him that Iran did not have the complete control of the movement of its oil that the Nigerian government believed it did, and simply could not 'turn off the taps to South Africa at will'.[105]

*****

Throughout the 1970s, Iran expanded its ties across West Africa. Senegal was the initial focus of Iranian diplomacy and was viewed as a like-minded ally in Black Africa that Iran could establish a special relationship with, to counterbalance its continued trade relations with apartheid South Africa. Senegal received development aid from Iran, as well as investment and loans. The volume of Iranian investment in Senegal increased exponentially after 1975, as relations between Senghor and the Pahlavi royal house grew ever closer. At the same time, the Pahlavi regime recognised the significance of Nigeria as the major political and economic powerhouse of West Africa. Although the civil war had prevented Iran from pursuing close relations with Nigeria prior to 1970, as Nigeria developed a petroleum economy in the years that followed, building closer relations became important in the context of cooperation through OPEC. Although Shāhrokh Firuz would have liked his grandiose ideas to have been taken more seriously, Nigeria was not a geographically strategic area of importance to Iran at this time. The role of ambassador was symbolic, reflected in the appointment of Firuz – a man with political connections, but no diplomatic experience.

Many states in Africa viewed Iran as an influential member of the Afro-Asian bloc, a wealthy oil-producing nation, and an emerging industrial power, which could be a market for their agricultural goods and other natural resources, but also a potential investor and technical assistance provider in the areas of industrial and agricultural development. But with the oil boom of the early 1970s came an expectation

[104] Wyman telegram, 2 April 1978, WikiLeaks Cable 1978LAGOS05071_d.
[105] Ibid.

from its new allies in Africa that Iran would have plenty of money to spare to distribute among them. Shāhrokh Firuz certainly expected that this would be the case when he put forward his proposal for a fund to be distributed in West Africa. Chapter 8 examines the issue of development aid in Iran's policy in Africa, and explores how Iran pursued its strategic goals in the region using a new tool: aid.

8 Distributing the Oil Wealth

Africa and Iranian Aid

In October 1974, *Newsweek* published an article on the shah, titled 'The Master Builder of Iran'. It began: 'His grandiose visions were once considered absurd daydreams ... Now, with visions of Persia's ancient grandeur dancing on his head, the Shah has set out to convert his immense oil wealth into geopolitical clout'.[1] The article asserted that the shah was using his oil wealth not only to develop a strong army equipped with the most sophisticated equipment, but he was also investing in business ventures and aid programmes around the world. This was, as the article claims, part of his soft power strategy 'to win friends and influence nations'. The article was illustrated with a map, showing the many places in the world to which Iran had sent aid, including $50 million in general aid to Syria, $100 million to Pakistan and $2 billion to Afghanistan.

Iran was able to invest this money because of the oil price hike of 1973, which meant that, as Ali Ansari puts it, 'Iran's economy was suddenly flush with money on a scale few could have imagined ... Iran's newfound status and the responsibilities it now aspired to demanded a whole new vision for the future which could not only be imagined but through the bounties of oil money, realised.'[2] Aware of Iran's recently acquired oil wealth and resulting political clout, leaders from all across the Global South travelled to Iran during the 1970s. Some viewed Iran as a political ally, some as a source of oil, and some as a connection to the United States. Others saw Iran as a potential source of investment; one without the history of imperialism that the European countries had, and one which appeared not to give aid, as the Soviet Union and the United States, merely with the expectation of receiving backing in the Cold War. African leaders were among those

[1] *Newsweek*, 14 October 1974.
[2] Ali Ansari, 'The Curious Case of the Nuclear Company of Britain and Iran', *Iran*, vol. 55, no. 1 (2017), 74.

who were optimistic about the possibilities Iran presented as a source of development aid. However, although Iran sought to project the image that it was prepared to use its oil wealth to aid the development of its allies in Africa, many countries found that in reality Iran was reluctant to part with its petrodollars. When aid was forthcoming, it was nearly always linked to Iran's strategic or resource needs.

Aid was not always equal to charity, nor was it given only to the Global South. Indeed, billions of dollars' worth of Iran's aid and development budget went to developed countries in Europe, including Britain, France and Italy. Aid also often came in the form of soft or concessional loans, rather than grants. For example, in 1975 Iran pledged to loan the government of Peru $100 million for the construction of the Norperuano pipeline and there are many other examples around the world.[3] Pledging these sums, whether in the form of grants, loans, or favourable prices on Iranian oil, helped to reinforce the image that the shah carefully cultivated during this period, articulated most explicitly during the imperial celebrations at Persepolis, of an Iranian renaissance, and of the shah as a wealthy and benevolent world leader. But the shah's desire to aid the development of his allies in the Global South clashed with his ambitions to bring about the rapid industrial development in his own country for the realisation of his Great Civilisation. Aid, whether in rhetorical or real terms, played an increasingly important role in Iranian foreign policy from 1974 onwards, so this chapter asks what can Iran's 'aid programme' in Africa – if such a programme existed – tell us about Iran's broader strategy in Africa during this period?

Princess Ashraf's Tour of West Africa (8 January–4 February 1976)

Just over a year and a half after his arrival in Nigeria, Iran's ambassador in Lagos, Shāhrokh Firuz, was asked to help arrange a tour by the shah's twin sister, Princess Ashraf, of West Africa. The foreign trips of Empress Farah, and the benefits they brought in promoting the Pahlavi monarchy around the world, have received the most attention

[3] *Kayhan International*, 1 February 1975, 1. See also, Fernando Camacho Padilla, 'Las relaciones entre Latinoamérica e Irán durante la última década de la dinastía Pahleví', *Anuario de Historia de América Latina*, vol. 56 (2019), 81.

by scholars. But other members of the Pahlavi family, such as Ashraf and her elder sister Shams, were also often sent on foreign trips as representatives of Iran on the international stage. Princess Ashraf was heavily involved in women's rights movements in Iran and abroad, and in 1970 was elected as the chairperson of the United Nations Twenty-Sixth Session of the Commission on Human Rights. Princess Ashraf's role in the United Nations gave her many opportunities to meet with world leaders and promote dialogue with Iran. In her autobiography, she referred to herself as 'a kind of unofficial, itinerant ambassador', and she travelled to many countries, including Indonesia, India and Russia.[4] In April 1971, she accepted an invitation to visit China, which was perceived by Premier Chou En-Lai as 'a gesture of friendship to our people'.[5] This was followed by the visit shortly after by the shah's younger half-sister, Princess Fatemeh,[6] and laid the groundwork for the formal establishment of diplomatic relations between the two countries in August 1971.[7] Empress Farah later travelled to China, in September 1972, along with Prime Minister Hoveydā.[8]

Princess Ashraf undertook her tour of West Africa from 8 January until 4 February 1976, visiting six countries – Senegal, Sierra Leone, Liberia, Ivory Coast, Ghana and Niger.[9] The princess had also intended to stop in Nigeria, but the Nigerian government claimed that it could not permit the visit for security reasons. Firuz failed to persuade Nigeria's president, Murtala Muhammed, to change his mind; indeed, in his memoir he implies that negative popular perceptions of Iran in Africa, might have been the real reason.[10] This hostility towards the Pahlavis was not only due to Iran's support of South Africa, but also because it was a monarchy. Many states in Africa, including Nigeria, had struggled to become independent from the British crown, and the institution of monarchy was perceived by some activists as representing imperialism,

[4] Ashraf Pahlavi, *Faces in a Mirror*, 175.
[5] *Peking Review*, 23 April 1971, 3.
[6] *Peking Review*, 7 May 1971, 30.
[7] *Peking Review*, 20 August 1971, 4.
[8] *Kayhan International*, 23 September 1972, 1.
[9] This tour immediately preceded Empress Farah's trip to Senegal in February 1976. It is not clear where the idea came from, but a document in the National Library and Archives of Iran shows that Princess Ashraf was invited by the government of Ghana in July 1975 to visit the country. It is possible that the idea for a tour of the region emerged from this invitation. ʿAbdol-Majid Majidi to Hādi Hedāyati, undated response to letter dated 1 Mordād 1354/ 23 July 1975, NLAI 220/4571.
[10] Firuz, *Zir-e Sāyeh-ye Alborz*, 767.

despotism and repression. While the shah presented himself to the Global South as a champion of human rights, some viewed this as a façade, and sympathised instead with those student activists in Western Europe and the United States who rallied against the Pahlavi regime.[11] Furthermore, although the governments of West Africa went to great lengths to make Princess Ashraf feel welcome during her tour, on occasion her attitude did little to endear her to her hosts.

The tour was ostensibly a goodwill trip to promote women's rights as part of Princess Ashraf's role as head of a UN committee overseeing International Women's Year, but she also used the trip to improve relations between her host countries and Iran.[12] Indicating the perceived importance of the trip for Iran's interests, Shāhrokh Firuz, as well as organising the programme, accompanied Princess Ashraf throughout.[13] Senegal was the first stop on the tour (8–13 January), and Princess Ashraf was received there with some fanfare. President Senghor was in Addis Ababa for an assembly of the heads of state of the OAU, so the princess was met at the airport by his wife, Colette Senghor, the prime minister, Iran's ambassador in Dakar, and several other political figures.[14] During the trip, dinners were held in her honour by both President Senghor (after he had returned from his trip) and Prime Minister Diouf, several 'prominently publicized' meetings on education and women's affairs were held, and the Senegalese minister of planning and cooperation gave a presentation to Princess Ashraf, in the presence of the prime minister, about the joint Irano-Senegalese city that was to be built north of Dakar.[15]

[11] On the student movement against the Pahlavis in the 1960s and 1970s, see Afshin Matin-Asgari, *Iranian Student Opposition to the Shah* (Costa Mesa, CA: Mazda Publishers, 2002); and Matthew Shannon, *Losing Hearts and Minds: American-Iranian Relations and International Education during the Cold War* (Ithaca, NY: Cornell University Press, 2017).

[12] Richard Helms to secretary of state, 30 December 1975, WikiLeaks Cable 1975TEHRAN12546_b.

[13] Firuz was not on friendly terms with Princess Ashraf, and although in public they were pleasant and professional to one another, in private the princess could not hide her dislike of him. According to him, she even made jokes and derogatory comments about the Qajar dynasty, much to the enjoyment of her entourage, but to the discomfort of Firuz. Firuz felt that she disliked him because of his brother, Mozaffar Firuz. See Firuz, *Zir-e Sāyeh-ye Alborz*, 768–769.

[14] *Ettelā'āt*, 20 Dey 1354/ 10 January 1976, 4.

[15] Orison Rudolph Aggrey to secretary of state, 23 January 1976, WikiLeaks Cable 1976DAKAR00445_b.

While the princess apparently showed great interest in Senegal, she did not maintain this level of enthusiasm in Sierra Leone, the next stop on her trip. According to the American ambassador in Freetown, Michael Anthony Samuels, Princess Ashraf received there 'a tumultuous welcome'. This was the first state visit of any country to Sierra Leone in over a year, so the government of Sierra Leone 'went all out to make [the] visit successful'. The visit received much attention in newspapers and radio, and 'was filled with ceremonial meetings'. Although the princess 'spoke frequently about general goodwill and [the] importance of [the] role of women' and inaugurated the first planned parenthood clinic in the north of the country, those who came into contact with her 'were not impressed'. According to the US ambassador's report:

> She seemed unwilling to make off-the-cuff speeches and, most noticeably with students at [a] visit to [a] university, almost showed disdain for [the] general public. She slept late practically every day[,] thus throwing off each day's delicately worked out schedule. She was impatient with the obvious problems that surround any travel in West Africa. She must not have like the food arranged for her at [the] State House because one evening she ignored her scheduled dinner to take her entourage to a local restaurant where she was observed dancing in a fashion unbecoming a princess with one of her travelling companions.

Local government officials suspected that the real purpose of the visit had been to produce a film of the princess touring West Africa, because so much footage was shot during the trip. Nonetheless, the government had expected some sort of aid to result from the visit, so was apparently shocked when, during their final conversation, the princess offered the president only platitudes. Indeed, the US ambassador speculated that the financial difficulties of the Sierra Leonian government had only been exacerbated by the traditional Sierra Leonean hospitality afforded the princess. The acting foreign minister confided in the ambassador that there was widespread 'glee that at last she had gone and they could return to normal business'.[16]

In Liberia, Princess Ashraf was granted the highest national honour, the Order of the Star of Africa by President William Tolbert, for her 'humanitarian service at the national and

[16] Michael Anthony Samuels telegram, 19 January 1976, WikiLeaks Cable 1976FREETO00165_b.

international levels', at a banquet held in her honour.[17] In Ivory Coast, with which Iran had just months earlier established diplomatic relations, she was received 'with lavish hospitality' and the trip received 'extravagant coverage' in the local press.[18] During the trip, she held meetings with women's association leaders and visited cultural sites. At a banquet speech delivered to the president, Félix Houphouët-Boigny, Princess Ashraf spoke of the close ties that bound the two countries. President Houphouët-Boigny stressed that although a huge difference separated them and they had only been friends for a short time, the relationship has thrived due to 'mutual understanding, mutual respect', shared struggles to maintain their independence and a desire to 'help one another'.[19]

The penultimate stop on Princess Ashraf's trip was Ghana. There, in addition to attending the expected state banquet, at which she was presented with the Star of Ghana, Princess Ashraf also visited charitable institutions and focused on meeting with women's groups.[20] Although she spent most of her time in the capital city, Accra, she also visited Kumasi, the capital of the sub-national constitutional monarchy of Asantehene, thus returning the visit of King Opoku Ware II, who had travelled to Iran the previous year. Throughout the trip, the princess continued to socialise. Indeed, the chief of protocol was ordered to make sure that no appointments were scheduled for mornings, 'as [the] princess liked to stay up all night and sleep most of the day'. In her report of the visit, the ambassador Shirley Temple Black noted that the activities of Princess Ashraf 'followed the same pattern as that reported by Freetown, although without adverse comment'. After one reception, she went to a local Chinese restaurant, 'surprising protocol chief somewhat by relishing sweet and sour pork'. On the day

[17] *Ettelā'āt*, 1 Bahman 1354/ 21 January 1976, 3.
[18] Goodwin Cooke telegram, 27 January 1976, WikiLeaks Cable 1976ABIDJA00849_b.
[19] *Ettelā'āt*, 4 Bahman 1354/ 24 January 1976, 32.
[20] In his memoir, Firuz recalls that Princess Ashraf gave a speech at the national university that was interrupted by protesters. Firuz was unsure why the protesters greeted the princess with such hostility, but he mused, 'perhaps this was an indication of the perception among intellectuals and public opinion in Black Africa of the illegitimacy of the Pahlavi monarchy'. Firuz, *Zir-e Sāyeh-ye Alborz*, 771. However, this episode does not appear in the US record of the visit (as it surely would have), and one diplomat who was present during the visit confirmed that it did not happen.

after, following a state dinner in her honour, 'she night clubbed' with her entourage 'until the wee hours'.[21]

Aside from Princess Ashraf's revelry, something each visit on her tour had in common was the expectation of aid from the host country. In Ghana, during preparations for the arrival of the princess, the Senior Principal Secretary was heard to complain 'mildly' about the extra work undertaken. 'But we need the money', he said.[22] In his banquet speech, hinting at possible Iranian help for Ghanaian development projects, Chairman of the Supreme Military Council, Ignatius Kutu Acheampong, said, 'Oil producing countries should adopt measures which would bolster the efforts of developing countries in their development process.'[23] Ultimately, the expensive hospitality and extra hard work undertaken for Princess Ashraf's visit were in vain, because to many of these countries, aid would not be forthcoming. The granting of aid was not even part of her brief. Moreover, contrary to the perception of Iran as a wealthy benefactor, by the time of Princess Ashraf's visit in 1976, Iran's aid and development strategy had changed. Iran no longer had either the money or the will to commit to the development of poor countries in Africa; at least not without the expectation of something in return.

Aid and Development

The oil price hike of 1973 redefined OPEC's relations with the Third World, transferred considerable wealth from the industrialised world to oil-producing countries, and as a result of the damage the increased oil costs inflicted on developing countries, in the words of Shireen T. Hunter, 'created new responsibilities for OPEC towards these countries'.[24] In May 1974, the Sixth Special Session of the UN General Assembly was held, which resulted in a declaration of the 'establishment of a new international economic order'. This declaration, intended to form a framework for future negotiations, contained provisions for the 'extension of active assistance to developing countries by the whole international community, free of any political or military

[21] Shirley Temple Black telegram, 30 January 1976, WikiLeaks Cable 1976ACCRA00793_b.

[22] Ibid. [23] Ibid.

[24] Shireen T. Hunter, *OPEC and the Third World: The Politics of Aid* (London: Croom Helm, 1984), 26.

conditions.'[25] At this event, Iran first put forward the idea for the creation of a special fund, for the purpose of providing aid to countries of the Third World, to which OPEC members would contribute.[26] Having not forgiven Iran for failing to join the 1973 oil embargo during the October War, Saudi Arabia did not support Iran's proposal. Other members, however, were amenable to the creation of such a fund, which was eventually established in 1976 as the OPEC Special Fund.

Given the shah's reluctance to support an initiative that was not entirely his own, as well as the diplomatic complications in contributing to such a multinational aid organisation, Iran focused instead on providing bilateral aid. During the period of 1974 to 1978, Iran committed no more than 0.1 per cent of its GNP to multilateral organisations, but provided as much as 1.79 per cent of GNP in Official Development Assistance.[27] In contrast to other OPEC member states, Iran did not create a special development fund, but rather its aid programme was set up under the auspices of the Ministry of Finance and was named the 'Organisation for Investment, Economic and Technical Assistance'.[28] Iran had a different definition of aid to other OPEC members. The shah was working towards his Great Civilisation and was insistent that Iran's new-found oil wealth would go towards development in Iran itself. For example, the budget of the Fifth Plan (1973–1978), which covered the period of these vast oil revenue increases, nearly tripled from \$44.1 billion to \$122.8 billion.[29] The shah stressed that every 'last penny' should be spent on Iran's development.[30] For this reason, the language of Iran's 'aid' was much different to that of other OPEC members, with an emphasis on development and funds focusing on certain countries in which Iran had specific interests. As Hunter writes, 'the limited nature of Iran's resources meant that it had to tailor its aid policy even more carefully than did some OPEC states

[25] 'United Nations General Assembly Sixth Special Session', *International Legal Materials*, vol. 13, no. 3 (1974), 718.

[26] Hunter, *OPEC and the Third World*, 32. [27] Ibid., 117–119.

[28] Ibid., 116.

[29] See Keith McLachlan, 'The Iranian Economy, 1960–1976', in *Twentieth Century Iran*, ed. Hossein Amirsadeghi (London: William Heinemann, 1977), 157.

[30] Hunter, *OPEC and the Third World*, 116.

with larger surplus resources, in order to advance its own political and economic interests'.[31]

Iran's aid budget for the Fifth Development Plan was set at $12 billion.[32] Some Iranian officials claimed that the figure would actually reach $15 billion.[33] This was loosely called 'foreign assistance', but included:

- Balance of payments assistance (e.g. to Egypt, Britain and France)
- Small amount of grant aid
- Credits to international organisations (e.g. the International Monetary Fund's (IMF) oil facility, which apparently the IMF considered to be Iran's 'monetary management')
- Foreign investment (e.g. in oil refineries)
- Investment in nuclear facilities abroad (e.g. $1 billion credits for France)
- Oil concessions granted by the NIOC to countries such as Sudan and India[34]

Between 1974 and 1976, the majority of Iran's bilateral aid went to powerful regional allies, such as India, Pakistan, Egypt and Syria. In 1975, India received the most bilateral aid, and in 1976, Pakistan accounted for 82 per cent of Iran's bilateral aid.[35] One of the clearest examples of Iran's foreign assistance funds being used to strengthen bilateral relations is its support for Egypt.

Iranian Aid to Egypt

One of the most important developments in Iran's foreign policy in the 1970s was its rapprochement with Egypt (see Chapter 5). This intensified after the Yom Kippur War in 1973. During that conflict, although Iran did not contribute militarily, it provided medical as well as logistical support to the Arab states, and did not allow Jewish volunteers from Australia to travel through Iran on their way to Israel.[36] Iran's

[31] Ibid.
[32] Helms telegram, 14 May 1976, WikiLeaks Cable 1976TEHRAN04911_b.
[33] Jack Miklos to secretary of state, 9 February 1975, WikiLeaks Cable 1975TEHRAN01248_b.
[34] Helms telegram, 14 May 1976, WikiLeaks Cable 1976TEHRAN04911_b.
[35] Hunter, *OPEC and the Third World*, 117.
[36] Ramazani, 'Iran and the Arab-Israeli Conflict', 418–419.

sympathies for the Arab states on this occasion was motivated by strategic calculations. It did not reflect a shift towards the Arab position, but rather the changing regional dynamics. The central motivation of Iran's regional foreign policy had throughout this period been, as Ramazani argues, 'the obstruction of Soviet power and influence of the Middle East. Iran assessed the regional balance or preponderance of power in 1973 as in 1967 primarily with a view to the achievement of that overriding objective.'[37] Whereas in 1967, Iran's cold war with Egypt and Syria prevented it from supporting the Arabs in the Six-Day War, now the emergence of a friendly government in Egypt had presented Iran with 'an Arab option'.[38]

Iranian investment was used to enforce relations and bring the countries even closer together. In April 1974, Iran's minister of economics and finance, Hushang Ansāri, travelled to Egypt to explore the types of projects Iran could invest in through the granting of credits on favourable terms. This resulted in the signing of an accord, which, according to *Kayhan International*, was inspired by the 'special desire of His Imperial Majesty [. . .] and the President of Egypt to consolidate and strengthen the friendly and brotherly ties existing between the two nations'.[39] This trip was quickly followed up by a visit to Iran in May of Egypt's deputy prime minister, Abdel Aziz Hegazi. The protocol signed at the end of this trip outlined possible loans and credits from Iran for joint projects, as well as imports, totalling as much as $870 million.[40] Though it was doubtful that the actual figures of investment would reach that amount, the Iranian press declared the accord to amount to a 'billion dollar agreement'. In spite of Iran's overly optimistic calculations – indeed, the US embassy considered that a 'substantial portion of [the] projects outlined in [the] protocol [are] likely to fall by [the] wayside' – the Egyptian delegation was impressed with the scale of Iran's ambitions. Indeed, Hegazi was said to have been 'pleased as punch' with the outcome of his visit to Iran.[41]

Iran's development assistance to Egypt was presented by the two sides a reflection of the countries' increasing closeness. In an interview with the newspaper *Ettelāʿāt*, Hegazi said that he felt that 'Iran and

[37] Ibid., 419. [38] Ibid., 420.
[39] Helms telegram, 18 April 1974, WikiLeaks Cable 1974TEHRAN03046_b.
[40] Miklos telegram, 27 May 1974, WikiLeaks Cable 1974TEHRAN04241_b.
[41] Ibid.

Egypt speak in one language'.[42] At the press conference announcing the signing of the protocol, he reiterated this message:

> Through each of the words mentioned in the agreement signed today, the long-standing and historical relations between the two countries is expressed. This is an historic opportunity in the lives of our two nations because it changes the course of relations between our two countries, and we are nations that have all the possibilities for progress.[43]

The newspaper *Āyandegān* also referred to the signing of the agreement as a turning point in the relationship between the two countries. While in the past 'the two countries were negligent in not developing closer ties with each other', Iran and Egypt were now 'two solid pillars that can prevent the region from falling into the hands of this or that power'.[44] The strengthening of this relationship was seen as central to maintaining the stability of the entire region, and thereby supported the foreign policy goals of both the shah and Sadat.

By 1976, two years later, some of the money had been disbursed and the agreed projects were progressing, albeit quite slowly. The projects included an Irano-Egyptian investment bank capitalised with $20 million, set up in Cairo to help channel funds towards the implementation of bilateral and multilateral projects and joint ventures; a $250 million loan towards the Port Said development, for which Iran had agreed to set up a joint Irano-Egyptian consulting and engineering company; and the construction of chemical manufacturing and cotton spinning plants.[45]

Aid to Sub-Saharan Africa

A US report from June 1974 noted that Iran's 'economic assistance agreements' with some eleven countries across Africa would not only improve Iran's political influence in Africa, 'simultaneously undercutting radical Arab influence in black Africa', and secure support for Iran in international forums, but would also 'provide Iran many needed commodities, access to markets for future industrial output, and

[42] *Ettelāʿāt*, 6 Khordād 1353/ 27 May 1974, 6.
[43] *Ettelāʿāt*, 5 Khordād 1353/ 26 May 1974, 16.
[44] Miklos telegram, 27 May 1974, WikiLeaks Cable 1974TEHRAN04241_b.
[45] P. J. Westmacott to A. J. Coles, 21 September 1976, FCO 8/2731.

constructive use for its surplus oil revenues'.[46] In the knowledge that Iran had money to invest, many African leaders travelled to Iran to request support for their development projects. The normal procedure was that a proposal would be made to the Iranian government, which would be forwarded to the relevant ministry to be studied. For instance, in 1975, the Iranian government received proposals for ten projects from the government of Upper Volta. These were subsequently passed on to the minister of economics and finance, Hushang Ansāri, for review.[47] On another occasion, the Gambian government requested Iran's assistance for the renovation and asphalting of 254 kilometres of roads. The proposal was passed on to the Plan and Budget Organisation to assess.[48] Proposals from the governments of Zambia and Kenya in the field of agriculture were passed on for assessment to the Ministry of Agriculture.[49] Once the proposal was assessed by the relevant ministry and a decision had been made, this decision was relayed to the government that had submitted it.

However, Iran's willingness to give aid to developing countries in sub-Saharan Africa was short-lived. In February 1975, Jamshid Ashraf, undersecretary in the Ministry of Economy and Finance in charge of foreign assistance, told the deputy president of the US Export and Import Bank for the Middle East and North Africa that Iran's export capital budget had been reviewed. The Iranian government now planned to reduce the budget, committing 'no more than $9 billion in both concessional and other lending abroad' during the Fifth Plan. The overriding criterion when considering whether or not to commit Iranian funds to projects abroad from now on would be 'what's in it for Iran?'[50] One year later, in an astonishingly frank assessment of Iran's situation in 1976, US ambassador Richard Helms wrote that 'Iran's tightened financial belt makes it difficult for it to deliver on its prior lavish extension of promises and credits'.[51] While the shah had previously revelled in his position as a wealthy

[46] Telegram from the Embassy in Iran to the Department of State, 26 June 1974, *FRUS, 1969–1976, Volume XXVII, Iran; Iraq, 1973–1976*, doc. 62.
[47] Majidi to Ansāri, undated letter, NLAI 220/4571.
[48] Shāpur Rāsekh (Plan and Budget Organisation) to Ministry of Foreign Affairs, 12 Esfand 1354/ 2 March 1976, NLAI 220/4571.
[49] Mostafā Bakāi to Plan and Budget Organisation, Ordibehesht 1354[?], NLAI 220/4571.
[50] Miklos telegram, 9 February 1975, WikiLeaks Cable 1975TEHRAN01248_b.
[51] Helms telegram, 14 May 1976.

benefactor, his priorities had shifted and he adopted the role of 'reluctant philanthropist'.[52]

The head of the foreign loans department of the Ministry of Economics and Finance had told the British embassy in Tehran that Iran would not be entering into any new overseas investment commitments. Only certain exceptions would be made, decided by the shah himself, based on 'political or important national grounds'.[53] The British ambassador in Iran, Anthony Parsons, said that this decision was taken as a result of a reduction in global demand for oil, a reduction in the price of oil since January 1974, and the slim prospect of a further increase in the price of oil in 1975, which 'meant that Iran would in the Iranian year (March 1975–76) need all her revenue for internal development and the meeting of existing overseas commitments'.[54] Iran's tightened purse strings meant that when African states made even modest requests for assistance from Iran, they were more often than not left disappointed.

By March 1976, $5.7 billion of Iran's foreign assistance budget of $9 billion had been disbursed. Of this, $1.6 billion (28.3 per cent) went to international organisations, $1.7 billion to developed countries (29.9 per cent), $680 million (12.2 per cent) to Eastern Europe, $1.2 billion (21.4 per cent) to developing countries in Asia and just $456 million (8.2 per cent) to developing countries in Africa.[55] More funds from Iran's 'aid' budget were allocated to developed countries, including Britain and France, than were allocated to developing countries in Asia and Africa. Moreover, in spite of increasing oil revenues, from 1975 until the revolution in 1979, Iran's aid commitments followed a downwards trajectory, from a height of $936 million in 1975 (1.79 per cent of GNP), to $807 million in 1976 (1.22 per cent of GNP) and $315.5 million in 1977 (0.38 per cent of GNP).[56] Indeed, by as early as the latter half of 1975, Iran had to be cautious in taking on additional foreign aid commitments due to shrinking reserves and prospective deficits. For example, net foreign exchange reserves fell from a height of $8.5 billion in February 1975 to $6.3 billion just one year later.[57]

Iran did not close the door completely to new areas of cooperation, but investment would only be forthcoming if it was of benefit to Iran.

[52] Ibid. [53] Parsons telegram, 27 March 1975, FCO/8/2501. [54] Ibid.
[55] Helms telegram, 14 May 1976, WikiLeaks Cable 1976TEHRAN04911_b.
[56] Hunter, *OPEC and the Third World*, 117.
[57] Helms telegram, 14 May 1976, WikiLeaks Cable 1976TEHRAN04911_b.

In March 1975, for example, an Iranian economic mission was sent to Ghana, Kenya and Zambia. The mission to Ghana was led by the head of the Plan Organisation, ʿAbdol-Majid Majidi, and discussed possible Iranian investment in Ghana's aluminium and timber industries, in order to increase production for export to Iran. While Ghana had some solid propositions to offer to Iran, the Kenyan leg of the mission was said by the head of African affairs at Iran's Ministry of Foreign Affairs, Shahbāzi, to have been 'disappointing'. The Kenyan authorities, although they treated the Iranian delegation 'like royalty', provided no concrete and cogent proposals. They suggested that Iran could provide $500 million to increase milk production in Kenya, but gave no specific details as to exactly how the project would work. Shahbāzi felt that instead of rolling out the red carpet, the Kenyan authorities should have spent more time putting together detailed proposals. According to Shahbāzi, 'the mission was left with the impression that the Kenyans expected them to be so overwhelmed by their reception that they would just "hand over the money"'.[58]

In the final years of Pahlavi rule, Iran prioritised countries that either had some strategic importance to Iran, or had resources that were of value. In negotiating with individual African countries, instead of playing the role of wealthy benefactor, Iran pushed to secure the best possible terms, often with the promise of long-term business. In the latter half of the 1970s, Iran became particularly interested in nuclear energy, and its search for regular and long-term supplies of uranium was tied to its overseas aid and investment policy. One example of such a relationship was Gabon.

Nuclear Energy and Gabonese Uranium

While the shah had long been intrigued by the prospect of Iran developing nuclear capabilities, investing in nuclear energy was extremely expensive. The oil price hike of 1973 presented opportunities to invest in the sector. The shah often spoke about the prospect of oil running out in the not-to-distant future. In his *Towards the Great Civilisation*, published on the eve of the revolution, the shah warned that 'the existing petroleum resources of the world will suffice for a

[58] Parsons telegram, 27 March 1975, FCO/8/2501.

period of only thirty-seven years at the present rate of consumption'.[59] Nuclear energy was seen as a viable option to meet Iran's long-term energy requirements in the absence of oil. The Atomic Energy Organisation of Iran (AEOI) was established in March 1974, headed by Akbar Eʿtemād, a respected scientist, who held a PhD in nuclear physics from the University of Lausanne in Switzerland and served as chancellor of Bu Ali Sina University.[60]

For the following five years, until the fall of the Pahlavi regime in 1979, Eʿtemād presided over what was considered to be one of the most ambitious nuclear power projects in the world; by 1994, the AEOI envisioned that 23,000 megawatts out of Iran's total generation capacity of 70,000 would be provided by nuclear power plants.[61] Iran purchased nuclear technology from various countries, and Iranian scientists were sent abroad to attain the necessary training.[62] To deflect criticism of its nuclear ambitions, particularly in light of India's successful nuclear test in May 1974 – Operation Smiling Buddha – Iran invested in nuclear infrastructure abroad to ensure a steady supply of enriched uranium. In 1974, for example, Iran loaned the French government $1 billion for the construction of a uranium enrichment plant in France called Eurodif, in exchange for a 10 per cent share in the plant, as well as the right to purchase 10 per cent of its production.[63] In the years that followed, Iran began to develop its own nuclear infrastructure. The German firm Kraftwerk Union, for instance, began work in 1975 to construct two 1,300-megawatt power stations near to Bushehr.[64] But Iran's long-term strategy was to acquire knowledge of the complete nuclear cycle, including uranium

59 Pahlavi, *Besu-ye Tamaddon-e Bozorg*, 22–23.
60 Afkhami, *The Life and Times of the Shah*, 347; *Iran Who's Who* [1972], 108. For a short biography of Eʿtemād, see Abbas Milani, *Eminent Persians*, vol. 1 (Syracuse: Syracuse University Press, 2008), 134–138.
61 US Embassy Tehran Airgram A-69 to State Department, 'The Atomic Energy Organization of Iran', 11 May 1977, 8. The National Security Archive, The George Washington University. Available online: https://nsarchive2.gwu.edu/nukevault/ebb268/.
62 Jacob Darwin Hamblin, 'The Nuclearization of Iran in the Seventies', *Diplomatic History*, vol. 38, no. 5 (2014), 1130. By 1977, there were approximately 300 students at nuclear centres abroad, primarily in the United States, Britain, France, Germany and Austria.
63 *Los Angeles Times*, 30 October 1986.
64 Hamblin, 'The Nuclearization of Iran in the Seventies', 1128.

enrichment, so that it would not be dependent on Western governments for a supply of enriched uranium in the future.[65]

Another one of Iran's priorities was now to secure mining concessions and supplies of uranium to power its planned twenty nuclear reactors.[66] One of the markets that the AEOI sought to exploit was the African market. Shāhrokh Firuz recalled in his memoirs that securing contracts for uranium in West Africa was among his most important tasks as Iran's ambassador to Nigeria (also Niger, Ghana and Sierra Leone) from 1974 until 1978.[67] When presenting his credentials as Iran's first ambassador to Niger in April 1976, Firuz discussed with the Nigerien president, Seyni Kountché, potential Iranian participation in a joint venture in uranium exploitation.[68]

Ghana was also identified as a potential long-term supplier of uranium. In meetings between Firuz and Ghanaian officials in Accra in February 1975, the potential purchase by Iran of Ghanaian aluminium bars, bauxite, lumber and, most importantly, uranium was discussed.[69] These discussions must have been quite positive because just three months later, a representative of the AEOI travelled to Ghana to investigate opportunities for investment in Ghanaian uranium projects.[70] To develop closer trade relations with uranium-rich countries, Iran offered them favourable terms on its oil. For instance, countries were normally required by the NIOC to complete the payment of oil purchases within sixty days, but Ghana was granted ninety days.[71] By establishing broader commercial, economic and technical agreements, Iran hoped to gain leverage in future negotiations over uranium.

[65] The shah was right to be worried about the supply of enriched uranium drying up. After the revolution, contravening the agreement signed with the French in 1974, the French Commissariat à l'Énergie Atomique refused to supply Iran with uranium. Hamblin, 'The Nuclearization of Iran in the Seventies', 1134.

[66] *Ettelā'āt*, 26 Mehr 1354/ 18 October 1975, 24. See also, US Embassy Tehran Airgram A-69 to State Department, 'The Atomic Energy Organization of Iran', 9.

[67] Firuz, *Zir-e Sāyeh-ye Alborz*, 717.

[68] US ambassador in Nigeria, Louis Douglas Heck, telegram, 27 April 1976, WikiLeaks Cable 1976NIAMEY01829_b.

[69] US ambassador to Nigeria, John Reinhardt, telegram, 18 February 1975, WikiLeaks Cable 1975LAGOS01507_b.

[70] Majidi to Ansāri, 27 Farvardin 1354/ 17 May 1975, NLAI 220/4571.

[71] Majidi to Nosratollāh Mo'iniyān, 17 Esfand 1354/ 7 March 1976, NLAI 220/ 4571.

Other parts of Africa were considered potential sources of uranium, including North Africa, particularly Morocco, and Southern Africa, primarily Zambia and Namibia (which was at this stage still under South African rule), as will be discussed in Chapter 10. However, Gabon emerged as one of the most promising prospects during this period. The initiation of formal political relations between Gabon and Iran can be dated to September 1975, when the shah's half-brother, Prince Gholāmrezā Pahlavi, travelled to Libreville on the invitation of the Gabonese minister for transport, Georges Rawiri, who had formerly served as the minister of foreign affairs and was a close friend of the president, Omar Bongo. Prince Gholāmrezā was ostensibly there to discuss private business ventures involving wood and pharmaceuticals, but was 'treated throughout his stay as GOG [Government of Gabon] official guest'.[72] He met twice with Bongo, who also hosted a dinner in honour of the Iranian prince. Bongo was due to travel to Iran in October, just weeks later, so hoped that the hospitality afforded the prince would help to enhance his image prior to his arrival.

During his five-day visit to Iran, Bongo was afforded, according to the British embassy, the 'full red carpet treatment'.[73] At the end of his stay, a communique was issued, which in addition to the usual pronouncements about the Indian Ocean and human rights, announced the signing of three bilateral agreements on commercial, cultural and economic/technical cooperation.[74] In terms of technical support, Iran offered Gabon assistance in the construction of a hospital and laboratory.[75] As part of the agreement on trade, Iran stated its intention to export as many as seventy different items, including buses, tractors, motorbikes, diesel engines and dates, to Gabon, and to import coffee, cocoa, manganese, marble and lumber.[76] One product that was not

[72] Andrew L. Steigman telegram, 26 September 1975, WikiLeaks Cable 1975LIBREV01545_b.
[73] P. J. Westmacott to P. K. Williams, 6 November 1975, FCO 8/2501.
[74] The Gabonese embassy had in September sent proposals to the Iranian government for economic, commercial and technical cooperation, which formed the basis of the agreements signed during the visit. Mostafa Bakāyi to Ministry of Foreign Affairs, 21 Shahrivar 1354/ 12 September 1975, NLAI 220/4571.
[75] Helms telegram, 21 September 1976, WikiLeaks Cable 1976TEHRAN09508_b.; Majidi to Khalʿatbari, 1 Bahman 1354/ 21 January 1976, NLAI 220/4571. Iran later pulled out of this project and it was completed with funding from the Philippines instead. Steigman telegram, 24 September 1976, WikiLeaks Cable 1976LIBREV01908_b.
[76] Helms telegram, 29 October 1975, WikiLeaks Cable 1975TEHRAN10546_b.

covered by press reports, but which was certainly discussed privately, was uranium.

In June 1975, President Bongo organised a meeting of OPEC members in Libreville to mark Gabon's accession to OPEC. It is thought that at a backroom meeting between Bongo and the Iranian representative, the subject of uranium was discussed, and Bongo offered to sell to Iran 520 tons of uranium.[77] The visit of President Bongo to Iran in October was likely planned a result of this proposal. Subsequently, in February 1976, Eʿtemād travelled to Libreville to examine both the procedure and terms for purchasing Gabonese uranium and the prospects of Iran's long-term cooperation in Gabon's uranium industry.[78]

President Bongo had initially offered to sell Gabonese uranium to Iran at the same reduced price (referred to as *prix africain*) that it gave to the French Commissariat à l'énergie atomique (CEA), which had been granted in return for the investment aid France provided to Gabon. However, the head of Gabon's negotiating team, the minister of state for mines, energy and water resources, Edouard Alexis M'Bouy-Boutzit, argued that as a new customer, Iran should pay the market rate. The Gabonese uranium distribution company Compagnie des mines d'uranium de Franceville (COMUF), in which the government Gabon owned a minority share (24.75 per cent), with the majority of the remaining shares (71.79 per cent) owned by a consortium of French companies,[79] offered the AEOI the going rate for a one-off purchase of $48 per pound of uranium.[80] Eʿtemād suggested that the AEOI was interested in a long-term collaboration, since to fuel its planned reactors, Iran would need 40,000 tons of uranium between 1977 and 1994. With this in mind, in addition to the agreements signed in Tehran the previous year outlining Iran's plans to assist in Gabon's development, Eʿtemād offered to pay $24 per pound – the *prix africain* that Bongo had originally offered to the shah.

[77] Gabrielle Hecht, *Being Nuclear: Africans and the Global Uranium Trade* (Cambridge, MA: The MIT Press, 2012), 131–132.

[78] 'Iranian Delegation Examines Uranium Cooperation Prospects', *Bulletin Quotidien de l'Agence Gabonaise de Press*, 16 February 1976, 6–8, cited in *Translations on Sub-Saharan Africa* (Joint Publications Research Service, 1976), 12–13.

[79] Guy Martin, 'Uranium: A Case-Study in Franco-African Relations', *The Journal of Modern African Studies*, vol. 27, no. 4 (1989), 633.

[80] Hecht, *Being Nuclear*, 132.

The COMUF and Gabonese officials rejected this proposal, but made a counteroffer of $39 per pound, apparently 'as a goodwill gesture by the Gabonese Authorities'.[81] The AEOI turned this down immediately. While these negotiations were ongoing, Iran continued to cooperate with Gabon in other areas. For instance, in 1976, the shah agreed to provide training for pilots from Gabon's Air Force in Iran.[82] But though the shah wished to maintain goodwill in Gabon, he also wanted results. In a meeting with ʿAlam in April 1976, the shah said that he would withhold financial assistance to Gabon until they had agreed to supply Iran with its uranium at below market prices.[83]

The threat of Iran either withholding aid, pulling out of future investments, or choosing to purchase their uranium from elsewhere was seemingly enough to convince the Gabonese to yield to the Iranians' demands. In October 1976, both sides agreed on a rate of $28 per pound of uranium, just $4 more than the *prix africain*. However, as Gabrielle Hecht writes in her fascinating account of this episode, Iran 'repeatedly prolonged negotiations by introducing new requirements and conditions'.[84] In a letter written to President Bongo, cited by Hecht, M'Bouy-Boutzit asked whether Iran was acting in good faith, or was merely attempting 'to profit excessively from your promise to the Shah?'[85] The deal looked dead and the Gabonese had begun 'plotting to withdraw from the negotiations without sparking a diplomatic incident', when early in 1978, out of the blue a deal was reached and a contract drawn up. However, in the Iranian political unrest in the autumn and winter of 1978, during which Eʿtemād resigned, the deal again stalled. The revolution was the final nail in its coffin.[86] The shah did not insist on receiving the *prix africain* just because that was the price he was initially promised by President Bongo. There was perhaps a sense of chauvinism in this insistence; that because of Iran's emergent position on the global

[81] Quoted ibid.
[82] Steigman telegram, 24 September 1976, WikiLeaks Cable 1976LIBREV01908_b.
[83] ʿAlam diary entry 19 Farvardin 1355/ 8 April 1976, *Yāddāsht-hā-ye ʿAlam*, vol. 6, 38–39.
[84] Hecht, *Being Nuclear*, 133. [85] Ibid.
[86] Firuz suggests in his memoir that the deal had already been cancelled by the beginning of June 1978. See Firuz, *Zir-e Sāyeh-ye Alborz*, 818.

stage, because of its history as a great civilisation, it was entitled to receive the same reduced rates as France.

*****

One of the goals of Iran's aid and development policy in the 1970s was to build some dependency relationships with countries in which Iran had either strategic interests, or which could provide resources that Iran needed. Shireen Hunter has argued that Iranian aid failed to create these types of dependency relationships for several reasons. First, Iran only developed a comprehensive aid and development strategy after the oil price hike of 1973, so it only lasted a little over five years until the revolution. During most of that time, essentially from late 1974, the global demand for oil dropped, and oil revenues decreased. Because the shah focused so much attention on domestic development, when revenues declined, industrial investment and military expenditure were prioritised over international aid. This was a remarkably quick turnaround. From as early as 1975, Iran was unable to meet its aid commitments and many African countries that came to Iran, or that invited Iranian trade envoys with the expectation of promises of aid, were left disappointed.

Second, in many cases the value of Iranian aid was not significant in comparison to that received from other countries. Third, because Iran was transparent in its eagerness to expand its influence around the world – as the *Newsweek* article cited in the introduction to this chapter noted – and purchase certain resources, recipients of aid were able to negotiate from a relative position of strength. This explains to some extent why negotiations over the price of Gabonese uranium took so long and why ultimately, after over a year of negotiations, Iran agreed to pay more, albeit only slightly, than the *prix africain*. Fourth, some of the countries that Iran provided aid to were equal or superior to Iran in some respects, for example, in military prowess, which also limited Iran's leverage. And fifth, Iran's regional oil-rich competitors in the Middle East also provided aid to some of the same countries as Iran. This undermined, in some instances, Iran's ability to influence them with aid.[87] For these reasons, Iranian development aid to Africa targeted specific countries, such as Egypt, Morocco, Tunisia,

[87] Hunter, *OPEC and the Third World*, 122.

Somalia and Sudan, that Iran enjoyed good relations with, or which had some strategic significance.

One country in Africa that was marked as a special focus of Iran's development aid was Senegal, where in the mid- to late 1970s, the shah pledged hundreds of millions of dollars to construct a refinery, phosphate mine and adjoining city. For some of the reasons stated above, most importantly the economic downturn which forced Iran to either suspend all together or scale down its international commitments, the project was not completed – in fact, it had barely started by the time of the revolution. However, the plans that were drawn up during this period provide evidence of the scale of the project, which would have been the biggest industrial undertaking in Senegal. Moreover, this project, had it been completed, may have provided the Pahlavis with a blueprint for creating other dependency relationships in Africa.

PART III

Africa and Pahlavi Iran's Grand Strategy (1976–1979)

9 Iran and Senegal

Building a Special Relationship in Africa (1975–1979)

By the middle of the 1970s, Iran had established extensive ties with countries across the whole of Africa. But one country in particular continued to receive special attention: Senegal. In the early 1970s, Senegal had been the main target of Iranian investment and development aid in West Africa. As the 1970s developed, Senegal became one of Iran's closest partners in Africa, politically, economically and culturally. The Pahlavi elite, in particular Empress Farah, did not merely see Iranian relations with Africa in political terms, but sought to raise awareness of African art and culture in Iran, and build cultural links between Iran and the countries of Africa. As a result, awareness of Africa among Iranian intellectual and artistic circles increased during the 1970s, and Senegal played a particularly significant role in this. Senegalese artists performed several times at the Shiraz Arts Festival, and during President Senghor's visits to Iran, Iranian intellectuals engaged with his literature and his idea of Négritude.

The bilateral relationship thrived due to a very particular set of circumstances, not least the friendly relations that developed between the Pahlavi and Senegalese political elites, in particular between the president, Léopold Sédar Senghor, and the shah and shahbanu. In Senegal, the constitution granted the president control over foreign affairs, national defence and the armed forces, essentially giving him sole prerogative to define foreign policy.[1] The shah, too, enjoyed complete control over Iran's foreign policy, so these personal friendships were important in the development of political relations. Another reason was the awareness among Iran's Francophile leaders of Senegal's unique position as a melting pot of African and European cultures. Indeed, during Empress Farah's visit in 1976, the Iranian press referred to Dakar as the 'Paris of Africa'.[2] The use of this

[1] Skurnik, *The Foreign Policy of Senegal*, 61.
[2] *Zan-e Ruz*, 23 Esfand 1354/ 13 March 1976, 31.

appellation indicates the attractiveness of Senegal's cosmopolitanism to Iran's elite; like Iran, Senegal had a rich native culture, but it also shared Iran's inclination towards Europe. Other factors played a role in drawing the two countries together, too. Iran had a motivation to develop strong links with a country in Africa which could help to counterbalance its extensive economic relations with South Africa, which were viewed negatively across the continent. Senegal was highly appealing in this regard since it had adopted a less confrontational stance towards the apartheid regime than other African countries.[3] Moreover, although Senegal was, like Iran, a Muslim majority country, religion did not occupy a central role in its national identity. Indeed, Senghor himself was Catholic.

The high point of Senegalese–Iranian interactions during this period was the Keur Farah Pahlavi project. This project aimed to build a refinery with an adjoining city, complete with port facilities and transport infrastructure linking it to other major cities and industrial centres. The city would have religious and cultural centres, which would blend the architectural styles of Iran and Senegal. The project was unlike anything else that Iran was involved in anywhere in the world during this period, both in terms of scale and expense. It was to be, in a sense, a physical manifestation of the close cultural, political and economic ties that had developed between Iran and Senegal.

Iran–Senegal Ties from 1975

In late January 1975, Senghor received a message from the shah asking him to meet him at his Swiss winter resort in St Moritz. On 8 February, news agencies in Senegal reported that 'President Senghor unexpectedly left Dakar' for talks with the shah.[4] It had been speculated that the shah wished to see Senghor to speak about a UNESCO-sponsored conference that had recently taken place in Dakar,[5] but apparently

[3] Richard Helms telegram, 29 April 1976, WikiLeaks Cable 1976TEHRAN04348_b. A.

[4] Entretien du President Senghor avec shah Saint-Moritz, 10 February 1975, CADN 184PO/1/531.

[5] The French reports simply refer to a 'conference', but presumably it refers to the Conference of Ministers of African Member States Responsible for the Application of Science and Technology to Development, which was organised by UNESCO, with the co-operation of the UN Economic Commission for Africa and the OAU, and took place from 21 until 30 January 1974.

the visit concerned primarily the issue of bilateral cooperation between Iran and Senegal.[6] The French ambassador reported that Senghor told him that the shah had spoken to him about the prospect of sending young Senegalese students to Tehran Polytechnic to study, and about potential areas in which Iranian aid could help realise some of Senegal's development projects.

It is likely that the prospect of an imminent trip by Senghor to Iraq was the real reason for this hastily arranged meeting in St Moritz.[7] The shah said that he saw 'no objection to the forging of relations between Iraq and Senegal', but gave Senghor a brief lecture on the nature of the dispute between Iran and Iraq, the Shatt al-Arab and the Kurdish movement. Whatever the motivation for hosting the meeting, it was apparently quite productive. Senghor and the shah decided that meetings would be held between their prime ministers every six months, with Diouf planning to arrive in Tehran just one month later.[8] The shah also invited Senghor to visit Iran the following year.[9]

Prime Minister Diouf, who had last been in Iran just months earlier, in June 1974, returned to Iran in March 1975. During this trip, a treaty of friendship and cooperation was signed by Hoveydā and Diouf, in which 'the two friends declare[d] their firm desire to establish between them sincere ties of friendship, cooperation, and durable peace'.[10] A 'mixed commission for cooperation' was set up, chaired by the head of government of each country, which would meet at least once per year, alternating between the two capitals, formalising what the shah and Senghor had agreed in St Moritz. The articles of this treaty appear to have been followed meticulously, and from this time until the overthrow of the Pahlavi regime in 1979, high-level visits frequently took place between the two heads of government.

An agreement was also signed on 30 April 1975 for the establishment of an Iranian–Senegalese company called Société Irano Sénégalaise des Pétroles et des Mines (Irasenco). The company was

6 Entretien du President Senghor avec shah Saint-Moritz, 10 February 1975, CADN 184PO/1/531.
7 Entretien du President Senghor avec le shah d'Iran a Saint-Moritz, 22 February 1975, CADN 184PO/1/531.
8 Ibid. 9 *Kayhan International*, 15 February 1975.
10 'Traite d'amitié et de coopération entre le gouvernement de la République du Sénégal et le gouvernement Imperial de l'Iran', 6 March 1975, NA 2.05.191/239.

capitalised with $80 million, 50 per cent of which was provided by Iran and the other 50 per cent by Senegal.[11] Iran granted a $40 million loan to Senegal to cover its half of the capital.[12] The remaining funds required to complete the proposed projects would be borrowed by Irasenco on the international money markets and from development institutions, with guarantees provided by the governments of Iran and Senegal.[13] The main purpose of Irasenco was to establish a petrochemical complex at Kayar, extract a new phosphate deposit near Kayar at Tobène, and construct a mineral/petroleum port. The idea was essentially that crude oil would be delivered to Senegal from Iran, and that the tankers would return with phosphates for processing in Iran. The new port would handle the shipments.[14]

In January 1976, shortly after the establishment of the company, the Iranian minister ʿAbdol-Majid Majidi and Senegalese minister in charge of financial and economic affairs, Babacar Ba, confirmed that the main purpose of the company would be to execute the following projects:

1. An oil refinery with an initial capacity of 1.5 million tons per year, which could be increased later to 2.5 million.
2. A majority shareholding of at least 61 percent in the operating facilities of the phosphate mine of Tobène, for a capacity of around 2 million tons of enriched phosphate per year.
3. The acquisition of 50 per cent of the distribution channels for oil products belonging to the Shell Company in Senegal.
4. Equity participation in the project to produce ammonia and urea belonging to Fertisen.[15]

The company also formally put in place plans for the construction of a town, built to house those employed at the refinery, which would be

[11] *Iran Economic News*, vol. 1, no. 1, January 1975, 7; Telegram: Visit to Senegal of Shahbanou of Iran, 4 March 1976, FCO 8/2766.

[12] *Ettelāʿāt*, 11 Esfand 1354/ 1 March 1976, 56; Movāfeqatnāmeh-e Māli, 26 April 1976, Majles-e Senā, NLAI 220/218.

[13] Wilfried Thalwitz to J. Burke Knapp, 19 March 1976, Contacts with Member Countries: Iran – Correspondence 03, 1771089, WB IBRD/IDA 03 EXC-10-4549S, World Bank Group Archives, Washington DC.

[14] Orison Rudolph Aggrey telegram, 13 May 1975, WikiLeaks Cable 1975DAKAR02766_b.

[15] Protocol signed by ʿAbdol-Majid Majidi and Babacar Ba on 20 January 1976, NA 2.05.191/239.

called Keur Farah Pahlavi. The port, which would be located in the town, would be called Port Sédar.[16]

Iran had granted substantial long-term loans for petroleum-related projects to other countries besides Senegal, but the scale of the project envisioned by Irasenco and the vast sums of money pledged by Iran were exceptional. The refinery alone, which would be funded by Iran and would give priority to the Senegalese market, would require nearly $120 million of investment between 1976 and 1980, and the planned improvements to the phosphate mine at Tobène would require $250 million of investment, at least 51 per cent of which the Iranian government had pledged to provide.[17] In response to a request from Senegal for a $57 million loan to cover the cost of the port infrastructure at Keur Farah Pahlavi, Iran agreed to cover half, on the condition that Senegal obtain the balance from the World Bank and Iran's portion not exceed $30 million. The Iranian government also agreed to fund a World Bank feasibility study for the port, not exceeding $290,000.[18] These substantial sums pledged serve to illustrate Iran's commitment to pursuing greater economic influence in sub-Saharan Africa during this period. Indeed, according to *Le Monde*, the Kayar project was 'undoubtedly the largest project ever undertaken in Senegal'.[19]

From this period onwards, the execution of the Kayar petrochemical complex and the adjoining town would be the primary concern of political contacts between Iran and Senegal. As far as the leadership of the countries were concerned, the project was far more than merely an industrial complex and adjoining town. It would be a cultural and tourism centre too, which would symbolise the close ties linking Iran and Senegal.

16 'Scope of Work and Proposal for Planning and Architectural Services in connection with the region north of Dakar, Senegal and the development of Keur Farah Pahlavi, Submitted to His Excellency Abdou Diouf Prime Minister of the Government of Senegal by Moshe Safdie and Associates Architects and Planners, Montreal, Canada', 1 October 1975, The Moshe Safdie Archive (henceforth Safdie Archive) B69.A PF1, McGill University, Montreal.

17 'Visit of Empress Farah Pahlavi: Economic Highlights', 5 March 1976, WikiLeaks Cable 1976DAKAR01348_b.

18 'Second Meeting of the Joint Iranian/Senegalese Committee', Tehran, June 1977, Report Dated 30 June 1977, Safdie Archive B69.A PF1.

19 *Le Monde*, 2–3 April 1978, 9.

The Keur Farah Pahlavi Project and Empress Farah's 1976 Visit to Senegal

Rapid urbanisation resulted in a significant increase of the population of Dakar in the years after Senegal's independence. The number of people living in the capital grew by 53 per cent from 374,400 in 1961 to 534,857 in 1970. By 1976, the population had grown to 798,792, a further 49 per cent increase in just six years. Other cities were affected by the general trend of urbanisation, too, though to a lesser extent. Senegal's second (Thiès) and third (Kaolack) most populous cities saw population increases of 29 and 11 per cent, respectively, between 1970 and 1976.[20] The construction of a new city in Senegal thus aimed to reduce the high population density in the capital; diversify and strengthen the economic and industrial bases of the country; and create an Iranian–Senegalese joint venture that would provide opportunities to expand bilateral trade and political relations.[21] When completed, Keur Farah Pahlavi would accommodate over 200,000 inhabitants, making it the second most populous city in the country by some margin, thus alleviating the strain on the capital.[22] Moreover, such huge programmes, or *grands projets*, several of which were incorporated into Senegal's Fourth Plan (1973–1977), and which required significant foreign investment, were designed to help achieve the desired diversification of the economy.[23] By the year 2000, Senghor aimed for Senegal to 'achieve the status of an industrial society, and all our efforts will be aimed at this objective'.[24] The Keur Farah Pahlavi project was intended to help accelerate the realisation of the industrial society Senghor envisioned.

The Israeli–Canadian architect Moshe Safdie was hired by the Senegalese government towards the end of 1975, almost certainly on the recommendation of Empress Farah, to design the architectural program of the new city.[25] Safdie's firm was also hired to provide

[20] *La Nouvelle Ville Keur Farah Pahlavi*, vol. 1, 25 February 1977, 10, Safdie Archive B69.A PF2.

[21] *La Nouvelle Ville Keur Farah Pahlavi*, vol. 4, 16 October 1978, 3, Safdie Archive B69.A PF2.

[22] Thiès had a population of 117,333 in 1976.

[23] Gellar, *Senegal*, 60–61.

[24] Quoted in Boone, *Merchant Capital and the Roots of State Power*, 113.

[25] Safdie was also hired directly by the Iranians to construct a housing complex, the Habitat Tehran El Ahieh, which would be similar to his Habitat in Canada, and in a private meeting in 1977, Empress Farah expressed interest in hiring him to

architectural and engineering services for the headquarters of Irasenco, which would be based in Keur Farah Pahlavi. At this early stage in the planning, work was geared towards identifying a suitable location and developing a schematic design in time for the visit of Empress Farah in February 1976, when she would take part in a ceremony at the site of the new city.[26]

This visit of Empress Farah was the highlight of the relationship between Iran and Senegal during this period. She arrived on 25 February 1976, less than two months after Princess Ashraf's visit to Senegal in January, to an extraordinary welcome. According to a British report, the reception accorded her was 'on the lines that are normal here for Heads of State and included all the characteristics of a full state visit'.[27] Local newspapers note the adoring crowds that gathered to welcome the empress on her arrival:

> Dakar, faithful to a long tradition of kindness and *teranga*,[28] felt obliged to outdo itself for the occasion. The applause from all sides, the smiles of the women who had come in great numbers to welcome her, the cheering of the children, the frenetic movements of the dancers, the tam-tam, all contributed to creating an atmosphere of celebration and popular rejoicing to which the Shahbanou did not remain indifferent. Standing and smiling next to President Senghor, she won over the Senegalese with her grace and simplicity, through the affectionate hand gestures she addressed to the crowd.[29]

The report continues: 'Senegal, as a whole, with a gesture of love and sympathy, will offer her heart and her friendship to the gracious Empress.'[30] During his visit to Iran two months later, Senghor recalled, 'None of the foreign figures who visited our country, even the late Georges Pompidou, president of France, who was my best friend, received such a reception.'[31]

carry out building projects in other cities across Iran. See 'Minutes of Meeting Held at the Royal Palace with Her Imperial Majesty, the Shahbanou and President Senghor, and the Members of the Iranian-Senegalese Committee for Keur Farah Pahlavi', 28 June 1977, Safdie Archive B69.A PF1.

[26] Reza Fallāh to Safdie, 15 November 1975, Safdie Archive B69.A PF1.

[27] Telegram: Visit to Senegal of Shahbanou of Iran, 4 March 1976, FCO 8/2766.

[28] Teranga is a Wolof word, which encapsulates the hospitality of the Senegalese people.

[29] *Le Soleil*, 26 February 1976, 1.

[30] *Le Sénégal, dans son ensemble, dans un geste d'amour et de sympathie, offrira son cœur et son amitié à la grâcieuse Farah l'Impératrice.*

[31] *Rastākhiz*, 9 Ordibehesht 2535/ 29 April 1976, 21.

The empress had cultivated an image of herself as a woman of the people, who freely mingled with all strata of society, and who showed sympathy to all whom she met.[32] This visit demonstrated the projection of this image. The women's magazine *Zan-e Ruz* published a seven-page-spread of the visit, including pictures of the empress greeting enthusiastic admirers. The front cover of the magazine featured an image of a beaming Farah holding a Senegalese child (Figure 9.1). Some women wore dresses adorned with the portrait of the empress and the admiration from the Senegalese appears to have been sincere. According to the US ambassador, 'Senegalese who came into contact with Shahbanou from Senghor on down appear to have been genuinely charmed.'[33]

Empress Farah was accompanied on the trip by Prime Minister Hoveydā, the president of NIOC, Manuchehr Eqbāl, and her mother, who had apparently visited Senegal before. Over the course of the five-day visit, the empress became the first woman to receive an honorary doctorate from the University of Dakar. Granting her the degree, the chancellor of the university drew attention to the 'exceptional merits of a woman who incarnates the "essence" of a country whose history goes back millennia and whose influence around the world is undeniable'.[34] She was also taken on a trip to the island of Gorée, which was supposedly the largest slave-trading centre in Africa from the fifteenth until the nineteenth century.[35]

The highlight of this visit was the ceremony to mark the unveiling of a ceremonial plaque at the site of the new city at Kayar. This took place on 27 February and was covered by the local media with apparently genuine enthusiasm. In the village beside which the new city would be constructed, the delegation was said by *Le Soleil* to have encountered 'a festive atmosphere'. The article continues:

> The ladies in their most beautiful boubous, the children of the schools waving small flags in the colours of the two countries. The men, in this region of cattle breeding, had abandoned their flocks for a while. No one

[32] On the image of Empress Farah in the press, see Liora Hendelman-Baavur, *Creating the Modern Iranian Woman: Popular Culture between Two Revolutions* (Cambridge: Cambridge University Press, 2019), 240–282.

[33] Orison Rudolph Aggrey telegram, 5 March 1976, WikiLeaks Cable 1976DAKAR01347_b.

[34] *Le Soleil*, 27 February 1976, 1.

[35] Previous Iranian visitors, such as Hoveydā, had visited the island. The journalist Amir Tāheri also reported on his trip to the island in June 1971, and introduced Iranian readers to the horrors of the Atlantic slave trade. See *Keyhān*, 20 Khordād 1350/ 10 June 1971, 6.

Figure 9.1 Empress Farah pictured on her trip to Senegal on the front cover of *Zan-e Ruz*, 23 Esfand 1354/ 13 March 1976.

would have wanted to miss this event about which people will later, in the evening around the fire, be able to tell their grandchildren.[36]

During the unveiling ceremony, Empress Farah delivered a speech in which she said:

> The laying of the first stone of an Iranian-Senegalese oil refinery is more than an economic gesture: it transcends the alliance of phosphate and petroleum and constitutes much more than a vow. This act of industrial infrastructure is the very symbol of our determination to build a world of brotherhood and hope.[37]

Senghor, echoing these sentiments, declared that the new city 'seals for eternity the deep friendship which binds the Senegalese and Iranian people'.[38]

The stone itself had the following words inscribed on its base: 'To commemorate the alliance between Xerxes and the eastern and western Ethiopians, in the presence of H.M. Farah Pahlavi H.E. Léopold Sédar Senghor, President of the Republic of Senegal'.[39] In many of Iran's relationships in East and North Africa, Iran stressed its historic, cultural and religious ties to the region. Iran had no such attachment to Senegal, so this inscription was an attempt to manufacture some historical connection. It also suggests that this was seen by the Iranians as more than just a bilateral partnership; in other words, the project was not just a commitment to Senegal, but to the whole of Africa.

Personal Connections and Cultural Engagement

The visit of Empress Farah to Senegal was reciprocated just two months later by President Senghor, who visited Iran from 25 to 30

36 *Le Soleil*, 28–29 February 1976, 1. 37 *Le Soleil*, 27 February 1976, 3.

38 Moshe Safdie, *Keur Farah Pahlavi: Ville nouvelle industrielle pour le gouvernement du Sénégal* (Montréal: Moshe Safdie et Associes Architectes et Urbanistes, 1976), 2.

39 Pour remémorer l'alliance de Xerxès avec les Ethiopiens orientaux et occidentaux, en présence de S. M. I. Farah Pahlavi S. E. Léopold Sédar Senghor, président de la République du Sénégal, ibid. The use of historical references in bilateral relations was common during state visits, particularly in speeches. Shojāʿ al-Din Shafā, who was responsible for writing most of these speeches, said that he often referred to materials in his extensive library to draw on historical or cultural links between Iran and the country in question, 'to make this exchange of expressions more personal and sincere'. Shojāʿ al-Din Shafā, 'Shojāʿ al-Din Shafā az Zabān-e Khodash', in *Yādnāmeh-ye Shojāʿ al-Din Shafā*, ed. Claudine Shafa (Paris, 2013), 82.

April, in what was said by the American ambassador, Richard Helms, to have been a 'very successful atmospheric display of Iran-Senegal friendship'.[40] Because of Senegal's hopes of Iranian investment in its oil industry, in addition to the standard excursions to Tehran's cultural sites, Senghor also visited the oil installations in the south of the country, including the Kharg island depot. During the receptions and gala dinners that were arranged in Senghor's honour, he was repeatedly praised by the shah for his cultural, as well as political, accomplishments.

To mark the visit, *Ettelāʿāt* dedicated a full-page spread to Senegal, in which Senghor was praised as 'a great poet, scholar and philosopher'.[41] On 26 April, an event was held at the central library of the University of Tehran dedicated to the poetry and philosophy of Senghor. During this event, the celebrated Iranian intellectual Mohammad ʿAli Eslāmi Nodushan gave a talk titled 'The Thought and Worldview of Leopold Sédar Senghor' (*andisheh va jahānbini-ye Liyupuld Sedār Sengur*) and the poet Nāder Nāderpur spoke about the characteristics of Senghor's poetry.[42] In his speech, Nodushan spoke about the 'resurgence' (*rastākhiz*) of Africa and the continent's growing importance on the world stage. Senghor, he argued 'is one of the most prominent speakers on this continent'. Nodushan then explained the meaning of Senghor's Négritude, comparing it to Persian mysticism. As Firoozeh Kashani-Sabet has argued, this event and Nodushan's speech reflect Iranian intellectuals' long engagement with issues of race and global struggles against colonialism.[43]

On 28 April, Senghor was granted an honorary doctorate by the University of Tehran, in the presence of Empress Farah. During the ceremony in Foroughi Hall, Senghor, spoke warmly about Empress Farah's recent trip to Iran, his first visit to Iran during the imperial celebrations in 1971, and about his love for Iranian literature, particularly the works of Saʿdi, Hafez, and Omar Khayyam. Senghor then accompanied the empress to inaugurate a new hall in the library,

[40] Richard Helms telegram, 29 April 1976, WikiLeaks Cable 1976TEHRAN04348_b.
[41] *Ettelāʿāt*, 6 Ordibehesht 2535/ 26 April 1976, 9.
[42] *Ettelāʿāt*, 7 Ordibehesht 2535/ 27 April 1976, 29.
[43] Firoozeh Kashani-Sabet, 'The Anti-Aryan Moment: Decolonization, Diplomacy, and Race in Late Pahlavi Iran', *International Journal of Middle East Studies*, vol. 53 (2021), 691–702.

named after the seventh-century historian and vazir Rashid al-Din Fazlollāh Hamedāni Tabib, and which also contained the library of Ebrāhim Purdāvud. At this inauguration, Empress Farah donated to the library six volumes of rare books on the history of Iran, written between the years 600 and 1700.[44] To further emphasise Iran's cultural sophistication, in the evening that Senghor was awarded his doctorate, Senghor and the first lady accompanied the shah and shahbanu to Rudaki Hall, where they were treated to a performance of André Hossein's ballet *Scheherezade*.

The shah enjoyed the company of intellectuals like Senghor, and frequently referred to him as a figure of cultural as well as political significance. Senghor certainly relished the opportunities these banquets presented to engage his hosts in intellectual discussions. Asadollāh ʿAlam was less impressed by Senghor's intellectualism. Of one such banquet, ʿAlam confided in his diary: 'He [Senghor] is a wise man, but he himself thinks he is very wise and talks a lot, he was almost a conversation hoarder. He talks about everything from race and religion and politics and Asia and Africa and Europe and everything else. The king looked at me and smiled.'[45] There are indications elsewhere in ʿAlam's diary that Senghor could be a source of affectionate amusement for the shah and his court minister. In May 1974, ʿAlam wrote, 'The speech of Senghor President of Senegal from China arrived, in which he referred to Mao as God. I was surprised by this and reported it to the king. He laughed a lot!'[46] This is perhaps an indication, too, that the shah was aware of the absurdity of some of the excessive flattery that was sometimes heaped upon statesmen such as himself, who wielded huge personal power.

During a banquet speech, the shah spoke fondly of his first meeting with Senghor in 1971: '[at Persepolis] I had the opportunity to get to know more and better your privileged, distinguished and cultural personality.'[47] According to the historian Gholam Reza Afkhami, Senghor was one of only a small number of leaders with whom the shah was on first name terms.[48] Senghor also spoke passionately

[44] *Ettelāʿāt*, 9 Ordibehesht 2535/ 29 April 1976, 3.
[45] Diary entry, 8 Tir 1356/ 29 June 1977, *Yāddāsht-hā-ye ʿAlam*, vol. 6, 517.
[46] Diary entry, 29 Ordibehesht 1353/ 19 May 1974, *Yāddāsht-hā-ye ʿAlam*, vol. 4, 104.
[47] *Rastākhiz*, 6 Ordibehesht 2535/ 26 April 1976, 17.
[48] Afkhami, *The Life and Times of the Shah*, 57.

about the shah and according to an article in *Le Soleil*, he 'never misses a chance to refer to the friendship that ties him to the Shah and the admiration he feels, as a scholar, for the fabulous history of Persia'.[49] It has been suggested that Senghor's relationship with Anwar Sadat, with whom both the shah and Senghor were very close, may have played a role in building trust between the shah and Senghor.[50]

Nearly as important as the relationship that blossomed between the shah and Senghor were the friendships between other members of the elite. These friendships were enabled in part by the francophone educational backgrounds and self-styled intellectualism of some key members of both Iran's and Senegal's political class. Some of the Senegalese elite felt that they belonged to *la francophonie* – a wider French-speaking community whose cultural heart is France.[51] Senghor in particular saw himself as much French as African, and for his contributions to poetry he became the only African to have been inducted into the *Académie Française*. His prime minister and successor as president, Abdou Diouf, also attended a French school in St Louis before studying law and political science at the Sorbonne, and going on to the Overseas Civil Service School.[52] Senior members of the Pahlavi regime shared this educational background with the Senegalese. Prime Minister Hoveydā, for example, had studied at a French school in Beirut and was enamoured with French literature and culture. In his diaries, Hoveydā regularly referenced European intellectuals, and as Milani notes, 'an essential component of the identity he envisioned for himself was one of an intellectual'.[53] According to Chehabi, the shah was appreciative of Hoveydā's 'cosmopolitan Francophilia' and from time to time even conversed with him in French.[54] Hoveydā travelled to Senegal on official visits three times and developed close bonds with both Senghor and his counterpart, Diouf (Figure 9.2).

49 *Le Soleil*, 26 February 1976, 1. 50 Gellar, *Senegal*, 80.
51 Schraeder, 'Senegal's Foreign Policy', 487.
52 Alan Rake, *African Leaders: Guiding the New Millennium* (London: Scarecrow Press, 2001), 193.
53 Abbas Milani, *The Persian Sphinx: Amir Abbas Hoveyda and the Riddle of the Iranian Revolution* (Washington, DC: Mage Publishers, 2000), 192.
54 H.E. Chehabi, 'A Cosmopolitan Dandy: Amir Abbas Hoveyda', in *The Age of Aryamehr: Late Pahlavi Iran and Its Global Entanglements*, ed. Roham Alvandi (London: Gingko Library, 2018), 155.

Figure 9.2 Senghor with Hoveydā, *Ettelāʿāt*, 21 Bahman 1352/ 10 February 1974, 1.

The Senegalese were perfectly aware of the importance of the French language in developing the bilateral relationship. In a letter to the president of France, Georges Pompidou, in 1971, Senghor decried the fact that young Iranians were no longer learning French, but studied English instead. It was most important to take the opportunity to improve the situation of the French language in Iran at this time because, he wrote, 'As you know, the generation currently in power – that of the shah and the prime minister – is the last francophone generation.' Senghor urged Pompidou to ensure that France took 'an active interest in the problem of the revival of French' in Iran.[55]

Empress Farah and President Senghor also developed a close friendship during this period. She later referred to Senghor as her 'old and dear friend' and her affection for him was certainly reciprocated.[56] During a speech in her honour, Senghor called Empress Farah 'one of

[55] Senghor to Pompidou, 30 October 1971, CADN 180PO/1/531.

[56] 'Her Majesty Shahbanou Farah Pahlavi's Address at the Symposium for the Festival of Arts, Shiraz-Persepolis Held at the Asia Society – New York', 5 October 2013. Available online: https://asiasociety.org/new-york/symposium-shiraz-arts-festival.

the most distinguished personalities in the world and a model for Senegalese girls to follow'.[57] He frequently referred to her as *l'Impératrice au sourire de soie*, the empress with the silken smile, while she called him *l'artisan impeccable du verb*, the impeccable craftsman of the verb.[58]

Senghor's approach to culture as a driver of development also appealed to the Pahlavi perception of the importance of Iran's own culture. In April 1966, Senghor held a huge cultural festival in Dakar, titled *Le Premier Festival mondial des arts nègres* (the First World Festival of Black Arts), in which thousands of writers, musicians, performers and artists from thirty African countries took part, in addition to delegations from other parts of the world.[59] The festival featured an impressive line-up of music, dance and theatrical performances, film screenings, exhibitions, including *L'Art nègre*, and a nine-day colloquium in which the idea of Négritude was debated. Facing criticism over the cost of the event – it made a loss of over $500,000 – Senghor argued, 'We ought not to regret the financial sacrifices the festival has cost us, because it is a matter of culture and, to repeat once again, culture is at the beginning and end of development.'[60] Empress Farah, whose own annual Shiraz Arts Festival commenced one year later in 1967, would undoubtedly have agreed with this statement.

The growing closeness of Iran and Senegal in the late 1970s stimulated an increasing Iranian interest in African culture and art, which was promoted by both sides. Empress Farah was particularly interested in increasing knowledge of African arts and culture in Iran, and as mentioned previously, African artists regularly performed at the annual Shiraz Arts Festival. Over the ten years of the festival's existence, artists from Egypt, Ethiopia, Nigeria, Rwanda, Tunisia and Uganda performed, giving many Iranians the chance to experience the traditional arts of Africa for the first time.[61] Senegalese musical performers appeared during two editions of the festival. The first

[57] *Ettelā'āt*, 9 Esfand 1345/ 28 February 1976, 25.
[58] *Le Soleil*, 27 February 1976, 3.
[59] David Murphy, 'The Performance of Pan-Africanism: Staging the African Renaissance at the First World Festival of Negro Arts', in *The First World Festival of Negro Arts, Dakar 1966*, ed. David Murphy (Liverpool: Liverpool University Press, 2016), 29.
[60] Vaillant, *Black, French, and African*, 323.
[61] Mahasti Afshar, 'Festival of Arts, Shiraz-Persepolis, 1967–1977', *Iran Namag*, vol. 4, no. 2 (2019), 5.

appearance was on 29 August 1970, when forty-five musicians and dancers from Le Ballet National du Sénégal, under the direction of Abdou Mama Diouf, performed traditional dances and songs 'displaying the rich ethnic varieties' of Senegal.[62] The same group performed two days later, on 31 August, a programme of Senegalese ceremonial dances and songs, incorporating a variety of traditional instruments.[63] Again six years later, at the penultimate festival in 1976, L'Ensemble Lyrique Traditionnel du Sénégal performed two concerts of traditional Senegalese music and folklore.[64]

During his trip to Dakar in 1974, Hoveydā visited the Museum of African Arts (Musée de l'Institut Fondamental d'Afrique Noire) where he was able to see the many examples of art from across West Africa on display, including pottery, basketry, silver bracelets, dolls, Snofu Loom pulleys, statuettes representing deities, women and fertility, tam-tams bearing mystical animals, an Ajemuba chief's loincloth from Nigeria, and Baoule masks for initiation rites (Figure 9.3).[65] Two years later, during Empress Farah's visit to Senegal, she observed several displays of African music and dancing, including the Saourouba, a typical Casamance dance.[66]

In late 1977, Empress Farah decided to hold a series of events in Tehran, billed as 'The Programme for Introducing the Arts of Africa' (*Barnāmeh-ye Āshenāyi bā Honar-e Afriqā*) (Figure 9.4). This programme was organised and sponsored by the Farah Pahlavi Foundation, in conjunction with Fārābi University and the National Radio and Television of Iran, and took place from 1 November to 16 December 1977.[67] The central point was an exhibition held at Bāgh-e Ferdows in Tehran, which was said by the Iranian press to be the first major exhibition of African arts held outside of Africa without the assistance of Western museums or cultural institutes. Because of the networks he had established during his time as ambassador in Lagos, Shāhrokh Firuz was asked to assist in finding

[62] Sheherazade Afshar Ghotbi and Arby Ovanessian, *Shiraz-Persepolis Festival of Arts (1967–1977): Detailed Catalogue of Events* (May 2021), 17. Available online: www.academia.edu/49073622/SHIRAZ_ARTS_FESTIVAL_Detailed_Catalogue_of_Events.

[63] Ibid., 18. [64] Ibid., 43–44. [65] *Le Soleil*, 11 February 1974, 3.

[66] *Le Soleil*, 1 March 1976.

[67] *Ettelā'āt*, 5 Mehr 1356/ 27 September 1977, 21.

Figure 9.3 Hoveydā at the Musée de l'Institut Fondamental d'Afrique Noire in Dakar. *Le Soleil*, 11 February 1974, 3.

artefacts.[68] More than 500 items were borrowed from 14 mainly West African countries,[69] with some of the more precious objects coming from museums in Abidjan, Accra, Dakar, Kinshasa, Lagos and Libreville.[70] The stated purpose of the exhibition was to help the public to 'gain a general understanding of the varied and remarkable range of African art' and arrangements were made for schools and educational institutions to visit in group tours.

The exhibition opened in the presence of the shah and shahbanu, along with the president of the Majles, the minister of court, the minister of foreign affairs, and the minister of culture and art.[71] In a speech to mark the inauguration, the empress said that she felt the

[68] Firuz, *Zir-e Sāyeh-ye Alborz*, 813–815.
[69] They were Senegal, Guinea, Mali, Ghana, Sierra Leone, Liberia, Upper Volta, Ivory Coast, Togo, Benin (Dahomey), Nigeria, Cameroon, Gabon and Zaire.
[70] *Ettelā'āt*, 25 Ābān 1356/ 16 November 1977, 21.
[71] *Ettelā'āt*, 11 Ābān 1356/ 2 November 1977, 28.

Figure 9.4 Advertisement poster for a lecture series as part of the 'Programme for Introducing the Arts of Africa', in *Gozāresh Az Barnāmeh-ye Āshenāyi bā Honar-e Afriqā* (Tehran, 1356).

exhibition was 'necessary' because although Iran had its own great history, civilisation and culture, it was not easy for Iranians to get to know other cultures from around the world.[72] The event received attention outside of Iran, too. Several African ambassadors were present at the opening ceremony, and the journalist Hoseyn Rāmtin, who had travelled extensively around Africa,[73] said in an article in *Ettelā'āt* that he had received letters about the exhibition from friends on the continent.[74] In the article, Rāmtin wrote that it was common for Iranians, and other people in the world, to associate Africa with slavery. He therefore expressed his hope that the exhibition would help to bring an understanding of African culture and would be 'the first and great step that paves the way for Iran and Iranians to cooperate and synchronise with the marginalised youth of Africa'.[75] A stamp was also issued to mark the occasion, depicting a ceremonial mask typical of West African art and culture. Such masks formed a central part of the exhibition itself and related published materials.

In addition to the exhibition, as part of the 'Programme for Introducing the Arts of Africa', African musicians and dancers performed at the City Theatre in Tehran, including groups from Ivory Coast and Zaire, and the Cameroonian songwriter and composer Francis Bebey. African plays were also performed, and a series of films by African directors were chosen to be shown both at Bāgh-e Ferdows and the Tehran Museum of Contemporary Art.[76] At the same time as the main exhibition, an international exhibition of books about Africa was held, containing, among other publications, several books that were published to coincide with the programme. This included 'a small book in simple language' on the arts and culture of 'Black Africa' for the benefit of the Iranian youth. A series of educational lectures and seminars were held at Bāgh-e Ferdows, organised by Fārābi University. The programme included three lectures by African scholars and four by 'world-renowned African experts' for the purpose of 'introducing different aspects of African culture' to Iranians.[77] Articles also appeared in the Iranian press. For example, in an interview in

[72] Ibid.
[73] His account of travelling to Nigeria is recorded in the memoir of his friend, Shāhrokh Firuz. See Firuz, *Zir-e Sāyeh-ye Alborz*, 809–812.
[74] *Ettelā'āt*, 12 Ābān 1356/ 3 November 1977, 26. [75] Ibid.
[76] *Ettelā'āt*, 5 Mehr 1356/ 27 September 1977, 21.
[77] *Gozāresh Az Barnāmeh-ye Āshenāyi bā Honar-e Afriqā* (Tehran, 1356).

Ettelāʿāt, the celebrated sculptor and professor at the University of Tehran Parviz Tanāvoli, discussed the diversity and value of African art.[78]

Keur Farah Pahlavi: The Meeting Point of Iranian and Senegalese Culture and Art

The cultural dialogue taking place between Iran and Africa was expressed most clearly through Keur Farah Pahlavi, and the city planning process was closely linked to other cultural exchange initiatives. Several members of the joint Irano-Senegalese committee that was established to oversee the project served on the African art exhibition's organising council. These included Jamshid Behnām, the chancellor of Fārābi University, who headed the council, and Parviz Tanāvoli. The membership of the Keur Farah Pahlavi committee reflected the importance of art and culture to the project; other Iranian members included Hushang Nahāvandi, chief of the Special Bureau of the Shahbanu; and Professor Mehdi Kowsar, architect and dean of the University of Tehran's Faculty of Fine Arts.

During the stone-laying ceremony of the city during Empress Farah's visit in 1976, Senghor expressed his desire that the city would 'create compatible harmony … between Iranian and Senegalese elegance'.[79] Aesthetics were of fundamental importance to the town, since they 'express the soul of a people, a nation, a civilization'.[80] He further stated his wish that Keur Farah Pahlavi would be a 'city which will complement our respective cultures … a Senegalese city in which the tectonic severity of Sudano-Sahelian art will respond to the warmth of Iranian art'.[81] The assignment to synthesise Iranian and Senegalese culture in the planning of the city as an expression of the development of the close political alliance became a pressing concern of the committee in the years that followed.

In addition to the money the Iranians pledged to industrial projects associated with the new city, they also offered to fund the city's public buildings and a cultural centre 'in honour of Her Majesty'. Nahāvandi even suggested that the Grand Mosque of the city be designed by an

[78] *Ettelāʿāt*, 19 Ābān 1356/ 10 November 1977, 25.
[79] Safdie, *Keur Farah Pahlavi*, 3. [80] Ibid. [81] Ibid., 1.

Iranian architect.[82] The extent of Iran's influence on the town's architectural style was a frequent subject of discussion among the joint Iranian–Senegalese committee. During one meeting held in June 1978 at the Senegalese embassy in Paris, when debating the prospective style of the bazaar, 'a rather intense discussion' took place 'on the nature, character and needs of the Iranian bazaar as compared between Africa and Iran'.[83] At the same meeting, Mehdi Kowsar gave a talk about the ways in which certain elements in urban texture could be selected 'to symbolize the link of friendship between Senegal and Iran'. He suggested that a neighbourhood park 'could be structured like an Iranian garden, or a water pond could be shaped in the quiet and elegant way of Iran', while the utilisation of African plants in these features could help to synthesise the two cultures.[84] Kowsar proposed that Iran's influence could also be imparted on the city by utilising Iranian ceramics, particularly blue tiles, in the making of street furniture, such as street signs and other minor components; by using water and landscaping; and by using geometric paving for walkways in the Iranian tradition.[85] During a meeting of the committee in Dakar, President Senghor spoke of public buildings as an area in which 'harmony between Iranian and Senegalese cultures could be realized'.[86] It was even suggested that a Senegalese architect travel to Isfahan to visit its Armenian churches and draw inspiration for the designs of churches in Keur Farah Pahlavi.[87]

The cultural centre of the city would include indoor and outdoor theatres, an art gallery, a library and a lecture hall.[88] In the final report of the Keur Farah Pahlavi project, published in October 1978, plans were even announced to hold an annual festival in the new city in

[82] 'Minutes of Meeting of Iranian/Senegalese Committee for Keur Farah Pahlavi', Dakar, 5 January 1978. Report Dated 11 January 1978, Safdie Archive B69. A PF1.

[83] 'Minutes of Meeting of Iranian-Senegalese Committee for Keur Farah Pahlavi', Paris, 2 June 1978. Report Dated 9 June 1978, Safdie Archive B69.A PF1.

[84] Mehdi Kowsar, 'Keur Farah Pahlavi New Town: Notes, Propose to the Discussion of the Working Group', Paris, 1–3 June 1978, Safdie Archive B69. A PF1.

[85] 'Minutes of Meeting', 2 June 1978, Safdie Archive B69.A PF1.

[86] 'Minutes of Iranian-Senegalese Committee for Keur Farah Pahlavi', Dakar, 5 January 1978. Report Dated 11 January 1978, Safdie Archive B69.A PF1.

[87] Ibid.

[88] *La Nouvelle Ville Keur Farah Pahlavi*, vol. 1, 41, Safdie Archive B69.A PF2.

conjunction with the Shiraz Festival of Arts.[89] Furthermore, at this time, the potential of the northern Senegalese coast as a tourist destination had been recognised. Keur Farah Pahlavi would offer opportunities to develop attractive beaches, construct hotels and ultimately bring tourists to the region.[90] Of course, the establishment of the cultural centre would also have a positive impact on the tourism sector.

The Petrochemical Project

In July 1978, the Senegalese press referred to the Kayar project as the 'jewel of the cooperation' between Iran and Senegal, and reiterated that the city would have a population of 200,000 and cover an area of 2,000 hectares.[91] Senghor himself repeated this information at every opportunity. In January 1978, for example, he said that he expected the city to become Senegal's second most populous by the year 2001.[92] However, despite Senghor's confidence, some of those working on the project doubted whether the targets set by the leadership were achievable. During a visit to Kayar in January 1977, when discussing the size of the city, one of the Senegalese representatives 'reiterated that he thought that 200,000 was unrealistic, though he acknowledged that with the President's position, he is not likely to challenge it.'[93] The Safdie experts concurred that though 'the number now is arbitrary … it seems to be unrealistically high'.[94]

As the 1970s progressed, some Iranian members of Irasenco also became less certain of the unassailability of Iran's investments. The chief NIOC representative of Irasenco, Homāyun Khosravāni, confided to the US ambassador that he was 'pessimistic even about the

[89] *La Nouvelle Ville Keur Farah Pahlavi*, vol. 4, 16 October 1978, 25, Safdie Archive B69.A PF2. The passage reads: 'Un festival annuel des arts devrait être organisé en conjonction avec la présentation du fameux festival Shiraz en Iran. Cet événement peut inclure un festival du film, du théâtre, de l'art Sénégalais et peut vraisemblablement devenir une coproduction Sénégalo-Iranienne.'

[90] *La Nouvelle Ville Keur Farah Pahlavi*, vol. 4, 26, Safdie Archive B69.A PF2.

[91] *Nation*, 19 July 1978, newspaper cut out in Safdie Archive.

[92] *Le Soleil*, 6 January 1978, 3.

[93] 'Report of Trip to Site of Keur Farah Pahlavi', 8 January 1977, Safdie Archive B69.A PF1.

[94] Moshe Safdie, 'General Notes on Committee Meeting and Trip', 14 January 1977, Safdie Archive B69.A PF1.

proposed oil refinery' and 'clearly sceptical of the entire Sedar project'.[95] One of the reasons for this was Iran's reluctance to pledge additional funds as its own financial crisis worsened. As a result, although Iran had agreed to invest in the port and the town, it declined to invest in other essential infrastructure, including roads and railway linking the port to the Tobène mine, or a power plant to serve the petrochemical complex and town. The cost of this infrastructure was reckoned to be as high as $300 million. As early as December 1976, Iran's minister of economy, Hushang Ansāri, had told the US ambassador in Tehran that 'unless the GOS can raise the money to finance the super-structure, the GOI will not want to pursue any of the projects such as phosphates, etc.'[96] A US report from 1976, just six months after the stone-laying ceremony, read that due to Senegal's inability to attract funding for infrastructure, the Kayar project was 'at [a] standstill' because Iran had demanded that before they commence construction on the refinery and mine, funds for infrastructure be assured.[97]

As time progressed, there were indications that the project was being scaled back. Following an Irasenco board meeting in April 1977 in Dakar, it was decided that the size and cost of the port be reduced and that the construction of the refinery be delayed 'for an interim period of time'.[98] The Iranians did suggest they would be willing to contribute $100 million towards infrastructure as long as the International Bank for Reconstruction and Development (IBRD), which was at that time completing its own feasibility report, also pledged $100 million. But even in its scaled down incarnation, the project was still 'unfeasible', according to the World Bank, which disassociated itself from the project in August 1978. By 1977, even the basic rationale of the project, to facilitate the exchange of Iranian oil for Senegalese phosphates, had to be reconsidered. First, depressed world markets for phosphates meant that the government of Senegal could not see the benefit in constructing a new mine. And second, an Irano-French firm had been prospecting for phosphates in southern Iran, which had

[95] Cohen telegram, 12 January 1978, WikiLeaks Cable 1978DAKAR00327_d.
[96] Richard Helms telegram, 6 December 1976, WikiLeaks Cable 1976TEHRAN12086_b.
[97] US embassy in Senegal telegram, 27 August 1976, WikiLeaks Cable 1976DAKAR05480_b.
[98] Aggrey telegram, 21 April 1977, WikiLeaks Cable 1977DAKAR02748_c.

yielded promising results. Should phosphates be found in Iran, this would negate the need for imports from Senegal.[99]

As a result of these developments, and the difficulty in securing funds for infrastructural development, the government of Senegal decided that it would delay exploitation of the Tobène phosphate deposits near Kayar, and instead increase production at the existing Taiba mine to two million tonnes per year. Iran's $12.5 million investment in the Taiba phosphate company, announced in February 1978, allowed this increase in production.[100] The Tobène mine, they announced, would only be opened in twelve to fifteen years, after the supplies at Taiba had been exhausted. This decision eliminated the need for a new port and additional infrastructure, since the road and railway links from Taiba to ports in Dakar were well-established. Additionally, the local Société Africaine de Raffinage (SAR) refinery announced that it would double its current 900,000 tonne capacity, which would 'clearly obliviate [the] need for new refining capacity for many years'.[101] Now, Senegal needed neither a new refinery, a new mine, nor a new port. A US report from 1978 noted wryly of the Keur Farah Pahlavi, 'perhaps it could be redesigned as a retirement community'.[102]

Curiously, is seems as though Senghor's spirits were not dampened by these complications. In an interview with the publication *Afrique Industrie Infrastructures* in January 1978, when asked about the reasons for the delays in implementing the Kayar project, Senghor responded,

> When a project is delayed, it is usually for one of the following reasons: preliminary studies that take longer or are more difficult than anticipated, the sourcing of funding, or a lack of will of the promoters. On this last point, we have no doubts whatsoever: the joint will of Iran and Senegal to realize this project has been reaffirmed recently, and with great force.[103]

In fact, the delay, which was, Senghor argued, 'not a very important delay', was caused by 'the complexity of the studies and the care taken to obtain suitable financing conditions'.[104] There was a strange

[99] Helms telegram, 13 September 1976, WikiLeaks Cable 1976TEHRAN09222_b.
[100] Cohen telegram, 24 February 1978, WikiLeaks Cable 1978DAKAR01450_d.
[101] Galanto telegram, 3 August 1978, WikiLeaks Cable 1978DAKAR05914_d.
[102] Cohen telegram, 12 January 1978, WikiLeaks Cable 1978DAKAR00327_d.
[103] *Afrique Industrie Infrastructures*, 1 January 1978, 28. [104] Ibid.

disconnect between the pessimistic attitude of Irasenco representatives on both the Iranian and Senegalese side, and the stubborn optimism of Senghor and the Iranian royal house. The leaders and the press presented the tough 'financial conditions' as mere glitches; bumps in the road that could easily be overcome. The joint Iranian–Senegalese commission that was charged with designing Keur Farah Pahlavi was meeting as late as July 1978, the final reports were submitted in March 1979, and Empress Farah was planning another visit to Senegal in January 1979. As it happened, these 'financial conditions' were a stumbling block that could not be overcome, and by 1978, the project in its original form was essentially dead.

In spite of the clear problems with the Keur Farah Pahlavi project, relations between Iran and Senegal continued to grow. Senghor travelled to Iran for the third time in July 1977, and again the following year in April 1978. The title of a report from the US embassy (perhaps sarcastically) reads: 'Senghor pays annual visit to Iran.'[105] Though these were ostensibly 'private visits', they were recorded prominently in the local press, and Senghor was accorded full honours. During his April 1978 visit, for example, he was both greeted and bade farewell at the airport by the shah and shahbanu and enjoyed several dinner banquets organised in his honour. During this trip, as with earlier visits, Senghor was taken to visit cultural sites, including the Reza Abbasi Museum, the Carpet Museum and the Museum of Contemporary Arts. He also flew to Kerman, where he visited several sites, presumably to become more acquainted with the types of traditional Iranian architecture that would be replicated in the Keur Farah Pahlavi, including the Malek Mosque, the Ganjʿali Khan Complex, the bazaar and the Shah Neʿmatollāh Vali Shrine (in Mahan).[106] Upon his return to Senegal after his 1978 visit, Senghor said that Senegalese foreign policy ascribed a 'large place' to Irano-Senegalese cooperation and once again stressed that the Kayar project was 'one of the best (examples of) cooperation which Senegal has with foreign countries'.[107]

[105] Sullivan telegram, 1 May 1978, WikiLeaks Cable 1978TEHRAN04111_d.
[106] 'Programme de la visite de son excellence monsieur le president de la republique du Senegal et madame Leopold Sedar Senghor en Iran', Safdie Archive B69. A PF1.
[107] Cohen telegram, 2 May 1978, WikiLeaks Cable 1978DAKAR03250_d.

Even during the unfolding crisis that would lead to the revolution, there were no indications that Iran sought to withdraw formally from the project, in spite of the economic problems Irasenco encountered. Was this because the empress herself had laid the foundation stone, rendering Iranian withdrawal virtually unimaginable? Was it because to Iran the project symbolised a bilateral relationship that was vital to its broader Africa strategy? Or was it because of the close personal bonds between the countries' leaders? It was probably a combination of these factors. In 1976, during Senghor's visit, the shah said: 'Thankfully, the relations between our two countries are based on increasing cooperation in all fields of economics, trade, science and culture. The existence of a new city now being created in the name of the Shahbanu of Iran in Senegal is a symbol of the extent of this friendship and the closeness of our two nations.'[108]

*****

Iranian–Senegalese relations in the 1970s illustrate how Pahlavi Iran used its relatively recently acquired financial clout to expand its political influence. When negotiating potential loans from the World Bank for the Keur Farah Pahlavi Project, Jahāngir Āmuzegār, who had served as Ambassador at Large and Chief of the Iranian Economic Mission in Washington, DC since 1963, proposed that for each sum required, a portion be loaned first to Iran. For example, if $20 million was needed, Āmuzegār suggested that $10 million be loaned directly to Senegal and $10 million to Iran to pass on to Senegal. When asked by the World Bank representative how this would provide additional benefit to Senegal, Āmuzegār responded that it would not; 'it would however provide certain political benefits for Iran vis-à-vis Senegal'.[109] In this way, Iran sought to maximise the political leverage it could gain through these projects.

An important factor in the development of the special relationship between Iran and Senegal was the genuine friendship that existed between the leadership of the two countries; not only the shah and

108 *Ettelā'āt*, 6 Ordibehesht 2535/ 26 April 1976, 40.

109 'Iran – Mr. McNamara's Meeting with Dr. Jahangir Amuzegar', 4 August 1976, Contacts with Member Countries: Iran – Correspondence 03, 1771089, WB IBRD/IDA 03 EXC-10-4549S, World Bank Group Archives, Washington, DC.

President Senghor, but also Empress Farah, Hoveydā and Diouf. Senghor appealed to the Pahlavi elite both as a world-renowned intellectual and poet and as a widely respected and forward-thinking, yet conservative, politician. He visited Iran four times between 1971 and 1978, more than any leader of an African country during this period. During these visits he was invariably honoured at banquets at the shah's palaces. During Senghor's first state visit, in a speech in his honour, the shah spoke of him as important 'not only as head of a friendly country, but also at the same time one of the most outstanding cultural personalities' and of his 'voice that resonates as the best contemporary African poetry'.[110] Most importantly, Senghor was considered not only to speak for Senegal, but for all Africans: 'Today you are not only the leader of an important African nation that under your leadership is heading towards comprehensive social, political and societal progress, but you are the spiritual spokesperson for the whole of Africa.'[111]

[110] *Rastākhiz*, 6 Ordibehesht 2535/ 26 April 1976, 17. [111] Ibid.

10 Southern Africa

The Politics of Race and Oil

In 1967, after the Six-Day War, not only had Iran not joined any Arab boycott of oil to those countries that recognised Israel, but it benefitted by increasing its supply to boycotted countries to make up for their shortfall. These countries included South Africa.[1] The closure of the Suez Canal during the war also increased the strategic importance of the Cape of Good Hope, and was one of the reasons for the establishment of political relations between Iran and South Africa at the consular level in 1970. Then, another conflict in the Middle East, the Yom Kippur War of 1973, again forced Iran to re-assess not only its relationship with South Africa, but the strategic significance of Southern Africa.

In response to American support of Israel in the Yom Kippur War, the Arab members of OPEC initiated an oil embargo against the United States, which led ultimately to a huge increase in the price of oil. Shortly after the initiation of the embargo, it was extended to South Africa, Rhodesia and Portugal, in the expectation that this would encourage independent African states to support the Arabs against Israel. As the historian Stephen Sparks has observed: 'The OPEC embargo against South Africa therefore had more to do with diplomatic horse-trading than anti-apartheid principle.'[2] Iran saw an opportunity to use the situation to sell even greater volumes of oil to South Africa. As a result, by the end of the 1970s, Iran supplied the vast majority of South Africa's crude oil imports; over 90 per cent annually between 1976 and 1978. South Africa also became a major trading

[1] In fact, a boycott had been announced against South Africa and Rhodesia before the war, which remained in effect during the blockade. M. S. Daoudi and M. S. Dajani, 'The 1967 Oil Embargo Revisited', *Journal of Palestine Studies*, vol. 13, no. 2 (1984), 71.

[2] Stephen Sparks, 'Crude Politics: The ANC, the Shipping Research Bureau and the Anti-Apartheid Oil Boycott', *South African Historical Journal*, vol. 69, no. 2 (2017), 257.

partner for Iran. A British report from 1975 stated that 'South Africa is now playing an increasingly important part in Iran's economic development. Since the establishment of relations between the two countries in 1970, trade has leapt.'[3] For the South African government, as it became ever more isolated within Africa and the wider world, Iran became ever more important as both a source of oil and a trading partner.

As the 1970s progressed, Iran paid increasingly close attention to the broader Southern Africa region, beyond South Africa. Iran was deeply concerned at the Soviet and Cuban support for nationalists in Angola, Mozambique and Namibia. Iran feared that deterioration of the political situation in Southern Rhodesia and the spreading of the civil war would present opportunities for the Soviets to intervene. This, the shah reasoned, might lead to the eventual victory of extremist nationalist forces in Rhodesia under the influence of Moscow. For this reason, when Britain and the United States, which shared Iran's concerns, sought to bring a diplomatic resolution to the Rhodesian crisis between 1976 and 1979, they found a willing ally in the shah.[4] But the shah was not a tool of British and American diplomacy; he was also looking after his own interests.

Moreover, the insurgency in Rhodesia was widely supported across Africa. Therefore, the shah could choose to take an active role in trying to bring about a resolution to the crisis, or else risk a backlash across Black Africa – where he had carefully cultivated ties for the past decade – for his support of South Africa. He chose the former option, and during the 1970s, Iran invited leaders of groups opposed to the Ian Smith regime to visit Iran, in particular Joshua Nkomo, who was considered by the shah the nationalist candidate most likely to oppose and prevent Soviet infiltration in the region.

Oil and Southern Africa

Iran had established relations with South Africa at the consular level in 1970 and thereafter developed close economic and security relations with the apartheid regime. In 1973, John Oxley was replaced as South

[3] R. J. Alston to J. M. O. Snodgrass, 28 April 1975, FCO 8/2501.

[4] Sue Onslow, 'The Cold War in Southern Africa: White Power, Black Nationalism and External Intervention', in *The Cold War in Southern Africa: White Power, Black Liberation*, ed. Sue Onslow (London: Routledge, 2009), 26.

Africa's consul-general in Tehran by the three-star general Charles 'Pop' Fraser. That such a decorated military figure was chosen to head South Africa's embassy is evidence not only of the significance South Africa attached to the relationship, but that he accepted the assignment is evidence of the attractiveness of the position to South African diplomats. In Johannesburg, Ahmad Tehrāni left his position in 1974 to pursue a career in the private sector.[5] He was replaced by Fereydun Sotudeh, a career diplomat, who had joined the Ministry of Foreign Affairs in 1950, and who would serve as consul-general in Johannesburg until 1978.[6] For the final months of Pahlavi rule, Mohammad Rashti, a founding member of the Iran Novin Party, took charge of the consulate.[7] Iran's choice of rather unglamorous, yet capable civil servants as consul-generals in the mid- to late 1970s emphasises the pragmatic nature of Iran's approach to South Africa during this period.

The cornerstone of Iran–South Africa cooperation during this period was oil. Throughout the 1960s and 1970s, Iran had consistently declined to participate in international sanctions against South Africa. In 1963, when the United Nations General Assembly voted to implement oil sanctions in response to South Africa's occupation of Namibia, Iran actually joined the majority in voting in favour of sanctions. However, at the same time, Iran declared that its vote did not mean that new sanctions would be imposed. As a result 'Iran's vote rang hollow', and it continued to supply the majority of South Africa's crude oil.[8] In 1967, Iran refused to join the Arab oil embargo, with the reasoning that politics should not interfere with trade relations, and in particular that oil should be separate from politics. In an interview in

[5] Tehrāni had received an official warning from Khalʿatbari about his conduct, after a report had accused him of criticising the Imperial Armed Forces of Iran, not observing the annual 28 Mordad commemoration in an appropriate manner, and womanising and gambling, among other things. Tehrāni strenuously denied all the accusations and complained to his friend, Zāhedi, at the injustice of punishing servants of the shah such as himself, without a fair trial. It is probable that this sense of injustice compelled him to leave government service and go into the private sector. See Khalʿatbari to Tehrāni, 14 Ordibehesht 1353/ 4 May 1974; Tehrāni to Zāhedi, 18 Farvardin 1353/ 7 April 1974; and Tehrāni to Zāhedi, 5 Ordibehesht 1353/ 25 April 1974, Zāhedi Archives, box 128, folder 6.

[6] *Iran Who's Who*, 383.

[7] Chehabi, 'South Africa and Iran', 693; *Iran Who's Who*, 338.

[8] Arthur J. Klinghoffer, *Oiling the Wheels of Apartheid: Exposing South Africa's Secret Oil Trade* (Boulder, CO: Lynne Rienner, 1989), 36.

1971 in the journal *Jeune Afrique*, the shah he said that 'while his Government had always condemned political racialism, politics should not be mixed with trade and he would, therefore, continue his contacts with South Africa.'[9] Iran was fairly consistent on this matter. Indeed, it continued to supply oil to Ethiopia after the revolution of 1974 and refused to support a potential Arab oil embargo of Ethiopia in February 1975, with the shah stressing that 'his country did not participate in oil embargos against other nations'.[10] Iran's stance, which it maintained throughout the 1960s and 1970s, was that one did not have to be friends with a country to trade with it. In December 1977, for example, Iran's representative to the Fourth Committee of the UN General Assembly, justifying its continued oil sales to South Africa, said that Iran had 'always considered oil as a commodity and not a political weapon'.[11]

Even if the political will had existed in Iran to join an Arab boycott, it is not certain that it would have been able to, or whether Iranian participation would have been effective. As part of the Consortium Agreement of 1954, signed in the aftermath of the oil nationalisation crisis of 1951–1953, 50 per cent of Iranian oil was distributed by the NIOC and the other 50 per cent was sold to members of an international consortium for international marketing. All five of the major oil companies (the so-called majors) with subsidiaries in South Africa were members of the consortium. In 1974, the year after the 1973 boycott, the consortium sold approximately 213,000 barrels of Iranian oil per day to South Africa, while an additional 38,000 were provided directly by the NIOC.[12] Iran had no intention of joining the Arab boycotts anyway, so we cannot argue that it was constrained by the consortium, and although the NIOC did not directly supply the majority of Iranian oil to South Africa, the Iranian government took a larger share of the criticism for oiling the wheels of apartheid.[13]

During the 1970s, in spite of pressure from the UN, Arab oil-producing nations and the OAU, the supply of Iranian oil to South

[9] Metrowich, *South Africa's New Frontiers*, 129.
[10] William Stoltzfus telegram, 24 February 1974, WikiLeaks Cable 1975KUWAIT00878_b.
[11] Martin Bailey and Bernard Rivers, *Oil Sanctions against South* Africa (UN Centre Against Apartheid, Department of Political and Security Council Affairs, December 1978), 77.
[12] Ibid., 27. [13] Chehabi, 'South Africa and Iran', 696.

Africa increased significantly. In 1972, Iran provided 54 per cent of South Africa's crude oil imports, with the remainder coming from Iraq (19 per cent), Saudi Arabia (16 per cent) and Qatar (11 per cent).[14] Because of the embargo placed on South Africa by the Arab oil producers in November 1973, South Africa lost a significant portion of its oil supply. Other suppliers, such as Qatar, Brunei, the United Arab Emirates and Kuwait, continued to provide small amounts of oil to South Africa, but Iran made up the majority of the loss of Iraqi and Saudi oil (Table 10.1). From 1974 until the revolution, Iran supplied on average 90 per cent of South Africa's oil imports.[15] In 1977, it was estimated that 91 per cent of South Africa's crude oil came from Iran, and it has been suggested that by 1978 the figure had reached 96 per cent.[16]

In the late 1970s, South Africa relied on liquid fuels – 90 per cent of which was oil – for 21 per cent of its overall energy consumption.[17] Iranian oil was thus a vital energy source for South Africa. Maintaining this supply was important for the preservation of not only South Africa's economy, but its military capabilities, too. It was reported, for example, that as a result of the breakdown of an Iranian tanker in November 1973, just as the Arab oil embargo began to bite, there was no fuel available to operate light aircraft.[18] Iran's exports to South Africa constituted just 4.7 per cent of Iran's total crude oil exports.[19] So, while Iranian oil was vital to South Africa, to Iran, South Africa was an important, yet not indispensable, customer.

Aware of this imbalance, the South Africans went to some lengths to make sure that Iranian oil executives were well looked after. In 1973, for example, the NIOC chairman, Manuchehr Eqbāl, was granted an honorary doctorate by the University of Stellenbosch. This was apparently ordered expressly by the prime minister, John Vorster, who

[14] Bailey and Rivers, *Oil Sanctions against South Africa*, 25.
[15] Although Table 10.1 shows that Iran supplied 85 per cent in 1975, it actually increased the volume of oil exported by 2,000 barrels a day.
[16] Bailey and Rivers, *Oil Sanctions against South Africa*, 26A; Chehabi, 'South Africa and Iran', 696.
[17] Mats Lundahl, 'Economic Effects of a Trade and Investment Boycott against South Africa', *The Scandinavian Journal of Economics*, vol. 86, no. 1 (1984), 69.
[18] Barbara Rogers, 'Southern Africa and the Oil Embargo', *Africa Today*, vol. 21, no. 2 (1974), 7.
[19] Bailey and Rivers, *Oil Sanctions against South Africa*, 27.

Table 10.1 ***Origin of South African oil imports in 1972, 1974 and 1975***

Country	1972 Quantity (thousand barrels per day)	1972 Percentage of total	1974 Quantity (thousand barrels per day)	1974 Percentage of total	1975 Quantity (thousands of barrels per day)	1975 Percentage of total
Iran	138	54	254	90	256	84
Iraq	50	19	15	5	–	
Saudi Arabia	41	16	–	–	–	
Qatar	28	11	13	4.6	36	12
Brunei	–	–	–	–	8	3
United Arab Emirates	–	–	–	–	3	1
Kuwait	–	–	1	0.4	–	–
Total	257	100	283	100	303	100

Source: Martin Bailey and Bernard Rivers, *Oil Sanctions against South Africa* (UN Centre Against Apartheid, Department of Political and Security Council Affairs, December 1978), 25A–25B

happened to be the chancellor of the university. The Dutch ambassador, in his report of a dinner organised by the consul-general on this occasion, seemed surprised by the influence exerted by Iran:

> On this occasion, the consul general [Tehrāni] organised a dinner in Cape Town, to which he had invited many prominent South African personalities, including the state president. My spouse and I had had the honour to attend this meal, and we witnessed how the state president, prime minister and many others were the guests of the consul general of Iran, a country, which … does not even have diplomatic relations with the Republic.[20]

The ambassador concluded that these close ties should be seen in the light of the interests of NIOC in South Africa, as well as South Africa's dependency on Iranian oil. One year after Eqbāl's visit, the president of the Iranian senate, Ja'far Sharif-Emāmi, headed a ten-man parliamentary delegation to South Africa on a twelve-day visit. South Africa must have felt that its efforts to affect the Pahlavi elite had achieved success, for during this visit, Senator Sharif-Emami insisted that Iran would not under any circumstances impose boycotts on South Africa. 'We have such friendly relations with you', he said, 'that I am sure we will continue not only to supply oil but any other commodities you may require'.[21]

Economic Relations

The government of South Africa was convinced that to maintain the flow of Iranian oil, it was important to develop closer economic relations in other areas. In a report of a conversation with the director-general of the South African Department of Foreign Affairs, Brand Fourie, on 6 December 1973, Ambassador Tehrāni wrote:

> While thanking the Imperial Government for its oil policy towards South Africa, the aforementioned [Fourie] said that the South African Government is willing to participate in Iran's Fifth [Development] Plan either through direct investment or through granting credit for a short period of time.[22]

[20] Dutch ambassador in South Africa, A. H. Hasselman, to Ministry of Foreign Affairs, 10 May 1974, NA 2.05.191/433.

[21] Metrowich, *South Africa's New Frontiers*, 130.

[22] Tehrāni to Khal'atbari, undated (December 1973?), box 128, Zāhedi Archive, box 128, folder 6.

Shortly after, Tehrāni held a meeting with Prime Minister Vorster, who said that 'South Africa will never forget the kindness of Iran' and was willing to cooperate with Tehran in various fields. Vorster added that 'he had made a firm decision and has ordered the relevant ministers to make every effort to help investment in Iran'.[23]

In the months prior, groups of South African industrialists had travelled to Iran to make preliminary assessments as possible areas for South African investment. As a result, shortly after Sharif-Emami's ten-man delegation had visited South Africa, an economic delegation from South Africa, headed by the South African minister of trade and industry, Owen Horwood, travelled to Iran, from 20 until 24 June 1974. During the trip, Horwood had an audience with the shah, and held meetings with the prime minister, Hoveydā, NIOC chairman, Eqbāl, minister of finance, Hushang Ansāri, the head of the Plan Organisation, ʿAbdol-Majid Majidi, minister of energy, Iraj Vahidi, the minister of commerce, Fereydun Mahdavi, and the minister of industry and mines, Farrokh Najmābadi. On the basis of these discussions, an agreement was signed, in which both sides pledged to increase their cooperation in various fields. One of these was mining. Horwood welcomed Iranian investment in coal mining in South Africa and South Africa agreed to cooperate with Iran in the exploration, exploitation and beneficiation of gold deposits in Iran. South Africa had been helping to train mining technicians in Iran, and agreed to continue this cooperation and expand the mining school at Nakhlak. Twenty bursaries were offered for Iranian students to study at Pretoria University. The first cohort enrolled at the beginning of 1975, and the first five to earn their master's degrees in engineering graduated in November 1976.[24]

Another area of particular attention was industrial development. As part of the agreement signed during Horwood's visit in June 1974, both sides pledged to cooperate in the establishment of pulp, paper and wood industries in Iran; and South Africa agreed to supply machinery and equipment for the production of cement, limestone and mining equipment, which Iran lacked. Later, in August 1974, it was announced that South African experts would help to establish and operate Iran's first copper alloy extrusion plant. These were planned to be the first of several South African industrial ventures

[23] Ibid. [24] Metrowich, *South Africa's New Frontiers*, 130.

in Iran.[25] Cooperation in the petroleum and petrochemicals industries was also an important part of cooperation. In 1974, South Africa proposed to increase the shares of NIOC in the Sasolburg refinery from 17.5 to 33.3 per cent; the Sasol company was willing to provide Iran 'on competitive terms' all the licences and training to convert dry gas to petrochemicals and petrochemical feed-stocks; and Sasol also offered Iran the opportunity to invest in a proposed petrochemical plant in South Africa based on steam cracking.[26]

Trade between the two countries also experienced huge growth during the 1970s. Iranian imports from South Africa, which were becoming increasingly important in the context of Iran's industrial programmes, had increased in value by 300 per cent between 1350 (1971–72) and 1352 (1973–74) alone.[27] These imports included farm produce, minerals, wool, paper products, ferrous metals and semi-manufactured steel products. In March 1974, South Africa's cement sector agreed to export over 200,000 tons of cement to Iran, representing 6 per cent of South Africa's total cement production.[28] Iran also accounted for 25 per cent of South Africa's total steel exports.[29] By 1975, South Africa was Iran's second largest supplier of asbestos and ferro manganese, provided 40 per cent of Iran's mica and 50 per cent of its tanning extract. As part of the agreement signed in June 1974, both sides vowed to expand further trade relations. South Africa pledged to supply Iran with larger quantities of cement, billet for Iran's rolling mills, and unrefined sugar. Both sides also agreed to explore the possibility of signing a trade agreement 'which will provide a further stimulus for the expansion of trade on a long term basis possibly leading to specific agreements of a bilateral nature'.[30]

The volume of trade continued to grow and in the two years before the revolution, there was a huge expansion in trade between Iran and South Africa. In 1355 (1976–77), Iran imported just over $100 million worth of goods from South Africa, representing 0.81 per cent of Iran's total import value. In the same period, it exported around one and a

[25] Ibid., 131.
[26] *Asnād-e Mo'āhedāt-e do Jānebeh-ye Irān bā Sāyer-e Duval*, vol. 1, 609–610.
[27] Alston to Snodgrass, 28 April 1975, FCO 8/2501.
[28] Metrowich, *South Africa's New Frontiers*, 131.
[29] Chehabi, 'South Africa and Iran', 698.
[30] For the complete text of this agreement, see *Asnād-e Mo'āhedāt-e do Jānebeh-ye Irān bā Sāyer-e Duval*, vol. 1, 605–613.

half million dollars' worth of goods to South Africa, representing 0.3 per cent of Iran's total export value. However, in the first nine months of 1356 (March–December 1977), the value of imports from South Africa was $142 million, or 1.4 per cent of the total, and the value of exports to South Africa was $17.6 million, or 5.6 per cent of the total.[31] Iran had become reliant on South African cement for its major construction projects. In 1978, South Africa exported 360,000 tonnes of cement to Iran for around $22 million.[32] The car manufacturer BMW had exported from its factory in South Africa more than 1,000 cars to Iran in 1978, and had just started delivery of an order of 3,000 more, worth up to $25 million, at the time of the revolution.[33] Iran also imported food products from South Africa; according to a British report, immediately after the revolution 'several big South African frozen chicken producers were hard hit by the disappearance of the Iranian market'.[34]

Iran was particularly interested in South Africa as a source of uranium and in 'tapping South Africa's nuclear know-how' and by early 1975, there were already some Iranians 'under training in South Africa'.[35] During the 1974 visit, the South African delegation 'offered its readiness to enter into a general cooperation agreement with Iran in all areas of atomic energy', and offered Iran the opportunity to invest in the uranium plant that South Africa was setting up. The agreement stipulated that Iran would consider South Africa's proposals after feasibility studies had been carried out. The following year, in October 1975, the press reported that Iran and South Africa were on the verge of signing a nuclear agreement that included the sale of 14,000 tons of South African uranium oxide, worth around $700 million, and Iranian investment in a South African enrichment facility.[36] Iran's 15 per cent share of the Rössing Company, which had the rights to the extraction of uranium in Namibia, was purchased for nearly $40 million and although no public announcement was made

[31] Vezārat-e Bāzargāni, 'Mobādelāt-e Bāzargāni-ye Irān bā Keshvar-hā-ye Qāreh-ye Āfriqā', 1977[?], NLAI 245/003909. In 1978, imports from South Africa were believed to amount to around $115 million. 'South Africa and the Shah: Oil Supplies at Stake', *MERIP Reports*, no. 73 (1978), 21.

[32] Sophia Lambert to P. Morrice, 27 March 1979, FCO 8/3373.

[33] Ibid. Apparently these cars were sent to Germany instead, where demand for the vehicles was high.

[34] Ibid.

[35] Alston to Snodgrass, 28 April 1975, FCO 8/2501.

[36] Kissinger telegram, 16 October 1975, WikiLeaks Cable 1975STATE246640_b.

at the time on Iranian purchases of uranium, it was understood that Iran signed a long-term contract for 16,000 tonnes over a period ending in 1991.[37]

Although Iran and South Africa did not raise the level of their representatives from consul-generals to ambassadors, relations between the two countries expanded considerably throughout the 1970s. Not only in terms of volume, but also diversity of trade, South Africa had become Iran's most important trading partner in Africa. However, even though Iran and South Africa enjoyed close economic and political relations, and in spite of the shah's assurances that he would not voluntarily impose an embargo on South Africa, it was widely believed that he would comply if the UN voted for a mandatory embargo.[38] Understanding this situation, Britain and the United States sought to encourage the shah to use the threat of withdrawing Iran's oil supply in negotiations with South Africa over the situation in Rhodesia.

Beyond South Africa

Petroleum was the main focus of relations with other countries in Southern Africa and for many of them Iran was a major supplier of oil. Angola had a refinery of its own, which produced eight million tonnes of crude oil annually. It exported 90 per cent of this, so was dependant on imports for two-thirds of its diesel fuel, half of its gasoline, and all of its lube oils and greases. Based on data from the first nine months of 1973, approximately 61 per cent of Angola's diesel imports came from Iran, as did 68 per cent of its gasoline and 30 per cent of its kerosene. [39] To Malawi, Iran exported all of its jet fuel requirements, and the vast majority of its aviation spirit, motor spirit, diesel and paraffin.[40] To Madagascar, in the first half of 1973, although all of its crude oil came from Qatar and Saudi Arabia, Iran

[37] Mohammad Taqi Ibn Sejād to ʿAbdol-Majid Majidi, 25 Dey 2535/ 15 January 1977, NLAI 220/010605; William Bowers, 'Note for the Record', 5 June 1979, FCO 8/3373.

[38] *The New York Times*, 18 June 1978, 6.

[39] Everett Ellis Briggs telegram, 18 January 1974, WikiLeaks Cable 1974LUANDA00037_b.

[40] Based on data for the year 1972. William C. Burdett telegram, 2 January 1974, WikiLeaks Cable 1974BLANTY00012_b.

exported 97 per cent of its refined products.[41] The situation was comparable in Mozambique, which imported all of its crude oil from Iraq, but a large percentage of its gasoline, kerosene, diesel and asphalt from Iran.[42] Although Iran did not have close political or economic relations with each of these countries, through petroleum it maintained a connection.

Landlocked countries, which lacked easy access to global markets, often relied on neighbours for access to oil supplies. For example, Zambia had achieved independence from Britain in 1964, but as a landlocked country, was reliant on other regional powers for access to the sea and trade. While many countries in Southern Africa naturally gravitated towards the economic powerhouse of the region, Zambia's first post-independence president, Kenneth Kaunda, engaged in what the journalist Stanley Meisler referred to as a struggle 'to free itself from the economic web of the white regimes in southern Africa'.[43] Zambia was a member of the non-aligned movement, to which Kaunda emphasised his commitment during the third summit, held in Lusaka in September 1970. The main focus of Kaunda's foreign policy was Southern Africa and working to bring about majority rule in every country in the region.[44] His support of liberation movements, in particular in Mozambique and Rhodesia, often raised tensions with Zambia's neighbours. In January 1973, for instance, Rhodesia closed its 400-mile border with Zambia to protest its refusal to stop exiled Rhodesian nationalist groups from carrying out raids from the safety of Zambia.[45] It was around this time, when Zambia was looking for economic partners to alleviate reliance on South Africa and Rhodesia, as well as sympathetic ears that would support their cause at the UN, that the first dialogue took place between Zambia and Iran.

Zambia was perceived as a potentially important ally in helping to maintain Iran's influence in the region when the regimes in Rhodesia and South Africa were eventually replaced. Kaunda's reputation within

[41] Not including greases and lubricants. Joseph Mendenhall telegram, 25 January 1974, WikiLeaks Cable 1974TANANA00104_b.
[42] Hendrik van Oss telegram, 3 January 1974, WikiLeaks Cable 1974LOUREN00003_b.
[43] Stanley Meisler, 'Zambia', *The Atlantic*, September 1970. Available online: www.theatlantic.com/magazine/archive/1970/09/zambia/661718/.
[44] Timothy M. Shaw, 'The Foreign Policy of Zambia: Ideology and Interests', *The Journal of Modern African Studies*, vol. 14, no. 1 (1976), 82.
[45] *The New York Times*, 10 January 1973, 8. The border opened one month later.

the non-aligned movement was particularly attractive to Iran, as ʿAlam noted in his diary.[46] He was perceived as the type of influential African leader with whom Iran should attempt to develop closer political ties. Iran and Zambia had established political relations early in 1974, and later that year, President Kaunda made a short 32-hour stopover in Tehran on his return home from a trip to Eastern Europe, where he had visited the capitals of Romania, the USSR and Yugoslavia.[47] On the day of his arrival, Kaunda had lunch with the shah, followed by a private discussion. During this meeting, the two leaders also spoke about the potentials for a trade deal, African affairs and the possibility of establishing a permanent Zambian embassy in Tehran.[48]

President Kaunda left Iran in November 1974 with a seemingly genuinely positive impression of the shah. On the way to the airport, Kaunda had said to ʿAlam that he had been 'so impressed by the shah' during their conversation and that he was 'overwhelmed with pride'.[49] In a speech given at a reception in Lusaka upon his return, Kaunda 'spoke with particular admiration and even some awe of [the] shah of Iran, whose personality apparently made a strong impression on him'.[50] The US ambassador remarked that it appeared as though Kaunda's meeting with the shah 'had opened [a] new chapter of cooperation'.[51] Eager to keep the shah's attention, Kaunda had said to ʿAlam in the car to the airport: 'Tell the king that we have uranium and we can discuss this issue in the economic negotiations.'[52]

The possibilities for securing uranium perhaps convinced the shah to pursue an economic partnership as a matter of urgency, for just

46 Diary entry 8 Āzar 1353/ 29 November 1974, *Yāddāsht-hā-ye ʿAlam*, vol. 4, 310.

47 Because the visit was non-official, Kaunda was met at the airport not by the shah, but the court minister, Asadollāh ʿAlam. Ibid. It is worth noting that the establishment of political relations between Iran and Zambia coincided with the initiation of President Vorster's policy of détente with Zambia in 1974. Onslow, 'The Cold War in Southern Africa', 15.

48 *Ettelāʿāt*, 9 Āzar 1353/ 30 November 1974, 4. At this time, the Zambian ambassador wasbased in Cairo and accredited in Tehran.

49 Diary entry 9 Āzar 1353/ 30 November 1974, *Yāddāsht-hā-ye ʿAlam*, vol. 4, 312.

50 Jean Mary Wilkowski telegram, 4 December 1974, WikiLeaks Cable 1974LUSAKA02486_b.

51 Ibid.

52 Diary entry 9 Āzar 1353/ 30 November 1974, *Yāddāsht-hā-ye ʿAlam*, vol. 4, 311–312.

months later, in February 1975, an Iranian economic delegation travelled to Zambia. This was followed by the visit to Iran of a delegation from Zambia in June of that year, during which a trade deal was signed. As part of the deal, Iran would trade goods such as fertilisers, agricultural tools, machinery and vehicles, and Zambia would trade corn, sugar and fruits. An important part of the deal was oil, and Iran agreed to give over one million tons of crude oil per year to Zambia.[53] At the same time as the Iranian press announced this agreement, it added that discussions between the two sides were ongoing concerning joint ventures in the development of copper and uranium mines in Zambia.[54] In September that year, the Zambian minister of industries and mines visited Iran and was received by the shah.[55] Uranium was almost certainly one of the main issues for discussion.

But while Zambia turned to Iran to alleviate its economic dependency on South Africa and Rhodesia, other countries in the region still relied on South Africa for its Iranian oil. For example, the majority of Botswana's fuel imports were refined in South Africa, and other refined products were imported from Iran via South Africa.[56] The situation was the same in Lesotho, which depended completely on petroleum and petroleum products from South Africa. Iran had established relations with Lesotho at around the same time as it opened its consulate in Johannesburg, and its consul-general was accredited ambassador in Maseru. The consul-general frequently visited Lesotho, and relations were generally friendly. The king of Lesotho, Moshoeshoe II, had attended the shah's imperial celebrations in 1971. As an expression of Lesotho's appreciation of the Pahlavis, in June 1974, the prime minister, Chief Joseph Leabua Jonathan, inaugurated an eighteen-bed clinic named after Princess Ashraf, in the presence of the Iranian ambassador, Ahmad Tehrāni.[57]

At the same time, the shah had shown a willingness to withhold promised aid to show dissatisfaction with his allies. In 1974, the Iranian government had offered Lesotho an aid grant of several millions of dollars. The following year, when a delegation came to Tehran

53 *Asnād-e Moʿāhedāt-e do Jānebeh-ye Irān bā Sāyer-e Duval*, vol. 6, 684.
54 J. W. Owen to S. W. Gardiner, 19 June 1975, FCO 8/2501.
55 Peter J. Westmacott to Peter K. Williams, 23 September 1975, FCO 8/2501.
56 Bradford Bishop telegram, 25 January 1974, WikiLeaks Cable 1974GABORO00135_b.
57 *Kayhan International*, 22 June 1974, 2.

to collect the money, the Iranian government said that they had changed their minds and the aid would be provided in the form of a loan instead. A few weeks later, the Iranians changed their minds for a second time and again promised a grant. But the funds were still not forthcoming. The British thought that the reason for Iran's wavering were reports of the imminent arrival in Lesotho of a Libyan delegation to discuss the supply of weapons and technical assistance to the police force, which had 'got back to the Shah's ears'. The report continues, 'The Shah's well known dislike of Qhadaffi [sic] could well lead him to instruct his Ministers to go slow on aid and investment negotiations with Lesotho and even stop them altogether.'[58]

One of Iran's most problematic and complicated relationships was with Rhodesia. It was widely understood that, in spite of comprehensive sanctions in place, Iran had for a long time been supplying Rhodesia's oil, which according to a report from the US secretary of state, Cyrus Vance, had been 'trans-shipped through South Africa'.[59] Iran turned a blind eye to this throughout the 1960s and 1970s, but as the situation in Rhodesia deteriorated towards the late 1970s, it sought to induce South African support for British–US proposals over the transition to majority rule by threatening to withdraw oil. The shah understood clearly that despite his oft repeated refrain that oil should not be mixed with politics, oil was deeply political, and was not only crucial to growing Iran's economy, but was also powerful leverage in achieving Iran's strategic objectives.

Iran and Rhodesian Sanctions

Southern Rhodesia had been established as a self-governing British Crown colony in 1923, structured to serve the interests of the white-minority European settlers who held control over its agricultural and mineral wealth. For a short while from 1953, the British administered a

[58] J. W. Owen to P. K. Williams, 25 June 1975, FCO 8/2501. This disagreement appears eventually to have been resolved, as in July 1976 an Iranian Air Force C-130 transport plane arrived In Maseru to deliver 'some eight or nine jeep type vehicles' to the Lesotho police force. Haught telegram, 7 July 1976, WikiLeaks Cable 1976MASERU00729_b.

[59] Cyrus Vance to President Carter, 14 February 1977, The National Security Archive, George Washington University. Available online: https://nsarchive.gwu.edu/.

federation consisting of Southern and Northern Rhodesia and Nyasaland, called the Central African Federation. During the era of African decolonisation, this agreement became less palatable to the native populations of these areas, who, inspired by what was happening in the rest of Africa, pressured the British to allow them to break from the federation. The British allowed Nyasaland to secede in 1962, followed shortly after by Northern Rhodesia in 1963. Malawi (Nyasaland) and Zambia (Northern Rhodesia) subsequently achieved independence in 1964 as majority-ruled countries.[60] Due to fears that it would be forced by the British to implement changes to its native policy, Rhodesia issued a Unilateral Declaration of Independence on 11 November 1965. The independent nation of Rhodesia thus came into existence, with a population comprising 4.1 million black people, 224,000 white, and 21,000 of other ethnic groups.[61]

Despite British prime minister Harold Wilson's warning that a unilateral declaration of independence would be tantamount to an 'open act of defiance and rebellion',[62] and the Labour government's sympathy towards the principle of majority rule, Britain was reluctant to use armed force against Rhodesia, opting instead to pressure the Ian Smith government through sanctions.[63] Rhodesia was immediately excluded from the sterling area, the import of Rhodesian tobacco into Britain was prohibited, as were weapons exports to Rhodesia. This expanded to a complete boycott in the months that followed.[64] Thirteen months after the Unilateral Declaration of Independence, the United Nations Security Council introduced mandatory economic sanctions (Resolution 232, 16 December 1966) for the first time in its existence to try to bring down the Ian Smith government. Some 90 per cent of Rhodesia's exports were subject to an international embargo,

60 Arthur Campbell Turner, 'Independent Rhodesia', *Current History*, vol. 58, no. 343 (1970), 131–132.

61 'Southern Rhodesia', Department of State, Washington, 23 January 1967, *FRUS, 1964–1968, Volume XXIV, Africa*, doc. 553.

62 *The New York Times*, 28 October 1964, 1.

63 Martin Bailey, 'Enforcing Oil Sanctions: A Comparison of the Rhodesian and South African Embargoes', in *Embargo: Apartheid's Oil Secrets Revealed*, ed. Richard Hengeveld and Jaap Rodenburg (Amsterdam: Amsterdam University Press, 1995), 225.

64 Johan Galtung, 'On the Effects of International Economic Sanctions, with Examples from the Case of Rhodesia', *World Politics*, vol. 19, no. 3 (1967), 391–392.

and members of the United Nations were forbidden from exporting to Rhodesia oil, weapons, vehicles or aircraft, or providing any kind of economic or financial aid 'to the illegal racist regime in Southern Rhodesia'.[65] Amid grave concerns that Resolution 232 had not been properly observed and that some states had 'failed to prevent trade with the illegal regime in Southern Rhodesia', a further resolution (Resolution 253, 29 May 1968) was passed, reaffirming the call for member states to break trade relations with Rhodesia.

Immediately after the Rhodesian declaration of independence, Iran put out a statement supporting the British government, which was printed in newspapers. A proclamation of independence 'prior to the amendment of the present constitution, the removal of all racial discrimination and the granting of full political rights to all the people of the country, would be in flagrant contradiction of the principles of the Charter and the World Declaration of Human Rights', it read.[66] Given that around 75 per cent of the oil for Rhodesia's Feruka refinery was supplied by Iranian oil, primarily through BP, Prime Minister Hoveydā ordered the consortium to suspend oil sales to Rhodesia – the first time Iran had attempted to interfere in the marketing problems of the consortium.[67] In August 1968, the Central Bank of Iran sent a message to all authorised banks in the country, ordering them not to 'deal in anything with, from or to Rhodesia', in compliance with UN Resolution 253. The government also passed a decree authorising compliance with the UN resolution.[68]

In spite of Iran's acceptance of UN resolutions forbidding trade with Rhodesia, it did not comply fully with these resolutions. In 1970, Iran was referred by the United Kingdom to the UN over suspicions that 30,000 steel billets it had purchased from a Franco-South African company were of Rhodesian origin.[69] The British report strongly implied that the Iranian Rolling Mills Company was fully aware that the steel was of Rhodesian origin, and could quite easily have opted to

[65] Resolution 232 (1966) / [Adopted by the Security Council at Its 1340th Meeting], of 16 December 1966. UN Digital Library: Call Number UNS(01)/R3. Available online: https://digitallibrary.un.org/record/90502?ln=en.
[66] *Ettelā'āt*, 10 Ābān 1344/ 1 November 1965, 16.
[67] Sivan to French Ministry of Foreign Affairs, 24 November 1965, CADC 367QO/59.
[68] *Echo of Iran*, 26 August 1968, Newspaper cut out in NA 2.05.191/467.
[69] British Mission to United Nations, 'Rhodesia Sanctions – Export of Steel to Iran', 10 February 1970, FCO 35/374.

buy steel from elsewhere, including South Africa. The attraction of Rhodesian steel was that it was much cheaper than other steel precisely because it was subject to a UN embargo.[70] The British had previously reported Iran to the UN Sanctions Committee for selling 'bulk ammonia' to Rhodesia.[71]

Iran did not appear to take heed of these criticisms, and in 1972 was again referred by the British to the UN committee. On this occasion, on 6 January a Norwegian-owned tanker was loaded at the Iranian port of Bandar Shapur with 'several thousand tons of anhydrous ammonia'. The ship arrived at the Port of Lourenço Marques on 23 January; however, it did not register the imported goods as required by Mozambique law. Furthermore, South Africa was self-sufficient in anhydrous ammonia, and figures obtained by the British indicated that Mozambique's requirement of anhydrous ammonia was less than 1,000 tonnes per year. The shipment was, therefore, the British concluded, 'destined ultimately for Southern Rhodesia'.[72] In response to these allegations, the Iranian Ministry of Foreign Affairs insisted that the National Petrochemical Industries Company of Iran had a deal in place with a company registered in Lichtenstein and 'does not know anything about any deals that may possibly be carried out subsequent to the said supply'.[73]

Iran was investigated by the British on several further occasions for breaching Resolution 253. In April 1973, for example, Iran had imported a consignment of sugar from a Greek-registered ship, which the British suspected was of Southern Rhodesian origin.[74] But in the same year, the British admitted that they had begun to withhold incriminating information on friendly countries.[75] In response to another investigation about the export of Rhodesian steel billets to Iran, the head of the Middle East department, Rex Hunt, urged his colleague to delay passing on the complaint to the UN Sanctions Committee, in light of the delicate negotiations that were taking place

70 R. A. Clinton-Thomas to Peter Tripp, 3 February 1970, FCO 35/374.
71 Ibid.
72 'Note to the Committee Established in Pursuance of Security Council Resolution 253 (1968)', 24 February 1972, FCO 35/507.
73 Iranian Ministry of Foreign Affairs International Organisations Department, 3 April 1972, FCO 35/507.
74 Douglas-Home telegram, 20 June 1973, FCO 36/1588.
75 T. T. J. Mound to Grattan, 6 March 1973, FCO 36/1594.

between Iran and the oil consortium. In fact, Hunt continued, 'In view of the commercial importance to us of good Anglo-Iranian relations, I wonder whether we should submit the notes at all.'[76]

Because Iran still enjoyed good trade relations with South Africa and South Africa did not restrict trade to Rhodesia, it was difficult for Iran to comply fully with the sanctions. This also made it also easy for Iran to circumvent these sanctions. It was not just the British who recognised Iran's non-compliance. In July 1976, the OAU issued a press release to condemn Iran for the alleged shipment of arms to Rhodesia. The press release cited *Newsweek* as the source of the accusation that Iranian-made ground-to-air missiles and machine guns had been flown by an Iranian aircraft to Durban, on the understanding that the weapons would be transported on to Rhodesia. The OAU statement read, 'Iranian arms collaboration with South Africa and Rhodesia constitutes a hostile act to OAU member states', and urged Iran immediately to halt 'this shameful and dangerous arms traffic with Rhodesia'.[77] It was widely understood that Iranian oil was also making its way into Rhodesia. In February 1977, the US secretary of state, Cyrus Vance, wrote to President Carter in 1977 that many nations 'pay lip service to the UN sanctions [on Rhodesia] but do little to enforce compliance... Rhodesia's oil supply originates in Iran and is transshipped through South Africa.'[78] This understanding of Iran's importance to both South Africa and Rhodesia encouraged the United States and Britain to seek Iran's help when attempting to secure a settlement with the Ian Smith government in the late 1970s.

Iran and British–US Initiatives in Rhodesia

Since Ian Smith's Unilateral Declaration of Independence in November 1965, successive British governments had tried and failed to bring about peaceful transition to majority rule. The British

[76] Rex Hunt to G. S. Turner, 6 April 1973, FCO 36/1594.

[77] Tienken telegram, 20 July 1976, WikiLeaks Cable 1976ADDIS08992_b.

[78] Cyrus Vance to President Carter, 14 February 1977, The National Security Archive, George Washington University. South Africa's oil supply became even more important for Rhodesia after the departure of the Portuguese from Mozambique in 1975 and the ensuing civil war, which cut off supplies from Mozambique to Rhodesia. On the background to sanctions on the Rhodesian oil embargo, see Klinghoffer, *Oiling the Wheels of Apartheid*, 79–85.

government under Harold Wilson adopted the principle of 'NIBMAR', meaning no independence before majority rule. Britain argued that rule must be returned to them on a temporary basis, so they could oversee a legal, peaceful and democratic transition of power to majority rule. The Smith government, on the other hand, had no intention of handing power back to the British and instead focused on cracking down on black nationalist groups and maintaining minority white rule. The result was that Rhodesia faced harsh economic sanctions from the UN, armed revolt from black nationalist groups, and the hostility of regional powers sympathetic to these groups.[79]

From the early 1960s, a civil war had been waged in Rhodesia between the Smith government and two nationalist opposition groups: the Zimbabwe African National Union, whose army was called the Zimbabwe African Nationalist Liberation Army, which was formed in Tanzania and based in Zambia, and was led by Robert Mugabe; and the Zimbabwe People's Revolutionary Army, also based in Zambia and led by Joshua Nkomo. The reverend Ndabaningi Sithole had played an important role in the Zimbabwe African National Union from its foundation until 1975, when the party divided into two factions, a moderate faction led by Sithole, which renounced violent struggle, and a militant arm, led by Mugabe. In report in August 1976, Kissinger declared that 'the prospects for Soviet expansion are good in Rhodesia' and that they were making strong inroads. The Soviets had a privileged position within the 'Marxist regime in Mozambique', which gave them 'a special ability to influence the crisis in Rhodesia'. Furthermore, Kissinger observed, 'the majority of Rhodesian guerrillas are positioned in Mozambique and are armed with weapons provided from communist sources'.[80]

The first real effort from Washington was Kissinger's initiative in 1976. Kissinger recognised early on the need to build a broad coalition of support for his efforts to unite the various factions and achieve a diplomatic victory. In April 1976 he thus embarked on a tour of Africa, which included stops in Kenya, Tanzania, Zambia, Zaire, Ghana, Liberia and Senegal. Kissinger also recognised the potential importance of Iran in his initiative. Speaking at a Security Council meeting on 11 May 1976 about his policy in Southern Africa,

[79] Robert Blake, *A History of Rhodesia* (London: Methuen, 1977), 395.
[80] Kissinger telegram, 1 August 1976, WikiLeaks Cable 1976STATE190448_b.

Kissinger remarked: 'I believe Iran would also be helpful. The Shah sent me a letter supporting my Africa trip.' The deputy secretary of defense, William Clements, replied, 'That support is very important.'[81]

While Kissinger's initiative was underway, in August 1976 Joshua Nkomo travelled around the world to the European capitals of London, Paris and Moscow, as well as Algeria, Saudi Arabia, Iraq and Iran to solicit support for his cause. Kissinger felt that Nkomo was the best nationalist candidate to take control of an independent Rhodesia because although he had received aid from the Soviets, he was not a communist. Furthermore, Kissinger believed that 'he commands the respect of all' and that he was 'the only political leader whose support cuts across tribal lines'.[82] Kissinger briefed the US ambassadors in Riyadh and Tehran to prepare them for the arrival of Nkomo. Subsequently, the ambassador in Tehran, Richard Helms, held a three-hour meeting with the shah at his guesthouse in Nowshahr, during which, among other things, the imminent arrival of Nkomo was discussed. According to Helms, the shah said he would 'see what he can do to help him [Nkomo] since he agrees with us that Nkomo represents a political element which we should support'.[83]

Kissinger met Ian Smith in Pretoria on 18 September 1976 and was able to convince him to accept the principle of majority rule. Smith communicated this decision in a television address on 24 September.[84] In recognition of the support the shah had shown, Kissinger wrote to him directly on 6 October. The letter began: 'Your Imperial Majesty: I recently returned from my mission to Africa and would like to bring you up to date on the status of our initiative.'[85] Understanding the shah's shared fears of the spread of Soviet influence in Africa, Kissinger stressed that the US objective was to bring about a government in Rhodesia 'strong and dedicated enough not to submit to Soviet

[81] Minutes of a National Security Council Meeting, Washington, 11 May 1976, *FRUS, 1969–1976, Volume E-6, Documents on Africa, 1973–1976*, doc. 44.

[82] Kissinger telegram, 1 August 1976, WikiLeaks Cable 1976STATE190448_b.

[83] Telegram from the Embassy in Iran to the Department of State, Tehran, 8 August 1976, *FRUS, 1969–1976, Volume XXVII, Iran; Iraq, 1973–1976*, doc. 183.

[84] Sue Onslow, '"We Must Gain Time": South Africa, Rhodesia and the Kissinger Initiative of 1976', *South African Historical Journal*, vol. 56 (2006), 123.

[85] Kissinger message to the shah, 6 October 1976, WikiLeaks Cable 1976STATE248116_b.

pressure'. He also hoped, through dialogue with other African states, 'to begin to build an understanding among those African states who oppose the extension of radical and Soviet influence'. He ended the letter:

> Many of Africa's moderate regimes face difficult economic problems and while I have no specific suggestions to make to you, I want you to be aware of the importance which the United States attaches to strengthening moderate governments in the continent.
>
> Iran and the United States share a common interest in African stability and I look forward to staying in close touch with you as specific opportunities emerge to which you can bring to bear your wise and constructive influence. I would also appreciate receiving your views on the African situation and our undertaking.

Kissinger appeared rather buoyant about the situation in Rhodesia, but although he had secured Smith's commitment to majority rule within two years, the Geneva Conference, held to negotiate a handover of power that was acceptable to all parties, ultimately ended in failure. US efforts to bring peace to Rhodesia would gain renewed energy under the presidency of Jimmy Carter.[86]

It was in February 1977, when David Owen became Britain's foreign secretary, that Britain decided to seek the direct support of the Carter administration in a new round of negotiations with Rhodesia.[87] In May 1977, the Anglo-American Consultative Group, consisting of the US ambassador to Zambia, Stephen Low, and the British diplomat John Graham,[88] arrived in Rhodesia for talks with the Ian Smith government.[89] At the same time, Owen visited Iran for his first meeting with the shah as foreign secretary, during the course of which, among other topics, the situation in Southern Africa was discussed. Owen agreed with the shah's earlier comment that he believed the South Africans would 'behave correctly' in Namibia and Rhodesia, but

86 On President Carter's Africa policy, see Mitchell, *Jimmy Carter in Africa*.

87 Nancy Mitchell, 'Terrorists or Freedom Fighters? Jimmy Carter and Rhodesia', in *Cold War in Southern Africa: White Power, Black Liberation*, ed. Sue Onslow (London: Routledge, 2009), 180.

88 Incidentally, shortly after, in January 1979, Graham became the British ambassador to Iran, where he tried to maintain British interests in Iran during the revolution.

89 Andrew J. Deroche, 'Standing Firm for Principles: Jimmy Carter and Zimbabwe', *Diplomatic History*, vol. 23, no. 4 (1999), 668–669.

stressed that 'they must change direction sufficiently to be able to return to full members of the international community'.[90]

From this period onwards, the British government made a conscious effort to solicit the support of the shah in their negotiations, and the ambassador, Anthony Parsons, was regularly briefed on how to approach the shah on this issue. The British strategy was, much like Kissinger's had been, to convince the shah that only through the joint British–American proposals could a communist takeover in Rhodesia be avoided.[91] In June 1977, just one month after the Graham-Low mission had begun, Parsons met with the shah to update him on its progress, and recount what had transpired at the Commonwealth Heads of Government Meeting earlier that month.[92] According to Parsons, the shah 'expressed considerable interest … and volunteered that he regularly received the South African consul-general here and he would continue in his efforts to persuade the South Africans to co-operate to the full over Rhodesia'.[93]

The British position vis-à-vis the shah and South Africa was set out in a report by the British ambassador to the United States, Peter Jay. The report read:

> [The] Central element of [the] current plan is our readiness to apply pressures to South Africa to induce it to exercise its influence on Smith to accept the settlement package. South African transhipment of oil to Rhodesia is [a] highly visible pressure point. [The] Shah's personal intervention to express to South Africa Iran's concern over transhipment of its oil to Rhodesia in violation of UN sanctions could be very helpful. Our hope is that Iranian reference to the problem will be constructed by South Africa as an important indication of US-UK-GOI commitment to the settlement effort and a signal of potential further pressures if South Africa does not exercise its authority to help achieve a settlement … The free flow of oil from South Africa to Rhodesia in violation of the UN's sanctions has kept the Smith regime alive … We believe that oil provides a key pressure point for our approach to the South Africans.[94]

90 Record of discussion between the Foreign and Commonwealth Secretary and His Imperial Majesty Mohammed Reza Pahlavi, Shahanshah Aryamehr at the Niavaran Palace, 14 May 1977, FCO 36/2001.
91 Parsons telegram, 5 August 1977, FCO 36/2001.
92 Parsons telegram, 22 June 1977, FCO 36/2001. 93 Ibid.
94 Peter Jay to British embassy Tehran, 6 August 1977, FCO 36/2001.

In recognition of South Africa's overreliance of Iranian oil and the influence that South Africa had over the Smith regime, the British position was, first through subtle suggestions and then more direct pressure, to invite the shah 'to action against South Africa should they be unwilling to cooperate'.[95]

On 12 August 1977, Secretary Vance and Foreign Secretary Owen were due to meet with the South African minister of foreign affairs, Pik Botha, in London to present the US–UK settlement proposals, and request Botha's assistance in convincing Smith to accept them. Ambassador Jay wrote,

> It would be most helpful if, prior to the Vance-Owen-Botha meeting, the South African government received a message from the shah indicating his concern over the increased violence in Rhodesia and desire that South Africa cooperate with the UK-US effort. In addition a general expression of concern about the possibility that a product of Iran, oil, may, in violation of the spirit and letter of the UN sanction resolutions, be entering Rhodesia, would be most welcome. No specific Iranian corrective or punitive action concerning this trade need be mentioned. The shah could simply ask for information or in some other manner indicate to the South Africans he is focussing his attention on the problem.[96]

In fact, the rumoured threat of Iran withdrawing oil to South Africa had already been discussed in political circles in South Africa. In response, Botha had travelled to Rhodesia in the first days of August to make it clear to Smith 'that it was one thing to keep his regime afloat against all the odds; it was quite another for South Africa to run the risk of losing access to their main source of oil supplies in its support'.[97]

On 9 August 1977, the British and American ambassadors in Tehran held a joint meeting with the shah. Parsons said to the shah that 'it was almost unprecedented in Iran for the American and British ambassadors to seek a joint audience. But we were in an unprecedented position.' With the joint proposals nearly complete, the United States and Britain were mobilising their allies. While they were not asking the shah at this stage to make any approaches to the South Africans, Parsons said 'we would be most grateful if he [the shah] would make

[95] E. A. J. Fergusson to Bryan Cartledge, 26 July 1977, FCO 36/2001.
[96] Peter Jay to British embassy Tehran, 6 August 1977, FCO 36/2001.
[97] British embassy in Pretoria telegram, 5 August 1977, FCO 36/2001.

it clear to Mr Botha that our proposals had Iran's support'. The shah responded that although he doubted whether Smith would agree to the proposals, he agreed that 'they were the only way forward'. He also offered to contact Botha through the consul-general after the Vance-Owen-Botha meeting and would even be willing to invite Prime Minister Vorster to Iran 'if we thought that it would be valuable at any stage'.[98]

The shah followed the negotiations closely, was given regular updates by the British ambassador, and frequently expressed his readiness to help. In a meeting in October 1977, for instance, the shah told Parsons that he had summoned the South African consul-general to stress 'the need for South Africa to bring maximum pressure on Smith to bring him into line'.[99] The shah's efforts apparently achieved some success, for in November 1977, the Iranian government received an assurance from the South African consul-general in Tehran which read: 'It is confirmed that no Iranian crude oil sent to Natref or products made from it are being or will be supplied to Rhodesia.'[100]

The shah also maintained dialogue with opposition figures. Bishop Abel Muzorewa, founder of the Zimbabwean United African National Council, visited Iran in autumn 1977 and again in September 1978, and the shah spoke to Reverend Sithole on his visit to Washington in November 1977.[101] Indeed, many of these figures sought the shah's support. In 1978, Nkomo, who had visited Iran in 1976, wrote to the shah requesting funds for Rhodesian refugees. Bishop Muzorewa requested the shah assistance in the military training of some of his followers. The shah agreed to accept 'five or six' of these followers for such training.[102]

As a result of these connections, the shah had gained a degree of influence among the opposition groups. This was recognised by the British. In August 1978, the British had proposed an all-parties meeting, but Bishop Muzorewa opposed such a meeting, for fear that it would merely embolden the Patriotic Front and further erode his

98 Parsons telegram, 9 August 1977, FCO 36/2001.
99 Parsons telegram, 17 October 1977, FCO 36/2001.
100 Miklos telegram, 12 December 1977, WikiLeaks Cable 1977TEHRAN10956_c.
101 Parsons telegram, 28 November 1977, FCO 36/2001.
102 I. T. M. Lucas to Mr Laver, Rhodesia Department, 16 June 1978, FCO 36/2236.

popular support 'and make it impossible for him to attain the political power he now sees within his grasp'. Foreign Secretary Owen felt that 'a message from the shah to the Bishop, urging his participation in an all-parties meeting might be instrumental in convincing Muzorewa that further negotiations with the patriotic front at an all-parties meeting would be worthwhile'.[103] Muzorewa subsequently travelled to Iran in September 1978, when, in exchange for the shah agreeing to supply funds, the shah 'was able to extract a promise from Muzorewa that he would not rule out completely his participation' in the proposed all-parties meeting.[104] This was the last contribution of the shah to the situation in Southern Africa before the revolution.

*****

Much of the scholarship on oil in the late Pahlavi period concentrates on how the generated income allowed Iran to invest in infrastructure and weapons, but comparatively little on how it was used to secure Iran's interests in the non-Western world. Southern Africa was a small market to Iran, but many of the countries there were heavily reliant on Iran as a source of oil. This allowed the shah to expand his influence in these countries. The shah presented himself throughout the 1960s and 1970s as being inherently sympathetic to African decolonisation movements, and even as ties developed between Iran and South Africa, the shah remained extremely critical of apartheid. However, the shah's foreign policy was essentially pragmatic, and although he kept South Africa officially at arm's length by keeping relations at the consular level, he identified South Africa as the most powerful country in the region economically and militarily, a key ally in the Indian Ocean, and, under the table, pursued relations with it quite boldly.

Since the shah had been so inflexible in the past about supporting international sanctions, the British exaggerated the threat of a Marxist takeover of Rhodesia to convince the shah to support their negotiating position with Ian Smith. That is not to say that this threat did not exist. As the historian Sue Onslow has observed, there were Marxist elements in the black nationalist movements in Southern Africa, and they did receive financial and political support from the Soviet Bloc.[105]

[103] Owen telegram, 24 August 1978, FCO 36/2236.
[104] Chalmers telegram, 12 September 1978, FCO 36/2236.
[105] Onslow, 'The Cold War in Southern Africa', 10.

The key goal of the Pahlavi strategy in Africa was to reduce Soviet influence, particularly in the areas that bordered, or were close to the borders of the Indian Ocean. Should a communist takeover succeed in Rhodesia, then it was feared this would embolden radical regimes and movements sponsored by the Soviets elsewhere on the continent. Thus, although the shah was undoubtedly happy to support his American and British allies, he was not merely a pliable instrument of these powers, nor was he easily manipulated by their arguments about a communist takeover. The shah's support for an amicable resolution that would bring a moderate government to power post-independence was fully consistent with his strategic goals. This was demonstrated in another major crisis in Africa in the same period; the Ogaden War of 1977–1978.

11 *Iran, the Ogaden War and African Security in the Late 1970s*

The Ogaden region of Ethiopia covers approximately 200,000 square kilometres, and though the majority of it is desert, it also contains two of the most populous cities in Ethiopia – Harar and Dire Dawa – and some of Ethiopia's richest agricultural land.[1] Until 1887, this ethnically Somali region, independent from Ethiopia, was ruled by the Muslim Emir of Harar. In 1887, however, buoyed by his victory over the Italians one year earlier, the Ethiopian emperor, Menelik II, forcibly occupied the Emirate and began to advance further towards the Indian Ocean. The Ethiopian advance was halted by France, Great Britain and Italy, who had come to assert their influence over the coastal regions. From this time, ownership of the Ogaden was negotiated between Ethiopia and the European powers.[2]

After gaining independence in 1960, the Republic of Somalia adopted an irredentist outlook. Its constitution stipulated a commitment to reunifying Somali-populated regions, and a five-pointed star was depicted on its flag. Each point represented a Somali-populated area, but only two of those were within Somali national territory; the other three were located in Djibouti, Kenya and Ethiopia's Ogaden region.[3] In opposition to Somalia's irredentist aspirations, the OAU, of which Somalia was a member, had explicitly proclaimed in 1964 that the existing postcolonial borders of Africa must be maintained. During the early years of Somalia's independence, Somali separatists, backed by the state, carried out attacks in Somali-populated regions in Kenya and Ethiopia against the state, leading in 1964 to fighting between

[1] Gebru Tareke, *The Ethiopian Revolution: War in the Horn of Africa* (New Haven, CT: Yale University Press, 2009), 184–186.

[2] 'Controverse territoriale somalo-éthiopienne, Aperçus historiques', CADN 437PO/1/70/DAM 9.1.

[3] James Mayall, *Nationalism and International Society* (Cambridge: Cambridge University Press, 1990), 60.

Ethiopian and Somali regular forces.[4] In 1969, Major General Siad Barre, an Islamic Marxist-Leninist, came to power in Somalia through a military coup. Barre's brand of Somali nationalism was predicated on a fervent desire to incorporate Somali-populated areas in Kenya and Ethiopia.

During the early part of the 1970s, Somalia had been supporting militant groups in the Ogaden and attacks on Ethiopian security forces there had increased in frequency and severity, until finally, in July 1977, Barre took the decision to launch a full-scale invasion. There were two reasons why this decision was taken. First, this was an opportune moment. Since the Ethiopian Revolution in 1974, Ethiopia had become politically and militarily weak; insurgents were gaining ground in several places and the armed forces had been purged of much of the top brass by the revolutionary Derg regime. Second, the Somali army, though numerically inferior to that of Ethiopia, was far superior in terms of firepower, as a result of the Soviet support it had received.[5] But Barre was also concerned that as Ethiopia edged closer to the Soviet Union, bolstered by Soviet support, its military would become more and more difficult to overcome. If Barre wanted to take the Ogaden, it was important to move quickly. In 1977, the Somalis still had the upper hand and as Gebru Tareke writes, Ethiopia 'could not withstand a full-scale invasion by a well-equipped army. It was a moment not to be missed and they [Somalia] seized it with relish.'[6]

The shah's response to this crisis initiated one of the most remarkable episodes in Iran–Africa relations. The shah had shown himself capable of supporting his regional allies militarily, as evidenced by his support of Sultan Qābus of Oman in his war against the Dhofari rebels between 1972 and 1975. But the nature of the conflict in the Horn of Africa was much different and the shah's involvement demonstrates how far he was willing to go to support his allies and defend Iran's interests beyond its immediate sphere of influence. Although the shah did not give Siad Barre the same backing he gave to Sultan Qābus, this was not because he did not want to, but rather because he was prevented from doing so by the United States. The Ogaden War is thus an example of not only the shah's ambitions in the Horn of Africa and

[4] Saadia Touval, 'The Organization of African Unity and African Borders', *International Organization*, vol. 21, no. 1 (1967), 111–119.
[5] Tareke, *The Ethiopian Revolution*, 183. [6] Ibid., 184.

the Indian Ocean, but also of his limitations in spite of the vast amounts of money he spent on Iran's military. Yet, as much as Iran was restrained by the United States, it was still able to influence to a certain extent the outcome of the conflict.

Iran's support for Somalia in the Ogaden War is also a clear example of how Iran's security policy in Africa was increasingly shaped in response to Soviet expansion. As discussed in Chapter 6, Iran's major objective following the withdrawal of the British from the Persian Gulf in 1971 was to ensure that the Indian Ocean remained free from imperial power competition. The Horn of Africa had become a particularly volatile region following the Ethiopian Revolution, and the shah was concerned not only by the increased Soviet presence, but also by the reluctance of the United States in its era of détente, and after its humiliating withdrawal from Vietnam, to become involved directly in conflicts in the Global South. By providing military support for Somalia in this conflict, Iran was filling the void left by the United States' retreat, but it was also to a certain extent serving US strategic interests.

The shah claimed that his support of Somalia was driven by fears of Soviet expansion in the region, but other African leaders pointed out the absurdity of this position, particularly since Barre had long benefitted from Soviet support. As one Kenyan newspaper argued:

> [I]t was Somalia who first invited the Soviet Union to secure a firm foothold in the Horn of Africa … now that the tide has turned, the world is being fed this hysterical claptrap about invasions, unholy alliances and the like.[7]

During the 1960s and 1970s, Iran had carefully cultivated an image of itself as anti-imperialist, a supporter of human rights, and advocate of majority rule in Africa. This image had already become more difficult to sustain as a result of Iran's continued relations with apartheid South Africa, but its support of an aggressor in a conflict further eroded trust in the shah's motivations in Africa. Iran came to be seen by some as just another imperial power, which had no genuine concern for Africa's struggles.

[7] Cited in Robert G. Patman, *The Soviet Union in the Horn of Africa: The Diplomacy of Intervention and Disengagement* (Cambridge: Cambridge University Press, 1990), 229.

Iran, Somalia and the United States

During the early 1970s, as Iran extended its reach across Africa, in particular Muslim countries, it adopted a cautious approach to Somalia. The two countries did establish diplomatic relations in 1972, and an Iranian embassy was opened in Mogadishu in February 1973, headed by a chargé d'affaires, but neither side appeared to attach much importance to the relationship.[8] This began to change in the latter half of the 1970s. In December 1975, a high-level delegation, headed by Iran's deputy minister of finance, Mustafa Mansuri, travelled to Somalia. Three months earlier, a member of the Supreme Council of the Revolution, Colonel Abdulrizak Mohamed Abubakar, had delivered a message to the shah in Tehran from Siad Barre, 'expressing the wish that Iran, in its capacity as a Muslim friendly country, would provide Somalia with economic and financial assistance to help it overcome the effects of drought'.[9] At first, the Iranian government 'turned a deaf ear' to the request, according to the French, but after 'an urgent approach' by Barre, agreed to send the delegation as a gesture of goodwill.

According to the French ambassador in Mogadishu, although the visit was cordial in nature, the Iranian authorities would 'have no intention of favouring a regime which they consider as totally subservient to the Soviets'.[10] But the fact that Iran allowed the visit, which took place just months after the suspected murder in captivity of the shah's ally, the emperor of Ethiopia, Haile Selassie, at all, may have indicated a slight shift in approach from Iran. The Iranian chargé d'affaires was said by the American ambassador to be 'vehemently anti-Soviet' and a 'hard-liner who personally opposes Iranian aid to Somalia' as long as the Soviets were so entrenched there. 'He favors immediate Somali reduction of Soviet power and influence as quid pro quo for Iranian aid'. The Americans thought that if Iran followed this approach and made it clear to the Somalis that Iranian aid was contingent upon a reduction of Soviet activity, 'then we believe [the] door will be closed to further discussions'.

[8] Robert Duvauchelle, French ambassador in Somalia to minister of foreign affairs, 19 February 1973, CADN 437PO/1/55.ANL 71.

[9] Jean Guerry, French ambassador in Somalia to minister of foreign affairs, 10 December 1975, CADN 437PO/1/55.ANL 71.

[10] Ibid.

On the other hand, [the] more realistic approach by [the] Iranians which reflects [a] better understanding of [the] Siad regime and his problems vis-à-vis USSR might ultimately benefit both Iran and U.S.

Iranian assistance to Somali economic development would first of all help demonstrate to Siad and his regime that us and its friends are not rpt not hostile to Somalia, as Soviet advisors allege, and do not rpt not see either Siad's downfall or Somalia's continued isolation, in Horn of Africa, in Arab League or in [the] area, which is a further page from [the] Soviet briefing book with Siad. Iranian participation in Somali economic development would help broaden Siad's sources of financial aid, would reduce his dependency upon [the] USSR and its satellites, and in our view further his ability to limit military concessions [that the] Soviets seek in Somalia and what they may obtain if Somali isolation and mistrust of us and Western intention grows.

Even if [the] attainment [of] these latter objectives seems somewhat remote at present, their importance is such that we believe [the] Iranian[s] should be encouraged to come to Somali in [the] same positive spirit in which our own recent decision to issue financial help to Somalia was made.[11]

At this stage, US policy in the Horn of Africa still concentrated on Ethiopia, and although the Soviets certainly sought a closer relationship with the Derg regime than had existed under the monarchy, they had invested heavily in Somalia, so were expected, as Henry Kissinger observed, to 'improve relations with Ethiopia only to the extent that this will not hurt their relations with Somalia'.[12] But there were indications that Iran and the United States were keeping lines open with Somalia and were ready to exploit any potential opportunities to lessen Soviet influence there.

Tensions in the Horn and the Arms Supplies

Given Somalia's long-standing claim to the Ogaden region, shortly after the Ethiopian Revolution, the Somali leadership 'made the crucial decision to implement by force its territorial claim against Ethiopia'.[13] The Government of Ethiopia had claimed to be 'in possession of

[11] US ambassador in Somalia, John Loughran, telegram, 10 November 1975, WikiLeaks Cable 1975MOGADI01567_b.

[12] Henry Kissinger telegram, 30 January 1976, WikiLeaks Cable 1976STATE023191_b.

[13] Note de l'Ambassade d'Ethiopie a Mogadiscio, 5 September 1976, 1, CADN 437PO/1/70/DAM 9.1.

irrefutable evidence' that this was the case; '[o]nly the timing and the mode of employment of force had been the subject of a continuing debate within the Somali leadership'.[14] According to a French diplomatic report, there were two lines of thought within the Somali leadership on what course of action to take. The first argued that, given the revolutionary turmoil across the border, 'there could not be a more propitious time' and thus argued in favour of 'the immediate commencement of hostilities against Ethiopia'. The second faction argued that overt Somali interference in Ethiopia 'would have the undesirable effect of uniting all classes and groups of people in Ethiopia against what can be considered a common enemy'. Therefore, they should wait until Ethiopia's 'internal conditions have deteriorated to the point when they could not be any more opportune for Somali territorial design'.[15]

Until around the summer of 1975, it was the second group that held 'a razor-thin majority in the on-going debate within the Somali leadership'. As part of this more cautious approach, the Somali government endeavoured to build up its military forces, while waiting for the situation in Ethiopia to deteriorate further. By the summer of 1975, however, the Somalis perceived that the situation had begun to stabilise and the Ethiopian leadership 'were consolidating themselves in growing measures'. A new majority view thus emerged among the Somali leadership that 'Ethiopia's internal conditions would deteriorate with longer time lapses', therefore the decision was taken 'to set in motion a process of hostile actions' which through a 'gradual process of escalation' would lead to a full scale war.[16] By the end of May 1976, 2,000 Somali soldiers were reportedly active in Ethiopian territory, rebel fighters were known to have received training in Somalia, and there had been a general increase in the number of attacks on Ethiopian forces in the Ogaden region.[17] Before launching the full invasion, however, Barre had to build up his army and ensure a steady supply of arms.

The removal of Haile Selassie from power in Ethiopia did not initially significantly alter the policy of the United States in the Horn of Africa. It still considered nurturing ties with Ethiopia as the key to

[14] Ibid. [15] Ibid., 2. [16] Ibid., 3.
[17] 'Somali infiltration and sabotage activities since January 1976', 2, CADN 437PO/1/70/DAM 9.1.

containing Soviet influence in the region, and the Soviets, although they sought to develop friendlier ties with Ethiopia, did not want to do anything that would harm their relationship with Somalia. However, eventually, in April 1977, as the Derg regime edged closer to the Soviet Union and the Carter administration became less tolerant of its human rights abuses and Marxist ideology, the US–Ethiopia alliance finally collapsed.[18] Subsequently, a significant arms deal between the Soviets and Ethiopia in May 1977 left Barre concerned about the implications of this Soviet support for the situations in Eritrea and the Ogaden. As a result, he reached out to Washington, and the Carter administration, aware of the strategic implications of a Soviet shift to Ethiopia, was open to talks. The United States thus agreed to supply defensive arms to Somalia and to encourage its allies to do the same. Even as the decision was being announced, however, in July 1977, Barre had already launched an attack on the Ogaden. As soon as the Carter administration found out, in August 1977, they cancelled the arms agreement, since Mogadishu had agreed that US weapons could not be used to destabilise or attack its neighbours.[19]

It was around the same time that Iran, aware of the rapprochement between the Carter administration and Somalia, increased its contact with the Barre regime. At the end of May 1977, Iran's foreign minister, Khalʿatbari, paid visits to Sudan and Somalia; his first such visit to the region.[20] During Khalʿatbari's meeting with Barre, the president informed him that 'he had no rpt no quarrel with the Soviet Union'. Somalia's only concern, he continued, 'was its growing relationship with Ethiopia and what this may lead to in terms of contested territories in Eritrea and Ogaden. For this reason and this reason alone, Somalia was again turning to the West for military and economic assistance.'[21] Although Somalia's requests to Iran for military aid were relatively modest, Khalʿatbari felt that 'Somalia was looking more intently and hopefully to us and other countries in the West to meet

[18] Jeffrey A. Lefebvre, *Arms for the Horn: U.S. Security Policy in Ethiopia and Somalia, 1953–1991* (Pittsburgh: University of Pittsburgh Press, 1992), 149–172.

[19] Ibid., 176. The Barre regime claimed that the United States was fully aware of Somali operations in Ethiopia, and even encouraged them to 'liberate' the Ogaden. *Newsweek*, 3 October 1977, 19.

[20] *Ettelāʿāt*, 2 Khordād 1356/ 25 May 1977.

[21] Miklos telegram, 2 June 1977, WikiLeaks Cable 1977TEHRAN04896_c.

its major military requirements'.[22] In addition to providing this equipment, it is possible that Khalʿatbari was invited to Somalia because of Iran's close ties to the United States, in the hope that he could encourage the Carter administration to follow his lead. The US ambassador in Somalia, John Loughran, reported that during a reception hosted by the Iranian embassy, Khalʿatbari 'went out of his way to introduce me to Vice-President Ahmed Suleiman and other senior Somali officials present'.[23]

The Carter administration was in a difficult position, for although it had shifted towards Somalia, it also recognised that Ethiopia was the preeminent power in the Horn, so kept the door open to future rapprochement.[24] This dilemma led to indecisiveness, which at times exasperated America's allies in the region, who wanted to intensify their support for Somalia and who were initially encouraged by the United States to do so, only then to be instructed by Washington to pull back. For example, in June 1977, Khalʿatbari had informed the US ambassador in Tehran that Iran would shortly be sending a military mission to Somalia to assess its needs.[25] Iran had been encouraged to do this by US Secretary of State Cyrus Vance during his visit to Tehran in May, and had 'been led to believe' that the United States was also sending a military mission.[26] One month prior to the departure of the mission, on 6 July, Iran's vice-minister of war, Hasan Tufāniān, sent a list to the United States of the arms they intended to send to Somalia and awaited approval.[27] This list had already been approved by the shah and included 12,000 semi-automatic carbines, 800 88.9mm bazooka launchers and 96 57mm recoilless rifles.[28] Three days later, the State Department submitted a series of issues they would like the Iranian mission to look into on the understanding that the 'Somalis not rpt not be told that information to be obtained by Iranian team would be shared with us'.[29]

22 Ibid.
23 Loughran telegram, 29 May 1977, WikiLeaks Cable 1977MOGADI00868_c.
24 Mitchell, *Jimmy Carter in Africa*, 378. 25 Ibid., 273.
26 William Sullivan to Warren Christopher, 9 August 1977, WikiLeaks Cable 1977TEHRAN07063_c.
27 Sullivan to Cyrus Vance, 11 August 1977, WikiLeaks Cable 1977STATE190575_c.
28 Sullivan to Vance, 6 July 1977, WikiLeaks Cable 1977TEHRAN05960_c.
29 Vance to Sullivan, 9 July 1977, WikiLeaks Cable 1977STATE159686_c.

In the same letter, Cyrus Vance set out the US position vis-à-vis the transfer of American-made weapons by Iran. He wrote that the issue was still under 'intensive study', and that the United States was

> bound by law to permit the transfer of U.S. [sic] origin arms only to a third country [to] which we ourselves would sell or transfer similar equipment at that time. At the present time Somalia is not eligible to purchase US defensive articles under the arms export control act or to receive military assistance under the foreign assistance act of 1961. It has not yet been decided whether a determination by the secretary of state to permit such transfers will be given.[30]

Iran had planned to send its military mission to assess the needs of Somalia in early July, but because the mission was expected to arrive with a supply of weapons, it was repeatedly delayed, until a final decision was made and clearance was given. Khalʿatbari had earlier said that Iran thought it was in their 'interests to help wean Somalia away from the USSR, and Iran would like to do its share'.[31] In this regard, it was felt that although the arms shipment was modest, Iran 'would hope that [the] gesture represented by transferring these items to Somalia would have benefit in terms of Somali political orientation'.[32] However, Iran would not proceed with the transfer before receiving clearance from the United States.[33]

On 21 July, President Carter approved 'in principle' Tufāniān's list.[34] Of course, the arms transfer would also have to be approved by Congress, but the US ambassador in Tehran, William Sullivan, argued that it 'would be natural, in these circumstances, for GOI [Government of Iran] to assume that appropriate clearance procedures were in train and that prior notification to congress had been made at [the] time of [the] President's decision'.[35] Shortly after, on 9 August, one month after the beginning of the conflict, two C-130 transport aircraft destined for Somalia were on standby at Mehrābād Airport; one containing the five-man military mission and the other containing a shipment of US-made military equipment. However, the aircraft

30 Ibid.
31 Miklos to Vance, 18 May 1977, WikiLeaks Cable 1977TEHRAN04400_c.
32 Sullivan to Vance, 6 July 1977, WikiLeaks Cable 1977TEHRAN05960_c.
33 Ibid.
34 Sullivan to Vance, 11 August 1977, WikiLeaks Cable 1977STATE190575_c.
35 Ibid.

containing the weapons was unable to take off, 'because of US block on transfer of arms', so the aircraft containing the military mission arrived in Mogadishu on 10 August empty-handed.[36]

Sullivan was promptly summoned to the Iranian Ministry of Foreign Affairs. There, the director of political affairs, Manuchehr ʿAzimā, told him that Iran was 'totally confused by the US position and now found themselves in [an] extremely embarrassing position. As they had carefully explained to us earlier, the Somalis had insisted that the arms and the military mission would have to arrive in Somalia together.' Concerned that Somalia would accuse Iran of 'bad faith', ʿAzimā 'urged that Washington, even though it might have to undertake further studies for [a] more extensive supply program, give immediate clearance for [the] current shipment'. No sooner had Sullivan returned to his office, having been urged by ʿAzimā 'not to delay message seeking Washington clearance', he reported that he was 'set upon by my volatile little Somali colleague', who 'likewise urged immediate Washington action to release the rifles'.[37] In his dispatch to the State Department, Sullivan requested that

> Since it was the US which got the Iranians involved [in] this whole exercise ... I see no repeat no alternative to an immediate release permitting them to send this load of rifles to Somalia. It seems to me that such a small delivery will have miniscule significance to the military balance, whether in Ogaden or elsewhere. On the other hand, it could have a truly significant effect upon the political scales which are currently being weighted in Mogadiscio while our Washington deliberations continue.

The deputy secretary of state, Warren Christopher, responded that the United States could not legally permit the transfer of US-made weapons to Somalia, but that it was 'not rpt not discouraging transfer of non-US origin arms by third countries'.[38]

Sullivan responded by reminding Christopher that it had been the secretary of state, Cyrus Vance, himself who had asked the shah to help in May. The Iranians had been completely transparent and a US objection could have been raised at any point since July; there was no reason why the administration should wait until the plane was loaded

[36] Sullivan to Vance, 10 August 1977, WikiLeaks Cable 1977TEHRAN07124.
[37] Ibid.
[38] Christopher to Sullivan, 10 August 1977, WikiLeaks Cable 1977STATE189617_c.

and ready to depart before reconsidering its decision.[39] To add to Iran's – and Sullivan's – frustrations, the US military mission that was supposed to arrive in Somalia at around the same time as the Iranian mission had also been cancelled.[40] Eventually, a solution was found, and on 14 August, the C-130 departed, loaded with 2,000 German-designed G-3 rifles manufactured by the Iranian Ministry of War, along with 2 million rounds of ammunition.[41] But Sullivan was nonetheless left frustrated by the conflicting messages he was receiving from Washington.

In response to the situation, a rather aggravated Sullivan wrote to Christopher that he was 'becoming increasingly bewildered by the various cables I am receiving concerning the supply of weapons to various countries in Africa'. At the same time as Sullivan had been instructed to tell Iran that it could not send US-made weapons to Somalia, the State Department had considered asking Iran to send weapons to Chad. 'Do I understand correctly', Sullivan wrote, 'that a US decision has been made to permit the transfer of MAP-supplied weapons to Chad? If so, it would be very difficult to explain to the GOI how the "legal questions" cited with respect to our indecision on Somalia have been resolved with respect to Chad'. He continues:

> The Iranian view, which is shared by most conservative Islamic rep [resentative]s here, is that the United States appears poised on the brink of a morass of indecision calculated to snatch defeat from the jaws of victory. It is their express concern that the situation in the Ethiopian-Somali area may end up with both countries effectively weakened by the current conflict, but with the Soviets firmly in control in both capitals.

Should these countries seek clarification on US-policy, Sullivan worried that he would be 'unable to articulate a US position because I have been unable to discern one from the signals I have received'.[42]

Iran was clearly constrained in terms of what they were allowed to give to Barre, given that they would need US permission to use or supply US-made weapons.[43] This did not discourage Barre from

39 Sullivan to Vance, 11 August 1977, WikiLeaks Cable 1977STATE190575_c.
40 Sullivan to Vance, 9 August 1977, WikiLeaks Cable 1977TEHRAN07063_c.
41 Sullivan to Christopher, 14 August 1977, Wikileaks Cable 1977TEHRAN07186_c.
42 Ibid.
43 'Minutes of a National Security Council Meeting', 23 February 1978, *FRUS, 1977–1980, Volume XVII, Horn of Africa, part 1*, doc. 62.

asking. In September 1977, for example, the shah informed Ambassador Sullivan, 'in confidence' that a special emissary had recently been sent to Iran from Somalia to request 'aircraft and pilots from the Iranian Air Force to fly them'.[44] The US position was fairly consistent throughout the conflict with regard to the use of US weapons; they accepted, even encouraged, the supply of defensive equipment and economic assistance to Somalia, but they would '*not* serve in a coordinating role'.[45] The United States also made it clear to Iran, as well as its allies Saudi Arabia and Egypt, that any unauthorised use or transfer of American arms would be contrary to bilateral arms agreements and could have 'a potentially adverse impact on Congressional approval' of future sales.[46]

Chad

At the same time that Iran was told not to give US-made weapons to Somalia, it was encouraged by Washington, as Sullivan alludes to in his frustrated dispatches to the State Department, to supply weapons to Chad. Chad had suffered from political unrest from the moment it achieved independence from France in 1960 and had been in a state of civil war since 1965. In summer 1977, Libyan-backed rebels armed with Soviet weaponry launched a major military offensive from northern Chad, where they had already established a strong powerbase. Fearing military defeat, the president of Chad, Félix Malloum, reached out to his French and American allies for support . By July, France had provided technical assistance and spare parts, and Egypt and Sudan, in fear of Libyan expansionism, sent military missions to assess the type of aid they could offer. In a letter to President Carter, his national security advisor, Zbigniew Brzezinski, argued that because the insurgency, if left unchecked, would 'directly affect the survival of the government ... it is in our interests to provide at least some military

[44] The shah 'politely turned them down'. Sullivan to secretary of state, 7 September 1977, WikiLeaks Cable 1977TEHRAN07895_c.

[45] 'Summary of Conclusions of a Special Coordination Committee Meeting', 16 March 1978, *FRUS, 1977–1980, Volume XVII, Horn of Africa, part 1*, doc. 75.

[46] 'Presidential Directive/NSC-32', 24 February 1978, *FRUS, 1977–1980, Volume XVII, Horn of Africa, part 1*, doc. 64.

assistance to Chad'.[47] One of the ways in which Brzezinski argued that US weapons could be provided was through third-country transfers.

Asked by Cyrus Vance about the possibility of Iran providing third-party transfers, Sullivan responded that the 'Iranian reaction to [a] Chadian request for [the] transfer of US-origin military equipment would probably be positive'.[48] However, Sullivan also thought it likely that should Carter renege on his pledge to sell to Iran a number of AWACS aircraft, 'the Shah will retrench significantly on his willingness to assume risks in his relations with the Soviets'. Should the AWACS transfer pass through Congress (on 5 August), Sullivan believed 'Iran will be willing to stand up and be counted for Chad'. Should it flounder, he added, 'Iran will probably abstain'. Vance added that Iranian assistance would be conditional upon other Islamic nations also taking part, most notably Egypt and Saudi Arabia.[49] Forwarding Sullivan's assessment to the US embassy in N'Djamena, Vance recommended that the ambassador approach the Chadian government to suggest they make a formal request to the Iranian government.[50] The US ambassador to Chad, William Bradford, made this approach, suggesting that Chad send a high-level delegation to Iran. Shortly thereafter, Chad's ambassador in France made an approach to the Iranian ambassador to request Iranian assistance.[51]

In a telegram to the secretary of state, Sullivan wrote that he was 'disturbed to note ... that we have assumed [an] active tutorial role in advising Chad how to approach [the] Iranians and what to ask of them in way of assistance'. His previous advice on the matter had concerned Iran's attitude towards providing aid to Chad, he said, 'not Iran's responsiveness to US prodding'. He advised that the United States should let France take a coordinating role, since 'there are reasons to believe [that] Iran might consider US initiatives on Chad inappropriate'.[52] Sullivan need not have worried, because in early September he was informed by an undersecretary at the Ministry of Foreign Affairs

[47] Memorandum from the President's Assistant for National Security Affairs (Brzezinski) to President Carter, 14 July 1977, *FRUS, 1977–1980, Volume XVII, part 3, North Africa*, doc. 18.

[48] Sullivan telegram, 26 July 1977, WikiLeaks Cable 1977STATE174328_c.

[49] Vance telegram, 30 July 1977, WikiLeaks Cable 1977STATE179388_c.

[50] Ibid.

[51] US ambassador to Chad, William Bradford, telegram, 6 August 1977, WikiLeaks Cable 1977NDJAME02687_c.

[52] Sullivan telegram, 7 August 1977, WikiLeaks Cable 1977TEHRAN06960_c.

that 'the Shah had agreed in principle to provide military equipment to Chad if USG wishes'.[53] Nonetheless, Khalʿatbari asked Sullivan for 'formal affirmation that US encouragement to Iran to respond positively amounted to US asking Iran to assist Chad'.[54] Vance advised Sullivan to respond that the US approach 'constitutes [a] formal request that GOI assist Chad by responding positively to requests from Chad'.[55]

General Tufāniān took steps to investigate what type of military equipment Iran might be able to supply, but by October 1977, Iran had still not received an official request from the Chadian government and was unwilling to reach out to Chad on its own initiative.[56] By December, an official request from Chad had still not been made, when an undersecretary at the Iranian Ministry of Foreign Affairs approached the US embassy in Tehran to inquire whether Iran was able to send US-made military equipment to the government of Mauritania to help it battle an insurgency in Western Sahara. Vance told the embassy to respond negatively to the request, since Mauritania was not eligible for US Foreign Military Sales (FMS). However, Vance added, it should be pointed out 'that one area where we hope they can be of immediate assistance is [the] provision of military equipment to Chad'.[57] However, at this point, Chad had still not sent a delegation to Iran to present a petition in person, and the Iranian Ministry of Foreign Affairs had still not decided whether they would grant any aid to Chad, should a request be made. Despite Sullivan's assessment, based on conversations with those in the Ministry of Foreign Affairs, including Khalʿatbari, that Iran would not provide any weapons for free, Vance insisted that the United States would not be able to provide any funding or replacement of equipment and that any Iranian aid would be considered a grant.[58]

Finally, after months of wavering, out of the blue on 18 February, Sullivan received a telephone call from 'a gentleman who said he was

53 Sullivan telegram, 7 September 1977, WikiLeaks Cable 1977TEHRAN07905_c.
54 Sullivan telegram, 18 September 1977, WikiLeaks Cable 1977TEHRAN08232_c.
55 Vance telegram, 20 September 1977, WikiLeaks Cable 1977STATE225966_c.
56 Sullivan telegram, 13 October 1977, WikiLeaks Cable 1977TEHRAN09041_c.
57 Vance telegram, 16 December 1977, WikiLeaks Cable 1977STATE300925_c.
58 Vance telegram, 17 February 1978, WikiLeaks Cable 1978STATE042952_d.

from Chad and needed to see me urgently'. The gentleman was General Negue Djogo and he was accompanied by the Chadian ambassador to Egypt. Sullivan recorded the meeting:

> The general produced what purported to be the text of a message relayed from Paris which said I had instructions to induce Iran to give Chad the military equipment it required and to tell the Iranians it should be in the form of a gift … Before leaving, the general, who is living in a suite at one of Tehran's more expensive hotels, with a three man mission occupying three separate additional rooms there, said he needed a little 'aide financiere' and asked me for twenty-five hundred dollars. I said I would ask Washington.

Sullivan was evidently frustrated again at the lack of proper direction from Washington. He ended his report:

> I am amazed by this tangible evidence that we are assuming active responsibility for the fate (and personal finances) of this residual French colony, of questionable significance or viability. When I am in Washington nextweek [sic] perhaps someone can explain this Nubian neocolonialism to me.[59]

One day later, Vance wrote to Sullivan to express his surprise at the presence of the Chadian delegation and to inform the ambassador that 'Chadian del[egation] is responsible for its own expenses. No rpt no USG financial assistance is authorized.'[60] Vance's position is curious, considering that just three days earlier, on 17 February, he had stated that such a delegation should be expected and that the 'embassy should provide assistance to Chadian delegation if requested'.[61]

The Chadian delegation met with Khalʿatbari on the afternoon of 19 February to make a formal request for military aid. Khalʿatbari said that while he 'assured them of Iranian sympathy with their need for military supplies to resist Libyan aggression', he was surprised by reports emanating from the region that negotiations had begun between Chad and Libya to bring a peaceful resolution to the fighting.[62] General Djogo responded that even if Chad reconciled with Libya, this would still not negate Chad's needs for arms. Before leaving, Djogo submitted his request, which essentially amounted to

59 Sullivan telegram, 19 February 1978, WikiLeaks Cable 1978TEHRAN01723_d.
60 Vance telegram, 20 February 1978, WikiLeaks Cable 1978STATE044127_d.
61 Vance telegram, 17 February 1978, WikiLeaks Cable 1978STATE042952_d.
62 Sullivan telegram, 19 February 1978, WikiLeaks Cable 1978TEHRAN01765_d.

furnishing an entire 3,000-man tactical brigade, including: their arms and munitions; transport and combat vehicles for them; and $5 million for the purchase of their food, fuel, lubricants and medicine. President Malloum also made a special request for 'missiles to use against tanks', which included not only smaller arms such as bazookas, but also heavier weapons, including B-26 bombers, despite the Carter administration making it clear to the Chadian government that the transfer of such weapons would not be authorised by the US government.[63]

In a conversation with US deputy chief of mission in Iran, Jack Miklos, the head of the Africa department at Iran's Ministry of Foreign Affairs outlined the reasons why the Iranian government was hesitant to accept Chad's request. First, Chad was a distant country, in which Iran had little strategic interest. Second, the logistics of airlifting vehicles to Chad would be complicated and the costs enormous. Seaborne shipments, meanwhile, would take so long that their usefulness in the current conflict would be questionable. Third, even if it were possible to airlift the vehicles to Chad, the cargo would have to fly over Sudan, which would potentially cause trouble for Sudan's reported attempts to rebuild ties with Libya. Fourth, Iran had already been accused of meddling in African affairs for its support of Somalia in the Ogaden War, particularly by Kenya (which will be discussed shortly) and it was felt that arming Chad could damage Iran's reputation further. Iran reasoned that it would be better if another friendly African country, such as Morocco, supplied the necessary arms. Fifth, Chad had indicated that it could defeat the rebels if they were not supported by Libya. Iran calculated that one shipment of Iranian arms would not be enough to counter the Libyans, should they remain committed to supporting the rebels.[64] For these reasons, Iran felt that Chad should push for a diplomatic solution instead.

Miklos wrote to the secretary of state, with notable frustration, that the 'chances of Iran coming through remain dim, as we have reported repeatedly over [the] past several months'. There was no surprise, then, when on 28 February, Iran's acting foreign minister, Manuchehr Zelle, after having spoken to the shah, confirmed that Iran did 'not wish to respond to Chad's request for military assistance'.[65] Miklos concluded

[63] Sullivan telegram, 21 February 1978, WikiLeaks Cable 1978TEHRAN01801_d.
[64] Miklos telegram, 21 February 1978, WikiLeaks Cable 1978TEHRAN01813_d.
[65] Miklos telegram, 28 February 1978, WikiLeaks Cable 1978TEHRAN02063_d.

that the Carter administration 'should stop prodding them for the moment and come back only if and when [the] developing situation in Chad provides strong new arguments for Iranian assistance'.[66] Nonetheless, while expressing sympathy for this stance, the US ambassador to Chad urged the embassy in Tehran to try one more time to induce Iran to 'arrange for the transfer of at least a token shipment ... [to] reassure [the] Chadians that we have not been leading them down the garden path for the last eight months'.[67] The embassy in Tehran appears to have ignored this request.

While the Carter administration assumed that Iran would be forthcoming in providing aid to Chad, this revealed a fundamental misunderstanding of Iran's position on the continent. Sullivan and Miklos, who were on the ground in Tehran and had regular communications with representatives of the Ministry of Foreign Affairs, were doubtful that Iran would agree to such a request from Chad. Iran's Africa policy was not merely an extension of US policy, as perhaps the Carter administration assumed; Iran would not provide weapons to an African country just because the United States requested it. Indeed, it is striking that at the same time as the Carter administration was encouraging Iran to give US-origin weapons to Chad, even though Iran had expressed no interest in the country, it banned the transfer of US-origin weapons to Mauritania and Somalia, which Iran was more amenable to. Moreover, while Iran had initially been encouraged by the Carter administration to support the Barre regime, as the war developed, their positions were reversed, and it was the shah who urged Carter to increase his support for Somalia.

International Diplomacy

Despite the lack of materiel support from the United States, the Somalis made significant progress in the early stages of the war, penetrating deep into Ethiopian territory in July and August 1977 and seizing the cities of Delo, Elkere, Filtu, Jijiga and Karamara. However, the Somali army failed to take Harar in a four-month battle lasting from September until January, due to determined resistance from the defending Ethiopians. In November, Barre, weary of the growing ties

66 Miklos telegram, 27 February 1978, WikiLeaks Cable 1978TEHRAN02011_d.
67 Bradford telegram, 1 March 1978, WikiLeaks Cable 1978NDJAME00858_d.

between the Soviets and Ethiopia, and wanting to prove to the United States and other regional allies such as Saudi Arabia his anti-Soviet, pro-Western credentials, broke off relations with the Soviet Union, expelled its military advisors, and abrogated the 1974 Treaty of Friendship.[68] During the lull in fighting in December and into January, the Soviets began a huge operation to transfer equipment and military advisors to support the Ethiopian war effort. In this period as many as 225 Soviet transport planes travelled to Ethiopia – representing as much at 15 per cent of its transport fleet – with an estimated $1 billion worth of arms.[69] As Tareke has noted, this arms transfer was similar in volume to the assistance the Soviets delivered to the Arabs in 1973 and to the MPLA in 1975.[70]

Iran would be frustrated with American wavering for the second time during this period, when in December the State Department, concerned that the Soviets were 'on the verge of mounting major upgrading of their military materiel and personnel assistance to Ethiopia', urged Iran, Pakistan and Turkey to refuse the Soviets permission to fly in their airspace.[71] Iran was eager to stop the planes from flying over, but at the same time was 'distressed and annoyed' with Washington for not relaying this request sooner, since it had already given permission for four Soviet planes destined for Ethiopia to enter its airspace.[72] Ambassador Sullivan was, in the words of the historian Nancy Mitchell, 'apoplectic'.[73] Writing to the State Department, he said: 'By sheer gall and because countermeasures have been neglected, the Soviets have already managed to send a number of flights to Aden ... If they [the Soviets] get away with this, they [America's regional allies, including Iran] will have a pretty low estimate of our resolve ... [and] be contemptuous of the quality of our leadership on this issue.'[74]

While the Soviet build-up in Ethiopia continued, Barre intensified his efforts to solicit military support from his regional allies under the

[68] Guy Arnold, *Africa: A Modern History: 1945–2015* (London: Atlantic Books, 2017), 494.
[69] Ibid., 497. [70] Tareke, *The Ethiopian Revolution*, 203.
[71] Mitchell, *Jimmy Carter in Africa*, 352.
[72] Sullivan to State Department, 11 December 1977, WikiLeaks Cable 1977TEHRAN10877_c.
[73] Mitchell, *Jimmy Carter in Africa*, 352.
[74] Sullivan to State Department, 11 December 1977, WikiLeaks Cable 1977TEHRAN10877_c.

Figure 11.1 The shah and his half-brother, Prince ʿAbdolrezā Pahlavi, with Siad Barre during his visit to Tehran. *Ettelāʿāt*, 8 Dey 1356/ 29 December 1977, 1.

banner of 'Islamic solidarity'. Over a short period in the end of December and the beginning of January, Barre visited Pakistan, Egypt, Sudan, Oman, Iraq, Syria and Iran.[75] Barre's trip to Iran took place in December (Figure 11.1). Accompanying him on the trip was a retinue of fifty high-level officials, and during the visit several meetings were held to deepen ties with Tehran and ensure the shah's continued support for Somalia in the conflict. This visit was particularly significant because President Carter was due to arrive in Tehran within days of Barre's departure, so this was an opportunity for Barre to urge the shah to put Somalia's case directly to the US president. During a banquet speech, the shah praised the 'friendly and fruitful' negotiations that had taken place. Framing Iran's interest in the Horn of Africa

[75] 'Soviet Foreign Ministry and CPSU CC International Department Background Report on the Somali-Ethiopian Conflict', 3 April 1978, TsKhSD [Russian Center for Preservation of Contemporary Documentation], f. 5, op. 75, d. 1175, ll. 13–23; translated by Mark Doctoroff, The Wilson Center, Cold War International History Project. http://digitalarchive.wilsoncenter.org/document/110975.

within the context of his Indian Ocean policy, the shah said, 'In these negotiations, in particular, we agreed that the Indian Ocean should be a region of peace and security.'[76]

The intensification of Soviet support for Ethiopia did not only cause concern for Barre, but the shah, too. He was worried that the Ethiopian army, bolstered by Russian arms and Cuban manpower, could continue its counteroffensive into Somalia, toppling the Barre regime and turning the whole of the Horn of Africa Red. During Carter's visit, the situation with Somalia was therefore at the top of the agenda. Describing the conflict in stark Cold War terms, the shah said that Barre 'sees his dispute with Ethiopia as a "Warsaw Pact problem" and part of a major Soviet drive'.[77] The shah assured the president that although he was keen to 'play a role' in bringing Ethiopia and Somalia together to discuss peace, 'Ethiopia should be reminded that if they are thinking of further encroaching on the internationally recognised borders of Somalia, it is not something that Iran can ignore.'[78] Carter, however, resisted subtle pressure from the shah to increase US support for Somalia, and rather in his New Year toast merely asked the shah to use his 'good influence' to encourage Ethiopia and Somalia to negotiate a peaceful resolution.[79]

In spite of the shah's insistence to Carter that he wanted to play a role in bringing a peaceful resolution to the conflict, Iranian newspapers focused on his statement that he would 'not remain indifferent to the invasion of Somalia' (Figure 11.2). This was not merely a message for the president of the United States, but for the Soviets, Cuba and Ethiopia, too. And the message was received. Shortly after, the Ethiopian ambassador to Nigeria, Kesate Badema, called on the US ambassador to discuss the situation in the Horn. Badema stated that 'his government was alarmed by recent statements by the

[76] *Ettelā'āt*, 8 Dey 1356/ 29 December 1977, 32.

[77] 'President's Meeting with Shah', State Department, 3 January 1978, WikiLeaks Cable 1978STATE000576_d.

[78] *Ettelā'āt*, 11 Dey 1356/ 1 January 1978, 4.

[79] Jimmy Carter, Tehran, Iran Toasts of the President and the Shah at a State Dinner, 31 December 1977. Online by Gerhard Peters and John T. Woolley, The American Presidency Project. www.presidency.ucsb.edu/node/242827; Donna R. Jackson, *Jimmy Carter and the Horn of Africa: Cold War Policy in Ethiopia and Somalia* (London: McFarland & Co., 2007), 57 and 85.

Figure 11.2 The shah in discussions with President Carter. The shah: 'Iran will not remain indifferent to the invasion of Somalia.' *Ettelā'āt*, 11 Dey 1356/ 1 January 1978, 1.

shah ... [and] worried that President Carter's talks with the shah may have included discussions of possible transfer to Somalia of Iranian weapons originally provided by the U.S.'.[80] Iran may not have been able to use or supply US-made weapons, but not everyone was aware of this and therefore the threat was taken seriously.

Another interesting dimension to the conflict was Israel's support of Ethiopia. Israel and Ethiopia had long been allies; drawn together, in the words of Jeffrey Lefebvre, 'by a mutual fear of Arab and Islamic encirclement'. While the likes of Iran and Saudi Arabia had ceased to support Ethiopia as it edged towards the Soviet Union after the fall of Haile Selassie, in the context of Israel's security policy, 'Addis Ababa's ideological orientation was of little importance'.[81] In fact, during the Ogaden War, Israel provided Ethiopia with spare parts for US-made weapons.[82] As Robert Patman has noted, this 'led to the apparently incredible situation whereby Tel Aviv briefly found itself on the same side as the USSR, Cuba, Libya and the PDRY [People's Democratic Republic of Yemen]'.[83] Had the conflict spread further, it could have proven detrimental to Iran's complicated relationship with Israel. Iran's support for Somalia in this conflict did, however, strain its relationship with one of its African allies – Kenya.

[80] 'Conversation with New Ethiopian Ambassador to Nigeria', US embassy, Lagos, 12 January 1978, WikiLeaks Cable 1978LAGOS00472_d.

[81] Lefebvre, 'Middle East Conflicts and Middle Level Power Intervention in the Horn of Africa', 395.

[82] Lefebvre, *Arms for the Horn*, 186–189; Patten, *Israel and the Cold War*, 147–148.

[83] Patman, *The Soviet Union in the Horn of Africa*, 229.

Iran and Kenya

Iran and Kenya had established political relations in November 1971, exchanged ambassadors in December 1972, and subsequently Kenya became a major consumer of Iranian oil.[84] Iran became one of Kenya's most important economic partners – by 1977 it was the second-largest provider of imports to Kenya (10 per cent of the total) after Britain (20 per cent).[85] As recently as May 1977, the Kenyans had approached Iran to express their fears of Somalian irredentism, which threatened also their Somali-inhabited north-east territories. The shah had agreed that there should be links between the intelligence services of Iran and Kenya to ensure that 'the Indian Ocean should be preserved from outside influence'.[86] But despite these close ties, Nairobi became increasingly troubled by Iran's support for Barre in the Ogaden War. On 10 January 1978, Kenya's foreign minister, Munya Waiyaki, arranged a meeting with Iran's ambassador in Kenya, Ahmad Tavakoli, during which he raised concerns about the shah's statements during Carter's visit to Tehran. The local press gave prominent coverage to the meeting, particularly Waiyaki's perception that the shah's statements 'encouraged Somalia's territorial claims not only in the Ogaden but in Kenya as well'.[87]

In response, on 30 January 1978, the Iranian embassy in Nairobi issued a press release which stated that Iran's 'National Independent Policy, with regards to the events taking place in the Horn of Africa ... has been misunderstood and even misinterpreted'. The statement articulated Iran's commitment to 'its traditional policy of solving international problems and disputes through peaceful means', but also reiterated the point that had been put to Carter, that 'Iran can not remain indifferent should Somalia be attacked and invaded within its

84 Bakhshi, 'Barresi-ye Tārikhi-ye Ravābet-e Khāreji-ye Irān va Qāreh-ye Āfriqā', 59–60.

85 *Keyhān*, 29 Bahman 1356/ 18 February 1978, 2.

86 'Record of Discussion between the Foreign and Commonwealth Secretary and His Imperial Majesty Mohammed Reza Pahlavi, Shahanshah Aryamehr at the Niavaran Palace on Saturday, 14 May 1977', 4, FCO 36/2001.

87 'Foreign Minister Waiyaki Expresses Concern about Shah of Iran's Recent Statements Concerning Conflict in Horn', US Embassy, Nairobi, 11 January 1978, WikiLeaks Cable 1978NAIROB00510_d.

internationally recognized borders'.[88] Despite Iran's claims that it had only provided medical aid to Somalia through its Red Lion and Sun Society, Waiyaki stated publicly that non-African powers like Iran had no right to interfere in African affairs.[89] In a private meeting in February, Ambassador Tavakoli told Waiyaki that 'Iran felt that [the] Kenyan press was taking a communist line on the affairs of the Horn ... and that the Russian threat in Ethiopia ought to be regarded by the Kenyans much more seriously than their fears of Somalia'.[90] According to the British high commissioner, Stanley Fingland, 'Tavakoli implied that if he could not get more satisfaction there was a possibility that the Shah might decide to withdraw him for a period of months or more formally.'[91]

At a press conference on 18 February 1978, Khalʿatbari announced that Iran was formally breaking off relations with Kenya and recalling its ambassador. Pushing back against some of the claims put forward by Waiyaki, he said, 'It is as if the African foreign minister is unaware of the presence of non-Africans in the conflict, or he considers Cubans and others involved to be Africans.' Besides, he added, as 'one of the founding members of the United Nations who had always participated in international affairs and world peace ... Iran cannot remain indifferent if a country's border is attacked'.[92] Iran's repeated insistence that it could not stand by while one country was attacked by another is remarkable considering its support for Somalia, which was the aggressor in the conflict.

The president of Kenya, Jomo Kenyatta, informed Tavakoli that 'he had been unaware of Dr Waiyaka's statements and that he wished the ambassador to know that he, Kenyatta, attached importance to Kenya's links with Iran'.[93] Fingland wrote that the Kenyans were 'puzzled by the suddenness of the Iranian decision', and although they wanted to maintain good relations with Tehran, did not think they owed an apology.[94] Tavakoli left Iran on 26 February, leaving the

[88] Press Release, Imperial Embassy of Iran, Nairobi, 30 January 1978, FCO 31/2328.
[89] The Red Lion and Sun Society (Anjoman-e Shir o Khorshid-e Sorkh-e Irān) was set up in the 1920s and was part of the International Red Cross and Red Crescent Movement.
[90] Stanley Fingland, 'Kenya-Iran Relations', 20 February 1978, FCO 31/2328.
[91] Ibid. [92] *Keyhān*, 29 Bahman 1356/ 18 February 1978, 2.
[93] Fingland report, 23 February 1978, FCO 31/2328. [94] Ibid.

British embassy in charge of Iran's consular interests in Kenya, with the presence of an Iranian chargé d'affaires.[95] The British and Belgians made some attempts to mediate over the following weeks and encouraged Kenya to send a high-level mission to Tehran to negotiate directly with the Iranian government. These efforts failed because Iran would only receive a mission if its purpose was to apologise and although Kenya was willing to send a mission, it would not do so 'if this could be interpreted as a Kenyan gesture of apology'.[96]

It seems strange that such a seemingly trivial matter could result in Iran suspending diplomatic relations, particularly with such a close economic ally, so what was the real reason for this diplomatic rift? Of course, it is entirely possible that the cause of the incident was that the shah considered criticism from Kenya as a personal slight. But is it conceivable that the shah was so thin-skinned that he would break off diplomatic relations with a friendly country over comments made by its foreign minister? Another event perhaps sheds some light on this. A few months after the split, Manuchehr Zelle telephoned the British ambassador, Anthony Parsons, to inform him that the shah had not received a response to his letter of condolence to the acting president of Kenya, Daniel Moi, following Kenyatta's death. The Iranians were considering whether to send another message to congratulate Moi on his inauguration, but 'did not wish to do so if Moi's failure to acknowledge the first message was deliberate'. Parsons was asked by Zelle for the high commissioner's advice, 'without consulting the Kenyans'.[97] The fact that Iran raised such a 'tedious point', to use Parsons' expression, demonstrates that the shah perhaps did feel genuinely aggrieved by Kenya's response to Iran's involvement in the Ethio-Somali conflict.

Personal feelings notwithstanding, the rift should also be seen in the broader context of the Ogaden War and Iran's policy in the Horn. Although Khalʿatbari maintained that the attitude of Waiyaki had been the cause of the closure of Iran's embassy, foreign newspapers speculated that this action was taken to demonstrate that Iran was taking a tough line and was willing to come to Somalia's defence if it were invaded by Ethiopia.[98] In other words, if Kenya's public criticism

[95] Fingland report, 28 February 1978, FCO 31/2328. The British continued to look after Iranian interests in Kenya until September 1980.
[96] George Chalmers report, 12 July 1978, FCO 31/2328.
[97] Anthony Parsons report, 11 October 1978, FCO 31/2328.
[98] *Keyhān*, 30 Bahman 1356/ 19 February 1978, 6.

was not challenged, then this could undermine the seriousness of Iran's threat to intervene in the Horn. On 15 February, at nearly exactly the same time as Iran announced the closure of the embassy in Nairobi, an Egypt Air plane en route to Somalia was intercepted in Kenyan air space by the Kenyan air force and forced to land at Nairobi. It was found to contain a cargo of munitions and according to the Kenyan government, this was the fourth Somali-bound Egyptian plane to enter its airspace in the past week.[99] In retaliation, Egypt seized two Kenyan aeroplanes in Cairo and arrested twenty-two crew members.[100] We know that Iran and Egypt were cooperating on matters of security in Africa, so it is surely no coincidence that these two diplomatic incidents occurred at the same time.

The shah's declarations during Carter's visit had also caught the attention of the OAU, which released a statement criticising Iran's role in the conflict:

> The recent statement of the government of Iran concerning the situation in the Horn of Africa is replete with very disturbing overtones. Iran had better address herself to the question of finding a peaceful solution to the crisis in the Horn of Africa and assist the OAU in this task.[101]

In 1968, during the shah's state visit to Ethiopia, the secretary general of the OAU had praised the shah for the role he 'plays in the great family of Asia and Africa'.[102] Ten years later, the tone was very different. Now, in its statement, the OAU declared that it had 'no room for any country whose consuming passion is to extend her sphere of influence to Africa by playing the role of a mini-power'. In spite of Iranian attempts to downplay the statement as the opinion of just one OAU administrator, a report by the US embassy in Addis Ababa concluded that 'while [the] statement is somewhat one-sided, [the] embassy believes it probably reflects [the] views of most OAU members'.[103] From the 1960s, when Iran first reached out to independent Africa, the shah had insisted that Iran was committed to

[99] 'Kenya Egyptian Plane Held', *AP Archive*, 15 February 1978, available online: www.aparchive.com/metadata/youtube/457d03e0f7aa4f0e3189a57e95d9b2f5.

[100] *The New York Times*, 17 February 1978, 3.

[101] 'OAU Press Release on Iran and the Horn of Africa', 20 January 1978, WikiLeaks Cable 1978ADDIS00310_d.

[102] See Chapter 3.

[103] US Embassy in Addis Ababa to State Department, 8 February 1978, WikiLeaks Cable 1978ADDIS00625_d.

combatting 'the remnants of colonialism', but this image was becoming increasingly difficult to uphold and some African leaders came to perceive Iran as merely another imperial power.

The Ethiopian Counteroffensive (January–March 1978)

In January 1978, the balance of the war shifted towards Ethiopia, as a result not only of Russian support, but also the presence of Cuban troops that had been airlifted in. Their numbers reached as many as 18,000 by February, half of which were transported directly from Angola.[104] The turning point of the war occurred on 22 January, when the Somalis launched their final attack on Harar. Armed with Soviet T-54 tanks and supported by Cuban ground troops and pilots flying jet fighter bombers, the Ethiopians routed the Somalis, killing as many as 3,000 and capturing tanks and weapons left behind on the battlefield.[105] From this time, the Somalis were on the back foot, and over the following weeks, the Ethiopian counteroffensive forced them to abandon all of the towns and cities they had taken in the early months of the war.

The Americans had seriously underestimated the number of Cuban troops in Ethiopia; by as much as 70 per cent.[106] By early February, when it became clear in Washington that the war had shifted in Ethiopia's favour, discussions took place over what to do if Ethiopia decided to continue its offensive into Somali territory. In a report by the director of the Bureau of Intelligence and Research, Harold Henry Saunders, the capabilities '(not the intentions)' of Egypt, Iran, Saudi Arabia and Sudan to provide assistance were evaluated. Saunders concluded that Iran was 'in a far better position than any other state in the area to provide a wide range of air support', would be able to provide technical and military advisors, and could logistical problems of transportation be overcome, the introduction of 20,000 Iranian and Egyptian forces 'would give the Somalis clear superiority over their opponents'.[107]

104 Gebru Tareke, 'The Ethiopia-Somalia War of 1977 Revisited', *The International Journal of African Historical Studies*, vol. 33, no. 3 (2000), 656.
105 Tareke, *The Ethiopian Revolution*, 205; Mitchell, *Jimmy Carter in Africa*, 374.
106 Mitchell, *Jimmy Carter in Africa*, 369.
107 'Briefing Memorandum from the Director of the Bureau of Intelligence and Research (Saunders) to Secretary of State Vance', 4 February 1978, *FRUS, 1977–1980, Volume XVII, Horn of Africa, part 1*, doc. 53.

Later in February, during a National Security Council meeting, President Carter asked the CIA chief, Admiral Stansfield Turner, whether Iran and Egypt would do anything to stop an Ethiopian invasion of Somalia. Turner told him they would not, but added that 'the Shah has discussed what he would do in the Horn and has said he would send help if the border was crossed'. The main problem for the United States was that as things stood, they were on the side of the aggressor. 'The key, therefore, is for us to get the Somalis out of the Ogaden', acting chairman of the Joint Chiefs of Staff, General David Jones stated. 'Once they are out, then we should support third country transfers.'[108] Although US policy was to find a diplomatic solution to the situation in the Horn, should this not be possible, they considered Iran to be key to preventing a Soviet-Cuban-backed Ethiopian invasion of Somalia. General Jones argued that 'the participation of the Iranians would give the Somalis a good chance to stop the invasion'.[109]

As the war approached its end, Iran continued to support Somalia publicly. As late as 6 March, a 'high official in the Shah's Government' said that Iran 'cannot permit the Soviets to conquer all Africa' and was resolved to commit military forces to Somalia if necessary.[110] However, in spite of the Iranian government's public pronouncements, it is clear that in private, the shah's position was beginning to soften, perhaps as he realised that the Carter administration would be unlikely to permit either the transfer of American-made weapons, or their use by a third country, such as Iran, in battle. In January, the shah had sent a message to Barre encouraging him to undertake 'an offensive for peace', and these messages became more urgent as the war dragged on.[111] At one point, the shah summoned the Somali ambassador in Tehran and reportedly said:

> I've had three messages from President Carter. You Somalis are threatening to upset the balance of world power. If you get out of the Ogaden we will see that you get all the aid you want, but it will be economic aid, not military. You must forget about the Ogaden.[112]

108 'Minutes of a National Security Meeting', Washington, 23 February 1978, *FRUS, 1977–1980, Volume XVII, Horn of Africa, part 1*, doc. 62.

109 Ibid. 110 *The New York Times*, 7 March 1978, 16.

111 Sullivan to State Department, 8 January 1978, WikiLeaks Cable 1978TEHRAN00190_d.

112 Heikal, *Iran: The Untold Story*, 116.

By early March 1978, it became clear that Ethiopia had won the arms race and Somali diplomats 'made known their disappointment with the shah's promises, which they claim have produced little of either financial or military value to their cause'.[113] On 9 March 1978, given the vast Soviet and Cuban support for Ethiopia, and Barre's inability to secure US-backing, Barre reluctantly informed Carter that he agreed to withdraw his troops from the Ogaden region. In fact, as the historian Donna Jackson notes, 'the "withdrawal" referred to by Siad was more like a rout'.[114]

Despite the failure of Iran, Egypt and Saudi Arabia to convince the United States to commit resources to the conflict in the Horn, their efforts were not entirely in vain. As the US historical record shows, Washington was aware that these countries were primed and ready to take action should America permit the use of third country transfers, or decide to send forces itself. Whether or not the shah was sincere when he repeatedly stated that Iran was ready to defend Somalia if it was invaded by Ethiopia, the message was taken seriously in Washington and Iran's potential to come to Somalia's aid was discussed at the highest level. It is entirely plausible that even if Iran did not shape American policy in the Horn as the war developed, it did influence it. It is also possible that the shah's public declaration to support Somalia played a role in the decision of the Ethiopians – and the Soviets – not to cross the border into Somalia.

*****

Roham Alvandi has shown in his *Nixon, Kissinger, and the Shah* that in the late 1960s and early 1970s, the shah was able to manipulate the Nixon administration, in a sense, by exaggerating the Soviet threat in Iraq in order to strengthen his case for increased US support.[115] But by the late 1970s, the situation had changed somewhat. No longer was the Soviet Union merely a faux threat exaggerated to elicit US support; it posed a direct challenge to Iran's immediate and long-term strategic goals. As the Ogaden War developed, the shah provided materiel and diplomatic support to Somalia, precisely because he feared an Ethiopian victory would

113 *The Washington Post*, 3 March 1978.
114 Jackson, *Jimmy Carter and the Horn of Africa*, 100.
115 Alvandi, *Nixon, Kissinger, and the Shah*.

spell the collapse of Somalia and leave the Soviets unopposed in the Horn of Africa. This would have implications for the shah's Indian Ocean policy.

With the absence of archival material, we cannot say precisely what arms Iran provided to Somalia during the conflict. Nevertheless, it is clear that throughout the war, Iran did supply the Somalis with weapons as well as logistical and medical support. According to one newspaper, in the first months of the war, Iran had provided light arms, trucks and hospital equipment.[116] Another claimed that in the first quarter of 1978, Iran provided over ten shipments of mortars, heavy artillery ammunition, and ground-to-air missiles, and as well as personnel.[117] The personnel were probably advisors. These weapons were not, for reasons already mentioned, the most recent technology produced in the United States, but 'obsolescent material' including American-produced M-48 tanks, which had reached Somalia via Oman.[118] Iran also provided 'financing for weapons bought on the free market'.[119] These included German mortars acquired through Turkey, and some anti-tank weapons.[120]

Throughout the conflict, there are indications that Iran was frustrated by the Carter administration's indecisiveness and failure to communicate its policy clearly.[121] Donna Jackson has argued that 'if events in the Horn of Africa had taken place ten or fifteen years previously, it seems unlikely that the American response to the usurpation of their influence by the Soviet Union would have been so calm'.[122] But the new administration was unwilling to get involved directly in the conflict, and rather than take sides, President Carter tried to play the role of peacemaker. He said, 'Those of us who have any influence at all must use it for this purpose ... We want Somalia and Ethiopia to be friends again.'[123] To his credit, Carter maintained this stance, even under pressure from some of America's most powerful Middle East and North African allies. The failure of these allies to

116 *The New York Times*, 1 January 1978, 1.
117 Saikal, *The Rise and Fall of the Shah*, 180.
118 Lefebvre, *Arms for the Horn*, 188.
119 *The Washington Post*, 3 March 1978.
120 Heikal, *Iran: The Untold Story*, 115.
121 Mitchell, *Jimmy Carter in Africa*, 295.
122 Jackson, *Jimmy Carter and the Horn of Africa*, 65.
123 *The New York Times*, 1 January 1978, 1.

secure US support prevented them from offering to Barre the type of assistance he needed to win the war. So, while Iran's support for Somalia in the Ogaden War demonstrates the aspirations of the shah to become a major power in Africa in the 1970s, it also demonstrates the limitations of his independent global policy.

Conclusion

In the autumn of 1978, the Iranian naval commander Bahman Minovi arrived in the Seychelles, the African archipelagic state in the Indian Ocean. Minovi's mission had begun in early September, when a squadron of six ships of the Iranian Imperial Navy visited several ports along the west coast of Pakistan and India. After reaching Cochin, half of the ships returned to Iran, but the other half, under the command of Minovi, proceeded on a secret mission to the Seychelles to ask its president, Albert René, whether he would allow Iran to build a navy supply base there. In view of the unease he felt at the large size of the Soviet and Chinese embassies in his country, René welcomed the prospect of a fellow Indian Ocean nation setting up there. In order to help him win over public opinion, however, René told Minovi that as a gesture of goodwill, Iran might consider funding the electrification of two outlying islands with clinics.[1]

The defeat of Somalia in the Ogaden War, the seemingly permanent shift of the Derg regime to the Soviet–Cuban camp, the suspension of relations with Kenya and OAU criticism had damaged Iran's prestige in Africa, and was detrimental to Iran's broader security strategy in the Indian Ocean. But the shah had policies in place to deal with this setback. He aided the rebels in Rhodesia and supported international initiatives to bring about a peaceful transfer to majority rule there, strengthened his allies with development aid, ensured that many countries relied on Iranian oil, and presented Iran's bond with Senegal as representative of broader connections between Iran and Black Africa. The seeking of new bases in the western Indian Ocean was in part also a response to Soviet inroads in the Horn of Africa, but it was not a knee-jerk reaction; it was by now a well-established part of Iran's

[1] From a telephone conversation between Houchang Chehabi and Bahman Minovi, 23 October 2018. I am grateful to Houchang Chehabi for sharing this with me.

strategy, as demonstrated through naval agreements with South Africa, and discussions with Mauritius about potential Iranian bases there in 1972.

In the 1960s and 1970s, Iran became a significant player in the politics of the Global South, particularly in areas that were impacted by the Cold War. As other scholars have argued, and this book has illustrated, the shah was a capable international statesman and knowledgeable in world affairs, who navigated the complex world of big power politics to devise a vision for the future of Iran in the modern world. The shah set out this vision for Iran's independent national policy in his final treatise, *Towards the Great Civilisation*, published in 1977, on the eve of the revolution.

> All efforts made under this policy are necessarily directed towards safeguarding the interests of the country and nation. In pursuing this path we have no need to resort to petty calculations and political acrobatics, or to seek the friendship or hostility of other countries for the sake of vague principles or special motives. Our actions spring from an enlightened and far-seeing appreciation of the real and palpable interests of the nation ... This policy also means that we do not need to resort to any noisy or showy actions, for such activities are often destructive rather than constructive. Actions tending to destroy are of course easy and nearly always have an exciting and attractive appearance, while constructive actions take place slowly and quietly and without any excitement. At any rate, this is the path that we have chosen, and we will follow it to the end.[2]

One of the qualities of a capable strategist is the ability to see the bigger picture and to deal with unforeseen events without losing the larger perspective.[3] It is not a coincidence that Iran responded to many of the major regional events of the 1960s and 1970s practically and with some measure.

The shah had a strong national ideology built around the idea of Iran's Great Civilisation, which was most powerfully articulated at Persepolis. But at the same time, he made use of Iran's Islamic identity in forging connections to Muslim-majority countries in the Global South. One of the shah's skills was the ability to adapt depending on who he was dealing with. To many Muslim-majority countries the

[2] Pahlavi, *Besu-ye Tamaddon-e Bozorg*, 234–235.
[3] For an introduction to the characteristics of grand strategists, see Gaddis, *On Grand Strategy*, 1–27.

shah was an Islamic representative, but to Léopold Sédar Senghor, he was a fellow secular-minded ruler of a majority Muslim country. The shah presented himself to the OAU members as a fellow member of the Global South and anti-colonial advocate, while at the same time forging close relations with the apartheid regime. To Haile Selassie, the shah was a fellow monarch in a troubling period for the global monarchical fraternity. The ability of the shah to adopt these apparently contradictory positions and play these roles convincingly was a key factor in the success of Iran's Africa strategy.

While the shah's generals and diplomats continued to work towards achieving Iran's strategic objectives across the regions bordering the Indian Ocean, the situation in Iran itself deteriorated. The shah left his country on 16 January 1979 for a life in exile. In February, the dissident cleric, Ayatollah Khomeini, returned to Iran, and shortly thereafter a referendum was held, after which the Pahlavi monarchy was replaced with an Islamic Republic. The shah first travelled to Egypt, where he was met at the airport by President Sadat and given a 'welcome fit for a friendly Head-of-State', complete with a guard of honour, twenty-one-gun salute and procession through streets adorned with Iranian flags and portraits of the shah and lined with cheering crowds.[4] Sadat urged the shah to remain in Egypt, but the shah planned to go to the United States to receive medical treatment for his cancer. Eager to 'lighten Sadat's burden' while he waited for arrangements to be made for his transfer to the United States, the shah accepted an invitation by King Hassan II to travel to Morocco.[5] The shah flew from Cairo to Marrakesh on 22 January, where his old friend graciously received him. But by the middle of March, as the revolution continued to unfold in Iran, the Moroccan king had become 'quite nervous about the shah's stay'.[6] On 30 March, the shah left Morocco for the Bahamas.[7]

While the shah was forced to make the adjustment from global statesman to outcast, his Africa strategy quickly unravelled. Even before he left Iran, on 11 January, the Bakhtiar government announced that it would stop supplying oil to South Africa and would be

[4] Houchang Nahavandi, *The Last Shah of Iran*, trans. Steeve Reed (Slough: Aquilion Ltd., 2005), 393.

[5] Afkhami, *The Life and Times of the Shah*, 531. [6] Ibid., 543.

[7] *The New York Times*, 31 March 1979, 3.

reviewing relations between the two countries.[8] On 4 March, just over one month after Khomeini's return to Iran, South Africa's consul general, General Fraser, had been summoned to the Ministry of Foreign Affairs 'and given his marching orders'.[9] But the close ties that linked Iran and South Africa could not easily be unbound and Iran still relied on South African technical assistance, particularly in the mining sector. Therefore, despite the break in relations between Iran and South Africa, the Ministry of Foreign Affairs had decided that three members of South Africa's consulate general could stay 'for an indefinite period, to wind up their affairs', while three members of the Iranian mission in Johannesburg would remain there.[10] The deputy consul, John Sunde, had been told by the Iranians that 'he could stay provided he kept his head down and observed a low profile'.[11] Sunde told the British that 'the Iranians believe that everyone looked upon Fraser as an Ambassador and, having expelled him, they now feel that they have made a gesture equivalent to suspending diplomatic relations ... and that no further move on the Iranian part is now needed'. By May, two months after Fraser's expulsion, Sunde reported that his mission was 'getting full cooperation from the Iranian authorities after a few initial hiccups'.[12]

In South Africa, Iran's acting consul-general, one Mr Seyedzādeh, initially had few contacts with the new regime in Tehran, and apparently at one time had to sell his Persian carpets 'in order to live'. By the middle of May, he reported that 'contacts with Tehran are now more or less normal', and that the new government was 'keen to maintain relations with South Africa'. This was particularly important because of Iran's shares in the Natref refinery in Sasolburg and the Rossing Uranium Company, commitments that the Iranian government could not legally withdraw from easily.[13] From October 1979 until the mid-1990s, Iran and South Africa agreed that their interests would be represented by Switzerland.[14] Iran maintained a small staff, based in the Reza Shah house in Johannesburg, to operate the Iran interests section at the Swiss embassy in Pretoria.[15] In spite of Iran joining the oil embargo against South Africa, it continued to supply oil to the

8 P. K. C. Thomas to P. Morrice, 15 March 1979, FCO 8/3373.
9 John Graham to Alan G. Munro, 5 March 1979, FCO 8/3373. 10 Ibid.
11 H. D. A. C. Miers to Munro, 1 May 1979, FCO 8/3373. 12 Ibid.
13 Sophia Lambert to Philip Morrice, 14 May 1979, FCO 8/3373.
14 Chehabi, 'South Africa and Iran', 704. 15 Ibid.

apartheid regime, though in reduced quantities. According to some estimates, by the time of the end of apartheid, Iran supplied between 65 and 90 per cent of South Africa's oil.[16] South Africa also supplied arms to Iran during the war with Iraq.[17] The revolution had changed Iran's foreign policy outlook in many ways, but the revolutionary regime, as the shah's regime, could not avoid developing strong ties to South Africa.

In contrast to the Pahlavi grand strategy, which sought to expand Iran's influence in Africa as a way to reduce the spread of communism and assert greater control over the Indian Ocean, the new regime's motivation was to spread the message of Khomeini's revolution. Whereas the shah generally avoided the more staunch anti-imperial regimes and movements across the continent in preference of moderate and pro-Western governments, the Islamic Republic's preferences were the opposite. Tanzania's revolutionary leader, Julius Nyerere, long shunned by the shah, congratulated Khomeini on the success of the revolution and shortly after, the Iranian government set up an office in Dar es Salaam. From that time, as Banafsheh Keynoush has written, 'Iran began viewing Tanzania as a frontline state in the fight against apartheid'.[18] Other states received this message, perceived the new regime in Iran as a partner in the struggle against apartheid and drew inspiration from Iran's revolution. In April 1979, a delegation from the Zimbabwe African National Union travelled to Iran to speak to its minister of foreign affairs, Ebrāhim Yazdi, and deliver a message of congratulations from the leader of the group, Robert Mugabe, to Khomeini. The head of the delegation, Simon Muzenda, claimed – 'somewhat sycophantically', a diplomat at the British embassy felt – that the delegation 'wished to familiarise themselves with the characteristics of the Iranian Revolution so this could be applied in Rhodesia'. A major reason for the visit was undoubtedly to solicit financial backing from the revolutionary regime in Iran.[19]

Whereas under the shah, Iran offered supported to the West in Africa, in the decade after the revolution, Iran posed a direct challenge to the

[16] Michal Onderco, 'A Battle of Principles: South Africa's Relations with Iran', *Commonwealth and Comparative Politics*, vol. 53, no. 2 (2016), 256.

[17] Chehabi, 'South Africa and Iran', 705.

[18] Banafsheh Keynoush, 'Revolutionary Iran's Africa Policy', *King Faisal Center for Research and Islamic Studies*, Special Report (June 2021), 129.

[19] Stephen Lamport to Robin Gorham, 6 May 1979, FCO 8/3373.

West and its allies throughout the continent. Many African countries had suspended or broken off their relations with Iran after the revolution, and as diplomatic ties were re-established, the nature of these relationships and Iran's priorities on the continent were redefined. Iran identified areas in Africa in which it might be able to export its Islamic Revolution; one CIA report warned of the dangers of 'the spread of Khomeini's gospel'.[20] This was felt particularly in countries with sizeable Muslim populations, in which 'Iran has begun to build networks of sympathisers'.[21] One of the targets of Iran's *propagande intégriste* was Senegal.[22] Iran's relations with Senegal had begun to sour shortly after the revolution. Iran immediately withdrew from the Kayar development project, but because of broader economic cooperation both embassies remained open. In November 1979, the Iranian ambassador in Dakar was summoned by the prime minister, Abdou Diouf, who expressed concern at the occupation of the US embassy in Tehran by revolutionaries.[23] On 28 November, President Senghor issued a statement condemning the taking of hostages in Tehran.[24]

In early January 1984, a new diplomat arrived at the Iranian embassy in Dakar. The Americans, whose embassy was located nearby, discovered that the man was Hamid Aboutālebi, whom they considered to have been 'one of the principal figures involved in the invasion of the American embassy in Tehran'. The American ambassador informed the Senegalese of his presence, and it was subsequently discovered that another Iranian 'diplomat' had earlier arrived in Dakar with his wife in November 1983. All three were ordered to leave, but went on hunger strike in protest. A few days later, the 'Senegalese authorities lost patience … and simply put them on board the Swiss Air flight to Geneva'.[25] According to the British ambassador:

> The Senegalese have been looking for an excuse to close down the Iranian mission here for some time. The reason is that its two members have been very active in stirring up trouble among the Shi'ite Lebanese here … They are

[20] 'Sub-Saharan Africa: Growing Iranian Activity', December 1984, General Records of the CIA, RDP85S00317R000300110005–1.
[21] Ibid. [22] Newspaper cutout, 6 February 1984, CADN 184PO/2/87/368/93.
[23] Newspaper cutout, 24–25 November 1979, CADN 184PO/2/87/368/93.
[24] 'Le Senegal condamne la prise d'otage de l'ambassade Americaine a Teheran', Dakar, 28 November 1979, CADN 184PO/2/87/368/93.
[25] P. L. O'Keeffe to Peter Wallis, 6 February 1984, FCO 8/5572.

Figure C.1 Commemoration of fifty years of Senegal-Iran diplomatic relations, Dakar. Photographed by the author, May 2022.

> also thought to have put up the money for an extremist Moslem weekly which made its first appearance a couple of weeks ago.[26]

In early February, the Senegalese Foreign Ministry announced that it had decided to close the Iranian embassy due to its engagement in 'undiplomatic activities'.[27] The expulsion of Iranian diplomats would have been unthinkable just eight years earlier, when Empress Farah had travelled to Senegal to lay the foundation stone of a city named after her; a city which would 'set in stone' the ties between the two countries.

In 2021, a poster was hung up outside the Senegalese embassy in Tehran, celebrating fifty years of diplomatic relations between Iran and Senegal (Figure C.1). Beside it were posters advertising the automobile factory, SenIran Auto, near to Dakar, in which the Iran Khodro Company holds a majority share. A short walk from the embassy is the former home of Léopold Sédar Senghor, now a museum, where, hung up on a wall outside his office, his woven portrait from the 1971 Persepolis celebrations is displayed. The revolution had a huge impact on Iran's relations with Senegal, but as with most other countries in Africa, these relationships were gradually redefined and gained new strength and meaning.

*****

[26] Ibid. [27] W. G. Clare to A. S. Collins, 8 February 1984, FCO 8/5572.

On 30 July 1980, Mohammad Reza Pahlavi was laid to rest in a marble tomb at the Al-Rifaʿi Mosque in Cairo. Anwar Sadat, had not only provided sanctuary for his 'true and dear friend' the exiled shah in his final months, but also granted him a full state funeral.[28] The first lady of Egypt, Jahan Sadat, later recalled: 'It was the most spectacular funeral that any of us in Egypt had ever seen.'[29] Egyptian soldiers led the funeral procession from Abdin Palace to Al-Rifaʿi Mosque, some playing instruments, some holding wreaths, with other officers mounted on horseback.[30] All of the shah's forty-five medals were brought to Cairo, but only three were on displayed at the funeral, on black velvet pillows in front of the shah's coffin; the Iranian Order of Zulfaghār, the Imperial Medal, and the Egyptian Nile.[31] According to the shah's chief of protocol, Amir Aslān Afshār, the inclusion of the Egyptian decoration was 'aimed at offering an emphatic homage to the testimony of immense friendship Egypt showed to Iran'.[32] It was also felt that it would be improper to display awards granted by countries that had 'behaved so basely towards the late Sovereign'.[33]

Leading the procession that followed the shah's coffin, which was draped in an Iranian flag and carried atop a carriage pulled by eight Arabian horses, was Anwar Sadat, the leader of the only country officially to mourn the death of the shah. Next to him were former president of the United States, Richard Nixon, the exiled King Constantine of Greece, and the Pahlavi family. As a mark of respect, some of the shah's Western allies sent their diplomatic representatives, but many more did not.[34] Having witnessed the seizure of the US embassy by revolutionaries in November 1979, the West feared for the safety of their own diplomats, as well as for their access to Iranian oil. King Hassan II of Morocco, for a long time the shah's closest ally

[28] *The Washington Post*, 30 July 1980.
[29] Jehan Sadat, *A Woman of Egypt* (New York: Simon & Schuster, 1987), 432.
[30] *The New York Times*, 29 July 1980, 8.
[31] Afkhami, *The Life and Times of the Shah*, 595.
[32] Amir Aslan Afshar, *Farewell Iran: A Century of Memories* (Bethesda, MD: Ibex Publishers, 2021), 335.
[33] Ibid.
[34] The countries whose ambassadors attended were the United States (Alfred Atherton), the United Kingdom, France, China, Israel and Australia. 'Editorial Note', *FRUS, 1977–1980, Volume XI, part 1, Iran: Hostage Crisis, November 1979–September 1980*, doc. 326.

in North Africa, sent his court minister; the only country in Africa, besides Egypt, to be represented at the funeral.[35]

It was fitting that the shah was buried in Cairo, since Egypt had played such a significant role in the shah's personal, as well as political life. Indeed, his first political act was to marry into the Egyptian royal house – an occasion at which Sadat had been present as a young soldier[36] – and the shah's first daughter was half Egyptian. Nasser had been the shah's sworn enemy in the late 1950s and throughout the 1960s, and the Iran–Egypt rapprochement that occurred under Sadat had allowed the shah to devise a security strategy that extended far beyond Iran's borders. It is equally fitting that the shah was laid to rest on the African continent; a part of the world that was integral to the shah's grand strategy until the very end of his reign.

[35] *The Washington Post*, 29 July 1980.
[36] Sadat would rejoice in retelling this story whenever he saw the shah. Afkhami, *The Life and Times of the Shah*, 530.

References

Archives

Ardeshir Zāhedi Archives, Hoover Institution Library and Archives, Stanford

British National Archives, Kew

Foreign and Commonwealth Office (FCO)

Foreign Office (FO)

Centre des Archives Diplomatiques de Nantes (CADN)

Centre des Archives diplomatiques du ministère des Affaires étrangères, la Courneuve (CADC)

Foreign Relations of the United States (FRUS): https://history.state.gov/historicaldocuments

The Moshe Safdie Archive, McGill University, Montreal

Nationaal Archief, The Hague (NA)

National Library and Archives of Iran, Tehran (NLAI)

Shojāʿ al-Din Shafā Archives, Bibliothèque universitaire des langues et civilisations, Paris

United Nations Archives: https://search.archives.un.org/

WikiLeaks Public Library of US Diplomacy: https://wikileaks.org/plusd/about/

Wilson Center, Cold War International History Project: www.wilsoncenter.org/program/cold-war-international-history-project

Wilson Center, Digital Archive: https://digitalarchive.wilsoncenter.org/

World Bank Group Archives: www.worldbank.org/en/archive/digital-collections

Periodicals

Afrique Industrie Infrastructures

Anti-Apartheid News

The Atlantic

Bingo

Echo of Iran

The Ethiopian Herald
Ettelā'āt
Iran Economic News
Iran Free Press
Le Journal de Téhéran
Kayhan International
Keyhān
Los Angeles Times
Le Monde
Nation
Newsweek
The New York Times
Nouvelles Du Cameroun
The Pakistan Times
The Palestine Post
Peking Review
Rastākhiz
Ruznāmeh-ye Jashn-e Shāhanshāhi-ye Irān
Le Soleil
The Star
Time
The Washington Post
Zan-e Ruz

Published Primary and Secondary Sources

'Abdoh, Jalāl. *Chehel Sāl dar Sahneh-ye Qazā'i, Siyāsi, Diplomāsi-ye Irān va Jahān: Khāterāt-e Doktor Jalāl 'Abdoh*, 2 vols. Tehran: Mo'assaseh-ye Khadmāt-e Farhangi-ye Rasā, 1368 [1989].

Afkhami, Gholam Reza. *The Life and Times of the Shah*. Berkley: University of California Press, 2009.

Afshar, Amir Aslan. *Farewell Iran: A Century of Memories*. Bethesda: Ibex Publishers, 2021.

Afshar, Mahasti. 'Festival of Arts, Shiraz-Persepolis, 1967–1977', *Iran Namag*, vol. 4, no. 2 (2019), 4–64.

Ajala, Olabisi. *An African Abroad*. London: Jarrolds, 1963.

Akhavi, Shahrough. 'EGYPT vii. Political and Religious Relations with Persia in the Modern Period', *Encyclopaedia Iranica*, VIII/3, 1998, 257–262. Available online: www.iranicaonline.org/articles/egypt-vii.

Akhtar, Iqbal. *The Khōjā of Tanzania Discontinuities of a Postcolonial Religious Identity*. Leiden: Brill, 2016.

Akhtar, Shameem. 'The Rabat Summit Conference', *Pakistan Horizon*, vol. 22, no. 4 (1969), 336–340.

Alam, Asadollah. *The Shah and I: Confidential Diary of Iran's Royal Court, 1969–1977*, ed. Alinaghi Alikhani. London: I. B. Tauris, 1991.

Ali, Mehrunnisa. 'The Second Islamic Summit Conference', *Pakistan Horizon*, vol. 27, no. 1 (1974), 29–49.

ʿĀlikhāni, ʿAli-Naqi ed. *Yāddāsht-hā-ye ʿAlam*, 7 vols. Tehran: Ketābsarā, 1393 [2014].

Alvandi, Roham. 'Muhammad Reza Pahlavi and the Bahrain Question, 1968–1970', *British Journal of Middle Eastern Studies*, vol. 37, no. 2 (2010), 159–177.

'Guest Editor's Introduction: Iran and the Cold War', *Iranian Studies*, vol. 47, no. 3 (2014), 373–378.

Nixon, Kissinger, and the Shah: The United States and Iran in the Cold War. Oxford: Oxford University Press, 2014.

'Iran in the Age of Aryamehr', in *The Age of Aryamehr: Late Pahlavi Iran and Its Global Entanglements*, ed. Roham Alvandi, 1–34. London: Gingko Library, 2018.

Ansari, Ali M. 'The Myth of the White Revolution: Mohammad Reza Shah, "Modernization" and the Consolidation of Power', *Middle Eastern Studies*, vol. 37, no. 3 (2001), 1–24.

'The Curious Case of the Nuclear Company of Britain and Iran', *Iran*, vol. 55, no. 1 (2017), 73–86.

Araujo, Ana Lucia. *Shadows of the Slave Past: Memory, Heritage, and Slavery*. New York: Routledge, 2014.

Arnold, Guy. *Africa: A Modern History: 1945–2015*. London: Atlantic Books, 2017.

Asgari, Nurmohammad. *Qolʿeh-hā-ye Qodrat dar du Daheh-ye Pāyāni-ye Dudemān-e Pahlavi (Shāh, Amir ʿAbbās Hoveydā, Ardeshir Zāhedi)*. Beh Āfarin, 1394 [2015].

Asnād-e Moʿāhedāt-e do Jānebeh-ye Irān bā Sāyer-e Duval, 10 vols. Tehran: Daftar-e Motāleʿāt-e Siyāsi va Beyn al-Melali, 1370 [1991].

Asserate, Asfa-Wossen. *King of Kings: The Triumph and Tragedy of Emperor Haile Selassie I of Ethiopia*. London: Haus Publishing Ltd., 2017.

Axworthy, Michael. *Revolutionary Iran: A History of the Islamic Republic*. London: Penguin Books, 2009.

Azizi, Arash. 'Iranians and the Vietnam War: Cold Warrior Enmities or Anti-colonial Solidarities?', in *Iran and Global Decolonisation: Politics and Resistance After Empire*, ed. Firoozeh Kashani-Sabet and Robert Steele, 199–235. London: Gingko Library, 2023.

Baghoolizadeh, Beeta. *The Color Black Enslavement and Erasure in Iran*. Durham, NC: Duke University Press, 2024.

Bailey, Martin. 'Enforcing Oil Sanctions: A Comparison of the Rhodesian and South African Embargoes', in *Embargo: Apartheid's Oil Secrets Revealed*, ed. Richard Hengeveld and Jaap Rodenburg, 225–233. Amsterdam: Amsterdam University Press, 1995.

Bailey, Martin and Rivers, Bernard. *Oil Sanctions against South Africa*. New York: UN Centre Against Apartheid, Department of Political and Security Council Affairs, December 1978.

Bakhash, Shaul. *The Fall of Reza Shah: The Abdication, Exile, and Death of Modern Iran's Founder*. London: I. B. Tauris, 2021.

Bakhshi, Ahmad. 'Barresi-ye Tārikhi-ye Ravābet-e Khāreji-ye Irān va Qāreh-ye Āfriqā', *Tārikh-e Ravābet-e Khāreji*, vol. 35 (1387 [2008]), 32–75.

Barseghian, Sergei. 'Malakeh-ye Mesri-ye Darbār-e Irān: Ezdevāj va Talāgh-e Mohammad Rezā Pahlavi va Fawziyeh', *Tarikh-e Irani*, 30 Esfand 1389 [22 February 2011]. Available online: http://tarikhirani.ir/fa/news/7102/ملکه-مصری-دربار-ایران-ازدواج-و-طلاق-محمدرضا-پهلوی-و-فوزیه.

Bayat, Asef and Baktiari, Bahman. 'Revolutionary Iran and Egypt: Exporting Inspirations and Anxieties', in *Iran and the Surrounding World: Interactions in Culture and Cultural Politics*, ed. Nikki R. Keddie and Rudi Matthee, 305–326. Seattle: University of Washington Press, 2002.

Beazley, Kim C. 'The October War, the 1973–1974 Arab Oil Embargo, and U.S. Policy on the Indian Ocean', in *The Indian Ocean in Global Politics*, ed. Larry W. Bowman and Ian Clark, 107–129. Boulder, CO: Westview Press, 1981.

Bechtold, Peter K. 'New Attempts at Arab Cooperation: The Federation of Arab Republics, 1971–?', *Middle East Journal*, vol. 27, no. 2 (1973), 152–172.

Bédrède, Thomas. 'Iran's Foreign Policy and the Algerian War of Independence 1954–1962', in *Iran and Global Decolonisation: Politics and Resistance After Empire*, ed. Firoozeh Kashani-Sabet and Robert Steele, 165–197. London: Gingko Library, 2023.

Bilinsky, Yaroslav. 'Moderate Realism in an Extremist Environment: Tunisia and the Palestinian Question (1965–1970)', *Revue de l'Occident Musulmane et de la Méditerranée*, vol. 13–14 (1973), 109–123.

Blake, Robert. *A History of Rhodesia*. London: Methuen, 1977.

Bonnefond, Philippe and Couty, Philippe. 'Agricultural Crisis: Past and Future', in *The Political Economy of Senegal under Structural Adjustment*, ed. Christopher L. Delgado and Sidi Jammeh, 31–45. New York: Praeger, 1991.

Boone, Catherine. *Merchant Capital and the Roots of State Power in Senegal 1930–1985*. Cambridge: Cambridge University Press, 1992.

Boussaid, Farid. 'Brothers in Arms: Morocco's Military Intervention in Support of Mobutu of Zaire during the 1977 and 1978 Shaba Crises', *The International History Review*, vol. 43, no. 1 (2021), 185–202.

Boye, François. 'A Retrospective Analysis of the Senegalese Economy', The Center for Economic Research on Africa, Montclair State University, 1990.

Brands, Hal. *The Promise and Pitfalls of Grand Strategy*. Carlisle, PA: Strategic Studies Institute, U.S. Army War College, 2012.

Bronson, Rachel. *Thicker than Oil: America's Uneasy Partnership with Saudi Arabia*. Oxford: Oxford University Press, 2006.

Camacho Padilla, Fernando. 'Las relaciones entre Latinoamérica e Irán durante la última década de la dinastía Pahleví', *Anuario de Historia de América Latina*, vol. 56 (2019), 66–96.

Chehabi, H. E. 'South Africa and Iran in the Apartheid Era', *Journal of Southern African Studies*, vol. 42, no. 4 (2016), 687–709.

'A Cosmopolitan Dandy: Amir Abbas Hoveyda', in *The Age of Aryamehr: Late Pahlavi Iran and Its Global Entanglements*, ed. Roham Alvandi, 147–167. London: Gingko Library, 2018.

'Royal Exile in the Indian Ocean: Reza Shah's Sojourn in Mauritius' in *Iran and Persianate Culture in the Indian Ocean World* ed. A.C.S. Peacock. London: Bloomsbury, 2025 [forthcoming].

Chittick, Neville. 'The "Shirazi" Colonization of East Africa', *The Journal of African History*, vol. 6, no. 3 (1965), 275–294.

Chubin, Shahram and Zabih, Sepehr. *The Foreign Relations of Iran: A Developing State in a Zone of Great-Power Conflict*. Berkeley: University of California Press, 1974.

Clapham, Christopher. *The Horn of Africa: State Formation and Decay*. Oxford: Oxford University Press, 2017.

Cohen-Tanugi, Gilbert. 'Tunisia', *The American Jewish Year Book*, vol. 67 (1966), 431–435.

Collins, Robert O. *A History of Modern Sudan*. Cambridge: Cambridge University Press, 2008.

Coulson, Andrew. *Tanzania: A Political Economy*. Oxford: Oxford University Press, 2013.

Daoudi, M. S. and Dajani, M. S. 'The 1967 Oil Embargo Revisited', *Journal of Palestine Studies*, vol. 13, no. 2 (1984), 65–90.

Decade of the Revolution: Resurrection of a Nation; A Miracle of Leadership, 1963–1973. [Tehran]: Central Insurance of Iran, 1973.

Deroche, Andrew J. 'Standing Firm for Principles: Jimmy Carter and Zimbabwe', *Diplomatic History*, vol. 23, no. 4 (1999), 657–685.

Dustdār, Yahyā and Tayyebāti, Hoseyn. *Ketābshenāsi-ye Jashn-e Shāhanshāhi-ye Irān*. Tehran: Showrā-ye Markazi-ye Jashnhā-ye Shāhanshāhi-ye Irān, [1351] 1972.

Ehteshami, Anoushiravan. 'Iran's Grand Strategy under the Pahlavis', in *Grand Strategy in the Contemporary Middle East*, ed. Tore T. Petersen and Clive Jones, 195–214. Berlin: Gerlach Press, 2022.

Elwell-Sutton, Laurence P. *Modern Iran*. London: George Routledge & Sons, 1941.

Erlich, Haggai. *Haile Selassie: His Rise, His Fall*. Boulder, CO: Lynne Reinner Publishers, 2019.

Falola, Toyin and Heaton, Matthew M. *A History of Nigeria*. Cambridge: Cambridge University Press, 2014.

Farmanfarmaian, Manucher. *Blood and Oil: Memoirs of a Persian Prince*. London: Random House, 1997.

Ferris, Jesse. *Nasser's Gamble: How Intervention in Yemen Caused the Six-Day War and the Decline of Egyptian Power*. Princeton, NJ: Princeton University Press, 2012.

Firuz, Shāhrokh. *Zir-e Sāyeh-ye Alborz*. Washington, DC: Mage Publishers, 2011.

Gaddis, John Lewis. *The Cold War*. London: Penguin Books, 2005.

On Grand Strategy. New York: Penguin Press, 2018.

Gāhnāmeh-ye Panjāh Sāleh-ye Shāhanshāhi-ye Pahlavi, 5 vols. Paris: Soheil Publishers, 1985.

Galtung, Johan. 'On the Effects of International Economic Sanctions, with Examples from the Case of Rhodesia', *World Politics*, vol. 19, no. 3 (1967), 378–416.

Ganji, Manouchehr. *Study of Apartheid and Racial Discrimination in Southern Africa: Report of the Special Rapporteur*. New York: United Nations Economic and Social Council, 1968.

Gasiorowski, Mark J. 'The Qarani Affair and Iranian Politics', *International Journal of Middle East Studies*, vol. 25, no. 4 (1993), 625–644.

Gelban, Mohammad, ed. *Dar Āyneh-ye Tārikh: Khāterāt-e Siyāsi-ye ʿAbbās Khalili (Modir-e Ruznāmeh-ye Eqdām)*. Tehran: Anusheh, [1380] 2001.

Gellar, Sheldon. *Senegal: An African Nation between Islam and the West*. Boulder, CO: Westview Press, 1982.

Gerges, Fawaz A. *Making the Arab World: Nasser, Qutb, and the Clash that Shaped the Middle East*. Princeton, NJ: Princeton University Press, 2018.

Getachew, Adom. *Worldmaking after Empire: The Rise and Fall of Self-Determination*. Princeton, NJ: Princeton University Press, 2019.

Ghani, Cyrus. *Iran and the West: A Critical Bibliography*. London: Kegan Paul International, 1987.

Gheissari, Ali. 'Unequal Treaties and the Question of Sovereignty in Qajar and Early Pahlavi Iran', *Durham Middle East Papers*, no. 106 (2023), 1–63.

Ghotbi, Sheherazade Afshar and Ovanessian, Arby. *Shiraz-Persepolis Festival of Arts (1967–1977): Detailed Catalogue of Events* (May

2021). Available online: www.academia.edu/49073622/SHIRAZ_ARTS_FESTIVAL_Detailed_Catalogue_of_Events.

Gleijeses, Piero. 'Truth or Credibility: Castro, Carter, and the Invasions of Shaba', *The International History Review*, vol. 18, no. 1 (1996), 70–103.

Goode, James F. 'Assisting Our Brothers, Defending Ourselves: The Iranian Intervention in Oman, 1972–75', *Iranian Studies*, vol. 47, no. 3 (2014), 441–462.

Gozāresh Az Barnāmeh-ye Āshenāyi bā Honar-e Afriqā. Tehran, [1356] 1977.

Griffith, William E. 'Iran's Foreign Policy in the Pahlavi Era', in *Iran Under the Pahlavis*, ed. George Lenczowski, 365–388. Stanford, CA: Hoover Institution Press, 1978.

Haile, Semere. 'The Origins and Demise of the Ethiopia-Eritrea Federation', *Issue: A Journal of Opinion*, vol. 15 (1987), 9–17.

Haile-Selassie, Teferra. *The Ethiopian Revolution, 1974–91: From a Monarchical Autocracy to a Military Oligarchy*. London: Kegan Paul International, 1997.

Halliday, Fred and Molyneux, Maxine. *The Ethiopian Revolution*. London: Verso, 1981.

Hamblin, Jacob Darwin. 'The Nuclearization of Iran in the Seventies', *Diplomatic History*, vol. 38, no. 5 (2014), 1114–1135.

Hecht, Gabrielle. *Being Nuclear: Africans and the Global Uranium Trade*. Cambridge, MA: The MIT Press, 2012.

Heikal, Mohamed. *Iran: The Untold Story: An Insider's Account, from the Rise of the Shah to the Reign of the Ayatollah*. New York: Pantheon, 1982.

Hendelman-Baavur, Liora. *Creating the Modern Iranian Woman: Popular Culture between Two Revolutions*. Cambridge: Cambridge University Press, 2019.

Henderson, Willie. 'Independent Botswana: A Reappraisal of Foreign Policy Options', *African Affairs*, vol. 73, no. 290 (1974), 37–49.

Horne, Alistair. *A Savage War of Peace: Algeria 1954–1962*. New York: New York Review Books, 2006.

Houshisadat, Seyed Mohammad. *Iran's Regional Relations: A History from Antiquity to the Islamic Republic*. London: Routledge, 2021.

Hunter, Shireen T. *OPEC and the Third World: The Politics of Aid*. London: Croom Helm, 1984.

Iran's Foreign Policy in the Post-Soviet Era: Resisting the New International Order. Santa Barbara, CA: Praeger, 2010.

Iran Who's Who. Tehran: Echo of Iran, [1972] 1976.

Jackson, Donna R. *Jimmy Carter and the Horn of Africa: Cold War Policy in Ethiopia and Somalia*. London: McFarland & Co., 2007.

Jones, Clive. 'Introduction: Grand Strategy in the Contemporary Middle East: The Concepts and Debates', in *Grand Strategy in the Contemporary Middle East: The Concepts and Debates*, ed. Tore T. Petersen and Clive Jones, 1–14. Berlin: Gerlach Press, 2022.

Karanjia, R. K. *The Mind of a Monarch*. London: George Allen & Unwin Ltd., 1977.

Kashani-Sabet, Firoozeh. *Conceiving Citizens: Women and the Politics of Motherhood in Iran*. Oxford: Oxford University Press, 2011.

'Colorblind or Blinded by Color? Race, Ethnicity, and Identity in Iran', in *Sites of Pluralism: Community Politics in the Middle East*, ed. Firat Oruc, 153–180. Oxford: Oxford University Press, 2019.

'The Anti-Aryan Moment: Decolonization, Diplomacy, and Race in Late Pahlavi Iran', *International Journal of Middle East Studies*, vol. 53 (2021), 691–702.

'Iran on Shaky Ground: Iran between Israel and Pan-Arabism, 1930–1970s', *Middle East Studies*, vol. 59, no. 6 (2023), 950–967.

'Global Civil Rights in Iran: Race, Gender, and Poverty', in *Iran and Global Decolonisation: Politics and Resistance After Empire*, ed. Firoozeh Kashani-Sabet and Robert Steele, 273–311. London: Gingko Library, 2023.

Heroes to Hostages: America and Iran, 1800–1988. Cambridge: Cambridge University Press, 2023.

Keddie, Nikki R. *Sayyid Jamāl ad-Dīn "al-Afghānī": A Political Biography*. Berkeley: University of California Press, 1972.

Kennedy, Paul, ed. *Grand Strategies in War and Peace*. New Haven, CT: Yale University Press, 1991.

Keynoush, Banafsheh. *Saudi Arabia and Iran: Friends or Foes?* New York: Palgrave Macmillan, 2016.

'Revolutionary Iran's Africa Policy', King Faisal Center for Research and Islamic Studies, Special Report (June 2021).

King'ei, Kitula and Musau, Paul. 'The Shirazi Influence on Swahili Language', in *Papers Presented during the First Conference on the Historical Role of Iranians (Shirazis) in the East African Coast: 2nd–3rd February 2001*, 83–94. Nairobi: Cultural Council of the Embassy of I. R. Iran, 2001.

Klinghoffer, Arthur J. 'US-Soviet Relations and Angola', *Harvard International Review*, vol. 8, no. 3 (1986), 15–19.

Oiling the Wheels of Apartheid: Exposing South Africa's Secret Oil Trade. Boulder, CO: Lynne Rienner, 1989.

Koehn, Peter. 'Ethiopia: Famine, Food Production, and Changes in the Legal Order', *African Studies Review*, vol. 22, no. 1 (1979), 51–72.

Kozhanov, Nikolay A. 'The Pretexts and Reasons for the Allied Invasion of Iran in 1941', *Iranian Studies*, vol. 45, no. 4 (2012), 479–497.

Kyle, Keith. *Suez: Britain's End of Empire in the Middle East*. London: I. B. Tauris, 2011.

Laitin, David D. 'The War in the Ogaden: Implications for Siyaad's Role in Somali History', *The Journal of Modern African Studies*, vol. 17, no. 1 (1979), 95–115.

Larmer, Miles. 'Local Conflicts in a Transnational War: The Katangese Gendarmes and the Shaba Wars of 1977–78', *Cold War History*, vol. 13, no. 1 (2013), 89–108.

Lee, Christopher, ed. *Making a World after Empire: The Bandung Moment and Its Political Afterlives*. Athens: Ohio University Press, 2019.

Lefebvre, Jeffrey A. 'Globalism and Regionalism: U.S. Arms Transfers to Sudan', vol. 17, no. 2 (1991), 211–227.

Arms for the Horn: U.S. Security Policy in Ethiopia and Somalia, 1953–1991. Pittsburgh: University of Pittsburgh Press, 1992.

'Middle East Conflicts and Middle Level Power Intervention in the Horn of Africa', *Middle East Journal*, vol. 50, no. 3 (1996), 387–404.

Lenczowski, George. 'United States' Support for Iran's Independence and Integrity, 1945–1959', *The Annals of the American Academy of Political and Social Science*, vol. 401 (1972), 45–55.

Lissner, Rebecca Friedman. 'What Is Grand Strategy? Sweeping a Conceptual Minefield', *Texas National Security Review*, vol. 2, no. 1 (2018), 52–73.

Lubeck, Paul. 'Nigeria: A Political Economy', *Africa Today*, vol. 24, no. 4 (1977), 5–10.

Lundahl, Mats. 'Economic Effects of a Trade and Investment Boycott against South Africa', *The Scandinavian Journal of Economics*, vol. 86, no. 1 (1984), 68–83.

Lüthi, Lorenz M. *Cold Wars: Asia, the Middle East, Europe*. Cambridge: Cambridge University Press, 2020.

Mahida, Ebrahim Mahomed. *History of Muslims in South Africa: A Chronology*. Durban: Arabic Study Circle, 1993.

Mamdani, Mahmood. *Good Muslim, Bad Muslim: America, the Cold War, and the Roots of Terror*. New York: Pantheon, 2004.

Mandela, Nelson. *Long Walk to Freedom*. London: Little, Brown and Company, 1994.

Marashi, Afshin. 'Performing the Nation: The Shah's Official State Visit to Kemalist Turkey, June to July 1934', in *The Making of Modern Iran:*

State and Society under Riza Shah, 1921–1941, ed. Stephanie Cronin, 99–119. London: Routledge, 2003.
Martin, Guy. 'Uranium: A Case-Study in Franco-African Relations', *The Journal of Modern African Studies*, vol. 27, no. 4 (1989), 625–640.
Mathews, K., 'The Organization of African Unity', *India Quarterly: A Journal of International Affairs*, vol. 33, no. 3 (1977), 308–324.
Matin-Asgari, Afshin. *Iranian Student Opposition to the Shah*. Costa Mesa, CA: Mazda Publishers, 2002.
Matthee, Rudi. 'Jamal al-Din Afghani and the Egyptian National Debate', *International Journal of Middle East Studies*, vol. 21, no. 2 (1989), 151–169.
Mayall, James. *Nationalism and International Society*. Cambridge: Cambridge University Press, 1990.
Mbodji, Mohamed. 'The Politics of Independence: 1960–1986', in *The Political Economy of Senegal under Structural Adjustment*, ed. Christopher L. Delgado and Sidi Jammeh, 119–126. New York: Praeger, 1991.
McLachlan, Keith. 'The Iranian Economy, 1960–1976', in *Twentieth Century Iran*, ed. Hossein Amirsadeghi, 129–169. London: William Heinemann Ltd., 1977.
McMahon, Robert J. 'Introduction', in *The Cold War in the Third World*, ed. Robert J. McMahon, 1–10. Oxford: Oxford University Press, 2013.
Metrowich, F. R. *South Africa's New Frontiers*. Sandton, SA: Valiant, 1977.
Milani, Abbas. *The Persian Sphinx: Amir Abbas Hoveyda and the Riddle of the Iranian Revolution*. Washington, DC: Mage Publishers, 2000.
Eminent Persians, 2 vols. Syracuse, NY: Syracuse University Press, 2008.
Milevski, Lukas. *The Evolution of Modern Grand Strategic Thought*. Oxford: Oxford University Press, 2016.
Miller, Susan Gilson. *A History of Modern Morocco*. Cambridge: Cambridge University Press, 2013.
Mirzai, Behnaz A. *A History of Slavery and Emancipation in Iran, 1800–1929*. Austin: University of Texas Press, 2017.
Mitchell, Nancy. 'Terrorists or Freedom Fighters? Jimmy Carter and Rhodesia', in *Cold War in Southern Africa: White Power, Black Liberation*, ed. Sue Onslow, 177–200. London: Routledge, 2009.
Jimmy Carter in Africa: Race and the Cold War. Washington, DC: Woodrow Wilson Center Press, 2016.
Murphy, David. 'The Performance of Pan-Africanism: Staging the African Renaissance at the First World Festival of Negro Arts', in *The First World Festival of Negro Arts, Dakar 1966*, ed. David Murphy, 1–52. Liverpool: Liverpool University Press, 2016.

Murray, Williamson, Richard Hart Sinnreich and James Lacey, eds. *The Shaping of Grand Strategy: Policy, Diplomacy, and War*. Cambridge: Cambridge University Press, 2011.

Nahavandi, Houchang. *The Last Shah of Iran*, trans. Steeve Reed. Slough: Aquilion Ltd., 2005.

Nkrumah, Kwame. *Africa Must Unite*. London: Heinemann, 1963.

Nmoma, Veronica. 'The Shift in United States-Sudan Relations: A Troubled Relationship and the Need for Mutual Cooperation', *The Journal of Conflict Studies*, vol. 26, no. 2 (2006), 44–70.

Onderco, Michal. 'A Battle of Principles: South Africa's Relations with Iran', *Commonwealth and Comparative Politics*, vol. 53, no. 2 (2016), 252–267.

Onley, James. 'Britain and the Gulf Shaikhdoms, 1820–1971: The Politics of Protection', *Center for International and Regional Studies, Georgetown University School of Foreign Service in Qatar*, occasional paper no. 4 (2009).

Onslow, Sue. '"We Must Gain Time": South Africa, Rhodesia and the Kissinger Initiative of 1976', *South African Historical Journal*, vol. 56 (2006), 123–153.

'The Cold War in Southern Africa: White Power, Black Nationalism and External Intervention', in *The Cold War in Southern Africa: White Power, Black Liberation*, ed. Sue Onslow, 9–34. London: Routledge, 2009.

Pahlavi, Ashraf. *Faces in a Mirror: Memoirs from Exile*. Englewood Cliffs, NJ: Prentice-Hall, Inc., 1980.

Pahlavi, Mohammad Reza. *Mission for My Country*. London: Hutchinson & Co., 1961.

The White Revolution. Tehran: Pahlavi Library, 1967.

Beh Su-ye Tamaddon-e Bozorg. Tehran: Ketābkhāneh-ye Pahlavi, 2536 [1977].

The Shah's Story. London: Michael Joseph, 1980.

Patman, Robert G. *The Soviet Union in the Horn of Africa: The Diplomacy of Intervention and Disengagement*. Cambridge: Cambridge University Press, 1990.

Patten, Howard A. *Israel and the Cold War: Diplomacy, Strategy and the Policy of the Periphery at the United Nations*. London: I. B. Tauris, 2013.

Podeh, Elie. 'The Drift towards Neutrality: Egyptian Foreign Policy during the Early Nasserist Era, 1952–55', *Middle Eastern Studies*, vol. 32, no. 1 (1996), 159–178.

Rahnema, Ali. *The Rise of Modern Despotism in Iran: The Shah, the Opposition, and the US, 1953–1968*. London: Oneworld Academic, 2021.

Rake, Alan. *African Leaders: Guiding the New Millennium*. London: Scarecrow Press, 2001.

Ramazani, Rouhollah K. 'Iran's "White Revolution": A Study in Political Development', *International Journal of Middle East Studies*, vol. 5, no. 2 (1974), 124–139.

Iran's Foreign Policy, 1941–1973: A Study of Foreign Policy in Modernizing Nations. Charlottesville: University Press of Virginia, 1975.

'Iran's Search for Regional Cooperation', *Middle East Journal*, vol. 30, no. 2 (1976), 173–186.

'Iran and the Arab-Israeli Conflict', *Middle East Journal*, vol. 32, no. 4 (1978), 413–428.

Richard, Yann. *Iran: A Social and Political History since the Qajars*. Cambridge: Cambridge University Press, 2019.

Rogers, Barbara. 'Southern Africa and the Oil Embargo', *Africa Today*, vol. 21, no. 2 (1974), 3–8.

Sadat, Jehan. *A Woman of Egypt*. New York: Simon & Schuster, 1987.

Safdie, Moshe. *Keur Farah Pahlavi: Ville nouvelle industrielle pour le gouvernement du Sénégal*. Montréal: Moshe Safdie et Associes Architectes et Urbanistes, 1976.

Saikal, Amin. *The Rise and Fall of the Shah: Iran from Autocracy to Religious Rule*. Princeton, NJ: Princeton University Press, 2009.

Samii, Abbas William. 'The Shah's Lebanon Policy: The Role of SAVAK', *Middle Eastern Studies*, vol. 33, no. 1 (1997), 66–91.

Schayegh, Cyrus. 'Iran's Global Long 1970s: An Empire Project, Civilisational Developmentalism, and the Crisis of the Global North', in *The Age of Aryamehr: Late Pahlavi Iran and Its Global Entanglements*, ed. Roham Alvandi, 262–291. London: Gingko Library, 2018.

Schraeder, Peter J. 'Senegal's Foreign Policy: Challenges of Democratization and Marginalization', *African Affairs*, vol. 96 (1997), 485–508.

Shafā, Shojāʿ al-Din, 'Shojāʿ al-Din Shafā az Zabān-e Khodash', in *Yādnāmeh-ye Shojāʿ al-Din Shafā*, ed. Claudine Shafa (Paris, 2013).

Shannon, Matthew. *Losing Hearts and Minds: American-Iranian Relations and International Education during the Cold War*. Ithaca, NY: Cornell University Press, 2017.

Sharifi-Yazdi, Farzad. *Arab-Iranian Rivalry in the Persian Gulf: Territorial Disputes and the Balance of Power in the Middle East*. London: I. B. Tauris, 2015.

Shaw, Timothy M. 'The Foreign Policy of Zambia: Ideology and Interests', *The Journal of Modern African Studies*, vol. 14, no. 1 (1976), 79–105.

Skurnik, W. A. E. *The Foreign Policy of Senegal*. Evanston, IL: Northwestern University Press, 1971.

Smith, William Edgett. *We Must Run while They Walk: A Portrait of Africa's Julius Nyerere*. London: Victor Gollancz, 1971.

'South Africa and the Shah: Oil Supplies at Stake', *MERIP Reports*, no. 73 (1978), 20–21.

Sparks, Stephen. 'Crude Politics: The ANC, the Shipping Research Bureau and the Anti-Apartheid Oil Boycott', *South African Historical Journal*, vol. 69, no. 2 (2017), 251–264.

Spiliotes, Nicholas J. 'Nigerian Foreign Policy and Southern Africa: A Choice for the West', *Issue: A Journal of Opinion*, vol. 11, no. 1/2 (1981), 41–45.

St John, Ronald Bruce. 'The Ideology of Muammar al-Qadhdhafi: Theory and Practice', *International Journal of Middle East Studies*, vol. 15, no. 4 (1983), 471–490.

Steele, Robert. 'Pahlavi Iran on the Global Stage: The Shah's 1971 Persepolis Celebrations', in *The Age of Aryamehr: Late Pahlavi Iran and Its Global Entanglements*, ed. by Roham Alvandi, 110–146. London: Gingko Library, 2018.

The Shah's Imperial Celebrations of 1971: Nationalism, Culture and Politics in Late Pahlavi Iran. London: I. B. Tauris, 2020.

'Iran's Golden Age of Tourism: The Development of the Travel Industry in the Late Pahlavi Period (c. 1960–1979)', *Journal of Tourism History*, vol. 14, no. 3 (2022), 239–262.

Sternfeld, Lior. 'Iran Days in Egypt: Mosaddeq's Visit to Cairo in 1951', *British Journal of Middle Eastern Studies*, vol. 43, no. 1 (2016), 1–20.

Takeyh, Ray. *The Last Shah: America, Iran, and the Fall of the Pahlavi Dynasty*. Yale: Yale University Press, 2021.

Takriti, Abdel Razzaq. *Monsoon Revolution: Republicans, Sultans, and Empires in Oman, 1965–1976*. Oxford: Oxford University Press, 2013.

Tareke, Gebru. 'The Ethiopia-Somalia War of 1977 Revisited', *The International Journal of African Historical Studies*, vol. 33, no. 3 (2000), 635–667.

The Ethiopian Revolution: War in the Horn of Africa. New Haven, CT: Yale University Press, 2009.

Tārtār, Mohammad Rezā. 'Negāhi beh tārikhcheh-ye ravābet-e Irān va Etiyupi', Report by the Cultural Counsellor of the Embassy of the Islamic Republic of Iran, Addis Ababa. Available online: http://icro.ir/index.aspx?pageid=32738&p=10&showitem=15370.

Titley, Brian. *Dark Age: The Political Odyssey of Emperor Bokassa*. Liverpool: Liverpool University Press, 1998.

Touval, Saadia. 'The Organization of African Unity and African Borders', *International Organization*, vol. 21, no. 1 (1967), 102–127.

Translations on Sub-Saharan Africa. Arlington, VA: Joint Publications Research Service, 1976.

Triplett, George W. 'Zanzibar: The Politics of Revolutionary Inequality', *The Journal of Modern African Studies*, vol. 9, no. 4 (1971), 612–617.

Turner, Arthur Campbell. 'Independent Rhodesia', *Current History*, vol. 58, no. 343 (1970), 129–134.

United Nations. *Final Act of the International Conference on Human Rights: Tehran, 22 April to 13 May 1968*. New York: United Nations, 1968.

'United Nations General Assembly Sixth Special Session', *International Legal Materials*, vol. 13, no. 3 (1974), 715–766.

United States Department of State. *The Suez Canal Problem, July 26–September 22, 1956: A Documentary Publication*. Washington, DC: The Department of State, 1956.

Vaillant, Janet G. *Black, French, and African: A Life of Léopold Sédar Senghor*. Cambridge, MA: Harvard University Press, 1990.

Watt, D. C. and Lyon, Peter. 'Notes on the Month', *The World Today*, vol. 21, no. 6 (1965), 223–228.

Westad, Odd Arne. *The Global Cold War: Third World Interventions and the Making of our Times*. Cambridge: Cambridge University Press, 2012.

The Cold War: A World History. London: Allen Lane, 2017.

Wright, Denis, in an interview with Habib Ladjevardi, Aylesbury, UK, 10 and 11 October 1984, Iranian Oral History Collection, Harvard University, transcript 7.

Yāri, Hasan ʿAli. 'Ravābet-e Siyāsi-ye Irān va Libi dar Dowreh-ye Pahlavi-e Dovvom (Ruyārui-e Shāh va Qazāfi)', *Nāmeh-ye Tārikh Pazhuhān*, vol. 24 (1389), 130–151.

Zabih, Sepehr. 'Iran's International Posture: De Facto Nonalignment within a Pro-Western Alliance', *The Middle East Journal*, vol. 24, no. 3 (1970), 302–318.

Zāhedi, Ardeshir. *Khāterāt-e Ardeshir Zāhedi*, vol. 3. Bethesda, MD: Ibex Publishers, 2020.

Index

Milton Keynes UK
Ingram Content Group UK Ltd.
UKHW021907160824
446834UK00007B/32

9 781009 473149